The publisher and the University of California Press Foundation gratefully acknowledge the generous support of the Simpson Imprint in Humanities.

AN AMERICAN LANGUAGE

AMERICAN CROSSROADS

Edited by Earl Lewis, George Lipsitz, George Sánchez, Dana Takagi, Laura Briggs, and Nikhil Pal Singh

AN AMERICAN LANGUAGE

THE HISTORY OF SPANISH IN THE UNITED STATES

Rosina Lozano

 UNIVERSITY OF CALIFORNIA PRESS

University of California Press, one of the most distinguished
university presses in the United States, enriches lives around
the world by advancing scholarship in the humanities, social
sciences, and natural sciences. Its activities are supported by
the UC Press Foundation and by philanthropic contributions
from individuals and institutions. For more information, visit
www.ucpress.edu.

University of California Press
Oakland, California

An early version of parts of chapter 2 appeared as
"Translating California: Official Spanish Usage in California's
Constitutional Conventions and State Legislature, 1848–1894,"
California Legal History 6 (2011): 321–56.

Chapter 10 is drawn from my previously published article,
"Managing the 'Priceless Gift': Debating Spanish Language
Instruction in New Mexico and Puerto Rico, 1930–1950,"
Western Historical Quarterly 44 (Autumn 2013): 271–93. doi:
10.2307/westhistquar.44.3.0271.

Library of Congress Cataloging-in-Publication Data

Names: Lozano, Rosina, 1978– author.
Title: An American language : the history of Spanish in the
    United States / Rosina Lozano.
Description: Oakland, California : University of California
    Press, [2018] | Series: American crossroads ; 49 | Includes
    bibliographical references and index.
Identifiers: LCCN 2017049892 (print) | LCCN 2017052400
    (ebook) | ISBN 9780520969582 (Epub) | ISBN 9780520297067
    (cloth : alk. paper) | ISBN 9780520297074 (pbk. : alk. paper)
Subjects: LCSH: Spanish language—History—19th century. |
    Spanish language—History—20th century. | Spanish
    language—Political aspects—United States. | Southwest,
    New—History—1848–
Classification: LCC PC4826 (ebook) | LCC PC4826 .L69 2018
    (print) | DDC 460/.973—dc23
LC record available at https://lccn.loc.gov/2017049892

Manufactured in the United States of America

26 25 24 23 22 21 20 19 18
10 9 8 7 6 5 4 3 2 1

For Nick, Walter, and Tomás

CONTENTS

ILLUSTRATIONS

Introduction

Quienes lean esta frase y entiendan lo que dice dominan, hasta cierto punto, un lenguaje específico, el español. Everyone who easily reads and understands *this* sentence has a certain level of fluency in a different specific language, English. Perhaps you read the first sentence and were confused or uncomfortable. Or you read it and patted yourself on the back for being able to understand it. Or you were so comfortable with the language that you read it as a native speaker and then had to switch gears to read the next sentence in English. Language affects both our perception of the text in front of us and our perception of ourselves. I open without italicizing the first sentence—often an invitation to skip over the words—to make precisely this point.

The relationship between language and identity forms the central theme of this book. Your ability to understand only one of the sentences at the beginning of this introduction or the ease with which you understand both mirrors the way language has shaped individuals' sense of belonging in the United States for over a century and a half. A time-lapsed map of the United States displaying its residents' mother tongues would include hundreds of American Indian languages that were encroached on by European imperial languages like French, Dutch, Spanish, and English. Additional European settlement and African slaves added to the mix with their own languages. Texas, New Mexico, California, and other states became part of the U.S. boundaries with Spanish-speaking settlers already in residence. This account is concerned with one of the most persistent languages on this map—Spanish—tracing how it moved from a language of governance in the mid-nineteenth-century

Southwest to a language of "foreignness" that has both served as the antithesis of American identity and supported the broadening hemispheric goals of the United States in the twentieth century.

An American Language uncovers the history of Spanish-language rights in the United States. Language rights are usually understood today by the United Nations and UNESCO as a category of civil or human rights that broadly represent the right of an individual to determine the language used in private and public settings.[1] In 1996, UNESCO issued the Universal Declaration of Linguistic Rights, which delineated protections for minority-language speakers. These protections included the "right to be recognized as a member of a language community, the right to the use of one's language both in private and public," the right to teach and preserve the language, and the right to have access to the language in media and official spaces.[2] These global guidelines on linguistic rights developed in a contemporary setting, but this does not mean that individuals did not advocate for language rights in an era that lacked the term. While the federal government did not explicitly specify any language rights historically, states, territories, and localities have extended various levels of protection to non-English speakers over the course of U.S. history. Sometimes states and territories made official, legal protections for different language communities. At other times, non-English-language speakers merely received some sort of recognition of their language needs and the state or territory left localities with the power to grant language concessions, which permitted residents a higher level of civic participation.

The United States remains one of just eight nations in the world that have no official language.[3] Congress has rarely discussed language in its federal laws, nor has it often interfered with state and local language choices. Measured in political and demographic terms, English has always been the dominant language of the nation, but the United States has never been an English-only society. The long multilingual experience of the United States has remained largely absent from popular understandings of the nation's history. The old joke—What do you call a person who speaks two languages? Bilingual. What do you call a person who speaks three languages? Trilingual. What do you call a person who speaks only one language? An American— is not only hackneyed but also historically inaccurate. In 1790, non-native English speakers made up one-fourth of the U.S. population.[4] European immigrants entered the country by the tens of millions throughout the nineteenth and early twentieth century and initially participated in civic life in various European languages, including German, French, Italian, Polish, and Hungarian.[5]

The enduring presence of Spanish within U.S. borders serves as a lasting and contemporary reminder of what has been a long national relationship with language politics. The Latino population has grown through immigration and birth by almost 49 million since 1965, a formidable demographic expansion that has demonstrably transformed the politics of language throughout the nation.[6] Spanish was by far the second most spoken language in the nation in 2009, with 35.4 million people speaking the language at home—and with many others having the ability to speak the language too.[7] In 2015, the Instituto Cervantes in Spain proclaimed the United States host to the second-largest population of Spanish speakers in the world and projected it would become the largest in 2050.[8]

Given the coverage of the topic in the contemporary media, a reasonable person might conclude that Spanish speakers are receiving unprecedented Spanish-language concessions in some courts and workplaces, on ballots and campaign material, and in bilingual schools. Most of these accounts suggest that Spanish is simply a language of recent immigrants. Some celebrate the spread of Spanish speakers as part of the nation's multicultural transformation. Others resist its use, fearing the debasement of an American culture that they view as built on the English language. In reality, these geographically limited allowances represent modest gains when considered historically. In the early years of the U.S. Southwest, Spanish was a language of governance required to build a U.S. political system. The omission of languages other than English in the larger historical narrative of the country has effectively eradicated a collective consciousness of multilingualism, which obscures the broader history of Spanish-language rights—a history that extends over centuries and that originated not in ethnic immigrant enclaves but in preestablished settlements.

Spanish in the United States is a colonial, indigenous, and immigrant language—the three major categories to which sociolinguists assign languages.[9] In the western hemisphere, Spanish started off as a colonial language that subsumed indigenous languages. After the passage of centuries, Spanish became the native language of Spanish settlements in Louisiana, parts of the future U.S. Midwest, and the future Southwest, and the lingua franca for many American Indians who lived among these Spanish-speaking settlements.[10] Over the course of the twentieth century, migration to the United States from

Latin American countries has replenished Spanish's place in the country and bolstered perceptions of Spanish as an immigrant language, distracting most from its earlier manifestations. This long exposure to the Spanish language makes it a part of the nation's fabric; echoes of each of these stages remain in state names like Colorado, in policies put in place determining who can serve on juries, in how we respond when hearing Spanish on the street, and in the way politicians reach out during political campaigns to the robust Spanish-language media.

A LANGUAGE OF POLITICS

Colorado state senator Casimiro Barela was born in El Embudo in Rio Arriba County, New Mexico, in March 1847. In 1889, he reflected on the incredible transition that his parents experienced when New Mexico became part of the United States on the conclusion of the U.S.-Mexican War the year after his birth. Barela recognized his parents as "among those who, owning [sic] to the commitment of this great government, gave up their status of citizens of the Republic of Mexico." One can imagine the leap of faith they took when they "renounced the government of their childhood and youth," all for a "solemnly extended" guarantee. Senator Barela regretted New Mexico's long wait for statehood and countered those who believed these former Mexican citizens incapable of self-government. After all, the people of New Mexico had formed a "deep loyalty to the principles of the American government."[11]

The history of Spanish-language politics in the United States began in earnest with the takeover of former Spanish lands, enveloping Spanish speakers like Senator Barela's parents. The most significant moment came in 1848 at the close of the U.S.-Mexican War. The Treaty of Guadalupe Hidalgo, which ended the war, recognized not just the land itself but also the people who lived on the land. These Mexicans were settlers on territory the United States now claimed but did not control due to the presence of autonomous Indians who raided newly arriving Anglos and long-standing Mexican settlers alike. Efforts to control the land required collusion between U.S. officials and the Spanish-speaking settlers who became elected officials and created the state and territorial systems bilingually, or in some cases, almost exclusively in Spanish. Joined increasingly by Anglos, the former Mexicans made up a demographically significant segment of the polity, which excluded American Indians from citizenship and suffrage. This reality encouraged the use of

Spanish in politics in the absence of any federal intervention or regulatory prohibitions. The upheaval caused by American Indian control over New Mexico's lands, a vast territory that included portions of the current states of Arizona and Colorado, made Mexican settlers a third player in the process of U.S. settlement.

I use the term "treaty citizens" to unite these former Mexican nationals annexed with California and New Mexico. Article IX of the Treaty of Guadalupe Hidalgo granted U.S. citizenship to the Mexican citizens residing in the ceded territory. In a single bold stroke, the treaty extended U.S. citizenship to approximately 56,000 individuals born in California and New Mexico, without a proviso regarding race or language.[12] Although the treaty claimed to accept all Mexican citizens as U.S. citizens, indigenous citizens of Mexico from California and New Mexico were not treaty citizens. The Mexican government recognized the Pueblos as citizens, but the United States did not, and Pueblos who lived in settlements near Mexican villages and towns in New Mexico found the treaty's promises especially hollow. *Californios* and *nuevomexicanos*—Mexican settlers living in California and New Mexico, respectively—became U.S. citizens who proved crucial to the initial creation of U.S. political institutions throughout the Southwest. Treaty citizens' origin point for citizenship also differed from the other major Mexican territory to join the United States in the 1840s—Texas. When Texas became a state in 1845 it already had an overwhelmingly Anglo population who controlled the state government and kept Spanish from becoming a language of politics. Language and citizenship together united treaty citizens.

Treaty citizens had legal citizenship and therefore could claim belonging as an "American."[13] For this reason, throughout the text I refer to people designated white, other than treaty citizens, as "Anglos" rather than "Americans." The treaty made no mention of language rights, but over time former Mexican citizens used the treaty to advocate for their right to access their own language. The treaty became a sort of amulet that treaty citizens gripped tightly and held up as proof of their rights in the years that followed the U.S.-Mexican War. They used the treaty largely metaphorically to support their claims to what they interpreted as the rights of "full citizens."

Treaty citizens and their descendants repeatedly returned to the treaty as their origin point as Americans. There is no evidence that the treaty was broadly circulated or studied, but its invocation in many speeches and petitions suggests it became well known as the arbiter of their civil rights. Into the late twentieth century, Spanish-speaking natural-born citizens pointed to the treaty to protest policies that made them second-class citizens and to highlight the illegality of the injustices that the U.S. government and political system directed toward them because of their racially ambiguous social status.[14] While the U.S. government legally and officially considered ethnic Mexicans white people, they remained nonwhite in the eyes of many Anglos.

Treaty citizens were the first geographically dispersed, politically significant, and racially ambiguous group to gain U.S. citizenship.[15] Historians should consider their dichotomous political and social status in conversations of how race or difference shapes citizenship—a discussion that often begins with the millions of former slaves who became citizens two decades after treaty citizens under the Fourteenth Amendment (1868).[16] Former slaves did not have racial ambiguity in the United States; over time, they were legally subjected to the one-drop rule. Whereas Blacks were black if they had any African ancestry, treaty citizens retained white status even though many Spanish settlers had relations—both forced and consensual—with American Indians, which resulted in a population that Anglos often categorized as mixed race. Use of the Spanish language became an important distinguishing factor for federal and territorial officials in determining who was a treaty citizen and who would receive federal services as members of federally recognized indigenous tribes. Treaty citizens' designation as legally white often resulted in political citizenship in the form of electoral protections and court proceedings but not social citizenship in the form of acceptance as fully integrated members of American society.[17] Treaty citizens' distinct cultural affiliations—including language—and their often darker skin marked them as separate in the nativist view of Americans as white and English speaking.

Aside from the treaty, treaty citizens had little in common. The majority of them could not communicate easily with one another across the vast territory and could do little to secure rights as a group. They did share the Spanish language though. When treaty citizens were absorbed into the United States they operated local governments, where they remained the majority, in Spanish out of necessity. After the initial unifying moment of 1848, the language experiences of treaty citizens in the Southwest diverged dramatically. California received statehood in the legislative political Compromise of 1850, whereas New Mexico remained a territory until 1912. New Mexico's boundaries shrank, as large portions of the territories of Arizona and Colorado were carved out of its territory in the 1860s. Colorado obtained statehood in 1876, while Arizona waited with New Mexico until 1912. Treaty citizens provide a point of commonality to gauge the conditions that created distinct language outcomes and permitted some regional dialect variations.

The comparison of states and territories is one of the book's major analytical threads. California's statehood status and demographic shift led to a rapid conversion to English in all aspects of life, which contrasts with the situation in New Mexico, whose long territorial status allowed its language use to remain distinct from the rest of the nation. New Mexico's treaty citizens dispersed across three states, each with dramatically different language concessions and language politics. The Colorado constitution included provisions for Spanish until 1900, while the Arizona legislature hardly gave any Spanish-language concessions. New Mexico's territorial status and demography enshrined Spanish as the default language of elected officials for decades. This legacy contrasts with California, where English was firmly entrenched in political and legal policies by the end of the nineteenth century. The 1879 state constitution revoked non-English-language rights in concert with the broader national tightening of requirements for citizenship and residency, including the end of Reconstruction protections for Black citizens and the start of Chinese immigration restriction.

Statehood became a major political goal for Anglo settlers who arrived in western territories during the nineteenth century. States could create an independently funded legislative, legal, and educational system; states, unlike territories, sent voting members to the U.S. Congress. In contrast, territorial status left residents under the governance of the federal, executive, and legislative branches. Congress paid territorial wages and printing costs and confirmed territorial laws.[18] The president chose the major territorial executive and judicial officials. Territories often lacked the funding to create robust educational systems.[19] A long territorial tenure like that experienced in New Mexico diverted political and organizational resources toward the drive to obtain statehood—energy and advocacy that could have been mobilized to achieve a more robust state government and infrastructure. The wait for statehood, however, had the effect of allowing Spanish speakers to retain political power in Spanish.

The politics of language provides a lens to view changes in how nationalism is practiced, for language has served and continues to serve as a marker of power. Americans' ideas of nationalism are constantly changing and being reassessed. Looking at how elected officials and the general populace respond to the presence of large numbers of Spanish speakers explains how different interpretations of "Americanness" are formed. The reasons for these interpretations range from the types of opportunities available to non-English speakers in the United States to their sense of belonging as full citizens of states with voting members in Congress. Territorial residents could remain distant from the more popularly accepted national expectations and had a different politics of language.

In the mid-nineteenth century, the desire for U.S. expansion or empire still defined and dominated the country's priorities, which outweighed a unified form of nationalism on language.[20] Anglo settlers and the government often saw eventual Anglo settlement as the solution to all "problems" in a territory occupied primarily by nonconforming citizens. Treaty citizens and their descendants would become diluted, many believed, as Manifest Destiny made its seemingly inevitable march across the continent. The federal government accepted Spanish-language use in the Southwest as an impermanent practice. Congress never discussed making the United States a bilingual nation like Canada, which officially embraced bilingualism in the 1860s.[21] Instead, federal officials assumed English was the inevitable dominant language in former Mexican lands, even though the legislature did little to support this transition in the nineteenth century. But once accepted, treaty citizens' use of the Spanish language was difficult to dismantle. As mainstream ideas of American identity solidified nationally at the turn of the twentieth century, belonging as an American included using the English language. This shift left treaty citizen families (the descendants of treaty citizens whose citizenship remained tied to the treaty even though they were natural-born citizens) torn between language and citizenship, two core aspects of how they chose to identify themselves.

The second major transition for Spanish-language speakers in the United States occurred half a century after the Treaty of Guadalupe Hidalgo, also because of a war. In 1898, the United States added the Spanish colonies of Puerto Rico, the Philippines, and Guam to its territories. The federal government also made Cuba a protectorate and had significant oversight over the Cuban government and educational system. The experiences of this new group of Spanish speakers tied to the United States show just how much the United States had shifted its views on Spanish by the start of the twentieth century. The changes moved Spanish increasingly from a regional language of politics to a language with political implications for the United States.

A POLITICAL LANGUAGE

Four distinct groups joined treaty citizen families as speakers of Spanish in the United States in the twentieth century: those added as a result of the Spanish-American War, those who crossed the border, those who lived in Latin America, and those who chose to learn Spanish. Spanish speakers added by the Spanish-American War used varying degrees of Spanish in different aspects of their lives. Elite Filipinos operated the Spanish colonial government and the islands' limited schools largely in Spanish, but most Filipinos spoke at least one of the over one hundred languages and dialects native to their archipelago. Puerto Rico, by contrast, presented a population of almost a million Spanish speakers. Mexican immigrants escaping the violence of the Mexican Revolution who took advantage of surplus agricultural and industry jobs became another new and large group of Spanish speakers starting in the 1910s. These Mexicans quickly came to outnumber treaty citizen families in the Southwest (though New Mexico received far fewer of these immigrants than its neighbors). U.S. political and economic interest in Latin America explains the final two groups of Spanish speakers. Latin Americans who visited the United States became watchdogs, with journalists sharing the conditions of Spanish speakers in the United States with readers in Latin America. Finally, Anglos across the country began learning Spanish in the hope of taking advantage of Latin American business or political opportunities, making Spanish the most learned non-English language in the early 1940s. Spanish speakers and interest in Spanish remained a constant presence in the United States throughout the early decades of the twentieth century.

As the influence of Spanish as a language of government in the Southwest declined, Spanish became a language with competing political meanings. New Mexico's use of Spanish as a language of governance largely disappeared in the 1930s. After nine decades, Anglo visions of English as the language of government prevailed but not to the complete cultural exclusion of Spanish. Citizenship did not bind these Spanish speakers; most Mexican immigrants lacked the ability to make claims to language rights as citizens. Mexican immigrant efforts to organize in Spanish came into conflict with a strong Americanization movement that sought to eradicate "undesirable" Mexican cultural traits and teach "American" ones, including the English language. The prevailing view of Spanish by U.S. citizens as the language of Mexican migrants, whom they deemed undesirable, shifted the politics of the Spanish language to discussions of eradicating a radical and foreign language. But Anglo views of Spanish encompassed more than just Americanization.

A countervailing view of Spanish opened up the possibility that Spanish served another purpose. Supporters of Pan-Americanism—both in the United States and in Latin America—encouraged Spanish-language instruction in order to prepare ambitious young people for economic and political opportunities available in Latin America. Spanish therefore became a political language that would help the United States attain power in the hemisphere and then globally in the twentieth century. In Puerto Rico, colonial subjects' (and after 1917, citizens') rejection of the English language allowed Puerto Ricans to use the Spanish language politically to distance themselves from the United States and to retain political and cultural autonomy.

Views of the Spanish language by elected officials and the general public in the Southwest and in Washington became increasingly contradictory in light of the simultaneous presence of the rhetorics of Americanization and Pan-Americanism. The politics surrounding those who spoke the language and the reasons they should be permitted to retain it or acquire it show that even when Spanish concessions disappeared from the law, the United States never escaped the political implications of the Spanish language.

LANGUAGE, NATIONALISM, AND MIGRATION

Examining the politics of Spanish-language use in the United States reveals how the idea of the nation has evolved over two centuries of global migration and integration. The United States is not a monolingual exception in a multilingual world; different states and localities have always acknowledged the presence of languages other than English. Historians and the general public have largely interpreted the early politics of Spanish as a history of minoritization, loss, or perhaps, for the more optimistic, continuity. I tell a different story here, one of migration and of how speakers of a nondominant language challenge citizens' understandings of their own nationalism.

I am fascinated by how the totality of Spanish-language politics offers an entry point into a story that not only transcends individual states, territories, and communities, but is larger than the United States. Focusing on Spanish shows the ramifications of persistent migration, which is the factor that sets Spanish apart from every other non-English language in the United States. While some immigrant language groups—especially German—experienced many decades of renewal, Spanish speakers have become the major story of the twenty-first century, due to Latin America's proximity to the United States and the sheer number of immigrants who have chosen to enter the country.[22] Their desires for recognition, to make a political impact, and to embody cultural or economic change encounter opposition from long-standing citizens. This fissure in ideas, values, and practices often precludes mutual understanding.

The story of how the United States has responded to the presence of a distinct language group that continues to replenish itself connects the country with the global movement of people—a trend that has become a global dilemma.[23] It may seem counterintuitive, then, that this book focuses on Spanish-speaking U.S. citizens. Yet without the original Spanish settlements, the treatment of Spanish in the United States would more closely resemble that of other immigrant languages. Through the experience of the treaty citizens, it is possible to interpret the ramifications of migration from Spanish-speaking countries for the politics of the Spanish language as a whole. Analyzing the role of Spanish-speaking institution builders grants a broader understanding of the arc and privileged position of the place of Spanish in the United States.

According to the 2000 U.S. Census, Latinos surpassed African Americans as the largest minority group in the United States. The last wave of immigration from Latin America, combined with internal migration from the Southwest, has resulted in Latinos becoming political players in such unlikely places as North Carolina, Georgia, and other areas not associated with long-standing Latino communities. The concerns with migrant belonging, cultural shifts and exchange, and generational upheaval are not unique to the Southwest or the United States. This longer history provides a new perspective that supplies evidence of Spanish having a historical role as a language of politics. This evidence counters the views of the media and federal officials who are involved in debates over the use of language in the country and who interpret Spanish solely as an immigrant or foreign language.

LIVING LANGUAGE

Jefferson Martenet, an Anglo migrant who arrived in California in 1852 from his native Baltimore, joined the xenophobic Know-Nothing party and the San Francisco Vigilance Committee of 1856.[24] At first glance, he would seem to have no real connection to *californios* or Spanish; if anything, one might expect that he was repelled by them. But in an 1853 letter home, he wrote about a "certain hombre" and the "Sierra Nevada (Snowy Mountains)" and used the terms *sombrero* and *zapatero*.[25] Martenet was just one of many Anglos who came to California with no previous knowledge of Spanish but adopted Spanish phrases or learned the language as a marker of their new home and as a means of transacting business with treaty citizens.

This flexible approach to language was, of course, a two-way street. The Civil War captain Porfirio J. Jimeno was educated on the East Coast and came from a prominent *californio* family.[26] In 1865, he wrote to his uncle Pablo de la Guerra, a *californio* statesman from Santa Barbara, using English more than Spanish but including what could be described as an early form of Spanglish. "Hemos tenido un lindo viaje de Drum Barracks a este punto.* 'Via hell!' alias 'Carrisso Creek,'" he wrote as he traveled through the Arizona territory.[27]

The history of Spanish-language politics in the United States is dynamic and nonlinear. Both Spanish and English are living languages and have regularly been altered by new speakers and writers who adopt words and phrases—either completely or in slightly altered form—from each other as well as from other languages. The languages themselves have never been uniform. The Spanish heard throughout the United States includes various regional vocabularies, along with the dialects stemming from the many countries and territories that are points of origin for the current Latino population. Spanish-language words or derivations are often spoken or written with no recognition of their Spanish origins. Place-names like San Francisco, San Diego, Nevada, Montana, and Colorado, along with common words including *patio, plaza, vanilla, canyon, tornado, mustang,* and *corral,* demonstrate the legacy of Spanish in the United States. Spanish itself has changed to such an extent that there is an Academia Norteamericana de la Lengua Española (North American Academy of the Spanish Language). This institution serves to preserve and draw attention to the particular "estadounidismos"—the specific uses of the language that originated in the United States—in a bid to convince the Dictionary of the Royal Spanish Academy to establish norms for this form of the language.[28] The mixing and melding of new concepts and forms of expression have left each language richer.

---

*"We have had a good journey to Drum Barracks to this point."

Spanish-language quotations throughout this book hint at the changing texture and flavor of the written language over a hundred-year period. By including the original Spanish, I hope to provide a small snapshot of both formal and more casual linguistic choices. The alternative—providing a translation without the original text—offers only one possible interpretation rather than permitting those who know Spanish to read and judge the sentiment and meaning for themselves. The quotations reflect regional variations in dialect, vocabulary, and slang but also show how even formal language changes over time. For these reasons, Spanish-language quotations appear as the authors wrote them, without editorial intervention. The best crowd-sourced English-language translations follow in parentheses or in notes.[29] This approach serves as a reminder of the presence of Spanish in political, economic, and social contexts and reaffirms the language choices made by the historical actors.

SOURCES AND SCOPE

In 1889, the treaty citizen and village teacher Jesús María Hilario Alarid published a poem on the virtues of using Spanish in the United States. Titled "El idioma español" (The Spanish Language), the poem reflected *nuevomexicano* pride in Spanish and argued for its retention broadly in the extensive Spanish-language press: *Que el inglés y castellano / Ambos reinen a la vez / En el suelo americano* (That English and Spanish / Both reign at once / On American soil). Alarid saw Spanish as the major language of culture that originated in Spain and should be kept even as the community learned English. His poem showcased a major argument for Spanish-language retention, even as he conceded English was the language of government.[30]

Treaty citizens' commitment to Spanish abounds in traditional sources like Spanish-language newspapers, but it also appears in sources more rarely explored by historians, including territorial and municipal records, state session laws and journals, federal official letters, political party collections, election rolls, and Senate hearings. While treaty citizens often initiated the discussions, federal officials also spoke of Spanish concessions among themselves and Congress determined federal programs or translation support for territories.

This book uses all of these sources to reconstruct a largely literate, and therefore often top-down, history of official policies for the Spanish language. While accents, vocabulary, and choices of language are highlighted throughout the book whenever possible, the vast majority of the sources uncovered are written, rather than oral, which means that literate male elites—state builders and officeholders of some privilege and means—dominate the sources and, by extension, this book. Nevertheless, I have attempted to incorporate individual desires and community language aspirations into this admittedly policy-driven history. I have endeavored to balance a broad range of Spanish-language politics and Spanish speakers' preferences to provide extensive coverage of the place of Spanish in the Southwest and the nation.

An American Language is a political history of language and identity organized in ten chapters in two parts. The first five chapters deal with the crucial factors that permitted Spanish to become a language of Southwest politics. The chapters together show how treaty citizens dealt with their new lives in the United States and explain why elite treaty citizens chose to invest their limited political capital in language rights and a U.S.-based political system. The primary and immediate motivating factor for treaty citizens was land, the focus of the first chapter. Treaty citizens prioritized their ties to the land over the draw of resettling in Mexico, which would have permitted cultural retention. Precarious elite landownership enabled Spanish to emerge as a language of governance in the Southwest, a display of power considered in the second chapter whose manifestation is most visible in the official translations commissioned at the state, territorial, and federal levels. The staying power of these translation concessions is explained in chapter 3, as it correlated with individual and collective opportunities to learn either Spanish or English. Chapter 4 recovers the formation of a bilingual form of political engagement from the legislature to elections to newspapers. The story of treaty citizens and language remained important in New Mexico, where it was largely undetected nationally until a well-publicized Senate visit in 1902, a story that unfolds in chapter 5. Part 1's five chapters follow the arc of treaty citizens and their descendants' use of Spanish as a form of political power and as a core marker of their identity.

Part 2 traces the shifting and competing political uses of Spanish in the United States. The five chapters in this part consider Spanish speakers who originated beyond the Southwest in relation to long-standing Spanish speakers in the first four decades of the twentieth century. Chapter 6 discusses how Spanish speakers used the language to create opposing identities as citizens and migrants. The gradual loss of Spanish as a major political language in New Mexico by the 1930s meant the end of Spanish as a language of government within the contiguous United States. While the loss was a victory for the idea of "Americanization," the long use of Spanish in New Mexico's government was also a testament to the staying power of bilingual governance in the country. Spanish speakers faced a formidable foe in the supporters of Americanization. Fiscal limitations and disinterest hindered educators' ability to adequately implement English-only preferences, as I describe in chapter 7. School districts often prohibited Spanish, but somewhat counterintuitively, they also often segregated Spanish-speaking students from English-speaking ones (often for racial, rather than language, reasons).[31] Americanization sentiments never fully dominated, however, in part because they were at odds with the rising interest in Pan-Americanism. Chapter 8 examines how Spanish speakers used the national interest in Pan-Americanism to elevate their native tongue's importance; it could now be employed as a form of U.S. nationalism. The competing efforts of Americanization and Pan-Americanism expose a contracted American self-image that increasingly disconnected speaking Spanish from U.S. citizenship, even as the country embraced the language in order to achieve new hemispheric economic and political goals.

These broader conflicting national Spanish-language policies and interests intensified during World War II and are the focus of the final two chapters. Chapter 9 turns to federal agencies that employed members of the ethnic Mexican community; the government agency archives at times offer a remarkable understanding of how geography and a region's relationship to Mexican immigration resulted in Spanish speakers' distinct relationships with the Spanish language and the nation. Chapter 10 continues with a close analysis of a 1943 Senate hearing in Puerto Rico that opposed Spanish-language use at the same time that New Mexico revisited compulsory Spanish instruction statewide. It argues that Spanish became a language of culture and a form of respect for the past in New Mexico, whereas in Puerto Rico it remained a language of government and a necessity in society. Finally, the epilogue turns to the post–World War II era, when the mass arrival of Latino immigrants transformed U.S. language politics in a number of ways.

The politics of the Spanish language in the United States began as a regional story but has become national. Stories of Spanish-language use, varied in topic and impact, emerge from all parts of the United States. Puerto Rico persists as a Spanish-speaking territory. U.S. cities owe their resilience and revival in large part to Latino and immigrant workers and their vibrant neighborhoods and businesses.[32] Scientists and educators have made an about-face; in the 1930s many concluded that bilingualism was akin to a disability that led to a lower IQ, whereas today bilingualism is embraced as a marker for a healthier, more elastic, and more agile brain for the old and a positive model for early language development in babies and youth.[33] In 2016, California repealed an anti–bilingual education proposition voted on in 1998; in 2017, it introduced legislation to permit diacritical marks in official records to be more cognizant of "family, tradition, and identity."[34] Affluent communities like Palo Alto, California, and Princeton, New Jersey, have joined districts in Santa Fe, New Mexico, and Miami, Florida, in creating Spanish-immersion elementary programs that support the values of bilingual education. And educators more generally espouse the benefits of bilingualism for all students.[35]

Despite these successes, the larger public and the government have almost exclusively treated Spanish as an immigrant language in the twenty-first century, with no perceived rights or precedence rather than as a partner in governance and society.[36] By the end of the twentieth century, Spanish's transition from a language of politics to a political language was largely complete. U.S. English, an organization hoping to make English the official language of the nation, and rising anti-immigrant sentiment in state politics won many successes in the 1980s and 1990s just as the largest boom in Spanish-speaking immigrants increased discussions about the need for and importance of bilingualism. While many academics, educators, and elected leaders in certain parts of the country see the presence of Spanish (and other languages) as a net positive, others denounce immigrants' use of foreign languages (particularly when those immigrants are undocumented). In 1995, Texas state district judge Samuel C. Kiser accused the mother of a five-year-old of effectively abusing her child by speaking to her only in Spanish. This was too much even for U.S. English, which denounced the judge's attempt to regulate the private language choices of a family.[37] In 2017, Oklahoma state representative Mike Ritze suggested all non-English-speaking children should be turned over to Immigration and Customs Enforcement (ICE), which would then determine their citizenship status.[38] Counties in states like Georgia are fielding (and at present denying) requests to offer bilingual ballots and other social services in Spanish.[39] These perpetually competing forces make language politics especially compelling; and this later clash, far from a brand-new development, marks the interaction and coexistence with Spanish speakers as a recurrent issue.

As these opposing reactions to the presence of Spanish-speaking immigrants show, the Spanish language is used by politicians, courts, and nativist organizations as a test of sorts, a test that determines who is deemed "American" in the United States. Spanish serves as a marker of difference and has become a factor in making racial assumptions. Hearing Spanish has drawn varied reactions across the nation. The scales have tipped at times in Spanish speakers' favor; at other times the scales have tipped significantly against them.

The long, deep, and varied history of Spanish in the United States is not well known. This oversight is understandable, since the major influx of Spanish speakers has occurred in the past forty years. These newer migrants join the descendants of treaty citizens and the children of early migrants, whose history can provide lessons on their long-held vision of belonging. Treaty citizens proclaimed their American citizenship while speaking an American language: Spanish.

PART ONE

A Language of Politics

1848–1902

CHAPTER I

United by Land

Los habitantes de California no habiendo tenido otra cosa à que dedicarse mas que à la vida campestre y pastoril, . . . oyeron con sorpresa y desmayo que por una acta del Congreso, se nombrò una Comision con la facultad de examinar todos los títulos, confirmar ò desaprobar . . . ha producido el efecto mas desastroso.*

—Antonio Ma. Pico et al., Petition, "Al Honorable Senado y Casa de
    Representantes, de los Estados Unidos de America," February 21, 1859

When José M. Gallegos, the first *nuevomexicano* terrritorial representative elected to Congress from New Mexico, took office in 1853, he resembled the vast majority of the citizens he sought to represent, in that he spoke only Spanish. Upon Gallegos's reelection in 1856, Miguel A. Otero, his bilingual and U.S.-educated opponent, appealed the results to Congress. Otero emphasized his ability to speak English, noting his willingness to address the legislature "in the language of its laws and its constitution."[1] Gallegos's impassioned self-defense was translated and read from the floor by Georgia representative Alexander H. Stevens. Gallegos protested the "sneers and jests" of "certain honorable members of this body" inflicted simply because he wished to "be heard by counsel (because of [his] inability to make a formal discourse in English)." He noted the "painful disappointment at these exceptions to the generous spirit which [he] had been encouraged to expect from all the representatives of a free and magnanimous people."[2] Otero emerged victorious

---

* "The inhabitants of California having had no other choice but to dedicate themselves to the rural and pastoral life, . . . heard with [surprise and] dismay of the appointment by Act of Congress of a commission with the right to examine all titles and confirm and disprove. . . . [It] has brought about the most disastrous effects."

from his appeal and began a five-year run as New Mexico's congressional representative.[3]

Gallegos, like other nonindigenous Spanish-speaking *nuevomexicanos*, had been granted citizenship in the terms of the Treaty of Guadalupe Hidalgo. As a member of a new class of treaty citizens, Gallegos had expected better treatment, both for himself and for his constituents. His treatment by Congress, however, suggests that those in the federal government had a more limited understanding of treaty citizens' rights and obligations.

In California, new treaty citizens encountered even more limits to their participation in political life. Nevertheless, they overwhelmingly chose to remain on their land after the U.S. takeover. As landowners, the treaty citizens—the majority of whom were Spanish speakers—required access to the language of power. Their desire to retain their privileges deepened their investment in the U.S. territorial or state system even as the English dominance of such a system led to loss of land and disrespect from Anglos.[4]

Never before had the U.S. government offered so much power to people who did not speak English or whose whiteness was in question. With the end of the U.S.-Mexican War, the United States acquired 525,000 square miles encompassing deserts, mountains, and canyons and populated largely by autonomous Indians. In New Mexico, *nuevomexicanos* comprised almost the entire settler population. In Northern California, *californios* found themselves overrun by Anglo settlers, whereas in Southern California they made up most of the settler population. The United States needed these treaty citizens to maintain control of the vast new territories it had acquired. These conditions permitted treaty citizens to establish social and political institutions that operated in Spanish—sometimes exclusively so.

This chapter explores the logic and limitations of treaty citizens' claim to Spanish through their fights to retain their land—a proxy for power. But because an understanding of their claims depends on their legal status, the chapter opens with a brief account of how the situation of Spanish-speaking citizens differed from that of other persons living in territories acquired by the United States. Even within the category of treaty citizens, however, landowners' experiences varied dramatically between California, which became a state immediately after its incorporation into U.S. territory, and New Mexico, which remained a territory until 1912. Treaty citizens in both California and New Mexico went to great lengths to retain their holdings, but their attempts to do so under different federal land confirmation criteria produced markedly different results.

A NEW KIND OF CITIZEN

The presence of a Spanish-speaking citizenry who preceded Anglos remains obscured in many stories of westward expansion. Rather than a "triumphant" story of inevitable national homogenization, that the United States set up territorial governments suggests regional fragmentation and disconnection. Granting citizenship through the Treaty of Guadalupe Hidalgo to former Mexican citizens is one major example of this diversity. This result was not predetermined. Uncertainty ruled all aspects of former Mexican citizens' lives as the war ended. What would happen to their land and possessions? Would they receive rights under the new government? How would they function in an English-speaking society? The nation could have imposed an English-language mandate as a prerequisite for holding office or for statehood. Instead, Congress legally incorporated former Mexican citizens based on geography.

Northern Mexican territorial residents encountered two distinct paths to U.S. citizenship. *Tejanos*, former Mexican citizens who had lived in tenuous settlements along the Río Bravo since 1749, received citizenship when Texas became a state in 1845.[5] By this point, however, the *tejanos* made up only one-tenth of Texas's population. The *empresario* system—which aided *tejano* economic ambitions and ensured their safety from autonomous Indians—brought an influx of Anglo and European settlers in the 1820s that left *tejanos* greatly outnumbered. *Tejanos* nevertheless survived through a set of rapidly shifting national allegiances to the Spanish Empire, Mexico, the Republic of Texas, the United States, the Confederacy, and finally the United States again. Upon its founding in 1836, the Republic of Texas swiftly dismantled Spanish and Mexican land grants, redistributing land based on length of occupancy. Many *tejanos* received the maximum allotment only to sell their properties to secure cash from speculators or rebuild after the war.[6]

Tejano appeals for the republic to recognize Spanish as a language of governance ended in frustration. The republic's governing structure included some *tejanos*—including three signatories to its constitution—who sided with Texas over Mexico.[7] During its second legislative session, a joint resolution requested that the Spanish language be used so as to accommodate "our fellow citizens" who were left "wholly ignorant" of laws for "which their obedience was required."[8] By the time the U.S. government ratified Texas statehood in 1845, the republic had experienced ten years of English-language rule disrespecting *tejanos* and their land rights.[9] The following year, the state legislature allowed Spanish translations of certain laws selected by the governor.[10] These realities of landownership and language separated the experience of *tejanos* from other residents of the Mexican northern territories.[11]

A year after Texas joined the nation, the United States began its military quest to take over Mexico's land. The campaign targeted a twenty-five-year-old nation whose adult citizens had lived through a major shift from the Spanish Empire to the Mexican nation.[12] In the generation following Spanish rule, land passed from Catholic missions to settler ranches that often extended beyond initial Spanish settlement. *Californios* received larger land grants, but female mission workers and neophyte Indians also received small grants.[13] In New Mexico, land grants clustered around access to waterways, with select individuals receiving large parcels that also housed non–grant holders. The Spanish crown and the Mexican government also deeded communal land grants to settlers and *genizaros* (culturally more Spanish Indians). The best and safest land often went to male settlers of higher status, though *genizaros* and women received grants too.[14]

In 1846, when U.S. general Stephen Kearney entered New Mexico, he placed a couple of *nuevomexicanos* in positions in the military government— a decision that appeased residents and foreshadowed future U.S. policy. His first public speech to residents reinforced the validity of an official use for Spanish. To assuage *nuevomexicano* fears, Kearney promised that "el fuerte, y el debil; el rico y el pobre; son iguales ante la ley[;] protegeré los derechos de todos con igualdad" (the strong and the weak; the rich and the poor; I will protect the rights of all with equality).[15] At first, New Mexico accepted the military occupation without armed resistance, but its residents reconsidered within a year. *Nuevomexicano* Pablo Montoya and Taos Pueblo member Tomás Romero led a revolt in 1847 resulting in the execution of Governor Charles Bent, his brother-in-law Pablo Jaramillo, Taos sheriff Stephen Lee, Judge Cornelio Vigil, attorney J. W. Leal, and a youth, Narciso Beaubien.[16] The presence of both Anglo and Spanish surnames among the dead shows how quickly *nuevomexicano* elites had become symbols of the new U.S. leadership system. Similarly, Southern California fought into 1847 as *californios* defended their autonomy. Both efforts ultimately failed.[17]

On February 2, 1848, Mexico ceded its northern region, which would become the U.S. Southwest, in the process creating a new class of U.S. citizens. Congress ratified the Treaty of Guadalupe Hidalgo on March 10, with Article IX stipulating, "The Mexicans . . . in the territories aforesaid, shall not preserve the character of citizens of the Mexican Republic, [but] shall be incorporated into the Union[,] . . . [with] enjoyment of all the rights of citizens of the United States."[18] This was hardly the first time that the United States had absorbed another empire's citizens in the process of its own territorial expansion—the Louisiana Purchase had, after all, offered U.S. citizenship to "inhabitants" (as determined by Congress) who lived in the 828,000-square-mile territory.[19] The administration of the treaty and its use by the former citizens differed drastically, however. Louisiana had a brief, twelve-year territorial status. Louisiana's state constitution only gave white male residents full political and voting rights.[20] As citizens of a fully incorporated state, Louisiana's white residents had no need to secure their rights through a treaty and those deemed nonwhite by the state had little recourse. For those granted citizenship by the Treaty of Guadalupe Hidalgo, even those deemed white often held an ambiguous racial status. U.S. government and elected officials portrayed the vast majority of treaty citizens as mixed race rather than white. The 1790 Naturalization Act limited naturalization to "free white" individuals, suggesting that treaty citizens sidestepped a more fraught naturalization process by being legally categorized by the federal government as white.[21] Treaty citizens became the first group of people considered ambiguously white to gain collective citizenship in the United States.

The Mexican government ratified the treaty on May 19 without seeking clarification on whether the treaty applied to all of its citizens or merely all white persons.[22] Mexico included indigenous peoples in their designation of citizenship, but the United States did not.[23] The ramifications of this choice emerged quickly when federal officials actively discouraged Pueblos from participating in territorial elections in exchange for allowing them to retain their culture and customs.[24] The United States consistently refused to view the Pueblos and autonomous Indians living in the region as worthy of citizenship, despite their arguable inclusion in the treaty as Mexican citizens.[25] In contrast, the 1850 federal census categorized Spanish-speaking treaty citizens as "white." For Mexicans in the northern territories, language and culture served as the major markers of race and citizenship.[26] U.S. officials likely followed these conventions when they chose whom to label "white."

Many of the treaty citizens had deep ties to the land that extended back centuries. For example, Santa Fe, founded in 1610, is the oldest capital city in the United States. The 1850 census counted approximately 100,000 Mexican citizens divided between New Mexico, Texas, and California.[27] New Mexico's 61,547 inhabitants, 95 percent of whom were born within the territory, represented the largest U.S. territorial population in 1850.[28] The majority of these *nuevomexicanos* lived rural and modest existences (the census recorded farmer, laborer, and servant as the top three occupational positions) in small settlements (fewer than 1,000 inhabitants) clustered along traditional Pueblo village sites where there was better access to water and developing trade routes.[29] Santa Fe, the largest town and a major center of trade, claimed just under 5,000 inhabitants.[30] Native-born *californios* clustered in small farming and ranching communities in southern counties like Los Angeles (the largest settlement, with 3,500 people) and Santa Barbara (1,185), far away from the mining regions to the north that were rapidly filling with Anglos.[31]

Elite treaty citizens wrote a mutually intelligible Spanish and shared their Catholicism and other cultural customs inherited from Spain.[32] While the presence of Spanish colonial authorities had increased the range of Spanish used in governance and trade over the centuries, Indian phrases and customs remained in use throughout the region into the Mexican period. The historical record obscures much of this multilingual reality by privileging European language sources over indigenous ones.[33] The absence of major cities and limited transportation options—when compared to those in central Mexico or the eastern United States—left the region's residents with few opportunities to form a common identity. As late as 1864, J. Ross Browne claimed it was simpler to execute a voyage from San Francisco to China than to Santa Fe.[34] While this was an exaggeration, the future states of California, Colorado, Arizona, New Mexico, and Texas developed in isolation, forming their own sense of identity and cultural customs. If united, citizens of the future Southwest might have learned from one another as their exposure to an English-speaking world occurred on different timetables.

RETAINING SETTLERS IN NEW MEXICO TERRITORY

When New Mexico became a U.S. territory, *nuevomexicanos* comprised almost the entire settler population. Without their leadership and aid, control of the territory would revert to the autonomous Indians who had led raids in the period leading up to and following the U.S.-Mexican War.[35] The prospect of losing settlers in New Mexico provided a strong incentive for the United States to acquiesce and support *nuevomexicano* cultural demands—including creating a political system in Spanish. The Mexican government's attempt to recolonize its former citizens magnified the threat.

Treaty citizens in New Mexico included those who owned no land, found no reason to learn English, or chose culture over the new form of government. As Francisco Ramírez of Los Angeles's *El Clamor Público* wrote, Mexico offered its former citizens a lot; after all, it was "donde están su idioma, sus costumbres, sus esperanzas . . . donde, en fin, van a gozar de los derechos del ciudadano libre" (where your language, your customs, your hopes reside . . . where, in the end, you will enjoy the rights of free citizens).[36] New Mexico's second governor, Donaciano Vigil (1847–48), embraced U.S. rule, but his correspondence with other elite *nuevomexicanos* lamented the loss of culture and language. At least one individual planned to avoid the loss by leaving for Mexico.[37] Countless others considered—and some actually attempted to move to Mexico immediately following the war—but they soon found that the federal government had no intention of encouraging mass resettlement. The United States chose retention when confronted with a decreasing number of treaty citizens.

Mexican president José Joaquín de Herrera—aware of former Mexicans' potential dissatisfaction—issued a recolonization plan in August 1848 promising economic resources and land for any former Mexican citizens who moved to Mexico.[38] Mexico employed three commissioners to recruit voluntary repatriates in California, New Mexico, and Texas.[39] The New Mexico commissioner, Father Ramón Ortiz, a Santa Fe native, encouraged resettlement by focusing attacks on *nuevomexicanos'* new inferior status as treaty citizens. He claimed, "Aunque sabían que, no obstante las garantías del tratado de paz, perderlan todas sus propiedades, querían perderlo todo más bien que pertenecer a un gobierno en el cual tenían menos garantías y eran tratados con más desprecio que la raza de África" (Although they knew they would lose all their property, notwithstanding the guarantees of the peace treaty, they preferred to lose all rather than belong to a government from which they had fewer guarantees and were treated with more disregard than the African race).[40] Ortiz received incredibly high support from *nuevomexicanos* in many villages—especially from San Miguel del Vado County, where 90 percent signed resettlement papers.[41]

Mexican officials, including Chihuahua's governor, Angél Trías, extended a generous welcome to potential repatriates.[42] As *nuevomexicanos'* enthusiasm for repatriation grew, official opinion in New Mexico worked to convince them to stay. "You will make the sacrifice of living with and suffering the cruel invasions of the barbarous," warned a Santa Fe newspaper.[43] The threat was real, as the Mexican government expected the settlers to fight the indigenous population from these border regions to make a stable permanent Mexican settlement.[44] Vigil responded by prohibiting Father Ortiz from registering recolonization candidates in Santa Fe. He required that repatriates sign a paper confirming their desire to retain Mexican citizenship, a provision that Father Ortiz found difficult to accomplish.[45] The next territorial governor, John Washington, put up other barriers for *nuevomexicanos* trying to claim Mexican citizenship and eventually expelled Father Ortiz and other recolonization boosters.[46] The U.S. secretary of war weighed in, claiming that the treaty's failure to mention repatriation procedures meant that it was prohibited.[47]

The U.S. effort to retain its treaty citizens seems counterintuitive. Here was an opportunity to have fewer Spanish-speaking inhabitants—a result seemingly welcome to nativists who refused to view the new population as white or American and consistent with the racially discriminatory views that prevented the United States from claiming the entire Mexican nation.[48] Yet treaty citizens, especially in New Mexico, served as the major claim the United States had on the territory. The federal government's inability to easily govern, oversee, or even access the territory elevated *nuevomexicano* power. The absence of treaty citizens risked autonomous Indians overrunning the territory as they continued to raid and push against the settlement throughout the 1850s.[49] A lack of laborers and residents would diminish U.S. land claims and endanger the lives of those citizens who remained.[50] The government therefore had incentive to support elite *nuevomexicanos* as local power figures who knew best how to govern the larger population.

Having squashed any remaining recolonization efforts, the United States appointed a surveyor-general in 1854 to determine land grants. Congress made no mention of language proficiency in its discussion of the bill creating the surveyor general—ignoring a potential language discrepancy between *nuevomexicanos* and the federal official.[51] While the surveyor-general approved the vast majority of land claims he considered, they languished in uncertainty without formal congressional approval.[52] Even without official land claims, *nuevomexicanos* remained on the land, keeping their demographic dominance.

Land claims were important not only for their obvious relationship to capital and water rights but also because they offered a layer of protection against Indian raids. *Nuevomexicanos* opposed Indian raids with force—the muster rolls of New Mexico's mounted militia reveal almost entirely Spanish-surnamed individuals—but when that failed, they filed claims for compensation.[53] The territorial legislature wrote a law accepting claims that detailed loss of property so as to recover raided property or receive payment if it was sold to others.[54] By filing claims, *nuevomexicanos* reasserted their rights as full citizens and indicated their acceptance of the U.S. government as a legitimate authority in the region. Monolingual Spanish speakers must have used mediators to navigate the system, because they learned of the law and submitted depredation claims mostly in English through Anglo lawyers.

The number of compensatory claims expanded during the Civil War, when Confederate forces raided *nuevomexicanos'* lands.[55] A series of claims in Spanish and English from small villages and ranches ranged from $50 to over $13,000, with livestock being the most common item "taken by force by Texan troops." Each of the sworn statements of loss included some variation of the following claim: "I beg to state that I am a citizen of the United States." Some mentioned their military responsibilities or war involvement, while others asserted that they "always have been loyal to the Government thereof."[56] Some *nuevomexicanos* expected territorial officials to understand their losses in Spanish.

New Mexico's position as an isolated buffer territory meant that land concerns and claims did not reach full force until the railroads arrived in the 1870s and 1880s. At that point, Anglo settlers, speculators, and lawyers—aided by some *nuevomexicanos* who desired more land—descended on the Spanish-speaking landowners.[57] With their hands tied, the New Mexico legislature turned to Congress through a legislative memorial: the protocol state or territorial legislatures use to petition Congress. The 1872 memorial confirmed that treaty citizens remained disproportionately affected by the ambiguousness of land claims when it proclaimed that any possible land confirmation procedure should include notices in both English and Spanish, because "very few of the parties interested . . . understand the English language."[58] Memorials by New Mexico's legislature to Congress further demonstrate their concern as they repeatedly requested a board of commissioners to settle land claims. Three such memorials appear in the 1880s Session Laws—a testament to *nuevomexicanos'* rising sense of urgency as Anglo settlers began to change the demographic makeup of the territory.[59]

The federal government finally created the Court of Private Land Claims to settle land disputes in 1891. Congress authorized a federally funded interpreter and translator to aid the court and also required notification of upcoming sessions along with the publication of the surveyor-general's survey in both English and Spanish.[60] As a territory, New Mexico lacked the representation or power in Washington to make land claim settlement a priority sooner. The commission also handled claims from former New Mexico lands in parts of the states of Colorado and Arizona.

Those who received confirmed land grants included *nuevomexicanos*. For those *nuevomexicanos* left unconfirmed, the fight to stay on the land did not end with the decision of the land commission.[61] *Nuevomexicanos* continued to operate locally on the land in Spanish. Comprising the majority of residents and an overwhelming number of residents in the northern counties in the territory, *nuevomexicanos* elected territorial officials who could bring their language concerns forward to Congress. Staying together on their settlements had strengthened their political power.

HOLDING LAND IN THE GOLDEN STATE

Californios faced the daunting task of living on land whose laws and regulations became foreign overnight. A deluge of over 58,000 miners—some Anglo, some not—entered California upon the discovery of gold, quickly outnumbering approximately 8,000 native-born *californios*. Combined with inhabitants born in Mexico, treaty citizens made up just under a quarter of California's population in the 1850 census.[62] By 1852, the new state's population more than doubled, to over 260,000 people.[63] Aside from the cultural shock of demographic change, California's immediate bid for statehood meant that treaty citizens encountered an entirely different legal, political, economic, and social system from the one they knew in Mexico. The *californios* who accepted U.S. citizenship focused their economic and political strength on retaining their land. The language difficulties these landed and politically connected *californios* encountered provides the first major example of how treaty citizens navigated the new English-language world.

Anglos recognized treaty citizens as part of the landscape they expected to find in California but did not always accept *californios* as part of the expected *American* future of California.[64] This early dismissal of Spanish by Anglo settlers was possible because of the influx of English-speaking settlers and the general belief in Anglo claims to the land. *Californios* meanwhile initially remained a significant force in California politics because of their landownership and concentration away from the mines and cities.[65] The vast majority of landed *californios* remained on land that was their principal source of livelihood and identity. *Californios* in the southern coastal regions also owned businesses and performed the needed manual labor for the community. Their presence sometimes enriched and aided rather than detracted from the new settler experience.

The rapid arrival of so many Anglos and immigrants gave the question of land claims urgency. The full text of the Treaty of Guadalupe Hidalgo included a provision, Article X, that ensured the rights of Mexican land-grant holders. When it approved the treaty, however, the U.S. Congress omitted Article X. Some congressional members believed it would have extended land protections to *tejanos* and voted it down.[66] Rather than streamline the process across the entire ceded territory, Congress implemented distinct processes of land confirmation for New Mexico and California. In principle, if *californios* provided evidence of Mexican governor-issued land grants, they received land confirmation. In practice, *californios* quickly realized that their status as Spanish-language speakers limited their ability to make their claims.

In California, the process of settling land claims was intimately connected to the demands of statehood. The California legislature depended on property taxes to fund the state government and implement its laws. The state government tied tax increases to land improvements, so it behooved the state to transfer "wild" regions into agricultural ones.[67] The gold rush had moreover introduced nearly 100,000 landless citizens within California's borders. Within his first month in office, California's first U.S. senator, John C. Frémont, prepared and submitted a bill to encourage the federal government to settle land claims in his new state. Congress acceded to California's needs— largely due to the presence of settlers eager to take over the land, not at the request of *californio* landowners. The so-called Gwin Act (named after California's other senator, William M. Gwin) created a three-person commission to examine and rule on California land claims.[68]

The commissioners, appointed by Congress, had little understanding of the Spanish language or the Spanish or Mexican legal system. With few English-speaking treaty citizens and a new U.S. legal system to learn, elite *californios* turned to English-speaking lawyers to handle their cases before the land commissioners. "I am led to fear that the law and the mode in which it is to be administered, will prove hardly less than a legal confiscation of the old estates in California," the New York-trained lawyer Eugene Casserly opined. He fore-shadowed the unscrupulous lawyers who would "extort from their unsuspecting clients, the most monstrous fees, or . . . wrest them of half their lands."[69] Smaller landholders, many of them women and American Indians who had obtained their land grants from former mission holdings, had even fewer options.[70]

Misunderstandings resulting from language differences abounded through-out each stage of the process. The first hurdle was hearing about and meeting the deadlines for confirming land, which one letter claimed were "posted up . . . in all prominant [sic] places in the frontier." Josefa Fitch received a letter in a language she did not understand from M. M. Sexton, who threatened her with the loss of her land: "No person will be allowed more than two Leagues of land in the frontiers. So at any rate your ranch in lower California will be curtailed."[71] If californios did not submit their land titles by the government-imposed deadlines, they lost their land by default.

The commissioners required several pieces of evidence to confirm a land grant. In addition to providing legal proof of a Mexican-issued grant, claimants had to document their continuous residence on the land and structural and pastoral improvements. Successful documentation ranged from a government-issued grant to a diseño (a hand-drawn map that showed the natural boundaries of the property) or testimony or statements from witnesses familiar with the land and its use during the Mexican period.[72] Letters relating to land claims suggest all documents needed to be submitted with English-language translations. As proceedings continued decades after 1848, californios found themselves respon-sible for translating documents. Writing from the Palace Hotel in San Francisco, Mariano Guadalupe Vallejo explained to his daughter the detailed process necessary to support his land claim on the Presidio: "Me cuesta mucho trabajo, y dinerito qᵉ· no tengo, para buscarlos en todas partes; y despues págán los 'affidevits' al notario de cada uno de ellos, traducirlos al inglés" (It requires a lot of work and money that I don't have to locate them [possible witnesses], and afterwards to pay for notarized affidavits and English translations for each).[73]

Californios had the added disadvantage of getting lost in legal misunder-standings—whether through language or unfamiliarity with U.S. legal tradi-tions. Even with lawyers who attempted to keep costs down, like the popular Halleck, Peachy, and Billings firm, the layers of legal interpretations compounded the difficulties and increased the cost. "The sale of that ranch is so long and so full of terms and phrases of Spanish jurisprudence that it is almost impossible to translate well in English," one land lawyer, Henry Hal-leck, complained. He asked Pablo de la Guerra if a similar translation existed from another case to save the owner $100 to $200 in translation fees, "to avoid all possible expense to the Californians."[74] Halleck's courtesy was an excep-tion; *californio* complaints about lawyers' exorbitant charges abounded.[75]

Traveling, awaiting a court date, and paying for witness expenses inflated the costs of the land confirmation process. The commission held its sessions in San Francisco, far from the many treaty citizen landowners who lived in Southern California. Court costs became insufferable after Congress imposed an automatic appeal in 1852. *Californios* in Southern California faced a daunt-ing, yet unexpected, average wait time of seventeen years for full confirmation of their claims.[76] Halleck complained that the wait stemmed in part from commissioner replacements: "Even when they come, they must *learn* their duties + study Spanish some; so the wheels are blocked again for 5 or 6 months at least!"[77] Even Anglos—both those who entered the territory prior to the U.S.-Mexican War and received their own land grants and those who pur-chased land grants speculatively—faced long waits and daunting costs.[78]

Rather than appoint commissioners familiar with both Spanish and Mexican legal procedures (who may not have existed), the United States passed the burden of translation and interpretation to *californios*. Even after transla-tion, the commissioners had ample opportunity to misinterpret the legal intentions of New Spain and Mexico, as they read the codices through a distinctly U.S. legal lens. The use of the land during the Mexican period dif-fered significantly from what lawyers in the United States expected, making translations at times impossible or inaccurate. "You should have seen the dismay of my bewildered countrymen . . . when they learned that gentlemen from Virginia or Illinois had commented on the Spanish word *cultivo* and decided that it meant the raising of a patch of corn," Pablo de la Guerra said.[79]

The commission nevertheless afforded *californios* the opportunity to testify in their native language—albeit with a translator—and even used them as a district court resource. For example, former Mexican governor Juan B. Alvarado testified in the district court in the case *Stafford et al. v. Lick et al.* in 1857 and answered questions about pre-U.S. period practices for the sale of property. He also discussed the intricacies of how the word *poder* might be misinterpreted, "The interpretation of the word 'poder' in connection with the 1st two lines is something like what we call 'empower' in english. I give power or right." Alvarado disagreed with this as a full interpretation and elaborated that *poder* "gives the person mentioned in the paper a very extensive power over the property." He also gave his opinion on the interpretation of *que tengo concidio* as pertaining to "an antecedent sale or grant."[80] As a *californio*, Alvarado provided the context necessary to interpret both government practices and legal language.

Californios' desire to secure their land led to their learning the intricacies of the U.S. court system. The landed *californios*, by necessity, used their money, literacy, and networks to gain this knowledge. The last Mexican governor of Alta California, Pío Pico, provides just one example of the legal learning curve. He experienced the land cases both as a landowner and as a plausible witness. In 1888, Juan Luco wrote Pío Pico in a way that demonstrated both men's understanding of the new legal system. Luco wanted to figure out "como remediar este gran mal, ultimamente encontramos que la decicion tenia una falta Constitucional" (how to remedy this great ill, ultimately we found the decision had a constitutional defect).[81] Pico never learned English but conducted business and participated in legal proceedings throughout the state of California through translations and lawyers.[82] His papers include other discussions of land grant cases, as do the collections of many other *californios*.

While *californios* worked to obtain knowledge of the U.S. court system, they encountered disrespectful and discriminatory attitudes to their use of Spanish. Santa Barbara landowner and respected *californio* Pablo de la Guerra retained his political power into the U.S. period and used his position as state senator and lieutenant governor to voice his critiques and disappointments with the government's mistreatment of his people. "Our veracity was questioned because we spoke Spanish," he asserted incredulously in an 1860 speech discussing land grant cases. De la Guerra noted the constantly shifting requirements for land confirmation: "Now the approval of the Departmental Assembly was held to be a condition *sine qua non* of confirmation and now the residence of the grantee in *propia persona* upon his land."[83] He used his speeches and political involvement to support the rights of monolingual *californios*.

Treaty citizens had accepted a new sovereign legal power in their land, but what, de la Guerra asked, did they get in return? *Californios*, he asserted, were "treated as a conquered and inferior race" by the United States.[84] Translators with an agenda could easily misconstrue, interrogate, or misrepresent a Spanish speaker's testimony. As de la Guerra explained, "A disgraceful distinction between *white* testimony and ours was indelicately paraded and the unfortunate witness whose simple statements reached the Court, only through an interpreter, was submitted to the tedious ordeal of a cross examination that lasted several days without producing any result except to manifest the patient ingenuity of counsel and their determination to force the witness to contradict himself."[85] De la Guerra, writing in English, distinguished "white" testimony from "ours." He unmistakably identified with the Spanish speakers and intricately linked concepts of race with language. De la Guerra did so even as he spoke in a "white" way. Equipped with the funds and educational opportunities that allowed him to navigate both the Spanish- and English-speaking worlds of California, de la Guerra continued in his role as *patrón*, protecting and mediating for others who could not speak English.

As the U.S. period lengthened, *californios'* ability to operate in a Spanish world within California became more limited and disconnected from the broader English-speaking country. María Ignacio Bale, a niece of Vallejo, found it very difficult to have her Spanish-language contracts honored as she attempted to sell goods off of her lands. As her nephew wrote, "En St. Helena nadie me quiere fiar en ninguna tienda porque no tengo escritura[.] [E]l papel que isimos en español no bale nada" (In St. Helena no one wants to give me credit in any store because I don't have it written down[.] The paper we did in Spanish is not worth anything.). He offered to get a contract written for her in English if she wished.[86]

Even with the system stacked against them, elite *californios* proved themselves resilient and willing to fight. In 1855, some Los Angeles landowners issued a subscription to fund commissioners who would find legal ways to fight for their land. They hoped to repeal the current law that "acusa de fraudulentos los titulos" (accuses the titles of being fraudulent) for lands "que nos fueron garantidos por el tratado" (that were guaranteed to us in the treaty). They committed to paying five commissioners (Abel Stearns, Benito [Benjamin] Wilson, Julian Workman, Pío Pico, and Agustín Olvera) "para asegurar los servicios de una imprenta publica" (to secure the services of a printing press) to broaden their supporters. "Un pronto reconocimiento de nuestros justos y sagrados derechos" (A quick recognition of our just and sacred rights) became their most immediate plea.[87]

The long fight became more difficult as squatters and other challengers meant that even settled claims were not necessarily secure. Once defeated miners came down from the hills, many desired access to the vast, "open," and fertile land of California. They looked to the federal government for affordable access—expecting the same distribution patterns as in other parts of the West.[88] Prospective settlers approached what they considered "virgin lands."[89]

When prospective settlers learned that the lands they desired were held up in court, they began squatting on ranchland whose use remained unfathomable to those used to small family farms. The squatters "improved" the land, which resulted in loss of wealth and higher taxes for landowners. María Amparo Ruíz de Burton fictionalized the culture clashes between the squatters and the *californios* in her 1885 novel *The Squatter and the Don*. Set in the early 1870s, the book immortalizes her troubles with squatters on her San Diego County ranch through the fictional Amaro family. The Hispanicization of "squatter" into the Spanish word *esquata*, exemplifies the phenomenon as new to the U.S. period.[90] In part because the state legislature depended on "improvements" to increase its property tax base, the California legislature generally supported the interests of squatters over landowners, a rare political pairing.[91]

In the midst of so many challenges, a much-awaited positive response from the commission yielded jubilation. In 1874, A. Garriza congratulated Mariano Guadalupe Vallejo after he received title to the lands that included Petaluma: "¡Gracias á Dios! . . . por la familia mas noble, mas antigua y (con pardon de los yankees) mas ilustre de California" (Thanks be to God! . . . for the most noble, established and [with apologies to the Yankees] most illustrious family in California). He saw the victory as one for "la raza española" (the Spanish people) and crowed, "la que pertenecerá á la raza mas gloriosa del mundo. . . . ¡Diganlo los siglos!" (which will belong to the most glorious people in the world. . . . It will be shared forever!).[92] More than twenty years after the passage of the Gwin Act, Vallejo's celebration was a long time coming.

The commission ultimately upheld the vast majority of land claims in California—for those who could afford to wait. Faced with property taxes (which increased dramatically as the land became more valuable), the legal costs of protecting their land, a glutted cattle market due to settlement in the Midwest, the loss of cattle to drought, and loans with astronomical interest rates, many *californios* sold their claims well before confirmation, effectively ending their rancho way of life.[93] The U.S. period compounded economic, political, and environmental pressures facing the *californio* elite. By the 1880s, very few held their original claims, and boosters began drawing scores of new Anglo settlers into Los Angeles and other treaty citizen strongholds.[94]

Land interests bound elite treaty citizens to the United States. Treaty citizens had lived through various imperial and national claims to the land they settled.

After all, they had already transitioned from the Spanish Empire to the new Mexican nation prior to being incorporated through war into the United States. Through it all, they also alternately battled and lived with autonomous Indians who constantly asserted their presence and power on the land. Still, they chose to stay and fight for their settlements. Elite treaty citizens largely made the case for their land in Spanish, a decision that inhibited their individual claims but simultaneously offered a form of cultural power that incorporated all classes of treaty citizens into the larger U.S. political and electoral system. Elite treaty citizens proved resilient in their fight for the extension of citizenship rights promised in the treaty.

Californios routinely interacted with the courts and the federal government in their efforts to confirm their land claims; in the process, they became invested in state politics. In New Mexico, where *nuevomexicanos* retained their demographic advantage, the treaty citizens retained their power through both landownership and presence in the territorial government. New Mexico's long tenure as a territory resulted in a much longer wait for land confirmation than was the case in California. Together, elite treaty citizens in California and New Mexico found themselves defending not just their own land but also treaty citizens' collective right to understand the U.S. governance system in Spanish. Translations proved crucial to this process, as they alerted treaty citizens to the current land situation and allowed them to make their case in court. As the next chapter demonstrates, translation concessions also became a very important marker of treaty citizen power.

CHAPTER 2

Translation, a Measure of Power

Afirmamos que estas verdades son evidentes en si mismas; que todos los hombres fueron criados iguales; y que están doctados por su criador con ciertos derechos inagenables; que entre estos se hallan la vida, la libertad y la prosecucion de la felicidad.

—El Clamor Público, July 3, 1855

Tenemos estas verdades por evidentes en si mismas: que todos los hombres son creados iguales; que son dotados por su creador con ciertos derechos enajenables, que entre ellos se hallan la vida, la libertad, y el procurar la felicidad.*

—1866 Laws of the Territory of New Mexico

The egalitarian principles of the nation ring true in any language, though they are not always properly or efficiently translated. The two epigraphs above, both translations of lines from the Declaration of Independence, interpret the same material differently. *El Clamor Público*'s translation uses *criado* (nurse) and *criador* (breeder) rather than the familiar *creado* (created) / *creador* (creator) that appear in the New Mexico territorial laws. While *El Clamor Público*'s version may include a typographical error (*doctado* was likely a mistake), the words do alter the meaning.

Treaty citizens, few of whom spoke English, required language translations to participate in U.S. political institutions. Ignorance of the law is not an excuse for an individual, but is the same true if the majority of a community remains ignorant because those in power issue laws in a foreign language?

---

*"We hold these truths to be self-evident, that all men are created equal, and they are endowed by their Creator with certain unalienable Rights, that among these are Life, Liberty, and the pursuit of Happiness." www.archives.gov/founding/docs.

Translations and interpreters—some officially sanctioned and funded by governmental authorities and some not—bridged the language divide and permitted the Southwest to function. Translation broadened the opportunity for both literate and illiterate treaty citizens to hear the news as literate family members, friends, employers, and neighbors passed along information they gleaned from publications in Spanish. Translations reached larger audiences when interpreters joined English speakers on public stages. That territorial and state authorities continued to provide language translations illustrates Spanish speakers' continued relevance to the political process.

It is the power behind the existence of political translations that guides this chapter rather than the translations themselves.[1] For the first twenty-five years after the U.S.-Mexican War, territorial and state officials in California, Colorado, and New Mexico simply assumed Spanish translations were a necessary aspect of governing. The decline thereafter in translations and Spanish-language rights coincided with the United States gaining full control over its continental territory, by forcefully removing most American Indians from the best land. Signs of this control are apparent in the completion of the Atchison, Topeka, and Santa Fe Railroad, which led to an increased Anglo presence in the Southwest. The railroad arrived in New Mexico in 1880 and started a rate war with the Southern Pacific upon reaching its terminus in Los Angeles in 1885.[2]

Throughout the U.S. Southwest, Anglo predominance in treaty citizen strongholds marked the moment when both regional and federal authorities explicitly reconsidered the role of Spanish in political institutions. The result was not always initially English-only policies. As Anglos arrived, so too did European, Latin American, and Chinese immigrants. The introduction of a larger German immigrant population in particular led to German-language translations alongside Spanish in both Colorado and California. The official demise of Spanish in California began in 1879, almost in tandem with the end of Reconstruction. The Gilded Age that followed resulted in state laws that began to repress the African American vote in the 1880s and 1890s. National discourse regarding language politics changed as the nation's borders hardened (both racial and territorial), due in part to the addition of immigrants and insular subjects in 1898 who did not speak English. The more permissive language politics of the mid-nineteenth century largely disappeared as federal and educational policies explicitly favored English.

State legislatures throughout the United States printed various types of official translations throughout the nineteenth century. While official federal translations never received the support of Congress before 1848, over a dozen states translated state legislative journals and/or session laws or required county notices to be published in immigrant languages before 1880.[3] Pennsylvania and Louisiana stand out as two of the earliest adopters of translation policies.[4] Louisiana began its territorial status with few language sanctions but began requiring translators at legislative sessions after statehood and with the new 1845 state constitution.[5] The loss of language rights in the late nineteenth century renders starkly visible treaty citizen families' (and often European immigrants') inclusion in larger national and regional exclusionary and discriminatory policies—such as Jim Crow laws, Chinese Restriction, and Indian relocation to reservations—that limited full citizenship to native-born, white residents.[6]

MAKING A (LIMITED) BILINGUAL STATE IN CALIFORNIA

California is the first major example of negotiations over language between Anglo and European settlers and treaty citizens. In California, unlike New Mexico, *californios* did not make up a majority of the elected officials at the state level or in northern counties. *Californios* nevertheless benefited from the somewhat flexible understanding of the relationship between language and citizenship that Anglo settlers from eastern states brought with them to California. U.S. officials needed the cooperation of *californios* to understand the political culture of the territories they had acquired, and *californios* needed access to Spanish to contribute to government on both the local and state levels. While California never officially established a fully bilingual government, the realities of early state government required translation both on the floor of the legislature and in publicizing new laws.

Outlawing Spanish was not an option for U.S. officials in Monterey, the Mexican capital of California and the territory's second-largest *californio* town, in 1848.[7] In Monterey, as in other treaty citizen towns, the transfer from Spanish to English in municipal leadership recognized both the prior and continued role of treaty citizens. Municipal officials used Spanish to issue warrants and liquor licenses and to provide receipts for services rendered.[8] They received Spanish-language letters from *californios* requesting reimbursement and complaining about land taxes.[9] Common council minutes discuss conducting translations of proceedings, and, perhaps most important, an 1851 Spanish special election notice shows how municipal officials informed and encouraged *californios* to vote.[10]

Evidence of the continued use of Spanish in municipal Monterey cannot overshadow the fact that town governance quickly shifted to primarily English. The language power gap was more pronounced on occasions when *californios* explained their ignorance of the municipal government's actions for acting "without having given notice in Spanish."[11] *Californios* reasserted their language rights in this rapidly shifting system, sometimes using a paid interpreter. Without Spanish translations, *californios* who had held positions of leadership in Mexican California could not aid others with the adjustment to the new system of government, compounding the difficulties of the transfer of power.

The textual evidence from Monterey's municipal archives provides few definitive conclusions on the role of Spanish in official town business during this period. The omission of the word *translation* on documents and the preference for English-language records may leave the impression that Monterey operated in English sooner than it actually did; archives, after all, are often kept in the dominant language regardless of the original language used. For example, Monterey court cases recorded the testimony of Spanish-surnamed witnesses in English without commenting on whether the testimony was translated. Records can only document the sounds of a courtroom or a town as well as the recorder. The speed with which Monterey's archives switched from Spanish to English—after 1853 few Spanish-language materials appear in the archive—is a testament to how language can disappear over just a few years on paper, silencing monolingual Spanish speakers and symbolizing their struggle in a new English environment. The rapidity of the shift away from Spanish in Monterey would prove to be an anomaly compared to the experience of most treaty citizens in California.

The national debate over California's admission to the Union, in the midst of a sectional crisis over slavery, encouraged Anglo advocates for statehood to bring a united front to Congress. The Treaty of Guadalupe Hidalgo added a huge swath of territory to the United States, triggering a new sectional controversy in Washington. Mexico had abolished slavery in 1829; outside of Texas, Black slaves rarely factored into the economies of the Southwest. Northern and Southern representatives in the U.S. Congress nevertheless took part in a furious argument over the legal status of slavery in the newly acquired lands. Eventually, California's 1849 convention produced a state constitution that banned slavery altogether. After much debate, Congress admitted California as a free state as part of the wide-ranging Compromise of 1850.

California residents agreed on abolishing slavery, but they faced their own political tensions between the newly settled mining-dominated and over-whelmingly Anglo northern districts and the ranching-dominated *californio* southern districts. Language concessions provided one culturally acceptable way for advocates for statehood to gain *californio* support. That priority emerged at the 1849 state constitutional convention, which took up the task of governing in two languages. Anglo convention members accepted the delegacy of *californios* as white state builders and supported their participation by requesting adequate translations prior to calling for a vote.[12] The convention made numerous attempts to support bilingual proceedings by endorsing generous interpreter wages and rejecting possible constitutional models that had not been translated.[13] At the end of the convention, delegates overwhelm-ingly voted to publish their proceedings in both English and Spanish and authorized a translator-certified Spanish version of the constitution.[14]

The bulk of those traveling to Monterey for the start of the convention on September 1 were new arrivals to California. The document signed on October 13, however, bore the mark of an older political elite: fourteen of the forty-eight signers had lived in California for a decade or more.[15] The proceedings noted that "a considerable portion of our fellow-citizens are natives of Old Spain, Californians, and those who have voluntarily relinquished the rights of Mex-icans, to enjoy those of American citizens."[16] With the exception of Mariano Guadalupe Vallejo, from the Sonoma district, and John Sutter, from the Sacramento district, all of the delegates with long-term residency hailed from regions south of San Francisco and the northern mines. These delegates rep-resented older settlers with interests that differed from those of newcomers.[17]

Most of the long-term residents did not speak English and participated in the convention through the services of a translator supplied by the convention. Those members included Vallejo (Sonoma), José María Covarrubias (San Luis Obispo), Pablo Noriega de la Guerra (Santa Barbara), Miguel de Pedrorena (San Diego), José Antonio Carrillo (Los Angeles), Jacinto Rodríguez (Mon-terey), Antonio M. Pico (San José), and Manuel Domínguez (Los Angeles). With the exception of the Spanish-born Pedrorena, all listed California as their place of birth.[18] The convention appointed William E. P. Hartnell, an established California settler linked to delegate Vallejo through marriage, convention translator on September 4.[19] Hartnell served as the intermediary between the two major language groups, a job he had held since the Mexican period, when he translated letters between English and Spanish speakers.[20]

Hartnell was assisted by W. H. Henrie, whom the convention had selected for "the office of Clerk to the Interpreter and Translator," at Vallejo's suggestion.[21] These non-native Spanish speakers took on the unenviable task of interpreting the floor debates while also translating the ideas, opinions, and arguments of Spanish speakers. Privy to discussions in both English and Spanish, the translators likely became uniquely intimate with the workings of the floor.

To pass the constitution and become a state, the convention required the southern delegates' support.[22] *Californios* used their power to advocate for voting rights for Indians, Spanish-language translation, more representatives from southern counties in state government, and local governance.[23] Carrillo even proposed the creation of a separate territory in the south instead of statehood.[24] Anglo allies, particularly those who owned large Mexican land grants, like Abel Stearns, Hugo Reid, and Pierre Sainsevain, often endorsed their efforts.[25] Anglo representatives from San Luis Obispo, Los Angeles, and San Diego joined Carrillo in advocating for territorial status in the south to provide long-standing residents control over local affairs.[26] These allies served as middlemen who ensured that the convention would not silence those with Mexican land grants.

The silences and choices of the Spanish-speaking delegates deserve a closer look, as the convention provides one of the only glimpses of how bilingual state-making operated in the first year after the U.S.-Mexican War. The proceedings record *californio* votes, but they also lay out the debates and daily discussions between members, allowing readers to follow who spoke and for what reasons, even if the information was filtered through an interpreter (although the bilingual delegates could ensure some accuracy). From the available evidence, it does not appear that the convention employed simultaneous translation. Instead, the interpreters summed up the arguments prior to the vote, with the opinions of Spanish speakers recorded only when they were solicited. The recorded proceedings must nevertheless be used with caution. It is impossible to determine, for example, whether Spanish speakers patiently waited for translations or whether they debated issues among themselves and then sent an emissary to relay their opinions.

Of the Spanish-speaking delegates, Carrillo, de la Guerra, and Vallejo appear in the proceedings most often, suggesting that they may have received a vote of confidence as intermediaries for other *californios*. They, along with Covarrubias, had the most experience with political leadership.[27] Even these men spoke rarely (de la Guerra, at fifteen times, spoke the most) and lamented their need for a translator: "Mr. Carrill [sic] felt a diffidence in addressing the assembly, from his ignorance of the English language. He claimed its indulgence, therefore, as he was compelled to speak through an interpreter."[28] Vallejo entered into the record a complaint about other delegates' inability to speak Spanish: "He regretted that his limited knowledge of the English language prevented him from replying to all the arguments adduced by those gentlemen who did not speak in his own tongue."[29] Covarrubias only spoke twice—aside from two motions—both times because he disagreed with a *californio*'s statement. His forceful interjections when he understood the dialogue portray an engaged and eager participant whose language skills limited involvement.[30] The muted moments of *californio* participation hint at larger unspoken opinions that could not be expressed because of language limitations.

Beyond their inability to fully participate in English-language deliberations, *californios* encountered disparagement and discrimination as the minority population.[31] Kimball H. Dimmick, from the Pueblo de San José, alerted the convention to egregious proceedings against *californios*.[32] "As to the line of distinction attempted to be drawn between native Californians and Americans, he knew no such distinction himself; his constituents knew none. They all claimed to be Americans," the convention minutes summarized. His viewpoint differed from William Gwin, a delegate from San Francisco, who used the term "American" synonymously with individuals born in "the old States of the Union," thus excluding treaty citizens from the "American" label. He backtracked after Dimmick's challenge and asserted he meant no distinction in terms of rights that the states granted to "Americans" or *californios*.[33]

The convention proceedings also bear witness to the limitations of California's commitment to bilingual governance.[34] There are recorded instances where the interpreters were absent and the convention continued. In one case, Spanish-speaking delegates could not follow the semantic discussions necessary for a constitutional document. De la Guerra requested that Spanish speakers abstain from a vote on the issue at hand, because "pues la cuestion parecia contraerse á ciertas palabras inglesas que ellos no entendian / the question appeared to be respecting certain English words, which they did not understand."[35] The convention voted on the semantics without the Spanish-speaking delegates, an action that confirmed that the convention drafted the state constitution in English, with Spanish being a mere translation. A truly bilingual approach to state making would have postponed discussions until adequate interpretation allowed all members to participate. It is unknown whether Spanish-speaking delegates read or debated the semantics of the translated version, though they requested adequate review time.[36]

On September 15, José Antonio Carrillo addressed the convention in the absence of both the translator and his clerk through the bilingual Stephen Foster. "Carrillo complained of incompetency and disrespectful language" by the clerk, which resulted in his replacement.[37] The absence of a translator facilitated Carrillo's proposal (perhaps he distrusted the clerk to translate his statement accurately or hoped to avoid a public denouncement in the clerk's presence), but the absence of both the translator and the clerk presents a serious breach in protocol for what was portrayed as a bilingual convention.

To be fair, *californios* only requested dismissal once due to their inability to follow discussions. A Monterey delegate, Charles Botts, halted the discussion "on the part of the Spanish gentlemen" but supported continuation of the discussion even when the proposed translator declined. He trusted them to find a translator and that the House would "reconsider any section passed . . . that might be objectionable."[38] The *californios* depended on friends to keep them abreast of major topics of discussion, and Botts halted the conversation again almost immediately when delegates began discussing the distribution of representatives: "They generally had very little objection to any of the provisions adopted by the Convention, but as this section was one in which they felt interested, and as they could not understand it without having it translated, and the arguments explained to them through an interpreter, they hoped at least that they would be allowed the privilege of a reconsideration, if it was deemed necessary."[39] The delegates briefly postponed the discussion. *Californio* delegates, especially Carrillo and de la Guerra, readily participated in the discussion when it resumed in the hope of keeping more representatives in Southern California.[40]

The convention supported translations for treaty citizens into statehood. On September 27, de la Guerra proposed a constitutional provision that would require the state to translate and publish all state "laws, decrees, regulations, and provisions" in Spanish. Delegate Botts objected, arguing that the new state government could handle Spanish-language translations without a constitutional provision. He worried about the "immense and permanent expense upon the people—an expense for which there will be no necessity in a few years." De la Guerra denounced Botts's stance, pointing out the real damage that the lack of translation had caused in the period of U.S. occupation. He explained how he had worked to translate materials for Santa Barbara residents even though he only had a cursory knowledge of English. "Deben publicarse todas las leyes en [u]n idioma que el pueblo entienda, á fin de evitar que los naturales de California incurran en gastos de intérprete / All laws ought to be published in a language which the people understand, so that every native Californian shall not be at the expense of procuring his own interpreter," de la Guerra argued. He reminded the floor of the new legal and political environment that "han de ser diferentes á las que anteriormente obedecian / will be very different from those which they obeyed formerly." Treaty citizens "no obedecerían las leyes á menos que no las entiendan / cannot obey laws unless they understand them."[41]

De la Guerra acknowledged that English, not Spanish or even bilingualism, would be the future of California. He agreed that interpretations might not be necessary after native Spanish speakers received educational opportunities in English. What he objected to instead was the imposition of a legal system in a language that current residents could not access. Gwin pointed out that Louisiana continued to publish its legislative documents in French and Spanish as well as English more than thirty-five years after obtaining statehood. With this, Botts "withdr[e]w any opposition," and the delegates unanimously passed the "reasonable" resolution.[42]

As approved at the state convention, Article XI, section 21, of California's constitution supported Spanish translations indefinitely and left open the possibility of a bilingual linguistic future.[43] (See figure 1.) The provision allowed treaty citizens access to state government and encouraged their political participation, which supported the rights guaranteed in the Treaty of Guadalupe Hidalgo to those deemed white. The U.S. Congress raised no objection to the bilingual provision.

With access to Spanish ensured in the state's constitution, *californios* like de la Guerra turned their attention to making sure the provisions were implemented at the first legislative session. At great personal cost, de la Guerra improved his English skills tremendously and traveled to Northern California to serve as a state senator who kept translations high on his priorities. Pablo was encouraged by his brother Antonio, who shared the situation of treaty citizens in Santa Barbara: "Aquí hemos visto varias leyes de esa legislatura pero a nada hemos hecho caso por no venir de oficio y estar en Yngles" (Here we have seen various laws of this legislative session, but we have paid them no attention since they are in English and not official). Antonio reminded Pablo that "no hai quien traduzca tal cual" (there is no one here to translate) and added, "Seremos los del sur los últimos en darles cumplimiento" (I believe that we of the South will be the last ones to comply).[44] *Californios* needed translations to aid fellow landowners, but translations also served as the only way for the larger treaty citizen community to become informed about laws.

De la Guerra lobbied to be included on a joint select committee charged with locating suitable candidates for the position of state translator; once appointed, he reported the committee's difficulty in finding an individual "fully competent to discharge the important duty [of] . . . translating, with minute accuracy, the laws of the State."[45] Unhappy with the skills of the temporary translator, William Lourie, de la Guerra requested that a joint committee be created to examine his accuracy.[46] Other *californios* kept the issue of the translator on the floor of the legislature. Covarrubias offered a resolution that emphasized that the southern half of the state was "almost entirely inhabited by people who do not know any other language than Spanish," who "felt very sorry for not knowing what was going on in the Legislature, as the information they received from their representatives was a very limited one, given by private letters."[47] A week later, the legislature elected Joseph H. Schull as state translator. He took the position with a budget for office rental and, if necessary, additional translators.[48]

The California legislature's first session stands out for its many documented discussions, reports, and acts on translations, as well as members' dissatisfaction when translations were delayed.[49] Both houses supported the employment of additional translators, as "there exists at present an urgent necessity for the translation of the laws into Spanish."[50] The high priority placed on the Spanish language resulted in prestige for the office. The state translator was one of California's nine major state offices, which included governor, secretary of state, comptroller, treasurer, and attorney general, whose salary was paid out of the general fund.[51] Only the governor, state treasurer, and supreme court justices earned more than the translator's salary, $8,000.[52]

Californios' success in bestowing high status to the position of translator proved short-lived. The second session of the legislature eliminated the state office for expediency and as a cost-saving measure.[53] By 1853 the legislature compensated the position at piecemeal rates. William Hartnell received less than $2.00 per folio of one hundred words and $0.50 per folio to be revised.[54] In 1876 the lowest contract bid for translation came in at $0.10 per folio.[55] That

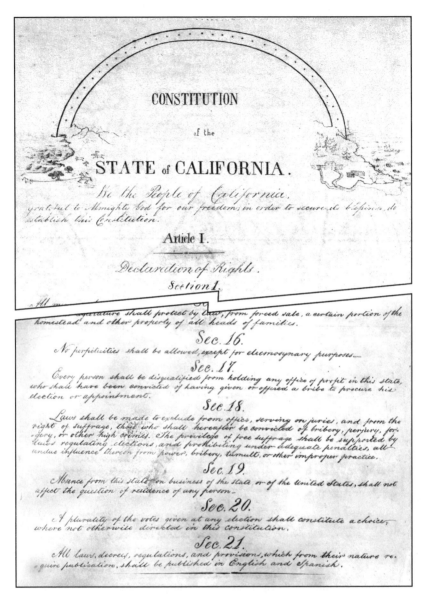

FIGURE 1. Printed in both English and Spanish, the 1849 California Constitution explicitly guaranteed Spanish-language translations. Records of the California State Constitution, 1849, California State Archives.

Constitucion
del
Estado de California.

Nosotros el Pueblo de California, gratos al Todopoderoso por el goce de nuestra libertad, y á fin de asegurar sus beneficios, establecemos esta Constitucion

impropias.

Sec. 19. La Ausencia de este estado, de cualquiera persona, á negocios del mismo estado ó de los Estados Unidos, no pondrá en cuestion su derecho de residencia

Sec. 20. La pluralidad de votos dados en cualquiera eleccion, constituirá eleccion, siempre que en esta constitucion no se disponga otra cosa.

Sec. 21. Toda ley, decreto, reglamento y disposicion que por su naturaleza deban publicarse, se publicarán en ingles y en Castellano.

same year, two women entered slightly higher bids; in 1878, Adelina B. Godoy's bid won the contract at $0.16 per folio.[56] The presence of bids from women suggests both that the availability of translators had increased in the generation after statehood and that the role had declined in prestige.

The state constitution included seemingly straightforward language that demanded translations of "all" state documents, decrees, and reports. Over time, however, as *californios'* representation in the legislature dwindled, translations and the constitutional interpretation became more limited and less respected. Each legislature determined which reports and messages would be translated into Spanish and how many copies of those would be printed and distributed. In 1869, for example, a joint resolution requested that the state translate and distribute 960 Spanish copies each of the reports of the controller, the surveyor-general, and the superintendent of public instruction. The legislature also endorsed 960 Spanish-language and 2,400 German-language copies of the governor's biennial message. The legislature approved no Spanish versions of the reports of the adjutant general, attorney general, state librarian, or state geologist but authorized 240 copies of the state treasurer's report.[57]

Members of the legislature distributed these Spanish-language copies almost exclusively to constituents along the coast and in Southern California. The legislative records do not explain how they determined the quantities to be published. Representatives from those regions likely advocated for these copies and estimated the quantity needed. In 1876 the counties of San Diego, San Bernardino, Los Angeles, Santa Barbara, San Luis Obispo, Monterey, Santa Clara, Contra Costa, Alameda, Marin, and Sonoma as well as the first, third, and seventh district judges received 240 copies of the Spanish-language translation of California's laws.[58] The state continued to order numerous Spanish copies of state documents up to 1879, although sometimes publication remained contingent on the availability of legislative funding.[59]

Notwithstanding efforts to get Spanish translations to its constituents, California was never a fully bilingual state. The tardy and inaccurate state translations thwarted day-to-day local interactions between the different language groups in local settings. Native Spanish speakers brought up missing translations on several occasions. In 1851 the legislature created an incomplete list of laws with Spanish translations.[60] During the ninth session a committee compiled an extensive list of translated laws still in effect. They hoped to create one comprehensive bound volume of laws in Spanish. Andrés Pico, the committee chairman, complained about the quality of the translations, which included many discrepancies and errors and which he found at times almost "enteramente ininteligibles" (completely unintelligible). He described the use of translations in legal proceedings and emphasized their pivotal rather than ceremonial role. Pico explained that Spanish speakers worldwide would read the translations "que haya habido tanta causa para criticar" (for which there are many reasons to criticize).[61] These concerns about quality and completeness implicate the legislature in failing the constitution's translation promises.

Even Anglo legislators intervened on the issue of the quality of translations in at least a couple of instances.[62] In 1876 a minority report of the joint committee delegating and checking on Spanish-language translations complained about José F. Godoy's reappointment as translator. They explained that they found the 1874 translations "grossly incorrect," with "a great many errors" that could not "be considered typographical." What's more, three bids had come in lower than Godoy's $0.16 per folio, including a previous "state translator" with fifteen years experience and no complaints.[63] Godoy's continued employment, under the circumstances, suggests that by the mid-1870s the appointment had turned into a patronage position. Inconsistent and error-prone translations created a muddled message and conflicting view of the state government for Spanish speakers.

At the county level, including Los Angeles, Santa Barbara, and San Diego, Spanish use continued in official government activities; many employed bilingual individuals. County officials in Santa Barbara—judges, sheriffs, notaries public, and clerks—alternated between Spanish and English on the same document, depending on the official's preferred language.[64] In 1866, G. A. Pendleton, a San Diego County clerk, distributed county legal documents and certified public posts completely in Spanish when necessary.[65] These practices reveal that bilingualism was not only tolerated, but routine for much of Southern California. While bilingual officials at times chose to cater to monolingual Spanish speakers, the presence of untranslated English in other documents shows that California did not always accommodate treaty citizens' language needs.

Treaty citizens' claims to a right to Spanish translation met increasing resistance after 1870. The state's linguistic diversity had increased during the gold rush as Europeans, Latin Americans, and Chinese immigrants arrived, and the *californios'* demographic and political importance declined over time. By the last quarter of the nineteenth century, Spanish had become one of many languages heard in California. A *San Francisco Chronicle* article from 1878 mentions over a dozen languages heard on city streets, with "English being of secondary importance, especially in the social affairs and domestic duties of life."[66] The census did not specify language use until 1890, and then did so only for first- and second-generation Americans, making it impossible to know the actual percentage of the population that was Spanish speaking. The situation was dramatically different in New Mexico.

NEW MEXICO'S BILINGUAL GOVERNMENT

Historians have access to only a handful of details on how language operated in the first legislative session in the territory of New Mexico, but hints at the culture clash between the legislators—almost all of whom spoke only Spanish—survive. W. W. H. Davis, a secretary of the territory in the mid-1850s, recalled stories in which Spanish-speaking members found themselves confused by the rules of order and their responsibilities in the legislature. One man reportedly asked, "Que quieres usted de mi, señor?" (What do you want of me, sir?), when called to vote. A second anecdote described a legislator abstaining on a vote by saying, "Blank." The next member called on to vote, a monolingual Spanish speaker, supposedly answered, "having confidence in his choice . . . [,] 'Yo voto para Señor Blank tambien. I also vote for Mr. Blank.'"[67] Elected by monolingual Spanish-speaking voters, New Mexico's territorial representatives required training and explanation in a language they understood in order to perform their duties. Davis, a member of the territory's presidentially appointed executive branch, blamed these misunderstandings on the supposedly authoritarian Mexican leadership that had prevented New Mexicans from learning the "modus operandi of making laws."[68] Another interpretation is that the logic of the proceedings was simply lost in translation. In New Mexico, both language groups soon came to realize that a functional legislature would require a bilingual approach.

In the dozen years following the U.S.-Mexican War, *nuevomexicanos* constituted more than 90 percent of the citizenry of New Mexico, making any English-only language requirement for the territorial government or legal system untenable. All three of the territorial government branches—judicial, executive, and legislative—recognized Spanish. At the judicial level, the 1846 *Laws for the Government of the Territory of New Mexico* stipulated that records of the superior and circuit court be kept in both English and Spanish; this practice continued into the twentieth century in some portions of the territory.[69] The legislature set a per diem rate for interpreters for district courts and grand juries.[70]

Hints of how Spanish operated in New Mexico's territorial government are available in the incomplete, English-language-dominated executive branch papers. These papers indicate that both the governor and the secretary of the territory (almost always Anglos from outside of New Mexico) adjusted to the Spanish-language environment. Some early legislative documents bear the markings of a "Translator's Office," signaling that they arrived at the executive branch having been translated from the original Spanish.[71] The executive branch received Spanish-language resolutions and letters from the legislature in the first decades and responded occasionally with engraved letterhead from the "Departamento de ejecutivo."[72] Governors often released proclamations in both English and Spanish in the same document.[73] Some governors chose at times to use the Spanish equivalent of their names on official documents— Henry Connelly became Enrique and William A. Pile, Guillermo.[74]

While hardly the norm, the executive branch files from the 1860s also contain printed forms offering Spanish-language oaths of office, including an oath of allegiance from the Civil War with a drawing of a bald eagle. Office-holders filled in forms of the "Territorio de Nuevo Mexico" to swear their "Juramento de Lealtdad al Gobierno de los Estados Unidos" (Oath of Loyalty to the United States Government).[75] (See figure 2.) In the absence of a Spanish-language form, oath takers completed English-language printed forms in Spanish by adding their office or title to their signature.[76] The federal government, through the office of the U.S. Comptroller and with the authorization of Congress, funded translations and institutionalized Spanish as a language of government. It had to, since legislators remained almost exclusively Spanish speaking in the first decades.

The legislative branch of the territorial government stands out as operating almost exclusively in Spanish during the first decades of U.S. rule. In 1850 it attempted to create a translator position with a $2,000 annual salary paid by the U.S. Congress, with the option to employ a clerk. Given that this was the first bill that the territorial government listed in its first submission to Congress, the office of the translator clearly held a prominent place in the minds of the legislators, as it had in California during its first session.[77] But in contrast to California, where the legislators had the power to create as many government positions as they could pay for, the New Mexico territorial

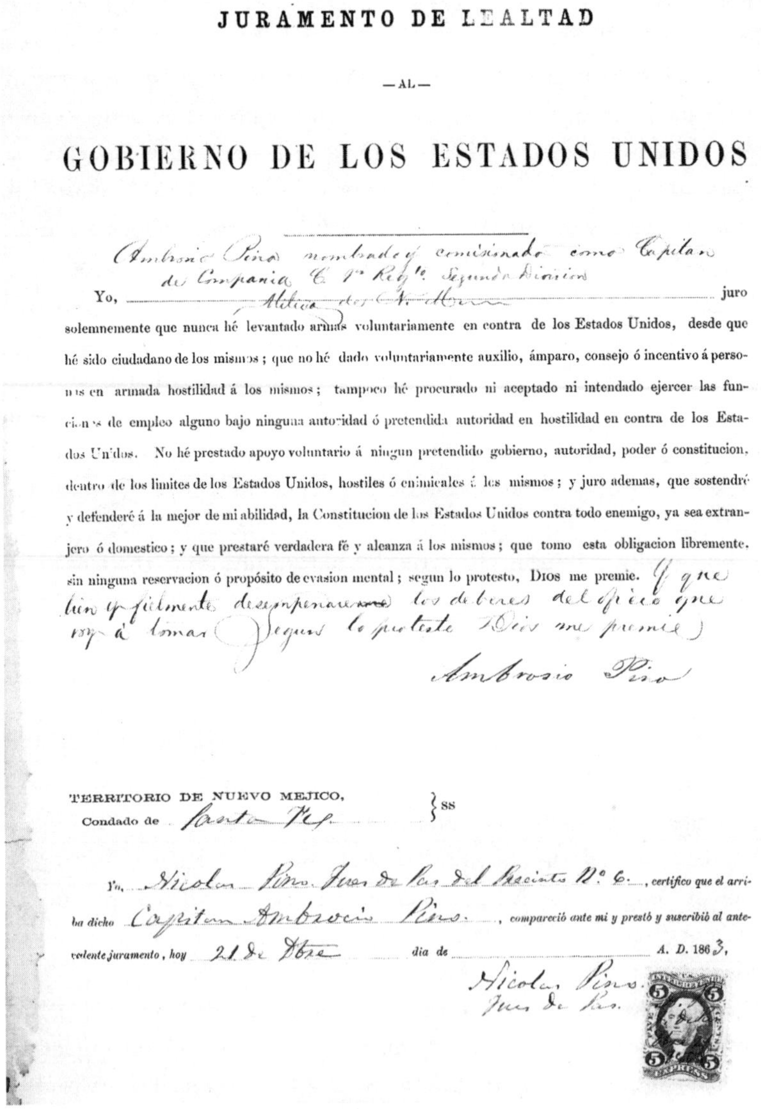

JURAMENTO DE LEALTAD

— AL —

GOBIERNO DE LOS ESTADOS UNIDOS

Yo, _Ambrosio Pino nombrado y comisionado como Capitan de Compania C 1° Reg.to Segunda Division Activa del_ _____ juro
solemnemente que nunca hé levantado armas voluntariamente en contra de los Estados Unidos, desde que
hé sido ciudadano de los mismos; que no hé dado voluntariamente auxilio, ámparo, consejo ó incentivo á perso-
nas en armada hostilidad á los mismos; tampoco hé procurado ni aceptado ni intendado ejercer las fun-
ciones de empleo alguno bajo ninguna autoridad ó pretendida autoridad en hostilidad en contra de los Estados Unidos. No hé prestado apoyo voluntario á niugun pretendido gobierno, autoridad, poder ó constitucion,
dentro de los limites de los Estados Unidos, hostiles ó enimicales á los mismos; y juro ademas, que sostendré
y defenderé á la mejor de mi abilidad, la Constitucion de los Estados Unidos contra todo enemigo, ya sea extran-
jero ó domestico; y que prestaré verdadera fé y alcanza á los mismos; que tomo esta obligacion libremente,
sin ninguna reservacion ó propósito de evasion mental; segun lo protesto, Dios me premie. _Y que
bien y fielmente desempenaré los deberes del oficio que
voy á tomar (Segun lo protesto Dios me premie)_

Ambrosio Pino

TERRITORIO DE NUEVO MEJICO, ⎱ ss
Condado de _Santa Fé_ ⎰

Yo, _Nicolas Pino, Juez de Paz del Recinto N° 6_, certifico que el arriba dicho _Capitan Ambrosio Pino_, compareció ante mi y prestó y suscribió al ante-
cedente juramento, hoy _21 de Dbre_ dia de _____ A. D. 186 _3_,

_Nicolas Pino
Juez de Paz_

FIGURE 2. In 1863 Captain Ambrosio Pino pledged his loyalty to the United States on a
Spanish-language form issued by Santa Fe County, New Mexico. RI 1215, William Ritch
Collection, The Huntington Library, San Marino, California.

legislators found that Congress limited their powers. As the comptroller for the U.S. Treasury, Elisha Whittlesey, explained in 1851, only Congress could create a permanent position in New Mexico, despite the fact that there "can be no question of the necessity of printing the laws and journals and bills also in both languages and of having a translator." The territorial legislators could only make temporary appointments.[78] Within a few years, however, Congress recognized translation as an indispensable service that allowed the territorial government to function. In March 1853 it authorized the employment of "a translator and interpreter, and two clerks" in each house. In addition, Congress required two clerks "qualified to write" in each language.

The secretary of the territory had two major responsibilities that placed him in direct contact with the territorial legislature: the office disbursed legislative members' "compensation and mileage" and printed and distributed territorial laws. Congress further delegated responsibility for approving expenditures and reimbursing territorial expenses—including legislative publications—to the comptroller of the U.S. Treasury.[79] Appointed to four-year terms, many secretaries arrived in New Mexico with little knowledge of the territory's social or political climate or with insufficient knowledge of Spanish. After Donaciano Vigil, no appointed secretary of the territory was native to New Mexico except for Miguel A. Otero in 1861.[80] The secretaries sought to convince the comptroller of the need for federal support of translations. While Whittlesey acceded to the legislature's request in 1851, funding for translation services remained contingent on the secretary in office.

W. W. H. Davis, secretary of the territory from 1853 through 1857, found his job impossible without an aide well versed in Spanish. Juan Climaco Tapia, a porter in Davis's office who was fluent in both English and Spanish, proved himself invaluable to the secretary. In 1855 Davis requested that Whittlesey authorize a salary increase for Tapia from $25 to $40 as "all the Secretaries have been obliged to make use of him as a clerk, a[t] which his whole time is employed . . . so indispensable are his services to the office that a Secretary could not do without him." In addition to his abilities as a translator, Tapia exhibited a deep knowledge of the Spanish-language archives. "The old records of the office are all in Spanish and frequently referred to," Davis explained. The massive archives spanned over two centuries, and Davis claimed that other employees could not "find a document from among this mass of papers, and decipher it, when found without his assistance."[81] Whittlesey agreed to the raise, convinced that "it would be exceedingly difficult for a Secretary at least appointed from the States, to do business efficiently and correctly without the aid of a person qualified to interpret." He nevertheless warned Davis that he did not intend to set a precedent.[82]

Davis's correspondence catalogs the roadblocks he encountered in transferring printed English-language journals of the territorial government to Congress. He explained the dominance of Spanish in New Mexico, his personal language limitations, and Whittlesey's unreasonably low ceilings on printing costs in a territory with few transportation options.[83] Davis contested the legislative translators' knowledge of and literacy in English, writing that some of them "cannot write a dozen lines, correctly, in any language." He asked for authorization to judge translators' qualifications in the future.[84] Whittlesey quickly blocked this attempt to circumvent the legislature's authority.[85] Davis pushed back against this decision, and his subsequent judgments regarding language merit in-depth examination.

The ongoing conflict between Davis and Whittlesey demonstrates the differing understanding of the role of language and translation. Whittlesey asserted the need for "proceedings reported correctly" and laws "consummated correct to the letter." Congress and the territory required that level of attention in order to gain "perfect confidence . . . in the proceedings."[86] For this reason, he preferred a translation that accurately reflected the words of the legislature, even if those phrases, in translation, violated standard expectations for a territorial government in the United States. Davis, in contrast, believed the legislators' Spanish was imperfect, though he could not speak the language himself. He described the House Journal as "kept in Spanish, badly written, worse grammar, and a still worse style. It is not fit to be copied or translated." He explained the "translator has to sit down and re-write the whole of the journal in Spanish changing the phraseology and putting it in regular journal shape, but without altering the substance." The translator used this version to produce an English-language version, after which Davis sent both "revised" versions to press.[87] Davis, in other words, aligned both the Spanish and English versions with his standards for a U.S. government document. This practice presumably undercut and perhaps even nullified the law. There is no evidence that the legislature approved the translated versions before the session laws were published.

Correspondence between Davis and Whittlesey reveals that in New Mexico "translation" referred to the practice of converting territorial legislative documents from Spanish into English, not the reverse. The United States held no other colonial possessions during this period, making the discussions surrounding *nuevomexicano* use of language and retention of culture a precursor for later ones in Puerto Rico, the Philippines, and other territories. From 1851 to 1870, the territory regularly printed its session laws with English on one side and Spanish on the opposing page, permitting easy comparison.[88] The continued dominance of Spanish throughout the territory appears in legislative journal orders for "doscientos en inglés y ochocientos en castellano / 800 in Spanish and 200 in English" in 1861.[89] As late as 1867, a legislative memorial to Congress requested printed copies of the U.S. Constitution and Organic Law of New Mexico in Spanish. The Council and the House explained this was necessary because 80 percent of the members of the legislature only spoke and wrote in Spanish.[90] The legislature approved the printing of 2,000 copies of the governor's message, with 500 copies in English and 1,500 in Spanish, and continued to request either an equal number of copies of various territorial reports in both languages or more copies in Spanish until 1893.[91]

As more Anglo settlers arrived in the territory and became members of the legislature, dual-language governance became more challenging. An 1871 memorial to Congress requested a longer legislative session on account of language differences, as "the time necessarily and unavoidably consumed in the transaction of business, is double that ordinarily necessary in legislative bodies."[92] The absence of earlier complaints suggests that earlier Anglo legislators either knew enough Spanish to not warrant this complaint or that they anticipated the need for extra time.

The transition from Spanish to English as the working language of the legislature seems to have happened fairly quickly in the period between 1874 and 1878. In 1874 the legislature determined that official law was the one voted upon, whether it was published in English or Spanish.[93] Until 1876 almost every English version of the session laws is marked as a translation; in 1876 the number of English and Spanish laws was almost evenly split.[94] From 1878 on, however, most of the official territorial laws are listed in English. Spanish remained a reality in the territorial legislature even as official laws were increasingly those written originally in English. The persistence of monolingual legislators is apparent from the legislature's continued employment of a translator, an interpreter, and, as more Anglos entered the territory, an assistant translator.[95]

The change in the preferred language for laws coincides with the rise of unrest in northern New Mexico over the privatization of commercial land, the rise of railroads, and the loss of traditional land grants and use. Most famously, the Gorras Blancas of San Miguel County cut fences, tore up the railroads, and challenged commercial ranchers in the late 1880s.[96] Legislators, much like these resisters, defended their way of life, which included retaining Spanish-language rights. The session laws of 1891 and 1893 explicitly mention Spanish- and English-language requirements for public notices informing residents of district court dates and land sales.[97] The erosion of bilingualism continued when the legislature required the secretary of the territory to publish Spanish printings of "bills, rules, reports, and documents" when ordered. Instead of guaranteeing access to Spanish translations, this law possibly *limited* Spanish printings; a truly bilingual territorial government system would automatically translate all documents.[98]

Nuevomexicanos benefited from Spanish-language policies that eased them into their lives as U.S. citizens. Even as political support for translations declined, it continued into the twentieth century. Those *nuevomexicanos* who lived in the portions of the territory that split off to create the territories of Colorado and Arizona in the 1860s, however, lost their Spanish-language privileges much sooner.

THE PERSISTENCE OF SPANISH IN COLORADO

After failing to create Jefferson Territory in 1860, Colorado became a territory in 1861. Much of the new territory's southern lands were carved out of New Mexico. No major settlements existed in those parts of Colorado during the Spanish and Mexican periods because Indian tribes controlled the land, but settlers slowly persisted in moving north. Beginning in the 1850s, increasing numbers of treaty citizen families moved into what would become the four southern counties, Costilla, Conejos, Huerfano, and Las Animas.[99] They continued to elect Spanish-speaking representatives after the counties became part of the territory of Colorado. These former New Mexican residents found themselves thrust into an uncertain territorial government run by Anglos. "Public officers elected at the last election are all Mexicans who do not understand english and can neither administer justice, collect taxes or perform any official duty until they obtain the Statu[t]e book of the Territory in the Spanish language," explained one territorial translator.[100]

The federal government's stance on translation for Colorado's Spanish-speaking officials clearly indicated that they saw the situation in New Mexico as anomalous. "The laws have been printed in the English language only except in New Mexico where 9/10th of the people are spaniards and use only this native tongue, and such printing was done by an Act of Congress," explained Whittlesey.[101] In 1862 the territorial legislature requested that the U.S. Congress grant a provision to print the territory's laws in Spanish, but Congress declined.[102] Lacking authority from the federal government, the Colorado legislature did not pass a translation law in either of its first two sessions. Federal officials refused Colorado's requests for translations of the governor's message and a House bill as well.[103]

Colorado's treaty citizens requested that New Mexico take control of their counties due to the lack of Spanish translations. In 1863 New Mexico's territorial legislature described to Congress how treaty citizen families expressed their misgivings to New Mexican legislators in "varias y energicas peticiones / various and urgent petitions." Residents of "Conejos, Costilla, y Culebra" complained about the unjust legal system "por ser las leyes en un idioma que ellos no entienden / [for] the laws [were] being published in a language by them not comprehended."[104] Officials in New Mexico resolved to raise the complaints in Congress in an attempt to restore the communities within its own borders. In response, the Colorado legislature prepared its representative in Congress to block the move.[105] The Colorado governor "earnestly recommend[ed]" that the legislature find funding for translations and printing from within the territory.[106] In March 1864, the territorial legislature authorized $7,000 to translate and print 500 Spanish-language copies of the territorial laws for distribution in the counties of Conejos, Costilla, and Huerfano.[107]

Without a set language policy for the territory's operating documents, each territorial session after 1866 began anew with discussions about Spanish translations. Despite these efforts, the funds allocated often remained in the treasury when the next territorial session met.[108] It is difficult to determine how often the legislature printed and circulated Spanish-language versions of its bills. Nor did the members of the legislature demonstrate much enthusiasm for those translations seen through to completion. A territorial audit completed in 1870 revealed that the territory paid approximately $39 for each translated document in 1864 and $25 for each copy in use in 1866. The "cost of a translation is very great, while the benefits of such translations are temporary and partial," the committee examining the auditor's report argued.[109] Mirroring the views of the federal government, the reviewers noted that English sufficed for millions of other immigrants who lacked state-sponsored translations.[110]

The territorial legislature disregarded these views in 1870 when it passed Council Bill No. 10, which supported Spanish translations of some laws. Governor Edward M. McCook vetoed the act on fiscal grounds, as it authorized $2,500 for translations and bids for printing, whereas he preferred bids for both. The bill failed to secure enough votes to overturn the veto.[111] Other territorial sessions included motions for translations, with no clear conclusion or follow-through for printing and distribution.

The territorial legislature's inconsistency encouraged treaty citizens to attempt to secure stronger protections as Colorado moved toward statehood. Colorado's state convention in 1876 included Spanish speakers. As in California in 1849, the delegates deliberated over whether to translate all of the state's documents into Spanish. One of two Spanish-surnamed delegates in attendance, Casimiro Barela (the other was J. M. García), argued that the Spanish-speaking settlers "need the publication of the laws in Spanish . . . and, in return, the people of southern Colorado will lend their support so that the Territory might be made a state."[112] Barela successfully lobbied for a more permanent commitment to Spanish in the state constitution. Treaty citizens threatened to withhold their support of statehood and involvement with the government until they received a promise of translations. Unlike California, Colorado's constitution stipulated a time limit of twenty-four years for Spanish- and German-language translations, until 1900.[113] With a constitutional obligation to Spanish, Colorado's first state legislative sessions centered on debates over the quantity and types of translations necessary.

Passage for these measures seems to have been limited primarily by cost considerations.[114] By the early 1880s, any Spanish print run faced tough hurdles. The increased availability of Spanish-language newspapers seems to have discouraged legislators from funding translations, as these newspapers could disseminate information at no extra taxpayer expense. Legislators expressed a more general concern about the high cost of printing materials in Spanish. In 1885 and again in 1887, Senator Antonio Archuleta moved to have the already translated session laws of 1883 printed. In 1887 he failed to add Spanish to the bill for the 1885 session law print run.[115] The 1887 legislative session marked a shift away from support for Spanish more generally, as the senate interpreter moved from the general floor to serving in the role of clerk for committees (presumably as needed).[116] By 1892 the interpreter position had disappeared entirely, without any discussion.[117] Support for Spanish in the Colorado legislature continued to decline until 1900, the date at which constitutional language protections officially expired.

Whereas California became a state when those desiring language protections could point to other examples, like Louisiana and Pennsylvania, Colorado's decision to privilege Spanish in the 1870s came during a different national mood. The fact that Colorado maintained translations as long as it did is a testament to the political strength of its treaty citizen families. They received language concessions even as the other territory that split from New Mexico, Arizona, ignored its citizens' language needs.

AMBIVALENCE AND AMBIGUITY IN ARIZONA

Most of Arizona joined the United States in 1848 as a large county of New Mexico populated almost exclusively by American Indians. Congress added the major Mexican settlement in Arizona in 1854 as part of the expansion of territory it made through the Gadsden Purchase. The settlers added, numbering only about one thousand, resided near the present-day border. The Gadsden Purchase offered the same rights to citizenship as the Treaty of Guadalupe Hidalgo, making these settlers treaty citizens too.[118] Anglo settlers began migrating to the region to take advantage of mining and other economic prospects. The county of Arizona split off from New Mexico in 1863, a separation encouraged by support for the Confederacy among the settlers. In contrast, the ethnic Mexicans residing near the border often held cursory allegiances to both the United States and Mexico. They saw themselves primarily as residents of the border.[119] Treaty citizens made up the majority of southern Arizona settlers in the decades before the arrival of the railroad, and they continued their cultural customs into the 1870s. The constant travel across the porous border meant that both treaty citizens and Mexican nationals resided in the territory from the beginning. As the internal migrant and immigrant population increased, settlers mostly relied on mines and ranches, or small mercantile ventures, for their livelihoods.[120]

Despite the continued presence of Spanish speakers, the Arizona territorial government demonstrated little enthusiasm or support for translations. The few calls for translations that did occur came from Yuma and Pima Counties, both located along the border with Mexico. A Spanish-surnamed legislative member sat on the state legislature during most territorial sessions until 1881.[121] In 1864 the territorial legislature approved translations of a compendium of the election law but only provided funds to print one hundred copies.[122] In 1865 Arizona hired two clerks with knowledge of Spanish and two with knowledge of English, but that was the only year this was done.[123] In response to a "reasonable" demand from "large and influential" taxpayers, Governor Richard C. McCormick encouraged the territory to fund translations in 1867.[124] The legislature reconsidered the issue, but once again translation efforts failed.[125] Token treaty citizen representatives and the disproportionate placement of political power north of Pima and Yuma Counties left the translation efforts with few allies.

In Arizona, Spanish-language translation remained an anomaly. Besides the limited 1864 printing, I have identified only three instances in which the territorial legislature published translations. When the legislature created public schools in 1875, a majority of the student population spoke Spanish, so the territory authorized 1,000 copies of the school law in Spanish and 2,000 in English.[126] Many of Arizona's school districts were established as a result of the efforts of Spanish-speaking parents and community members, which necessitated translations for local trustees.[127] The second and third exceptions came with the publication in Spanish of the governor's message of 1877 (500 copies) and 1879 (300 copies).[128]

The former *nuevomexicanos* of Arizona must have marveled at their rapid loss of rights, the change of language of their elected officials, and their demotion to second-class citizens. In many ways, their experiences—so different from their neighbors in New Mexico—mirrored that of treaty citizen families in California in the last decades of the nineteenth century.

THE DECLINE OF TRANSLATIONS IN CALIFORNIA

In 1878 lawmakers gathered in Sacramento for California's Second Constitutional Convention, with dire consequences for the state's Spanish-speaking citizens. While the status quo did not guarantee translations, the patchwork system in place allowed local municipalities to conduct official business in Spanish if convenient. California state law mandated English-only for the language of instruction in schools and for pawnbroker records, but Spanish support continued in some county court proceedings and through translations and printings of select state publications.[129] The constitution adopted in 1879 completely dismantled all Spanish-language privileges throughout the state.

In contrast to the state convention in 1850, *californios* and Latin American immigrants (not to mention American Indians) had no representation at the 1878 convention. Joseph Brown, the representative from Tulare County, attempted to seat Major José R. Pico "as a representative native Californian." Aside from Major Pico's personal achievements, Brown asserted, "I believe he is the only man of that race, that once possessed this whole country, that is on hand here." He emphasized the place of the "Spanish and Mexican population" in the state and estimated that their population "amounts to twenty-three thousand."[130] The delegation declined to seat Major Pico. With *californios* spurned by the convention, Anglo delegates from the southern counties attempted to obtain support and language privileges for treaty citizen families. While their rights were already eroding prior to the convention, delegates effectively ended treaty citizen families' language claims on the state government in the new constitution.

Nativist delegates opposed the state's continued support for bilingualism.[131] Most delegates expected English-language use in the schools, among electors, and by all participants in government. They confirmed this position by proposing constitutional amendments that would disenfranchise non-English speakers and those "unable to read English intelligently."[132] These requirements signaled a move away from tolerance for voting in languages other than English or as illiterates, a practice that began in Massachusetts and Connecticut in the 1850s and had become common nationally.[133] The proposition failed, but delegates easily passed the amendment dismantling Spanish translations: "all laws of the State of California, and all official writings, and the executive, legislative, and judicial proceedings shall be conducted, preserved, and published in no other than the English language."[134]

Constitutional delegates Horace Rolfe, Charles Beerstecher, and James Ayers all spoke in support of Spanish-language proceedings and translations in local venues. Rolfe, a representative of San Diego and San Bernardino Counties, pointed out that monolingual Spanish-speaking judges presided over some courts, arguing that halting this practice would hinder local justice. Ayers explained, "There are townships in Southern California which are entirely Spanish[;] . . . Justices of the Peace are carried on sometimes exclusively in the Spanish language." Aside from being a long-held practice, he believed "it would be wrong . . . for this Convention to prevent these people from transacting their local business in their own language." After all, the practice did not "harm . . . Americans."[135] Even delegates who rallied for Spanish-language use for longtime occupants marginalized and isolated Spanish speakers as not American or equal to Anglos.

In defense of *californios* in the areas they represented, Ayers and Beerstecher invoked the protections of the Treaty of Guadalupe Hidalgo. Removing Spanish-language privileges, they argued, went against the promises of the treaty. Sensing a disregard for the treaty, Beerstecher mentioned that Michigan, Wisconsin, and Pennsylvania published versions of their laws in other languages—a tactic that had worked at the first convention but failed to sway opinion this time around, when new internal migrants and other immigrant delegates worked together to the exclusion of Spanish speakers. "We ought not to put any Know-Nothing clause into the Constitution," he appealed to delegates. When W. J. Tinnin of the Third Congressional District claimed that there was no reason to support "tons and tons of documents published in Spanish for the benefit of foreigners," Rolfe responded by asking if Tinnin called the native population foreign. Tinnin replied that they had "ample time to learn" English. Rolfe ended his case by reminding delegates that "the Americans, or English speaking people," were the newcomers and migrants who took the land "when Spanish was universally the mother tongue of the people. They are a conquered people." He believed the state, having taken their land and promised them equal citizenship status, had an obligation to "give them an equal show." The delegation resoundingly dismissed Rolfe's argument and rejected his amendment to limit English-only to the state legislature and not localities, 27 to 55. They subsequently defeated two final attempts to restore Spanish-language rights.[136]

Delegates' disdain for Spanish speakers emerged one other time, during a lively exchange over a "petition"—one they asked to be read. The record states, "The secretary read the petition down to the names, and then hesitated, as they were mostly Spanish names, difficult to pronounce." "Cries of 'Read!' 'Read!'" filled the chamber. Byron Waters of San Bernardino rose to defend the petition and attempted to calm his fellow delegates, resulting in laughter. "I know every man whose name is appended to that petition. They are electors of that county, and have been for the last twenty years and more," Waters offered in vain. He then volunteered to read the names of the long-standing voters. Ayers supported Waters, saying, "They are just as good names as if they were all 'Smith.'" The convention ignored the arguments and never read the names.[137] Language in the form of surnames, even absent any physical characteristics, served as the primary discriminatory indicator. *Californios* had little standing in the state in 1879.

———————

Language barriers remained a huge obstacle for Spanish-speaking constituents' full inclusion in U.S. citizenship. At least in the first decades after the Treaty of Guadalupe Hidalgo, state and territorial governments offered concessions—some more than others—to monolingual Spanish-speaking citizens and lawmakers in the form of publicly funded translations. But while these translations represented a victory, they did not address many of the harsh realities that treaty citizens faced. As a disillusioned Francisco Ramírez complained in 1857, "No importa mucho en que lengua sean publicadas—en Kanaka ó en Chino es lo mismo—si siempre serémos gobernados por la ley de Lynch" (It does not matter much what language they are published in—in Hawaiian or in Chinese is the same—if we are always governed by Lynch Law).[138]

Territorial and state governments' support for translations traces the political involvement and power of treaty citizens. Advocates for language rights included Anglo representatives who benefited politically from treaty citizens' votes. Across the lands that formerly belonged to Mexico, elite treaty citizens with financial resources obtained English-language fluency and received political and economic advantages due to their newfound knowledge. Rather than abandon treaty citizens, most of the elite kept their political relevance by advocating for the retention of Spanish in official settings. Their reasons for doing so ranged from practical necessity to cultural pride. While individual state and territorial support for translations followed distinct time lines, each legislature decreased language concessions as treaty citizen families' demographic standing declined.

Treaty citizens rarely received concessions as a separate racial entity but instead sought and received political recognition and governmental action through language. Even as they gained political recognition, the government's acceptance of translations marked them as perpetually foreign in the nation. No other language group (with the occasional exception of German) received official government-recognized translations in the Southwest. Treaty citizens won language concessions, which elevated their status as the "natives" in the region. The Anglo "foreigners" needed the treaty citizen "natives" in order to secure the land for the United States.

Although brief, government support for Spanish translations in the Southwest reveals the changing views of language rights and race in the United States in the last half of the nineteenth century. The decline of translations follows a larger historical trajectory that redefined what it meant to be American and who should be excluded. As Jim Crow laws disenfranchised African American voters and Chinese restriction acts villainized Chinese immigrants, treaty citizen families largely lost their ability to be viewed as part of the U.S. polity if they retained their Spanish language. Quickly forgotten was the reality that without its Spanish-speaking citizens the United States could not have taken over or established such a stable system of governance in its Southwest.

While California, Colorado, and Arizona retained few provisions for Spanish as the nation exited the Gilded Age, *nuevomexicanos* kept Spanish as their everyday language. Political campaigns, the legislature, the courts, and the schools all persisted completely in Spanish in parts of the territory well after the treaty citizen families in other places could hope for concessions. An important indicator of the use of Spanish came down to demographics and schooling opportunities in English. Treaty citizen families collectively adjusted to a broad range of language policies and schooling options, which conversely resulted in either their diminished or continued need for translations.

CHAPTER 3

Choosing Language

Cuida mucho á Marmita y dile que no pierda tiempo de leer y escribir en ingles y en espa-
*ñol. Lo mismo Matias.**

—José Matías Moreno to Pudenciana López de Moreno, August 1, 1861, HRL

"¿How yous like my ingles? ¿You understan it? if not tell me the truth about it."[1] Mariano Guadalupe Vallejo, a former Mexican military officer and the owner of extensive Mexican land grants, was a symbol of an older California. He continued to receive respect during the U.S. period but never mastered the English language. Vallejo's attempt at English, written in a letter to his daughter in 1864, unambiguously displays his discomfort with the language but also his willingness to write in it. In 1876 Vallejo explained to his grand-daughter, "Grandpa curses and reviles them [squatters] in Spanish because he doesn't know how to do it in English."[2] Despite (or perhaps because of) his insecurity with language, Vallejo's friends and family encouraged him to write in English more often. He obliged in small portions of letters but explained that he could not avoid writing in Spanish as "es necesario probar ya en uno, ya en otro idioma, puesto que the principal object of the languages are for communicate our thoughts, and understand each other."[3] Vallejo's measured, almost philosophical response to his family's prodding allowed him to accom-plish what the new California required of him: conversing with Anglos. One can imagine conversations between two friends when neither person spoke solely in the other's native tongue and needed to use vocabulary and phrases from his or her preferred language to express ideas.

---

* "Take care of Marmita and tell her to make haste with reading and writing in English and Spanish. The same to Matías."

The personal letters of *californios, nuevomexicanos,* and settlers are concrete examples of how Anglos and treaty citizens attempted to learn each other's language in the first decades after *la invasión norteamericana* (the North American invasion) and the ways that choice affected their lives.[4] Tracing the linguistic transition of one Northern California family, the Vallejos—from Spanish to a hybrid world of Spanish and English—richly documents the societal constraints on language, how language itself changed based on generational use, and how decisions about language altered family relations. Correspondence between other elite treaty citizens further complicates the story, providing a glimpse into the educational options available in other parts of the Southwest and the different choices other treaty citizens made.

The United States never mandated that treaty citizens master the English language, and the government provided few resources to support its acquisition in the former Mexican territories. Access to traditional public schools did not exist uniformly throughout the Southwest, which hindered the language choices available to treaty citizens even as some knowledge of English became increasingly necessary for political and economic success. This ambiguity surrounding language permitted treaty citizens a certain level of agency in their language preferences, even if their choices sometimes had consequences. Anglo settlers similarly could decide whether learning Spanish would further economic prosperity or political ambitions—a decision they faced without having to consider the relationship between language and their position in the nation. This chapter unravels individuals' choices and opportunities to learn languages in formal and informal educational settings, because language acquisition is a central part of the politics of language. The choices that individuals made dictated how persistent the Spanish language would be throughout the Southwest.

ELITE *CALIFORNIOS* IN AN ANGLO WORLD

The Vallejos' abundant letters detail one elite family's wavering commitment to Spanish in the second half of the nineteenth century. General Vallejo and his wife, Francisca Benicia Carrillo, had sixteen children, of whom ten survived to adulthood. They took great pains to educate all of them. At the apex of his financial and political power, Vallejo relied on private tutors and boarding schools to educate his children (his main home was a ranch away from town settlements). Even after financial ruin, Vallejo sent his youngest daughters to the local public school and later to Catholic boarding schools, which facilitated their opportunities in an English-speaking world.[5] The large size of the Vallejo family, their geographic dispersion, and their literacy means that the archive of the correspondence includes not only letters from parents to children and vice versa but also letters between siblings, cousins, aunts, uncles, and grandchildren. Whereas siblings might correspond with one another primarily in English (or an early form of Spanglish), they might elect Spanish when writing to parents or older siblings. These layers of relationships, mediated through language, make the Vallejos' correspondence particularly compelling.

The educational choices available to General Vallejo and his family closely mirror those available to other treaty citizens (though his residence in Northern California truncated somewhat the transition to English). In some rural parts of the Southwest, it took a hundred years for public instruction in English to become available, so treaty citizen parents availed themselves of other educational opportunities. Many sent their children to schools in major towns or outside of their territory; others hired private tutors when no local schools existed. Vallejo's family history displays all of these schooling options.

Vallejo, educated by private tutors, became a firm believer in classical education and acquired books throughout his adulthood. After studying about Napoleon and the works of Shakespeare and Plato, he gave his sons illustrious names: Napoleon, Andrónico, and Platón.[6] A man of great pride, Vallejo demanded that his wife and children receive an education, even though few of Francisca's contemporaries were formally educated. Because Francisca's literacy was limited, she asked her children or her husband to write most of her letters. Vallejo chastised Francisca for her self-consciousness and the literary silence it produced, telling her she should not be ashamed of her language skills: "Ya sabes escribir bastante, y aun no me escribes de tu misma mano. . . . ¿Me tienes acaso verguensa?" ('You now know how to write well enough, yet you still do not write me in your own hand. . . . Are you by chance ashamed?').[7] Francisca Vallejo's obvious discomfort regarding her literacy did not necessarily transfer to her daughters.

The distribution of language ability and preferred use among Vallejo's children can be attributed to both age and gender. Vallejo's older children, who approached adulthood during the period of the U.S.-Mexican War, did not benefit from formal instruction in English. His eldest daughter, Epifania (Fannie), married the Anglo John Frisbie when she was sixteen, the year after California's statehood.[8] (See figure 3.) Frisbie acquired fluency in Spanish

FIGURE 3. Fanny Vallejo Frisbie, eldest daughter of Mariano
Guadalupe Vallejo, ca. 1865. Photograph collection of family members
and descendants of General M. G. Vallejo [graphic], BANC PIC
1978.195:11--PIC. Courtesy of The Bancroft Library, University of
California, Berkeley.

during the Mexican period and presumably spoke to his wife and her family
in Spanish, at least at first. Fannie's letters leave no trace of English writing
ability, as surviving letters to her father and siblings are all in Spanish. She
left California in 1853 when her husband accepted employment in New York
and later Mexico, where he made a fortune serving under Porfirio Díaz in the
1870s and 1880s.[9]

Fannie Frisbie's Spanish-language letters offer two possible historical
interpretations. While it is possible that she could neither write nor speak

English, this is unlikely, since she entertained and was well spoken of by her Anglo friends and her in-laws. At one point, she attended a ball with President Abraham Lincoln, and her children wrote in English to family members from New York.[10] Life in New York would have required some English-language skill but not necessarily English literacy. It follows that Fannie may have chosen to write to her family in Spanish out of respect or preference, because she knew her family would understand her and she preferred the language of her formal education. Letters may have offered a way for Fannie to keep the Spanish world that she loved alive while living on the East Coast. Or she may simply have felt ill equipped or embarrassed to write in English.

Fannie's siblings expressed more enthusiasm for and confidence in English. Vallejo actively promoted English-language learning from early in the statehood period, particularly for his sons. In one letter he singled out his nine-year-old son, writing "á Platon que no deje de hablar ingles" (that Platón should not stop speaking English.)[11] Vallejo recognized early the new practical reality that California's political, business, and social dealings would be conducted in English. In 1851 Vallejo's eldest son, Andrónico, wrote about his proficiency in English. He proudly professed, "Yo estoy ablando el Ingles todo el Dia con todos lo que quiero" (I am speaking English all day with whoever I want).[12] Andrónico secured access to native English speakers by leaving home. He saw this as noteworthy, yet wrote of it in Spanish.

Vallejo's younger sons complied so successfully with their father's wishes that, by the time Napoleon wrote from the university in 1868, he pointed out the novelty of writing in Spanish to his monolingual mother: "Este es mi primer esfuerzo que yo hago en escribir en Español" (This is the first effort that I have made in writing in Spanish.)[13] In contrast to Andrónico, who wrote in Spanish with ease and spoke of his many opportunities to use English, Napoleon, born sixteen years after his older brother, attended Santa Clara University where he wrote in English. The brothers' educational experiences acquiring language varied significantly. Henry, an older adopted son of Vallejo, wrote in Spanish to his brother, Platón, in 1861, while the younger Uladislao wrote in English about his inability to write to his mother in Spanish in 1860.[14] Elite treaty citizen children across the Southwest acquired language skills at different rates.

Vallejo's investment in learning the English language was an important strategy for retaining his family's upper-class status. By providing his children with an English-language education, Vallejo broadened his (and his children's) options beyond Spanish-speaking contacts or a Spanish world. In 1878, thirty years after California became part of the United States, Vallejo continued to use his daughter María as his translator for important documents and letters: "Tengo que hacer muchos escritos, primero en Español y luego entre yo y Maria los traducimos al inglés, y esto me salva de pagar á los traductores por cada papel, veinte y cinco ó treinta pesos" (I have to do much writing, first in Spanish and afterwards between María and I we translate them into English, and this saves me from paying for translations for each paper, twenty-five to thirty pesos).[15] María Vallejo's translations allowed her father to conduct business in an English-language business world, saved him money, and ensured a level of discretion and trust.

Platón especially flourished in a U.S. English-speaking world. (See figure 4.) In the early 1860s, he studied medicine in New York, where he found few opportunities to write in Spanish. He ended his first letter to his mother in "Castellano," expressing a reluctance to commit more errors.[16] In 1877 Platón's insecurities about using Spanish remained, and his parents reassured him that his letter to his mother "is in very good Spanish."[17] In an 1880 letter, Vallejo explained, "Mi hijo el Doctor, Don Platon, á quien envie su carta para q^e. le escribiera en español, me autoriza p^a. decirle, primero, que no sabe escribir en el idioma castellano, solm^{te} el inglés: p^o. q^e. por mi conducto pueden entenderse" (My son the doctor, Don Platón, who sent his letter to me so I could write you in Spanish, authorized for me to say first that he does not know how to write in the Castilian language, only in English: but through me you can understand each other).[18] Despite Platón's academic success, he never mastered corresponding in Spanish, but the expectation that he could exemplifies California's hybrid language culture. While he was an unqualified success by U.S. standards, Platón's inadequacy in Spanish meant that he, like his father, relied on family members to meet the social expectations of those who only spoke one language.

Vallejo's expectations for the social requirements of language were gendered. He instructed Platón's wife, Lucy (whom he addressed as Fabiola), to "make an effort to write to me in Spanish. It doesn't matter that you make mistakes." He explained, "I am old and don't want to set out *now* to write English, which although I can do so slowly, I can't do it correctly as my own language."[19] Vallejo's code of respect and conduct required that Platón's Anglo wife learn his language. No such letters exist for Vallejo's Anglo sons-in-law or even Platón.

The Vallejos accepted the English language with pragmatism because they lived in Northern California, where by 1850 Anglos greatly outnumbered

FIGURE 4. Mariano Guadalupe Vallejo and his son, Platón Vallejo, late nineteenth century. Autry Museum, Los Angeles; 2002.1.4.13.

californios. Their language choices supported this environment. The majority of Vallejo's children wrote to him in English in adulthood. Fluent in spoken Spanish, they peppered their correspondence with Spanish phrases and sometimes combined the two languages. "Si puede—compreme a little box of drawing pencils si puede!," María Vallejo exclaimed to her father.[20] She signed a letter to her mother, "I remain your querida hija Maria."[21] María mastered the English language to such an extent that, like her brother Platón, she recognized her comparative limitations in Spanish. "Tell Mama I do not write to her, as I have become such a '*gringa*' that I cannot write her in Spanish as my heart would dictate," she lamented.[22] The adult children's tentativeness with Spanish demonstrates how quickly a new language can replace the old, even if the written evidence does not tell the full story. All of the children presumably could still speak to their parents in Spanish.

Letters from the waning years of Vallejo's life demonstrate generational variations in Spanish language use. New generations of *californios* born in the United States learned English as their first language. Vallejo's grandchildren eagerly reclaimed their sense of pride in their heritage when they chose to learn Spanish. They expressed excitement about writing to their grandparents in their native language. One grandchild wrote, "My next letter to you, I will write you in Spanish, not only to let you know what progress I have made in the language, but because I think it would please you to receive a letter from your oldest grandson in your native tongue."[23] Vallejo's grandchildren proudly related their progress in learning Spanish from their disparate locations in upstate New York, California, and Mexico. Their path to learning Spanish followed a cultural, rather than a practical or an economic, logic. A card sent to Vallejo on his eightieth birthday demonstrates the great variety of language preferences among his extended family. Over a dozen salutations carried out over four pages of writing include as much English as Spanish. His daughter Adela writes in both Spanish and English, and Fannie writes in Spanish. These birthday wishes, sent from Mexico, fully display the family's mixed language preferences and how they changed over time.[24]

The Vallejos were atypical in that they mastered English so quickly. As members of the *californio* elite they had the financial resources to create an English-language future even before public schools reached their rural location. Later, they benefited from the establishment of public schools for principally English speakers. Conversely, treaty citizens in Southern California kept Spanish as their primary language for a longer period. Other families prioritized raising fully bilingual children. But regardless of the exact timing of the change, the Vallejo family's trajectory in English-language acquisition foreshadowed the experience of treaty citizens across the Southwest. Especially in California, families increasingly moved toward English for their business and social interactions and Spanish for family and home. Whether the transition occurred within a particular family in thirty years, as happened for the Vallejos, or almost a hundred, as it did for some families in the villages of northern New Mexico, each treaty citizen family has in common a distinct story of how they mediated language use across generations.

Treaty citizens' choices about language reflected their relationship to, and understanding of, power. Choices about language could, for instance, signal disapproval of the United States or a solid preference for retaining cultural ties to Spain, Mexico, or the local monolingual treaty citizen community. "Our sweet Castilian tongue has given place to the unpronounceable English jargon—bless the Almighty I have not learned it," Soledad Ortega Argüello, the wife of a Mexican-period governor, explained.[25] Rosalia Vallejo Leese, Vallejo's sister, also never learned English. She believed doing so distanced her from General John C. Frémont and his men, whom she viewed as "brutes": "Since I have not wanted to have anything to do with them, I have refused to learn their language."[26] Her language choice manifested as a political act, which she could afford to do since she was a woman of some means; others, however, would have suffered politically and economically from such a public stance against English. Her bold proclamation to Henry Cerruti, the interviewer supplied by the historian Hubert Bancroft, who was collecting documents and testimony on the Mexican period, further solidified the symbolic importance and political meaning of her stance.

The *californio* Pablo de la Guerra was not yet proficient in English in 1849 when he required a translator at California's constitutional convention, but he learned to write the language by 1851. His mastery of English enabled his ascent to seats of power in California as a judge, state senator, and lieutenant governor (1861–62).[27] He dedicated sustained amounts of time to its study—a luxury most wage-earning treaty citizens could not afford. De la Guerra's letter to his lawyer, Archibald Peachy, shares his doubts and challenges during the process. He expressed conflicted views about his new "Yankee," English-speaking identity (despite retaining some wealth and status) and the ill-fitting language more generally: "The english (in which I have to write to you) the idiom of birds, I do not know it with such a perfection as I have neither beak nor wings, things both I believe, inherent to every Yankee, and notwithstanding that I am one of them, yet its deficiency in me I think is, because I am an unwilling one."[28] Rather than exhibit weakness, de la Guerra's apologetic rendering of English—in conventional grammar and syntax—showcased how rapidly he mastered the language. He used his newfound ability to make a poetic political statement that asserted his difference from the "Yankees." The letter stands out for its critique of the new situation, veiled in apologies about his deficiency in the language. De la Guerra related that he had to "employ several hours to write a few lines in this language." He further confessed that he had previously needed a grammar or dictionary to write in English. Recognizing his unnecessary wordiness, de la Guerra wrote in wonder, "Behold! How many words to say what? That I am a poor english scholar."[29] If de la Guerra had kept silent about his doubts, few would have guessed his struggle with English.

These confessions about language spotlight the importance of English-language correspondence, as treaty citizens accepted the time-intensive challenge of expressing themselves in a new tongue. They placed great importance on ensuring their respect and relevancy in the new U.S. state, an effort that is starkly apparent if one imagines the countless letters they composed in English. It is even possible that de la Guerra used this letter as an active attempt to make Peachy recognize the great difficulties and efforts that native Spanish speakers made to address him.

For treaty citizens, choosing English could be a sign of grudging acceptance, rebellion, or calculated purpose; whatever the reason, it had to benefit them enough to warrant the effort. Spanish, in contrast, underlined their pride and cultural connections to other treaty citizens and even, for some, to God. De la Guerra proclaimed Spanish was an unalterable part of his identity and called it "the language of God." Rather than quietly accept the supremacy of English, he preferred to write in Spanish, "which I understand tolerably as I intend to become a Saint one of these days."[30] While expressed partly in jest, this view of language use goes much deeper than just using an idiom for communication. Language served a purpose beyond business and politics or as a means of participating in society. For de la Guerra, Spanish was the irreplaceable language of faith and the afterlife. Each language held distinct purposes, and the reality for most treaty citizens involved code-switching between both languages or mixing the two.

Spanish remained a presence in the lives of many of those treaty citizens who outwardly (in the personal letters that exist) wrote only in English. De la Guerra's papers provide only one example of a cultural world often lost to historians. Many *californios*, like de la Guerra, retained a preference for writing in Spanish to family members and other Spanish speakers. They worshipped in Spanish, thought in Spanish, greeted their neighbors on the street in Spanish, and spoke Spanish in the home. The likely strength of Spanish in these personal spaces serves as a reminder of the cultural vigor and strength of *californios* in the U.S. state of California.

NEW MEXICO'S EXPECTATION OF BILINGUALISM

Like de la Guerra and Vallejo, elite *nuevomexicanos* recognized that learning the language of their new nation would be a crucial weapon for transmitting and retaining power. There was, however, an important difference. While *californios*, surrounded by Anglos, increasingly saw English as the language of politics and business, *nuevomexicanos* assumed that their local affairs would continue to be conducted in Spanish. English was for the federal authorities, not for territorial affairs. For this reason, elite *nuevomexicanos* insisted that their children learn perfect Spanish at the same time that they perfected their English.

New Mexico's future leaders on the national stage all benefited from their facility with English. The father of J. Francisco Chaves, New Mexico's three-time territorial representative to the U.S. House of Representatives between 1865 and 1871, prophetically advised him in 1841, "The heretics are going to overrun this country. Go and learn their language and come back prepared to defend your people."[31] This quote—whether apocryphal or not—has been described as the "most famous" in New Mexican history and places language at the center of the transfer of power from Mexico to the United States.[32] Chaves's collegiate career at St. Louis University mirrored that of other *nuevomexicanos* of means who attended Missouri boarding schools and colleges to ensure they would become fluent in English. Francisco Perea, Mariano Otero, Tranquilino Luna, and Francisco Manzanares, all future New Mexico representatives to Congress, attended Missouri schools.[33]

But while Chaves's national career depended on his ability to speak English, he won the support of New Mexicans with his elegant Spanish. He became a member of the territorial legislative assembly (1859–60; 1875–1904) and territorial delegate to Congress (1865–67; 1869–71) and held the office of territorial superintendent of public instruction (1901–3). When he died, newspapers praised his rhetorical skill in both languages, a feat that won him great political success. A summary of Chaves's distinguished career lists his many elected positions alongside his language abilities: "Es uno de los mejores parlamentarios y oradores públicos del sudoeste, expresándose con igual fluencia y propiedad en ambos idíomas inglés y castellano" (He is one of the best parliamentarians and public orators in the Southwest, expressing himself with equal fluency and propriety in both English and Spanish).[34]

Nuevomexicanos certainly recognized the political and economic benefits of speaking English in the United States, but their commitment to English was accompanied by the expectation that their sons would retain and perfect Spanish-language skills as well. Juan Armijo, attending St. Mary's College in Missouri, received letters correcting his Spanish grammar from his father,

Nicolás, in 1880. One of them read, "Tu letra esta muy buena, pero se pone llevado no llebado—dice no dise murió con el acento, estuviera no con b" (Your penmanship is very good, but you put *llevado*, not *llebado—dice*, not *dise murió* with an accent, *estuviera*, not with a b). The letter continues with news from home, but Armijo could not move away from the Spanish spelling errors and returned for further adjustments: "Pon cuidado en lo que te corrigio para que te acuerdes.—hago no ago—llevarme no con b" (Take my corrections seriously so that you remember them.—*hago*, not *ago*—*llevarme*, not with a b).[35] While Juan received these corrections from his father, his formal education was conducted in English, which helps to explain some of the errors found in Spanish-language texts in the territory. The educated men taking up major political and economic leadership roles in Spanish across the territory had not necessarily received formal training in that language.

Succeeding in politics in New Mexico required flawless speaking and decent writing skills in both English and Spanish. The territory's political position allowed *nuevomexicanos* a much longer opportunity to adjust—to language at least—than in California, where the Vallejos and de la Guerra scrambled and pushed English as a necessity as early as 1850. These differences were also reflected in the public school systems slowly opening across the U.S. Southwest.

DIVERGENT FORMAL EDUCATION SYSTEMS

The initiation of a public education system in the U.S. Southwest provides one concrete explanation for the divergent language preferences of *californios* and *nuevomexicanos*. The language in which an educational system conducts its work can either validate or dismiss citizens' claims to language as a right. The degree to which treaty citizens could fund, implement, and regulate a Spanish-language educational system would determine the degree to which that language would be tolerated in a political, legal, and economic system dominated by English.

California's status as a state gave its legislature the power to create a comprehensive school code and raise funds to support the system. Political leaders' concern over the large number of Spanish speakers in the state led them to create a system in the 1850s that was more centrally organized than that in any other part of the country in the nineteenth century, including the states and cities on the East Coast. This centralization covered all aspects of education that related to language choice or local control, from teachers to textbooks to administrative regulations and curriculum, all in the service of creating properly trained U.S. citizens.[36]

During the earliest debates over the language of instruction in California's public schools, politicians and educators alike assumed that students primarily required instruction in languages that they would encounter in everyday life. In 1851, the year of California's first school legislation, John Marvin, the first state superintendent (1851–53), argued that Greek and Latin should be eliminated from public schools in favor of Spanish and French. He reasoned that "desirable . . . ancient languages . . . would be less practical and useful to the growing youths of our State, then the living Languages."[37] The question of what languages to teach, however, was a rather different question from that of the language of instruction. At least before the 1870 law instructed schools to only use English in primary education, California's schools faced the dilemma of selecting a language for instruction: the language their students currently spoke or the language they needed to speak in the future.[38]

Language of instruction debates hint at the relative importance of Spanish to settlers and treaty citizens in different communities. In Southern California, Spanish persisted as a language of society at least into the 1870s. Students often learned English in the classroom. In 1851 "about one-fourth" of students came from Spanish-speaking households.[39] For the first generation after statehood, many schools—especially rural ones and those in towns with a strong treaty citizen presence—lacked qualified English teachers. Unfortunately, no archives exist to allow a calculation of how many schools taught their students in Spanish following statehood. An 1852 Report of the Superintendent of Public Schools singles out the use of Spanish in Santa Cruz, Santa Barbara, and Bodega schools, but this list must be considered incomplete since most local officials failed to state the language of instruction or neglected to submit a report.[40]

One report complained that the lack of English-language skills challenged the county's ability to create stable schools. James D. Hutton, a San Luis Obispo County clerk, described a "great part of" the local children as having "American fathers" but explained that "none speak the English language," though their parents eagerly awaited schools that could teach them. The reality of the students' language environment created "the difficulty—that of getting a teacher who understads [sic] both English and Spanish—the situation not being sufficiently remunerative for a person having those requirements."[41] Hutton's characterization of the community suggests that mothers played a key role in retaining Spanish as the language of society and the home even when the fathers' native language was English. The situation in San Luis Obispo exemplifies that in the more southern and rural parts of California, Anglo settlers from the Mexican period who became Mexican citizens and intermarried with *californianas* retained Spanish as their language in the home.[42]

Other schools' commitment to Spanish-language instruction attracted less criticism from the state. Parents in Santa Barbara enrolled their sons and daughters in separate English- and Spanish-language public schools in 1855. As late as 1887, a full two-thirds of Santa Barbara's student population spoke Spanish and students learned grammar in both languages, suggesting that the state education regulators had limited powers to enforce the English-only code.[43] Los Angeles's first three public schools reflected the language spectrum of its inhabitants—one taught bilingually in Spanish and English, while the other two taught just in English or Spanish.[44]

Treaty citizens' desire for Spanish-language instruction held sway in these communities, in part, because they either sold or donated the land for some of the early sites of instruction. Los Angeles community members chose Judge W. G. Dryden (whose first wife was a *californiana*) to approach a *californio* for land to build a new school because of his ability to speak persuasive Spanish.[45] Although both Anglo and *californio* parents recognized the need for proficiency in English in the new state, they desired instruction in Spanish, and many supported schools that taught both languages.[46] The presence of both languages in the community made bilingual individuals powerful mediators and ensured that Spanish remained as a subject of instruction (though not as the language of instruction for all subjects) at least into the late 1870s.[47]

California had a diverse population composed of European, Asian, and Latin American immigrants. Not all of the language groups present in communities became formal subjects of instruction. In 1864 San Francisco created Cosmopolitan Schools that supported the instruction of German and French in the primary grades, reflecting the large demographic shift in San Francisco after the gold rush that had left Spanish-speaking immigrants and *californios* outnumbered by immigrants from France and Germanic states.[48] These schools exposed students to languages their parents spoke or that they heard in the streets of the city. John Swett, founder of California's teacher's union and superintendent of public instruction from 1863 to 1867, suggested that multilingual skills supported students' ability to acquire jobs; for this reason, he praised the San Francisco Cosmopolitan Schools' multilingual approach.[49] No schools after 1870 were permitted to use any language other than English for instruction, but San Francisco's Cosmopolitan Schools were explicitly permitted to teach modern languages as separate classes.[50] By 1872 the San Francisco School District taught German and French—but not Spanish—in almost every school.[51] While commonly in use among Latin American immigrants in San Francisco, Spanish did not have political advocates in Northern California to keep the language in the schools.

Treaty citizens advocated for their children to be taught modern languages besides English and Spanish as well. The del Valle family of Rancho Camulos in Southern California felt it was very important for their son, Reginaldo, to learn both English and French in addition to his native Spanish. At the behest of his father, twelve-year-old Reginaldo translated a portion of his father's letter to his godfather, Joseph Lancaster Brent, from Spanish to French and English in 1866.[52] *Californio* youth in Northern California who attended Santa Clara College found a similar emphasis on language instruction. Instructors taught classes in orthography, reading, and grammar in both Spanish and English in the early 1850s. And French and the ancient languages were part of the basic curriculum.[53] California's robust and growing public school system helped make the case that the state's future would be conducted in English— or at the very least, not Spanish alone.

As residents of a territory, *nuevomexicanos* lacked the ability to amass debt, which included passing bills to manage common schools.[54] This congressional barrier granted local communities nearly complete autonomy over what was taught in the schools since individual counties raised the funds to pay for their own schools. By 1875, *nuevomexicanos* held thirty-three of the thirty-nine school commissioner positions; a full two-thirds of the territory's public schools operated solely in Spanish. Only 5 percent of the territory's schools offered instruction solely in English.[55] This system of local control continued through the 1880s, with some counties even choosing to pay the salaries of Catholic nuns and priests. *Nuevomexicanos* resisted Anglo educational reform efforts to standardize or secularize the schools in New Mexico.[56]

Paradoxically, this opposition to centralized territorial schools safeguarded Spanish instruction and its place in society. The bilingual instruction students received at Santa Fe's St. Michael's College, for instance, created an entire generation of journalists who formed the backbone of the territory's Spanish-language press in the 1880s, which only expanded once the railroad made it possible to lower printing expenses.[57] In New Mexico, in contrast to California, monoglot Spanish speakers maintained access to political and economic opportunities, even if they were unable to attend Missouri schools or learn English.

Anglo reformers succeeded in enticing large landowners and the New Mexico legislature to pass a territory-wide public school law in February 1891.[58] As New Mexico's first superintendent of public instruction, Amado Chaves, summarized the situation fourteen years later: "Prior to 1891 we had very few schools in this Territory, in which the English language was taught. At that time the great majority of our people were of Spanish descent, and spoke Spanish only."[59] The new school code mandated English as a subject of instruction and stipulated that the territory support textbooks in English or in both Spanish and English but not just in Spanish, upsetting the existing practices in rural districts.[60] In New Mexico, educators held up bilingual teachers as the ideal for native Spanish-speaking students. The pedagogical point of using Spanish, however, was not to ensure that the children would maintain literacy in their native language but rather served as a transitional process to help the students learn English.[61] In practice, it was logistically impossible to implement the new law's language stipulations throughout the territory, as rural village teachers lacked knowledge of English and the territory could not recruit enough native English speakers willing to teach in remote Spanish-speaking regions.[62] In a concession to native Spanish speakers, the territorial school code required all school "forms and blanks" to be provided in both Spanish and English—ensuring parents' understanding.[63]

The first four superintendents of public instruction worked to maintain a Spanish language experience for Spanish-speaking children. All hailed from *nuevomexicano* families. They included Amado Chaves, who served two non-sequential terms (1891–97, 1904–5); Plácido Sandoval (1897–99); Manuel C. De Baca (1899–1901); and J. Francisco Chaves (1901–3). Each received territorial and national correspondence in both English and Spanish, and the superintendent's office responded at times in Spanish. Their support for Spanish, at the very least to aid in acquiring English, remained constant through this period, if gendered. In 1893 Chaves explained that "many women are now unable to understand any English," yet "few" men could not "transact the ordinary business of life" in English.[64] Four years later Superintendent Plácido Sandoval attempted to quantify New Mexicans' ability to speak and understand English. The 1890 census recorded that 61.1 percent of the territory's residents could not speak English, but Sandoval believed that, after six years of territory-wide schooling, the numbers "will not at the utmost exceed fifteen per cent." These predictions are generous; they make no mention of gender. Earlier in the report he spoke of official county visits where "nearly all the pupils understood nothing but Spanish" and were under the instruction of a monolingual English teacher. He labeled this arrangement "ridiculous."[65]

Despite the push for English, Chaves praised the practicality of his native language:

> Spanish is, after English, of paramount importance on the whole continent of America, of far greater practical value to our children than the rest of modern or dead languages. . . . It is a crime against nature and humanity to try and rob the children of New Mexico of this, their natural advantage, of the language which is theirs by birth-right, to deprive them unjustly [of the] advantages, great and numerous, which those have who command speech in two languages.[66]

Nuevomexicanos never lost sight of *hispanoamerica*; they capitalized on the concept that Spanish is a language of the Americas.

The superintendents' admirable support for Spanish ensured that students had access to their native language, but it did not guarantee their access to the language that Chaves deemed most important to their future and that the legislature had insisted be taught: English. Despite the 1891 law, Spanish remained the language of instruction and society in many rural villages, necessitating in 1907 a Spanish fluency requirement for the assistant superintendent of instruction.[67] The appointment of the fifth and sixth superintendents, Anglos Hiram Hadley and J. E. Clark, signaled a shift away from Spanish-language support, a phenomenon that mirrored the broader national mood against non-English-language instruction. The years surrounding World War I fed xenophobic and Americanization efforts.[68] In New Mexico, the realities of monolingual Spanish speakers, *nuevomexicano* political power, and the continued support of many prominent Anglos slowed the push for Americanization, but by the first decade of the twentieth century, their influence was waning.

ANGLO APPROPRIATION OF SPANISH

In the U.S. Southwest, both Anglos and Spanish speakers alike were interested in learning each other's language, albeit for different reasons. At a very basic level, Spanish place-names and choice phrases became part of the everyday lexicon. Others discovered that political and economic success in the former Mexican territory required investing in Spanish. Still others opted to learn the language out of interest or to foster social connections. Most migrants making these language decisions were adults learning the language in informal settings.

For some Anglos, the Spanish language served as a symbol of the Southwest's unique cultural heritage. Consider, for example, a Spanish-language oration that Vallejo delivered to the California Pioneer Society on July 5, 1886. He began by acknowledging his preference for speaking in Spanish: "Permit me, gentlemen, to express in my native tongue, in the beautiful idiom spoken by the discoverers of this continent."[69] Vallejo's use of language not only connected Spanish-speaking listeners to him, personally, but also connected all those in attendance to the language's legacy in the state. Organizers and attendees alike found themselves transported to a different time that fed their connection to the land, with themselves depicted as bringers of great progress. The Spanish language—like the culture of Mexico and its people—could be viewed as part of the past. At times, Vallejo provided Anglos with the Spanish-language names for geologic formations and explained early California history.[70] Anglos saw Vallejo as having a vital role in preserving the state's Spanish and Mexican history; some, out of curiosity, even sent him translations of his speeches to review prior to publication.[71] His knowledge of the past served as a commodity for Anglos, and their respect for his expertise permitted Vallejo to continue to use Spanish even after the language had no official role in California politics or economics.

Letters from Anglos to their East Coast friends and family included Spanish names with authority. One migrant, Addison A. Pollard, provided a bit of a lesson to his wife, Susy, in 1870, writing, "The valley is some ten or fifteen miles across and extends up & down the San Bonita (Good Saint) Creek. The creek used to be San Juan (St. John) so I suppose putting this & that together that same St. John of the Spanish calendar was the 'good Saint.'"[72] The true Western settler peppered his correspondence with Spanish words. Words and phrases like *cañon, hombre, mesa, patio,* and *que lástima* became commonplace among those who spent time in the West. As Charles Botts of Virginia said at the state constitutional convention of 1849, "I am willing after the Spanish fashion, to leave it to those *buenos humbres* in Congress and our Legislature to decide."[73] Having lived in the region for just a year and a half, Botts adopted the Spanish-language phrase for "good men." It is unlikely that congressional representatives in his native Virginia used "buenos hombres" in official settings.

Anglos altered the language as they learned it, making it uniquely their own. Gertrude Atherton, the self-proclaimed first California-born writer, weighed in on a newspaper discussion about whether something could be described as Californian. She offered the appropriation of the Spanish language by native Anglo Californians as proof. "We have taken kindly to San José and scorn those who say San Jose; but even this favored word has had its pruning," she explained. "We do not say San Hosé, but San Ozé."[74] Californians' pronunciation became foreign to both *californios* and other Anglos.

Standard—or as close to standard as possible—Spanish-language pronunciations became an expectation of Anglo settlers, even those outside of the Southwest. An article published in the *Cleveland Leader*, for instance, poked fun at a Pasadena visitor's difficulty with pronouncing "the letter 'J' in Spanish" (e.g., La June-tah instead of La Hoon-tah). "Darn the language; it breaks me all up," he exclaimed after receiving numerous corrections. He then overcompensated at the Carlton Hotel when he ordered everything with a "Spanish" pronunciation (he used "ham" instead of "jam"). When the restaurant patrons erupted in laughter, the man further emphasized his ability to "speak" the language, "Spanish? I can sling more Spanish in a holy minute. . . . My name is Jeremi—I mean Heremiah Hones from Hacksonville, Illinoy." The man, escorted out of the restaurant by his friends, could not comprehend why the diners "played" him for a "greeny."[75] This humorous anecdote shows that Californians' pronunciation of Spanish was familiar. Mastering it granted Westerners the right to claim pioneer status, or at the very least, that of a well-established settler. Pronouncing words according to Spanish-language convention became part of the reality and charm of the West.

Some Anglos mastered the Spanish language beyond pronunciation, certain phrases, and place-names. "Tengo miedo, querida Señora, que U. no podra entender lo que escribo" (I am scared, dear mistress, that you will not be able to understand what I write), Leonard Ver Mehr wrote to María Ignacia Bale de Soberanos in St. Helena.[76] In another letter, he sought the company of Spanish speakers: "Ay un mes que estoy en San Francisco, y me parece un año. En todo ese tiempo no he hablado ni leido español, y me parece que he olvidado todo. Me parece que no puedo escribir ni un palabra" (I've been in San Francisco for one month, and it feels to me like a year. In all this time I have not talked or read in Spanish, and I think that I have forgotten it all. I think that I cannot write even one word).[77] Rural spaces often increased the opportunity for Anglos to interact with Spanish speakers and likely encouraged their desire to use the language.

At times, English speakers entered Spanish-language households to master the language. A *Voz del Nuevo Mundo* ad requested employment in the form of sewing, painting, or caring for children. A seemingly well-off young woman eagerly hoped to learn Spanish prior to embarking on a trip to Mexico. "Solo desea que por su buen trabajo se le trate bien" (All she wants for her good work is that she be treated well), the ad elaborated.[78] Another example comes from an Anglo suitor who sought the hand of a *californiana*. The draft of William Leighton's letter to his hopeful intended's father, Agustín Olvera, is marked with corrections: "q^e· yo dijo [diga] claro[a] y franco[camente] q^e· yo la amo y con toda[o] mi corazon y mi fuerza. No sé si [esta pasion es reciproca] recipi-rocado mi pasion" (that I tell you clearly and frankly that I love her with all my heart and being. I don't know if my passion is reciprocated).[79] To make his intimate request, Leighton needed assistance with his Spanish.

Mastery of Spanish signaled Anglos' long tenure in the territory and often their political and economic importance. Joseph Lancaster Brent, who was completely accepted by the *californio* community, became *padrino* (godfather) to many *californio* children and received letters in Spanish wishing him well even after he left California. Ysabel del Valle wrote to Brent of her husband's death in an effort to renew their friendship: "será un consuelo para mi despues de la muerte ser compadre" (it would be a consolation after the death to be your compadre).[80] Other Anglos shared familial ties with treaty citizens through intermarriage, a common occurrence throughout the Southwest. The 1860s teenage diary of Mary Refugio Carpenter, daughter of an Anglo father and a *californiana* mother, suggests an active social life between landed Anglos and *californios* in Southern California that required bilingualism in order to communicate among the generations.[81]

Whereas *californios* and some of their neighboring Anglos actively sought a Spanish world, the situation in New Mexico forced politically ambitious settlers to learn Spanish, whether they wanted to or not. Thomas Benton Catron relocated to New Mexico in 1866 while the shadow of the Civil War still hovered over the eastern states. Looking forward to starting life anew, Catron bought a Spanish grammar and dictionary and began learning the language on his sixty-day journey overland on the advice of his tutor, travel companion, and later law partner, Stephen Elkins.[82] On his arrival in New Mexico, Catron discovered his quick study of Spanish was insufficient for his political ambitions. The territorial governor, Robert B. Mitchell, promised Catron that when he mastered Spanish he would be rewarded with a district attorney position. Catron purposefully moved to the village of Alcalde in Rio Arriba County, where he stayed with the family of Elias Clark, to immerse himself in the Spanish language.[83] "For five years he lay awake every night conjugating Spanish verbs," the *Washington Herald* reported in 1914.[84]

Catron's behavior was not typical for a settler headed west. Most westward-bound settlers had no need to learn a new language unless they came from Europe, in which case they eventually had to learn some English. Most went to communities where the vast majority of the population was other settlers and frontiersman who spoke English or their own European language. In New Mexico, in contrast, native English speakers made up a small but politically and economically connected population with an intimate knowledge of the United States. Anglos "who aspired to power and wealth as Catron did," and who wanted "to cultivate worthwhile acquaintances and inspire their confidence," found it necessary to learn Spanish, not just colloquially, but well.[85]

As promised, Mitchell made Catron a district attorney in 1867. In 1869 he was promoted to attorney general. "The business of our courts was translated into English, but most of our jurymen and witnesses were Mexicans and interpreters were necessary. Attorney[s], however, were permitted to address the juries in Spanish," Catron remembered in 1914.[86] With Spanish being unavoidable in the courtrooms of New Mexico, an individual on the path to a successful legal career could only advance with the support of native Spanish speakers. Having achieved fluency, Catron became one of the most successful and notorious politicians and large landowners in New Mexico, serving a term in the U.S. Senate.

In learning Spanish, Anglo settlers in New Mexico forged a different path from those settling in other Mexican-ceded territories. Albert Fall, Bradford Prince, and Stephen Elkins, among others, became political and economic forces in New Mexico in part because they mastered the Spanish language and gained the trust of native Spanish speakers.[87] *Nuevomexicanos* remained the majority in the New Mexico territory until around 1940.[88] Anglo social lives, business interactions, and even educational opportunities placed them in contact with monolingual Spanish speakers who retained local and territorial political power. Not all settlers chose to learn Spanish, but those who did—especially the early ones—benefited greatly from that choice. Margaret Hereford Wilson, an early Anglo and rare female settler who later joined her husband, the businessman Benjamin Davis Wilson, in California, noted the difference in cultural opportunities in her letters to family back East. She wrote that her son was "learning to speak the Spanish language very fast, much faster than the rest of us." Despite the ease with which the younger generation learned Spanish, Wilson avoided interacting with the "Spanish" families, no matter how genteel or elite. She mingled with just one "Spanish" woman, who, she wrote, "has tried very hard to learn sister and myself to speak Spanish." Rejecting *nuevomexicano* society had its costs, as Wilson chose to attend only "American Parties" and not "fandangos."[89] Self-ostracized, Wilson chose less social engagement in the Spanish-dominated territory.

––––––––––

The language map of the Southwest in the last decades of the nineteenth century remained varied, the product of individual preference, ambition, and uneven educational opportunities. The map was never stable, and the gradations of language ability shifted over time, even for individuals. Those choices could benefit or hinder one's economic and political prospects, which could prompt a person to reevaluate their decision. The clues in the written sources suggest that both languages lived somewhat together throughout the Southwest. One can imagine a mixture of both languages or the use of a form of Spanglish to get ideas and sentiments across. English speakers adopted Spanish words, and Spanish speakers of course adopted English words and phrases too, producing new forms of both languages.

Even as new state and territorial laws marginalized the use of Spanish in official government business, some treaty citizens not only survived, but thrived in the new U.S. legal, political, business, and social worlds—often while retaining the language they knew best—whereas others found their use of Spanish pushed aside in classrooms and business or politics. No simple statement can capture the state of language in the Southwest during this time period. Not everyone moved from Spanish to English, or did so easily or willingly. Like the Vallejos, sometimes individuals in the same family made different choices and had distinct opportunities related to language. At times, Anglo settlers chose to learn Spanish, further making it possible for some treaty citizens not to have to learn English. Language acquisition was a nonlinear process with multiple avenues of development. It was messy and community specific. Individual choices mattered and reverberated in the formation of structures of governance in the region.

CHAPTER 4

A Language of Citizenship

Que demandaremos en todo tiempo nuestros justos derechos, los privilegios é inmunidades
comunes á todos los ciudadanos de esta república, la cual fué fundada sobre la idea sublime
de justicia é igualdad. Tampoco olvidaremos ni dejaremos de exigir aquellos otros derechos
garantizados á nosotros como un pueblo por el solemne compacto y tratado . . . conocido
como el Tratado de Guadalupe Hidalgo.*

—*Noticias*, March 1, 1884, Fernández, *Biography of Casimiro Barela*

In 1859 over one hundred *californios* signed a document outlining the ways that
Anglo settlers and the new state government had abrogated their rights as
U.S. citizens. The document, sent "al honorable senado y casa de representantes de los estados unidos" (to the honorable U.S. Senate and House of
Representatives), explained how the encroachment of *norteamericano* settlers
contributed to the loss and destruction of their land. But their losses were
more than material: the *californios'* petition recounted the social disruption
of being "tirados . . . entre los extraños à su idioma, costumbres, lees y usos"
(thrown . . . among strangers [with] their language, customs, laws, and habits).
The nation ought "amparar, proteger, y sostener los tratados de Guadalupe
Hidalgo, de los que depende" (to respect, protect, and uphold the treaties of
Guadalupe Hidalgo, on which we depend). Further, the *californios* argued that
the former Mexican citizens remaining in the Southwest deserved respect
because they "asumieron al momento la posicion que les ofrecio de ciudadanos

---

* "We demand our just rights at all times along with the privileges and immunities that are
common to all citizens of this Republic founded on the exalted idea of justice and equality. We
also do not forget to demand those additional rights guaranteed [by the agreement] . . . known
as the Treaty of Guadalupe Hidalgo."

de los E.U. . . . [y] han mantenido con celo y fidelidad" (immediately assumed the position of American citizens offered them . . . [and] have maintained it with zeal and faithfulness).[1]

In theory, the Treaty of Guadalupe Hidalgo granted treaty citizens "all rights and privileges as citizens." In practice, each territorial and state government in the former Mexican territory chose what that citizenship looked like.[2] This situation arose not only because of the different legal status of areas (state versus territory) but also because the United States did not possess a universal view of citizenship in the mid-nineteenth century.[3] Throughout the nineteenth century—and to a certain extent today—individual states held the right to determine electoral requirements, and individual states made wildly divergent choices—upwards of thirty-five states chose to extend the vote to noncitizen immigrants who intended to become U.S. citizens.[4] These states and territories included Colorado (until 1902) and Texas (until 1921) but not Arizona, California, or New Mexico.[5] The ratification of the Thirteenth, Fourteenth, and Fifteenth Amendments in 1865, 1868, and 1870, respectively, altered and solidified definitions of citizenship in the United States. While the Thirteenth Amendment abolished slavery, the Fourteenth extended citizenship rights to all persons born or naturalized in the United States. The Fifteenth Amendment promised to protect the vote for millions of former slaves. These promises of full citizenship proved fleeting for African Americans when, with the end of Reconstruction, individual states passed laws that suppressed and disenfranchised the new citizens. The Fifteenth Amendment did not spell out who could participate in various aspects of civic life. In a period with political machines and patronage positions, state and territorial officials determined who could run for office, serve on a jury, or testify in court. Each state and territory was largely left to determine the parameters of inclusion for these civic positions, and they chose very different paths when it came to language requirements.

While historians have produced rich scholarship on the changing meanings of citizenship in the United States in the nineteenth century, they have not adequately considered how the existence of another group of persons whose full citizenship was in doubt and did not speak English—treaty citizens— affected the debate.[6] The Treaty of Guadalupe Hidalgo, signed twenty years before passage of the Fourteenth Amendment, granted a new form of citizenship defined in a negotiated treaty between two sovereign nations. This new category of citizenship was made explicit in Arizona, whose 1877 territorial election law permitted "every male citizen of the United States, and every male citizen of Mexico; who shall have elected to become a citizen of the United States under the treaty of peace" to vote. This categorization kept treaty citizens perpetually separate and removed from the category of natural-born citizens.[7]

The existence of this new category of citizens, the vast majority of whom did not speak English, required local, territorial, and federal officials to reassess who could be considered a legitimate member of the nation. The treaty left the rights and privileges of citizenship undefined. By failing to explicitly detail the rights of its treaty citizens, Mexican officials left the citizens they "voluntarily abandoned" without specific universal rights.[8] Those categorized by the U.S. government as American Indians lost their citizenship status because of ambiguity, and most treaty citizens became second-class citizens. This story of second-class citizenship with inadequate access to the political and legal system is a familiar one for historians of the United States, but the specific story of the treaty citizens shows how language use became another marker for different political treatment in the U.S. Southwest.

Access to the Spanish language is one measurable index of treaty citizens' incorporation in the U.S. polity. Whether in California, Colorado, Arizona, or New Mexico, treaty citizens throughout the Southwest largely accepted the form of the U.S. political system, with its parties and expectations of electoral participation, but they participated in these institutions primarily in Spanish. For treaty citizens, Spanish became a negotiated right. This chapter explores how treaty citizens participated in U.S. civic life during the second half of the nineteenth century and reveals where that participation encountered limits. It does so by probing the ways language policies of state and territorial legislatures intersected with Spanish-speaking citizens' ability to participate in elections, courts, and juries. It concludes by considering the broader meanings of participating in citizenship in Spanish in the United States during a time when its meaning was very much in flux.

THE LIMITS OF PATRONAGE POLITICS IN CALIFORNIA

Francisco P. Ramírez, the precocious teenage editor of *El Clamor Público*, the first full-length Spanish-language newspaper in Los Angeles, used his platform to educate new treaty citizens on the importance of their electoral involvement. "Dejar las elecciones al acaso es uno de los errores mas funestos para los pueblos" (To leave elections to chance is one of the most dismal errors for the people), he railed during the 1857 campaign. Ramírez chastised Spanish-speaking citizens for giving up the right to vote by either failing to participate in elections or by allowing their vote to be purchased. He believed these practices led to the great ills of society. By not participating in elections, *californios* were "abandonàndolas a hombres corrompidos, que dueños del campo falseaban la voluntad del pueblo, es evidente que se hubieran ahorrado al país muchos errores, muchos desaciertos y muchos crímenes" (abandoning them to corrupt men, who as owners of large estates falsify the will of the people. [Had they not done this,] the country would have been able to avoid many errors, many mistakes, and many crimes). As a new citizen, Ramírez placed his faith in the power of electoral politics; he remained a true believer in the country's founding documents. He had not yet become disillusioned by the day-to-day reality of the legal and voting policies and practices of the nation. And, as a newspaper editor, he believed in the power of the press: "La prensa està en su derecho intentando guiar é ilustrar el espíritu público en la lucha electora" (The press is, within its right, attempting to guide or illustrate the spirit of the public in the electoral fight).[9]

Ramírez faced an uphill battle. Throughout the former Mexican territory, attempts to buy the votes of Spanish-speaking citizens abounded. The story is most familiar in Texas, where *patrones* dictated the vote. *Patrones* often drove their largely monolingual Spanish-speaking workers to the polling station and watched as they cast their votes.[10] Ramírez expressed his disgust for the kind of vote buying that occurred in California: "Cuando llega el tiempo de ejercer el primero de los derechos, sois arrastrados por las calles en los carruages de los candidatos, y no quereis votar a menos que se os *compren vuestros votos!*[11] / When the time comes to vote, the first of your rights, you [are dragged] about the streets in the carriages of [the] candidates, and you will not cast your votes unless *you are paid* for them!"[12]

Stories of vote buying proliferate in early settler accounts. Treaty citizen voters are described in Anglo sources as uninformed, impressionable, and unconscientious voters who wasted their new voting privilege. These views likely arose from the idealism of new citizens and immigrants to the West who held the United States to its written ideals rather than to the reality of the national practice of getting out the vote. The pattern of writing about widespread vote buying of treaty citizens resembled the larger view of national electoral politics of the time.[13] U.S. politics in the late nineteenth century was characterized by mass mobilization, high voter participation, and intense party loyalty. Party politics infiltrated all aspects of social and even religious life.[14] Party supporters perfected the tactics of rewarding the vote with alcohol, free rides to the polls, help with naturalization, local patronage positions, or local improvements.[15] Political parties vetted and approved of candidates and shared their choices with loyal party members, who, in return, benefited from favors, patronage posts, or even candidacy.[16] Preprinted party ballots predominated across the country when the U.S.-Mexican War ended. A standardized ballot, also known as the "Australian" or secret ballot, widely replaced preprinted party ballots between 1887 and 1896.[17] The political parties could not function if they gave up a large segment of the population simply because they spoke another language.

Harris Newmark, an early German immigrant to Los Angeles, corroborated Ramírez's views of Los Angeles's early voting situation. Instead of desiring better voting practices for monolingual Spanish speakers, he believed the group voted illegally and skewed the election results. Newmark suggested that candidates unduly influenced Spanish-speaking prospective voters, therefore impeding the democratic process. Candidates' use of languages other than English in political campaigns challenges the standard narrative of apathetic voters. Newmark recounted what he perceived as the facetious story of William H. Workman, a non-Democratic candidate for county clerk. Workman's brother attempted to secure votes for him using the common tactic of buying alcohol and corralling a group of "docile, though illegal voters," whom Newmark viewed largely as "Indians," for the night. When "prominent Mexican politicians led by Tomás Sanchez" learned of Workman's attempts to buy the election, they rode over to where Workman held the men, broke in, and "made such flowery stump speeches in the native language of the horde that, in fifteen or twenty minutes, they had stampeded the whole band!"[18]

Newmark's description of Sánchez's intervention inadvertently demonstrated that these supposedly complacent men changed course and voted for the Democratic Party because Sánchez had convinced them of its superiority in Spanish.[19] Los Angeles County overwhelmingly voted Democratic in the first decade after statehood; Newmark's anecdote suggests one reason was that elite *californios* spoke to potential voters in their native language.[20] Candidates in much of the former Mexican territory excluded monolingual Spanish speakers from political life in the first decades after the U.S.-Mexican War at the peril of losing elections.

Political operators in California, a state with a fast-growing population, did not need to court the Spanish-speaking electorate for long. *Californios'* political power in Los Angeles declined in the mid-1870s, then plummeted in the 1880s. One visitor returned to Los Angeles in 1874 after a seven-year absence and commented that in the interim it had become an "American City."[21] It is difficult to estimate the city's demography with any accuracy, since *californios* counted as white and the census only began asking about language use in 1890. In California, 8.2 percent of the state's population over the age of ten could not speak English. Just over three thousand individuals of native parentage could not speak English in a state with almost a million residents.[22] By the 1890s, California's population bore little resemblance to that of the pre-treaty period. With adequate Anglo voters and schools that taught ethnic Mexican children English, there was little need for candidates to continue to reach out to the shrinking base of Spanish-speaking voters.

By the 1880s, ethnic Mexican voters were facing some of the same exclusionary tactics that immigrant voters faced in the Northeast and Black voters faced in the South.[23] An 1880 law required all election officers to be "able to read, write, and speak the English language understandingly."[24] Political candidates could court them if they wished, but they were under no obligation to go out of their way to inform non-English speakers about their platforms or aid them at the polls. In 1894 the legislature officially disenfranchised non-English speakers under the age of sixty. The law made an exception for most treaty citizens due to the age specification but made no provision for their descendants or for naturalized immigrants who may not have known English.[25]

Other aspects of treaty citizens' rights, including their access to legal information and court proceedings, also diminished with the loss of *californio* demographic power. As discussed in chapter 2, the state provided limited support for translations of legislative proceedings during the first thirty years of statehood. Witnesses in California "who d[id] not understand or speak the English language" were entitled to an interpreter.[26] In several counties, the state required that defendants receive summons in Spanish so that they understood the charges against them. In Santa Barbara, San Luis Obispo, Los Angeles, San Diego, Monterey, Santa Clara, Santa Cruz, and Contra Costa Counties, laws permitted courts, "with the consent of both parties, to have the process, pleadings, and other proceedings" in Spanish.[27] By limiting Spanish to counties with significant numbers of *californios*, however, the state legislature discriminated against Latin American immigrants who settled in the mining regions along with other non-English speakers like the French. Until the late 1870s, *californios*, as treaty citizens, carried political clout; immigrants did not.

Spanish-language privileges—for both *californios* and more recent immigrants—declined rapidly between 1870 and 1894. Just one year after California signed its second constitution, legislators further narrowed their language preferences toward an English-only stance. State laws dictated English-language requirements for certain professions, regardless of local community preferences. For instance, pawnbrokers were legally required to keep their records in English. Those who did not keep accurate records risked a misdemeanor charge.[28] An 1880 state law required that police officers have the ability to read and write in English.[29] That same year the legislature passed amendments to the code of civil procedure that required all judicial proceedings and written court documents to be in English. Once this requirement for the judiciary had changed, jurors were also required to demonstrate "sufficient knowledge of the English language."[30] By 1899 English-language literacy requirements existed for those holding positions as police officers, firemen, and election board members, along with their clerks.[31]

The privileging of the Spanish language that occurred in the first few decades of statehood no longer merited discussion in the state legislature by the 1890s, demonstrating a blatant disregard and dismissal of the rights of any remaining voters who lacked English skills.[32] A similar loss in political power occurred throughout county and state governments too. Treaty citizen families largely turned their organizing strength to their own businesses and communities.[33]

REGIONAL POWER IN COLORADO

Colorado became a state in 1876, just a few years before California began rescinding some of its treaty citizens' rights. Spanish speakers in the new state benefited from their numerical supremacy in southern counties, which made them a threat to political candidates who opposed their right to vote. Treaty citizens elected representatives who secured their rights as electors, as they had the political strength to help set territorial (and later, state) policy.

Colorado's most vocal advocate for treaty citizen families, Senator Casimiro Barela, served Las Animas County citizens in the state senate for thirty-seven consecutive years, providing stability and a consistent voice for Spanish speakers. Unanimously elected president pro tem of the senate in 1893, he had deep political connections and was skillful at gaining the support of English-only legislators through political compromise that ensured that many of his bills supporting his constituents' language rights passed.[34] While in office, legislative accomplishments on behalf of his Spanish-speaking constituents included encouraging Spanish-language instruction in Colorado's schools, the hiring of a legislative interpreter, and continued publication of official government translations.

With prodding from Barela, the Colorado legislature supported the voting rights of monolingual Spanish speakers into the twentieth century. In 1891, when Colorado adopted the secret ballot, Senator Barela proactively pushed through a bill that required precincts to supply interpreters for voting. "Election judges may select two persons, one from each political party, who shall act as interpreters and . . . may assist such persons who cannot speak or read the English language in making up their ballots," the final law promised.[35] The bill's passage suggests that even at this late date the legislature valued the presence of Spanish-speaking voters and remained committed to high electoral turnout. In his introduction to Barela's biography, *nuevomexicano* Benjamin Read credited legislative aid to monolingual Spanish-speaking voters to Barela's efforts: "Don Casimiro aseguró por 25 años los derechos civiles de miles de sus conciudadanos que iban á quedar descalificados . . . por no poseer el conocimiento del idioma Inglés" (Don Casimiro secured for twenty-five years the civil rights of thousands of his fellow citizens that would have been disenfranchised . . . on the basis of not knowing the English language).[36]

Outside the statehouse, Senator Barela mobilized Spanish speakers around issues that concerned their community. Barela joined many of his constituents, for instance, in a *junta de indignación* (mass meeting of indignation) after a threat to limit monolingual Spanish speakers' rights in the courts emerged. Treaty citizen families in New Mexico and Colorado used spontaneous *juntas de indignación* to air their grievances—often concerning racial discrimination—and to send demands to public officials. They were organized and led by treaty citizen families and not necessarily elected leaders or the elite.[37] In September 1883, just eight years after Colorado became a state, Judge Caldwell Yeaman of Las Animas County (a county Barela's biographer described as mostly comprising residents who spoke Spanish exclusively) ruled that monolingual Spanish-speaking jurors could no longer serve in his court. The leaders of the county's Spanish-speaking community led a massive civic demonstration to protest the ruling. On March 1, 1884, an estimated 1,500 people (in a county of approximately 10,000) gathered to hear the speeches of eleven prominent Spanish speakers, including Senator Barela. With the Trinidad courthouse filled to capacity, about 500 of the demonstrators listened from outside.[38]

The meeting produced a series of unanimously adopted resolutions. The *junta* not only protested Judge Yeaman's specific ruling against monolingual Spanish speakers but also opposed restrictions on jury duty service for any group. To strengthen their demands, they invited the legislature to compare the results of court cases with Spanish speakers against those conducted solely in English: "Deseamos si fuese necesario que fuesen examinados y escudriña-dos. . . . [L]os hechos de los llamados jurados mexicanos, cotejan bien cuando menos, con la conducta y decisiones de jurados compuestos de aquellos que se arrogan á sí mismos el nombre de Americanos / We would welcome the scrutiny. . . . [T]he record of Mexican jurors compares favorably to the conduct and decision of juries comprised of those who [arrogate] for themselves the name of Americans." They saved their tried-and-true argument for last, reminding their audience of "aquellos otros derechos guarantizados á nosotros . . . por el solemne compacto y tratado / those additional rights guaranteed to us by the solemn compact and treaty" while also reaffirming that "Mejicanos somos nativos del suelo en que vivimos, y no extranjeros / Mexicans are native to the soil upon which we live and are not foreigners."[39]

These resolutions exhibit the high level of treaty citizen families' engagement in civil rights issues in Colorado, as well as their political sophistication. Colorado's treaty citizen families had a broad commitment to the political system and believed their place in it was guaranteed by the treaty. They also understood the channels of power, combining a mass demonstration at a courthouse with a written statement that solidified and recorded their complaints and demands. At least 10 percent of the county's population attended the *junta*.[40] This number is far higher than the estimated number of elite in the county, suggesting that language rights fueled the interest of the larger Spanish-speaking community and triggered activism against language abuses.

The activism encountered some English-only backlash. As the *Colorado Springs Gazette* opined, "Our jury system is bad enough as it is." The editorial emphasized that "the Mexicans should . . . learn the language of the country and then they will not suffer this disadvantage."[41] For some, language exclusion served as the stand-in for the legal exclusion of the treaty citizen families of Las Animas County.

Senator Barela took the fight for jury eligibility back to Denver. He introduced and successfully passed a bill that nullified Judge Yeaman's ruling. The bill explicitly mandated that "no county commissioners, judges, or other State or county officers, shall . . . reject or challenge any person, otherwise qualified, on account of such person speaking the Spanish or Mexican language and not being able to understand the English language."[42] Barela explained before the senate that even though he had mastered the English language and the provision could not affect him personally, "I have my relatives and I have that immense majority of honorable Spanish-Americans who are fellow citizens and they are of my same race. They have the same rights and prerogatives I have, and I cannot allow them to be dispossessed of them." He reminded the senate of the full citizenship status of those prohibited from jury service and that the state's constitution included a twenty-four-year requirement to translate state laws into Spanish.[43] The debate over Judge Yeaman's ruling, which temporarily stripped monolingual Spanish speakers' rights to serve on a jury locally, is a telling illustration of why explicit statewide support for language rights was so important.[44]

Just as the March 1 *junta de indignación* resolutions had suggested, monolingual Spanish speakers' previous record in court aided their cause. A federal judge, Moses Hallett, was quoted by Barela to support his argument. Hallett opined that "Spanish-Americans as jurors [were] the most convenient [and were] . . . not corruptible, [and] they act with complete impartiality and in conformity with their conscience while keeping the considerations of the court in mind." Barela further assured the senate that "knowledge of English is not needed to act in conscience, righteousness, equality and justice. Conscience and common sense do not require a language."[45] Barela's longevity in the state senate was uncommon and required the mobilization of Spanish-speaking voters. He, in turn, earned their confidence by supporting full citizenship rights for Spanish speakers.

The broad support for Spanish speakers in Colorado does not match up with its demography. In 1890 only 5 percent of individuals in the state could not speak English. Other language communities were included in this statistic, meaning the monoglot Spanish-speaking population was a small one. Their concentration in just a few counties in southern Colorado significantly increased their political clout.[46]

INVISIBLE IN ARIZONA

The political visibility of treaty citizens in southern Colorado contrasts with the experience of the largely forgotten treaty citizens of the other major territory to split from New Mexico: Arizona. When the first legislature of the Arizona territory met, it created four counties—Mohave, Pima, Yavapai, and Yuma—in a territory still populated more by autonomous Indians than settlers.[47] The only two counties that ever elected Spanish-surnamed representatives in the nineteenth century were Pima and Yuma, but even there the majority of elected legislators in the first session were Anglo.[48] While still an important demographic of the territory, the early treaty citizen settlers were quickly outnumbered by Anglo settlers who arrived seeking mining, ranching, and other economic opportunities.

In the generation following Arizona's establishment as a territory, treaty citizen families—and the territory's other Mexican inhabitants who naturalized—voted with no legal restrictions, regardless of their language preference. But while the territorial government made few attempts to restrict these Spanish-speaking residents' access to the franchise, neither did it do much to ensure their participation. Aside from requiring the territorial government to create a compendium of translated laws (which included the election law) in 1864, there is no evidence that the territorial legislature discussed language preference in establishing the rights of the electorate and citizens.[49] During the first three years of the territory's existence, elected officials who represented Spanish-speaking communities attempted to pass legislation requiring the territory to translate official publications, but the bills languished or failed.[50]

The one major exception to Arizona's policy occurred in the courts. The legislature voted in 1875 to permit interpreters in all courts of the territory at the rate of $5 a day upon the request of the presiding judge. Relatedly, in 1887, the legislature permitted police officers to employ an interpreter for taking depositions. The use of interpreters in the courts may have worked from Spanish to English as well as from English to Spanish. At least some local justices of the peace lacked English-language skills, leading the territory to authorize the translation and printing of five hundred copies of a Spanish-language version of court laws in 1881. The proceedings unfortunately offer little commentary on why this project was undertaken so late or what the general practice was prior to the 1881 translation.[51]

Two laws passed in 1889 and 1891 suggest significant ambivalence within the legislature about Spanish-speaking treaty citizen families' status as full citizens. The first instructed the Board of Supervisors to withhold a certificate of election or appointment for any official at the territorial, county, precinct, or district office level who did not know English.[52] This law circumvented voter choice, severely undermining local control of public positions and the political interests of the Spanish-speaking community. Two years later, however, the Arizona legislature signaled its support for monolingual Spanish speakers' ability to vote. A second law passed in 1891 granted aid to any voter who declared that he could not understand the English-language ballot.[53]

The ambivalence in language discussions may have come from a rising immigrant population—many of whom were not Mexican. In 1890 about 28 percent of Arizona's population over the age of ten could not speak English. Only 5.5 percent of the white native-born population, which included treaty citizen families, could not speak English.[54] Arizona's stance on language largely mirrored that of California, where *californios* saw a gradual erosion of their rights. Overall, legislators determined the parameters for civic participation and they responded to political pressures. Outside of New Mexico, the changing demographic reality of settlement patterns in the increasingly Anglo Southwest left policy makers with few reasons to see Spanish as compatible with U.S. citizenship.

A BILINGUAL TERRITORY IN THE SOUTHWEST

Of the four states eventually formed from the territories added after the U.S.-Mexican War, New Mexico is exceptional. The territory of New Mexico is the sole example of a Spanish-dominated political and legislative system in the continental United States. Monolingual Spanish-speaking citizens became accustomed to being addressed in their mother tongue in speeches, newspapers, and campaign appeals. In return for their participation in elections and party loyalty, *nuevomexicanos* secured local patronage positions and favors for their small villages and towns, where most of their true allegiances lay. While the U.S. government initially had little objection to this arrangement, over time some federal officials and Anglo settlers voiced increasingly loud objections to New Mexicans' use of Spanish.

In New Mexico, Spanish-surnamed individuals filled the lists of territory-appointed positions, including justice of the peace, postmaster, notary public, census collector, sheriff, state senator, and jury members.[55] While other states began requiring English literacy to hold office, New Mexico's legislature opted in 1889 to permit officeholders to demonstrate literacy in either Spanish or English.[56] They established generous per diem rates for court interpreters and encouraged all citizens to serve on juries regardless of their facility in English. This occasionally required the use of interpreters at grand juries as well as the district courts.[57] Some local courts operated solely in Spanish.[58]

The mere existence of so many Spanish-speaking officials for decades proves the degree to which *nuevomexicano* families enthusiastically embraced the political party system. In the 1850s, they rapidly joined the Democratic Party. The territorial Democratic Party split between those in favor of statehood and those opposed, respectively labeled the American Democrats and the Mexican Democrats.[59] As former secretary of the territory W. W. H. Davis wrote in his memoirs, the territory was completely anti-Whig during its early years. New Mexicans, he explained, acted as if "the weal of the Territory would be eternally sapped should a single Whig obtain a place in either branch."[60] Once formed, however, the Republican Party gained the support of many *nuevomexicanos*. To remain competitive in the territory, both parties engaged monolingual Spanish speakers in the political process.

Office seekers acknowledged and respected the reality of New Mexico's Spanish-language environment. Voting in the territory could not have begun or been implemented with any kind of legitimacy without Spanish. Scrolls from Valencia County show how the process, with Spanish-language voters, candidates, and election officials worked. The records detailed the election of "4 del mes de Septiembre de Mil ochocientos sesenta y cinco" (September 4, 1865) for the representative to Congress and the territorial senator and other major territorial positions. The final tally submitted by the "secretarios" (secretaries) and "jueses de la mesa" (precinct captains) stood by the results—"certificamos que lo de arriba es legal" (we certify that the above is legal)—before sending them to the territorial government.[61] The precinct's ninety-inch roster tallied each of the votes cast by the 241 voters, alongside their names. The rolls include just ten non-Spanish surnames; they stand out for their distinct handwriting, suggesting that they were recorded in the voters' hand. Other "Libro[s] de Matricula de Eleccion" (election or poll books) submitted by Valencia County during the 1860s also appeared to have been kept in Spanish and show overwhelmingly Spanish-surnamed voters.[62] Though few rosters survive for other precincts across the territory, there is no reason to think that Valencia County's experiences were atypical.

Campaigning for office necessarily required candidates to woo Spanish-language voters. As of 1890, 65 percent of New Mexico's population over the age of ten could not speak English, including 70 percent of the white native born.[63] It was simply not an option for the political parties to ignore Spanish speakers if they wished to remain competitive.

The election of 1892 provides a fairly typical example of the routine, and expected, presence of Spanish in New Mexico's territorial elections.[64] This election took place more than forty years after the creation of treaty citizens, meaning many of the Spanish-speaking voters were children and grandchildren of treaty citizens and, therefore, natural-born citizens. Yet even at this late date, Spanish continued to be absolutely necessary for serious candidates to court, convince, support, and employ Spanish speakers.

In 1892 L. Bradford Prince, a Republican, held the federally appointed governorship. A mix of Spanish- and non-Spanish-surnamed individuals held the other major territorial positions. The territorial auditor was Dometrio Perez, the superintendent of public instruction was Amado Chaves, and the librarian was Facundo Pino.[65] Chaves used his position to focus on the cultural and practical value of the Spanish language in the territory.[66] *Nuevomexicanos* remained a visible presence in territorial posts and served as party officials, which extended their influence beyond local communities. At the local level, they held even more power as election officials and local party committee members and held most of the appointed offices. Local position holders answered to higher-up party officials and kept their posts by delivering the party-line vote and appeasing the demands and concerns of local voters.[67]

Although 1892 was a presidential election year, the election in New Mexico focused largely on the race for the territorial representative to Congress. As a territory-wide position, this race drew the most ink.[68] Two political veterans vied for the position. The seven-year incumbent was a Democrat, Antonio Joseph, who had been born in New Mexico to a Portuguese father; his mother was from New Orleans. His Republican challenger was Thomas B. Catron, lawyer, land mogul, and Republican Party stalwart.[69]

The Republicans held their convention on August 25 in Las Vegas, New Mexico, with invited delegates hailing from every territorial precinct. Spanish-speaking delegates received a letter certifying their invitation to the convention in Spanish from two Spanish-surnamed secretaries, Jesus Lucero and

Demostenes Martínez.[70] These Spanish speakers made up the majority of the convention's delegates and also held important party positions. The convention selected Catron as permanent chairman and Larkin G. Read as permanent secretary. The brother of Benjamin Read, who later published a Spanish-language history of New Mexico, Larkin was the son of a *nuevomexicana*. The convention vice presidents were Clemente P. Ortiz, Stephen H. Hale, and Agustín Mestas.[71] The leadership alone emphasizes the strength of *nuevo-mexicanos* in the Republican Party structure.

The Democratic convention had a similar leadership distribution pattern, with two Spanish-surnamed vice presidents and two elected interpreters.[72] The county conventions, which selected delegates for the larger statewide elections, included interpreters, a position that is listed matter-of-factly, even in the English-language press.[73] Some local county Democratic conventions included Spanish-language speeches with no English-language translations, demonstrating the party's lack of concern about conducting political affairs in Spanish.[74]

After the Republican convention, Catron began campaigning in earnest. His contacts across the territory wrote to him with specific suggestions on how he might appeal to the monolingual Spanish-speaking vote. In contrast to California, corralling the voters or swaying their votes through bribes did not come up. Instead, Catron addressed each local community based on what he believed would convince them to vote for him, especially in an ugly campaign. One supporter advised Catron that Democrats in Cerrillos had proposed discrediting him by distributing "25000 copies of Spanish + hundreds of comments on your public record." Lamenting the use of these tactics, the supporter surmised, "If Joseph proposes going into personalities would it not be well to publish in Spanish his early history?" The letter ended with an explanation of how local campaign workers would be distributed, recommending one campaign worker for the "Mexicans" and others for the miners and townspeople—not as a form of discrimination, but as a form of economic campaigning by language and occupation.[75]

Campaign workers viewed Catron's fluency in Spanish as the asset that would convince voters to stick with the Republican ticket in small towns. J. C. Berry, Georgetown, New Mexico's postmaster, wrote asking that Catron make an appearance there. He explained that local Democrats had spread rumors that Catron believed "all the Mexican women were whores, prostitutes etc. and all the men were thieves." Berry continued, "A few words from him in

[the] Mexican language will do wonders."[76] A Socorro election worker, Samuel C. Week, wrote to Catron's campaign headquarters three weeks before the election, urging Catron to get a "translation of Joseph's Bill No. 3371 with reference to the Irrigation scheme." He argued that "scattered among the Native people [it] would work a miracle, between now and Nov. 8th." Week asked that Catron's office send a thousand copies of the document and reported that Socorro election workers had distributed among *nuevomexicanos* the issues of the *New Mexican* that Catron had sent.[77] Week believed once voters read the bill, they would eagerly vote for Catron. A letter from Gallup urgently requested a Spanish speaker to help campaign there before Catron lost his advantage; Democrats lobbied for "50 Mexican votes." "Can you send a good worker to Gallup, one who can influence these voters," the letter implores.[78] This form of political strategizing points to issue-driven, well-read—or at least well-informed—voters who were expected to respond to printed bills, pamphlets, and speeches.

With only one side of Catron's correspondence available, it is difficult to know how he responded to particular pleas, but his public actions acknowledged local voters' preference for Spanish. When writing to John Daily of Golden, New Mexico, about notices calling for a Republican convention, he explained, "I do not send them in English, because the most of the people understand Spanish." Saddled with the cost of printing, Catron opted to publish campaign documents in the most well understood language among both Anglos and "Mexicans" in the region.[79] These inside campaign letters suggest that English speakers kept abreast of the campaigning among Spanish speakers in their towns and that all of them accepted the strategy of using Spanish to secure votes for their candidate. No one discouraged Catron from using Spanish in the campaign or encouraged behavior that disenfranchised Spanish-speaking voters.

Getting at the individual local opinions of Catron or Joseph is impossible, but one opportunity to uncover Spanish speakers' viewpoints is the Spanish-language press. Local Spanish-language newspapers flourished in New Mexico in the last two decades of the nineteenth century. Political news, both local and national, along with commentary, was lucrative enough to sustain a Democratic and a Republican newspaper in almost every town.[80] Editorials lambasted candidates of opposing parties, and editors added Spanish-language captions to political cartoons originally published in English. One political cartoon in Santa Fe's heavily distributed Democratic newspaper, *La Voz del*

Pueblo (The Voice of the People), lampooned the gold standard during the 1892 campaign and included the caption, "Los republicanos con el ante cristo, sus pompas y sus obras" (The Republicans with the Antichrist, his pomp and his works)—a decidedly partisan take repeated throughout the paper. Partisan papers published ruthless attacks on candidates in the weeks preceding the election. An anti-Catron editorial translated "palabras que salieron de la boca de Catron" (words that came out of Catron's mouth) and included citations to the date and page number of the *Legislative Assembly Journal*. The paper concluded, "Desde ese tiempo estaba aproximandose el Antecristo [Catron] para correr de delegado" (Since that time he [Catron] was imitating the Antichrist in order to run as a delegate).[81]

Party funding meant limited political autonomy for these Spanish-language newspapers, but editors wrote their own articles that critiqued politicians and corrupt policies while providing clear and informed opinions on the major territorial and national political issues of the day. The newspapers included articles of particular interest to the local Spanish-speaking community, such as editorials, poetry, literature, social commentary, gossip, and advertisements.[82] Newspapers often covered the politics of Latin American countries and news with great enthusiasm, familiarity, and a sense of hemispheric political and cultural affiliation.

Party-supported newspapers filled their most important columns with election coverage that both lobbied for the candidates and stood up for *nuevomexicano* rights. In the Democrat-supported *Estandarte de Springer* (*Springer Standard*), an editorial lambasted the injustice of New Mexico's territorial status by criticizing particular U.S. senators for voting for statehood for Idaho and Wyoming and against statehood for New Mexico. The same editorial praised the incumbent, Antonio Joseph, who continually defended the territory and encouraged statehood.[83] Democratic-leaning papers accused Catron of working to disenfranchise *nuevomexicanos*.[84]

In 1892, the voters of New Mexico reelected Antonio Joseph as their representative in Congress. But more important than the specific outcome of the election is the prominent, and apparently uncontroversial, role of Spanish in the campaign. Spanish remained essential to the electoral process in New Mexico up to and past the turn of the century. With such a far-flung population, New Mexico's political system remained local, small-scale, and Spanish.[85] While information on the day-to-day dynamics of parties at the village level is difficult to uncover, Catron's campaign correspondence makes clear that village campaign workers kept the central campaign up to date on the varied politics of each place. *Nuevomexicanos'* use of Spanish in most communities was absolute; in their home villages and local communities they lived their lives with little or no need for English. During their first decades as treaty citizens, *nuevomexicanos* privileged local citizenship over territory and territory over nation. Their limited and largely locally based inquiries and requests to federal territorial officials—frequently submitted in Spanish—suggest that *nuevomexicanos* remained loyal to their local communities and participated in the larger territorial and national political process with specific local demands. In this, *nuevomexicanos* mirrored the behavior of citizens across the country who continued to put their community ties ahead of state and national ones.[86]

In contrast to these elected officials, the governor received few letters in any language during the last decades of the nineteenth century, suggesting a disconnect between citizens and the federally appointed governor.[87] Official correspondence between the legislature and the governor in the first decades of territorial status was sometimes written in Spanish.[88] In other cases, *nuevomexicanos* joined with other residents in English-language petitions to the governor.[89] One case, an 1866 petition from Socorro County requesting the pardon of Cecilia Lucero López's husband, included her mark along with the signatures of supportive *nuevomexicanos* and English-surnamed court officials.[90] The governor at the time—Henry Connelly—used Spanish-language stationery and corresponded in Spanish with the territorial legislature, but the senders may not have been aware of his openness to Spanish, or they lived in a community where few individuals possessed literacy in English or Spanish.

The other major occupant of the executive branch, the secretary of the territory, received English-language letters with some regularity from *jueces de prueba* (justices of the peace) and legislators. These letters often requested Spanish-language documents that would allow monoglot Spanish speakers to conduct their work (someone may have been hired to write them).[91] Other *nuevomexicanos* wrote to the secretary on local issues of grave importance in Spanish.[92] Community members wrote to reinforce their claims to the land—especially when they concerned grievances against American Indians.[93] In doing so, they frequently invoked their rights as "citizens." Other letters addressed public grievances. An 1890 letter written by "el Pueblo Reunido en Masa" (the Town Gathered En Masse) demanded that the secretary of the territory stop a company from taking water from the town's sources: "De ninguna manera este pueblo permitira que ni una pulgada de agua sea tomada de dicho Río por ninguna companía" (This town will not permit for any reason even one inch of water to be taken by any company from this river).[94] Their request languished in the secretary's files, because the claim of a united people was belied by the absence of signatures.

Many *nuevomexicanos'* letters to government officials throughout the nineteenth and into the early twentieth century concern patronage posts, suggesting that they considered themselves fully deserving of all the perks of citizenship. Lucas E. Gallegos, a loyal Republican Party member, appealed to the governor for his first local patronage post with clear awareness of what was owed to him: "Creo que tengo derecho a pedirle al partido Republicano alguna vez, alguna cosa, he trabajado por el partido Republicano y nunca he aseptado ninguna oficina local" (I believe I have the right to ask the Republican Party sometime for something, I have worked for the Republican Party and have never before accepted a single local position).[95]

The limited number of patronage positions in small villages made the position of postmaster a particularly attractive appointment.[96] In 1901 Governor Otero received letters in Spanish from grateful appointed postmasters, from disappointed individuals passed over for the position, and from those hoping to influence a future appointment.[97] Also in 1901, New Mexico's congressional representative B. D. Rodey wrote to the Fourth Assistant Post Master General in Washington, DC, about retaining a Santa Fe County village post office position. "I think there ought to be no Post Offices abolished, and as many established as possible. The Government does not pay out any too much for New Mexico anyway," he wrote when he forwarded his letter to the governor.[98] Rodey's assertion that the federal government owed New Mexico more monetary aid and patronage positions allied him with his constituents.

Territorial officials agreed that *nuevomexicanos* had rights irrespective of what language they spoke, and they defended attacks on Spanish. Few complained about the prevalence of Spanish, given Spanish-speaking citizens' continued political power and their role in the origin of territorial politics. Long-standing settlers saw language concessions as the norm, whereas new settlers—particularly those who arrived after the 1880s—had to grow accustomed to them. As calls for statehood increased, however, New Mexicans found that their preference for Spanish placed them at a disadvantage. Federal authorities consistently cited the presence of so many monolingual Spanish speakers as a reason to reject the territory's bid for statehood. The prospect of statehood was not universally endorsed by New Mexicans.

Advocates of statehood tried to gain the status numerous times beginning in 1848. In 1872 and 1879, *nuevomexicano* voters helped defeat drafted constitutions at the polls. In 1850 and 1876, Congress rejected statehood attempts.[99] The possibility of statehood for New Mexico came up repeatedly in Congress and resulted in various reports that often highlighted and denigrated *nuevomexicanos'* cultural practices—including their use of the Spanish language.

In 1888, both the U.S. House and Senate Committees on Territories recommended that Congress admit New Mexico as a state.[100] A dissenting minority report from William M. Springer, Illinois, disapproved of residents' use of Spanish, the culture of New Mexico, and the Catholic faith, each of which he viewed as a valid reason for denying statehood.[101] Kansas senator John Ingalls backed Springer's dissent by entering a petition into the congressional record from Anglo New Mexican citizens who opposed statehood. The petition was signed by seventeen individuals from Albuquerque "and thousands of others if necessary." The petitioners concluded that "New Mexico is at present totally unfitted for the responsibilities of statehood, because first, the greater part of her population are unfamiliar with the English language." The petitioners placed language disparities at the forefront of a petition that included numerous other complaints, from corrupt political dealings to an embarrassing legislature.[102] For these seventeen individuals, *nuevomexicanos'* use of Spanish meant ignorance of their role as citizens.

Although he was not a voting member of Congress, Representative Joseph opposed these attacks against his constituents' bid for statehood. He rejected the minority opinion of 1888 by emphasizing New Mexican patriotism.[103] In at least three statements before Congress delivered between 1889 and 1894, Joseph opined that the territory deserved statehood regardless of language, asking the rhetorical question, "Can the Congress of the United States refuse admission as a state because a part of the people of the proposed State speak the Spanish language?"[104] He pointed to the promises of the Treaty of Guadalupe Hidalgo and the territory's material ties to the United States as reasons Congress could not deny statehood.[105]

New Mexicans had proved their citizenship through self-governance for decades, but their critics dismissed this evidence, as it was manifested in Spanish. Until native territorial Spanish speakers learned English or English-speaking settlers dominated, they faced Anglos who viewed them as "no more Americanized than . . . the day the country was wrestled from Old Mexico" rather than rightfully as American citizens.[106]

In the 1880s, with the completion of rail lines through New Mexico and the arrival of an increasing number of Anglo settlers, criticisms of Spanish began to emerge locally as well as nationally. Some of the new settlers, who viewed the prevalence of Spanish as foreign, challenged *nuevomexicanos'* claims to citizenship. In 1888, the *Las Vegas Optic* made numerous statements about Spanish speakers that newspapers had used forty years earlier to describe *californios*. The editors claimed that those who are ignorant of the English language "are a quiet, inoffensive people, with as little activity in development and progressive ideas as they have in wrong doing."[107] They persisted in this view in 1889: "The only way to make American citizens is to teach the youth the English language, so that they will think and talk in the common tongue of the United States."[108]

As Anglos increasingly expressed their preference for English, *nuevomexicanos* bemoaned the loss of their culture. As José Escobar (aka Zig Zag) wrote in *El Nuevo Mundo* in 1897, "progress and advancement" were not entirely positive. "Spanish-American people have found only the source of their ruin and the foundation of their degradation in being reduced, politically and socially, to zero, or its equivalent—nothingness!," he complained. Published in Anglo-dominated Albuquerque, Escobar's lament was prophetic but not accurate across the territory at the turn of the twentieth century. Escobar himself still had hope: "If America is for Americans, then let us say: New Mexico for New Mexicans."[109]

Although New Mexico's territorial status limited its citizens' expressions of self-government, its residents paradoxically also had more freedom in some domains, particularly in their language sovereignty. *Californios* understood this, which is why at the state constitutional convention in 1849 they along with some southern delegates proposed splitting the state in two—a northern state and a southern territory—to better serve their interests.[110] A united state would confine treaty citizens to a small minority of the population. In contrast, territorial status would have created a place where *californios* continued to hold political power. The transition to statehood, so eagerly sought by Anglo settlers from other states, further incorporated treaty citizens into the nation—removing opportunities for self-government at the local level.

The federal government unwittingly endorsed the use of Spanish in New Mexican territorial affairs by permitting its people to elect monolingual

Spanish speakers, which in turn made the Spanish language a normal part of the territorial political process. Having retained political positions and therefore power, *nuevomexicanos* considered themselves an integral part of the territory and, by extension, the United States. This equal footing allowed *nuevomexicanos* to develop a more limited understanding of the role of the English language in U.S. identity than developed in the rest of the country.

While the federal government condoned or even expected some of the Spanish-language policies that New Mexico adopted at the start of the territorial period, it undoubtedly did not anticipate the staying power of a language other than English in a U.S.-controlled territory. *Nuevomexicanos,* although American in name, failed to follow Anglos' preconceived vision of what an American looked or sounded like. Simply by operating their territorial legislature, their courts, and their schools in a language other than English, the majority of New Mexico's population rejected aspects of America's dominant culture. While this occurred to a smaller extent in southern Colorado, Spanish had little staying power as a language of citizenship in the rest of the Southwest.

In the last decades of the nineteenth century, Anglos narrowed their understanding of language and citizenship. They increasingly refused to tolerate languages other than English as being part of an acceptable American identity. By 1900 other states had joined California in implementing English-only requirements for voters. In this context, New Mexico's struggle for statehood became a national debate over what it would mean to accept a territory in which the majority of the inhabitants did not speak English.

CHAPTER 5

The United States Sees Language

*El Senador de Indiana ha venido á Nuevo México y Arizona, preocupado por la cuestion de raza é idioma; en vez de asomarse á la ventana de la justicia y del sentido comun.**

—P. Pino de la Huerta, "La Admisión de Nuevo Mexico," *El Tiempo*
  (Las Cruces, NM), December 6, 1902

The element of surprise landed most forcefully in Las Vegas, New Mexico, forty-six miles east of Santa Fe on the Atchison, Topeka, and Santa Fe Line. Four U.S. senators, members of the Senate Subcommittee on the Territories, arrived on Wednesday, November 12, 1902 (after a planning session in Chicago), purportedly to test the fitness of the territory's inhabitants for statehood.[1] They did not share their itinerary with anyone; their secrecy even led newspapers to report incorrectly that they headed to Oklahoma first.[2] As the senators rode through town in a carriage, they noticed that the signs on the grocery stores and meat markets were more often written in Spanish than in English.[3] They heard people speaking to one another in Spanish. They met a group of children, and when they attempted to speak to them in English, the children could not respond.[4] If the senators had walked into the post office in West Las Vegas, they would have been greeted in Spanish by Enrique Salasar, the postmaster and a twenty-four-year veteran newspaperman. His paper, *El Independiente*, with a circulation of 1,800 copies a week, served New Mexico's five largely rural northeastern counties: San Miguel (which included Las Vegas), Mora, Colfax, Union, and Guadalupe.[5] (See figure 5.) The senators asked detailed questions, and they marveled at their findings.

---

* "The Indiana Senator has come to New Mexico and Arizona, concerned about the question of race and language, rather than casting his glance toward justice and the common sentiment."

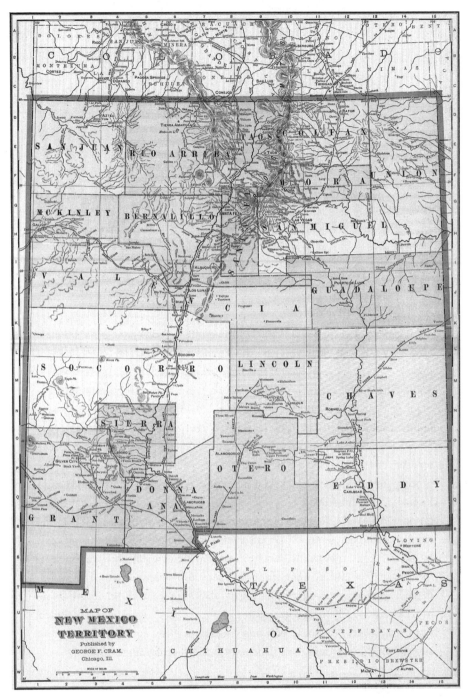

FIGURE 5. County map of New Mexico, 1901. George Franklin Cram and Eugene Murray-Aaron, originally published G. F. Cram, New York, Courtesy of David Rumsey Historical Map Collection, www.davidrumsey.com.

The subcommittee's interrogations inadvertently provided the best snapshot historians have of the use of Spanish throughout New Mexico territory at the turn of the twentieth century. In addressing elected officials, the territory's Anglo boosters wildly inflated the prevalence of English. For example, less than six months before the visit, Bernard Rodey, the territorial congressional representative, shared his perspective on language use in front of the committee: "You may travel all over the Territory hundreds of miles along the railroads and unless you take special pains about it . . . you will probably not hear a word of Spanish spoken the whole distance."[6] Statehood boosters deemphasized Spanish both to attract new Anglo settlers and investors and to persuade outsiders that New Mexico was ready for statehood. In 1897, for example, the superintendent of education estimated that all but 15 percent of the population could conduct business in English—a statistic flatly contradicted by the subcommittee's findings.[7] New Mexico's use of Spanish remained an open secret in Washington, with few focusing on the details about what it meant for a continental territory to operate in Spanish. The territory's representative to Congress and those in the executive branch could all address federal officials in English.

The senators were there to investigate what they viewed as the anomalies of *nuevomexicanos'* form of citizenship. For the senators, and many other national politicians and the white electorate more generally, citizenship was increasingly bound up with culture. By the first decade of the twentieth century, the dominant Anglo middle-class view of citizenship in the United States emphasized moral understandings of cleanliness, propriety, and "American identity" as much as it did legal or constitutional status.[8] Treaty citizens, along with their U.S.-born children and grandchildren, unapologetically saw themselves as U.S. citizens, albeit U.S. citizens who happened to speak Spanish. But to Anglo settlers and some *nuevomexicanos* who strove to put forth an image of New Mexico in compliance with national norms of cultural citizenship, the persistence of Spanish was alarming and possibly threatened the territory's claim to statehood. The United States had no legal reason to keep New Mexico from statehood on the basis of language use or culture, but congressional denigrations of *nuevomexicano* cultural and religious practices appear repeatedly in New Mexico's numerous statehood attempts as reasons for Congress to deny statehood.[9] The polygamous practices of a segment of the Mormon population in Utah are the other major example of cultural restrictions on statehood. Utah did not become a state until 1896 because of national opposition to polygamy.[10] While such cultural differences were not a legal impediment, downplaying them would help in the effort to gain statehood.

The probing questions of the visiting senators in November 1902 confirmed that the territory's residents still used Spanish in everyday life. It was the sole language of their villages and communities, and the territory's monolingual officeholders often preferred it. *Nuevomexicanos* saw nothing out of the ordinary in using Spanish as the primary language and defended it long after the senators left New Mexico and judged it as foreign. Although the senators' visit was not the principal reason that the 1903 Congress denied the territory statehood, their findings helped turn national public opinion against New Mexicans as aberrant, inauthentic citizens. The visit and subsequent negative press made language policies a major point of contention within the territory, precipitating policies that dislodged Spanish from the place of honor it had held in the territory's self-governance for half a century.

INADVERTENT ARCHIVISTS

This trip was the first and only time that members of the U.S. Senate interviewed territorial citizens in their territory of residence in order to judge fitness for statehood.[11] Technically, the visits of the Senate Committee on the Territories, chaired by Indiana senator Albert J. Beveridge, were Senate hearings. Instead of calling elite witnesses to testify before them in the ornate chambers of Congress, these unusual, more informal hearings took the senators through the neighborhoods of typical residents in New Mexico, Arizona, and Oklahoma. The hearings had broad goals and included interviews questioning irrigation capabilities, use of land, taxes, and educational opportunities. But without a doubt, the main purpose of the trip was to investigate the suspect moral and cultural habits of the residents of these remote, sparsely occupied territories.

The idea for this sort of visit originated with the territories themselves, as delegates for "half a century in New Mexico's case" had encouraged a visit to the territory, "contending that no unprejudiced committee could report against their admission as states after a visit."[12] It was ironic that Beveridge became the first senator to heed this call. New Mexico faced a formidable gatekeeper in the young—he had just turned forty—austere, and ambitious Indiana Republican. Known best as a supporter of U.S. imperialism for his fiery 1898 "March of the Flag" speech, Senator Beveridge delivered a speech to Congress in 1900 that trumpeted the annexation of the Philippines as an opportunity for the United States to claim power over the entire Pacific. He was also a vocal opponent of Filipino self-rule.[13] Beveridge took a fact-finding visit to the Philippines during the summer of 1899 and according to some "posed as an authority" on the archipelago when he returned. When Beveridge announced the subcommittee's visit to New Mexico, his recent trip to the Philippines was fresh in both local and national reporters' minds.[14]

Beveridge's plans for the visit attracted national controversy, as Republican leaders had already pledged their support for statehood for all three territories. He would be traveling with fellow Republican senators Henry E. Burnham of New Hampshire and William P. Dillingham of Vermont and Idaho populist Henry Heitfeld.[15] Beveridge's strong opposition to the admission of New Mexico and Arizona was well known. He actively resisted New Mexico's appeal for statehood, primarily on the basis of language; his role as chair gave him a national platform to broadcast his views. Newspapers across the country followed Beveridge's lead in explaining the terms of the debate surrounding statehood. One area of concern, the New York Times reported, was the small population in all three territories. But more ominously, the paper also noted that "one ground of objection is that New Mexico and Arizona are largely Mexican in population."[16]

Beveridge and the other senators became the first federal officials to systematically listen for and document the Spanish that had existed for over half a century in New Mexico, since the United States took over the territory. Prior to their visit, the national press and, by extension, the general public had little understanding of the extent of Spanish's use within the territory of New Mexico. It was, of course, an unavoidable reality for those who visited and for the limited pool of federal officials who handled the territory's business on a day-to-day basis. Once word of New Mexico's Spanish-speaking culture leaked out, it "rather staggered some of its [statehood] supporters."[17]

Aside from brief carriage tours to key landmarks and geographic features, the senators spent most of their visit in private sessions with territorial citizens. They maintained an inordinate amount of secrecy about the specifics of their schedule, which prohibited the fanfare usually accompanying visiting national political figures and angered their potential hosts. "Not much can be done in the way of preparation until more is known of the plans of the visitors," an Arizona reporter complained. Beveridge explained to territorial officials, and to national critics who believed his visit was a junket, that while he appreciated "all intended courtesies," the short duration and important purpose of the visit "requires us to devote ourselves exclusively to work."[18] The senators continued this "secrecy" at each stage of the trip, informing hosts in the towns they visited a few hours before and only then announcing the site of their next visit.[19] They initially employed a bilingual stenographer, a topographer, and a geologist to aid their work, only later adding a translator.[20] The workers were reportedly "groaning" at the fast pace and turnover expected of them.[21]

The hearings highlight the Senate subcommittee's focus on behavior and culture and exhibit its biases about what constituted the proper and expected practices for citizens of a prospective state. New Mexico experienced the longest and most difficult interrogation by far, not only because of the length and number of interviews, but also because it had the misfortune of being the first stop.[22] The transcripts clearly convey the senators' preconceived biases against statehood, but they also shed light on the territory's day-to-day language practices. The senators' aversion to and fascination with *nuevomexicanos'* use of Spanish provides an opportunity to glean how Spanish operated throughout the territory. Elected and appointed territorial officials answered explicit questions related to what language meant over a specific two-week period.[23] The visit therefore allows the historian to map the use of language across New Mexico, uncovering what sorts of language skills were necessary to navigate daily life in different parts of the territory.

A transcript of a sitting senator questioning a Spanish-speaking citizen is not, of course, an ideal source, and the uneven power dynamics of the interviews are troublesome. The senators' questions and interpreters' translations mediated *nuevomexicano* voices. In some cases, private citizens' anxiety about being questioned privately by elected federal officials is visible on the page.[24] As an Arizona newspaper suggests, the questions—while professional—could also be unrelenting: "All of the senators, and especially Senator Beveridge, would succeed as reporters."[25] The testimony is nevertheless priceless, in that it includes the perspective of those outside New Mexico's political establishment. Former governor L. Bradford Prince lamented the fact that the senators' choice of interviewees overlooked "many of the most intelligent and well-informed citizens who were close at hand."[26] By selecting less elite individuals, the Senate visit uncovered how New Mexico's general population perceived language and citizenship. These Spanish speakers unabashedly saw Spanish as a cultural right alongside their national pride.

DAY 1: LAS VEGAS, NEW MEXICO

The senators left no known rationale for their trip's itinerary, but it is likely that they stopped first in Las Vegas because they came to it first on the train. That meant that Las Vegas had the least warning and also possibly the most apprehension about the visit. (News of the impending visit spread throughout New Mexico and Arizona, leading some elite boosters to later present prepared statements.)[27] The hearings began at the recently opened Castañeda Hotel, built in the mission revival style right along the rail line in the new and growing part of town. The senators quickly found they could not conduct interviews without an interpreter.[28] They took no "special pains" to locate written or oral use of Spanish, as territorial representative Rodey suggested was necessary in prior testimony to the committee.[29] Instead, Beveridge's committee became the first federal body to encounter the reality beyond statehood boosters' rosy proclamations downplaying the prevalence of the use of Spanish in New Mexico.

Las Vegas could not hide its use of Spanish if it wanted to; the town split geographically according to language use. (See figure 6.) Each half had its own post office, schools, businesses, and social circles. East Las Vegas's English-speaking respondents lacked respect for their Spanish-speaking neighbors. Justice of the peace H. S. Wooster criticized the quality of West Las Vegas's language use: "They speak the Spanish language, or try to; but I understand that it is not a pure Castilian; it is a sort of jargon of their own." Wooster insisted that if the senators went out and listened, they "could not understand a word." While likely the case, as none of the senators appeared to understand "Castilian" or any other kind of Spanish, Wooster's attack on a regional dialect, even though he himself did not speak Spanish, exhibits a deep-rooted prejudice against all aspects of the "Mexican" language and culture.[30] It also brings forth a local Anglo perception of New Mexican Spanish as nonstandard or uneducated—a prejudice in evidence at least since the 1850s when Secretary of the Territory Davis translated the legislative journals into "good Spanish." Northern New Mexican Spanish did have its own regionalisms that drew increasing academic interest in the following decade, fueling the career of a *nuevomexicano* Stanford professor, Aurelio Espinosa, who argued its differences largely resulted from medieval Spanish archaisms.[31]

Wooster, while Anglo, spoke as a minority citizen. He was a member of Las Vegas's new but growing Anglo settler community. Other witnesses

FIGURE 6. Bilingual advertisements and signs in Las Vegas, New Mexico, circa 1900. Rex Studio, Courtesy Palace of the Governors Photo Archives (NMHM/DCA), 070808.

described the population of the five northeastern counties as predominantly Spanish speaking. The senators estimated language breakdown by county, asking census takers and the federal judge who presided over the five counties for their impressions of language use. The senators pressed census enumerators on language use, in addition to population demographics.[32] While the census enumerators' statistical recall rarely corresponded to the reported census figures (which is understandable, as they did not have time to review their work), their memory of the language used for interviews is more credible. After all, census takers needed to employ translators to complete their survey if they did not speak the language of the residents. Or at the very least, they would have remembered their struggle to conduct their work in a less familiar language. The census enumerators called to testify largely came from San Miguel County and reported that the residents of small towns like Old Las Vegas ("practically all"), El Aguilar (estimated at 80 percent Spanish speaking), and many others were overwhelmingly Spanish speaking.[33]

Given this demographic reality, the residents of surrounding villages who traveled to Las Vegas to trade and buy goods required Spanish as a language of commerce. For this reason, the schools in East Last Vegas—the Anglo part of town—included Spanish classes in the curriculum. While it was not taught in elementary schools, the high school (almost exclusively attended by Anglos) taught Spanish. The East Las Vegas superintendent of public schools confirmed the senators' understanding of the importance of Spanish-language instruction: "Q. Your purpose . . . is that pupils may be taught Spanish so that they may teach Spanish or transact the business life in a Spanish population? A. Yes, sir; that is the idea exactly."[34] The residents of West Las Vegas confirmed that newspapers and public signs were in Spanish and that interactions in the post office, courts, and homes all took place in Spanish.[35] The residents' preference for Spanish alarmed the senators, especially when justice of the peace for Plaza Vegas, Felipe Baca y García, expressed an unexpected need for court interpreters, indicating, "When they are English I have an interpreter here."[36] Or when they heard school-age children speaking Spanish among themselves, even when they putatively knew English. Over a dozen hearing questions centered on the languages students used in the home and off school grounds.[37]

The senators left Las Vegas that evening and continued to Santa Fe, where they resumed their session at the Palace Hotel the next morning.[38] As they recommenced, their vocabulary betrayed a big shift in their thinking. In Las Vegas, the senators had asked individuals if they were "a native of New Mexico" or referred to "Spanish children." These word choices distanced *nuevomexicanos* from Mexico, making them more European.[39] Just one day later, they spoke of native or "Mexican" citizens and foreign or "American" ones, while often double-checking for confirmation of meaning, "as those terms are used down here."[40] As William Mills clarified in Las Vegas, "The term 'American' includes everybody that is not a 'Mexican.'"[41] Beveridge himself distinguished between the "foreign and so-called American population" and the "native" population.[42] New Mexicans pushed to be described as "natives" to emphasize their place on the land (and to rewrite the space for themselves rather than American Indians). By recasting Anglo settlers as foreigners, New Mexicans also created a distinction that reinforced Beveridge's view of *nuevomexicanos*, and specifically Spanish speakers, as not part of the nation.[43]

This set of categories designated European immigrants as "American," regardless of their citizenship status, and *nuevomexicanos* as "not Americans," even as they held positions only open to legal citizen voters. *Nuevomexicanos* used national labels racially rather than as terms of nationality. As Enrique

Armijo of Las Vegas explained, "We use the term 'Mexican' to distinguish from the Anglo-Saxon."[44] The subcommittee members embraced this racial designation wholeheartedly, but they ignored the actions and statements of Spanish-speaking citizens that emphasized their place in the nation.[45] New Mexico's elites accepted the reality of Spanish speakers as an important voting bloc, but their choice of language in describing them marked them as not-quite American.

By virtue of the Treaty of Guadalupe Hidalgo, treaty citizens enjoyed the status of citizens; their descendants claimed birthright citizenship. Their statements and record in New Mexico demonstrated that they took on the major political roles expected only of citizens in all nonfederal sectors of New Mexico's territorial government and society. When asked, *nuevomexicanos* quickly claimed allegiance to the United States despite their preference for the Spanish language. As former justice of the peace, José María García, explained, "I like my own language better than any other, the same as I like the United States better than any other country in the world."[46]

DAY 2: SANTA FE

Even though they must have been aware of the impending visit, individuals in Santa Fe had little time to prepare their testimony after learning they would be called before the senatorial hearing. Those summoned waited together in the lobby of the Palace Hotel.[47] Still, the fact that they had any warning at all may have produced slightly toned down responses, or more attempts to appease the senators. José D. Sena, who served as an assistant court interpreter and had interpreted for a recent Republican territorial convention, answered questions that pertained to both public and private use of Spanish. Sena described families who spoke in English except in the company of their Spanish-speaking mother—suggesting generational and gendered differences in language use. He implied a class divide in language acquisition by claiming, "Poorer people are very anxious to learn the English. They learn it as fast as they can." "American boys will try to speak the Spanish and try to learn it, but the little boys won't let them." When Sena encountered individuals who worked for English-speaking families on the street and addressed them in Spanish, he found "they will answer me in English."

Sena's report of locals' language choices suggests that New Mexicans engaged in code-switching, depending on the circumstance, and that language preferences could serve as an indicator of social status. This was an angle that interested the senators, who followed up with more pointed questions about class and the difference between Las Vegas and Santa Fe. Sena explained the cultural and spatial division as racial: "There seems to be a race prejudice there [in Las Vegas] more than in any other part of the world." He saw this sort of race prejudice as a thing of the past, as something that was "dying out." But while Sena pointed to "race," his answers specified language as the great divider. When asked explicitly if he knew of other towns like Las Vegas, Sena admitted that Old Town Albuquerque and its new town were similarly separated by language.[48] He acknowledged that early settlements remained divided by language but suggested that Santa Fe and other, more modern towns no longer followed this old pattern.

Other witnesses pointed to print language as evidence of the region's preference for Spanish. Postmaster Paul A. F. Walters explained that while "the average man in the city can understand English," he estimated that Spanish-language newspapers made up half of those sent through the post office.[49] Newspaper publisher James Hughes substantiated this guess by stating that 1,900 copies of the Spanish-language newspaper *El Nuevo Mexicano* circulated weekly.[50] Aside from newspapers, Walters also noted that "the natives are great letter-writers. Most of their mail is in the Spanish handwriting."[51] Spanish appeared in court archives just as it did in the post office. The senators pressed Justice of the Peace Charles Conklin on his reasons for keeping his docket in Spanish. They expressed incredulity since both Conklin and his son who helped him could understand and write in English. "It was the custom of the justice of the peace that was before me. He always kept the record in Spanish," Conklin explained."[52]

The senators showed interest in the language of territorial court proceedings throughout the visit. Senator Burnham admitted to a reporter of the *Santa Fe New Mexican* his difficulty with the Spanish-language courts during what was an otherwise tight-lipped committee visit (senators did not share their opinions with local newspapers). "It is a little hard for us to grasp how an interpreter can follow along just a few words behind the speaker, how speeches can be made at the same time and yet be followed," he confided. A bilingual court or political system was beyond his ability to comprehend: "Back in my state a speaker in a convention or an attorney is expected to get excited. How do you arrange that here?"[53] New Mexicans, whose daily political lives and experience in the courts entailed simultaneous translations as the norm, responded that the interpreter got just as excited, if not more, and often gave

a better speech than the original.[54] Recognizing the skilled nature and absolute necessity of the court and political interpreters, New Mexicans highly
valued their work.

Santa Fe's census enumerators similarly evoked a geographically separated
community, split by language preference. Camilo Padilla described his district
of 1,500 to 1,700 residents as consisting of almost entirely Spanish speakers,
with just a smattering of English, German, and Italian speakers.[55] Ambrosio
Ortiz estimated that two-thirds of the slightly more than 3,000 residents
that he surveyed were "Mexican." "We always use the Spanish language," he
explained.

The senators interviewed five census takers in Santa Fe County who provided a greater understanding of the region surrounding Santa Fe (the county
encompasses an area slightly over 1,900 square miles). These census takers suggested an even more lopsided language landscape. Facundo Ortiz and Barbara
Perea y [Y]risarri claimed to conduct their business in the environs of Agua
Fria, La Cienega, Cerrillos, and Madrid almost totally in Spanish. They encountered few "Americans."[56] Of the other "scattered houses" visited by Clementa
P. Ortiz in San Ildefonso and Española, about three-fourths contained Spanish speakers, with the remainder of residents either American Indians, "Americans," or Germans. Ortiz did not follow territorial racial conventions in
responding to Senator Dillingham's questions; she used "Spanish," rather than
"Mexican," and distinguished between English-speaking Anglos and German
immigrants.[57] Joseph P. Conklin described the mining region in the southern
portion of the county as two-thirds Mexican. In explaining residents' language
use, he invoked generational status and occupation. Conklin described the
elderly generation as "too old now" to learn English and claimed that farmers
knew less English than Mexican mine workers.[58] The census takers' testimony
painted a geographically divided language map, with individuals' opportunity
to interact in English growing as they moved to towns or worked in mines. The
rural portions of the county remained overwhelmingly Spanish speaking.

While in Santa Fe, the senators interviewed Pedro Sánchez, the seventy-
year-old, monolingual Spanish-speaking census supervisor. Through an interpreter, Sánchez answered questions related to the approximately seventy-eight
census enumerators he selected—all of whom, he believed, could speak both
English and Spanish. The senators, incredulous, asked how he determined
that applicants were bilingual when he himself could not speak English.[59]
"They wrote to me that they all spoke English," he countered. When Beveridge

told of encountering non-English-speaking census enumerators in Las Vegas, Sánchez replied, "In that case they lied to me." Sánchez justified his choice of a largely Spanish-speaking or Mexican group of enumerators by explaining that the majority of people they encountered spoke Spanish, especially in the country districts.[60] He did employ some Anglos, however, because in "some cases the population were more American." But even with the Anglos hired, Sánchez had to authorize the hiring of thirteen Spanish-language interpreters to complete the census.[61]

After the visit to Santa Fe, local newspapers confirmed that "the committee seemed chiefly interested in to what extent Spanish [wa]s used in the intercourse of citizens of New Mexico."[62] Santa Fe's residents described a bilingual town whose citizens used either Spanish or English as the occasion warranted. Compared to those in Las Vegas, Santa Fe's English speakers appeared more receptive to *nuevomexicanos* and did not emphasize racial difference. Spanish speakers could reply to or at least understand when they encountered English speakers on the street, at the post office, or in a business establishment. Yet they lived in largely Spanish-speaking communities, where they wrote to one another and conducted most of their legal and political proceedings in Spanish.[63]

Outside of town, the county's residents, including ranchers, farmers, and laborers, largely spoke Spanish and most had no understanding of English. When they visited Santa Fe for trade or to make purchases, as many villagers did, these residents could easily conduct their business because the town itself was bilingual.[64] Las Vegas and Santa Fe remained equipped to aid rural Spanish-speaking travelers. Villages with populations under one hundred, along with ranches and farms, comprised over three-fourths of the territory's 195,310 residents in 1900, which explains why visits to town remained crucial for acquiring goods and for trade.[65] In Albuquerque, rural Spanish-speaking residents had to take greater pains to find Spanish speakers.

DAYS 3 AND 4: ALBUQUERQUE

The next stop on the senators' itinerary was the largest town in New Mexico, Albuquerque. Including Old Town, it comprised around 7,000 residents, with 1,300 voters counted in the previous election.[66] The senators spent two days interviewing in Albuquerque, using the railroad to summon individuals from Socorro County.

When the senators arrived in Albuquerque, they were greeted by a host of Anglo supporters of statehood, including the U.S. territorial representative, Bernard Rodey. Rodey, an immigrant from Ireland, spoke at length before granting the floor to several prominent community members he had chosen. Each of these speakers delivered prepared statements on New Mexico's financial and economic attributes, and each emphasized that, in the words of one, the "younger generation understands English as well as I do. We ought to have statehood."[67] They attempted to control the damage of the testimony delivered in Las Vegas and Santa Fe by reinforcing previous boosters' claims that English was commonly heard throughout the territory.[68] In their zeal, they stretched the truth, particularly about language.

The senators received these comments with skepticism. They questioned lawyer and former Albuquerque mayor O. N. Marron: "Is it not a fact that the Mexicans, as a rule, in their own homes very largely use the Spanish language?" Marron conceded, "That, I think, is the fact, Senator. There is no question about that," though he provided no evidence to support his conclusion. He recovered quickly by emphasizing that both English and Spanish speakers were "very anxious for statehood."[69] For those eager to boost New Mexico's chances at statehood, Albuquerque represented the last chance to convince senators that they had heard misleading testimony in the territory's smaller cities. Rodey even dismissed the census results, claiming that "the census gives us no information on the subject."[70] Still, despite their best efforts, the boosters could not prevent the senators from encountering more evidence of the prevalence of Spanish in New Mexico's largest settlement.

The testimony from Albuquerque's residents suggested that while New Mexicans continued to use Spanish, a generational language shift was under way. Senator Dillingham told twenty-seven-year-old interpreter Antonio A. Sedillo (future chief interpreter of the territorial assembly), "You use good English."[71] His comment suggests that Sedillo likely had a clearly understandable English that compared favorably to the other translators' broken English.[72] Sedillo deflected the compliment: "I think I use better Spanish than English; I use Spanish most of the time."[73] We cannot know Sedillo's motives for contradicting Senator Dillingham. Perhaps he wanted to reinforce Rodey's suggestion that Albuquerque's bilingual residents spoke Spanish in the private sphere but knew English well and used it in the official realm.[74] Or perhaps Sedillo's statement should be read as a demonstration of his cultural pride, a way for him to reinforce the idea that Spanish ruled supreme in his life, whereas he associated English solely with work. Or perhaps he was merely modest. Whatever motivated Sedillo's response, similar admissions from other witnesses led the senators to believe that Albuquerque's Old Town residents considered themselves primarily Spanish speakers.

Albuquerque's census takers described significant numbers of Spanish speakers in the town and surrounding areas. Seferino Crollott, former superintendent of schools, who married a "Spanish" woman and had seven children, spoke of the districts encompassing Alameda and Sandia, which he remembered as having between 1,400 and 1,500 people.[75] Crollott suggested a high rate of intermarriage in these districts, estimating that between 110 and 150 families consisted of half Anglo and half Mexican households, with the rest of the population Mexican. He also described a more recent shift to English in the schools, though he acknowledged that the shift had not yet occurred in homes. Crollott explained that young people between the ages of eight and twenty-one "speak pretty fair English." He encountered some English speakers among people 45 or 50 years of age, but almost no one "from 65 up could speak it at all."[76] The generational patterns for language use in Albuquerque corresponded to the town's Anglo growth and serve as a reminder of how quickly youth can acquire a language, once taught.

Several witnesses made claims on behalf of residents' English-speaking abilities that could not hold up to questioning. Census takers Modesto C. Ortiz and Eslavio Vigil, for instance, confirmed that they had used Spanish to interview residents of Old Town and Los Barelas but only after having first claimed that they used English.[77] Vigil, a native Spanish speaker, only did so after Beveridge exclaimed, "Do you mean to tell the committee that you used the English instead of the Spanish in taking that census?" Vigil backed down, saying, "No, sir; no, sir."[78] New Mexico–born G. W. Metzgar finally admitted after contradictory statements that most of the eight hundred people he interviewed in Corrales, a country district eight miles from Albuquerque, spoke Spanish to one another, even though he spoke English to some of them.[79] In this case, the testimony of the census takers may have presented a skewed picture of language use in Albuquerque and the region; Beveridge mainly summoned those from primarily Spanish-speaking populations.

Other officials, particularly those from the surrounding area, were more forthcoming about residents' preference for Spanish. Nestor Montoya, a court reporter (and future newspaper editor and congressional representative), described the residents of Bernalillo County, his lifelong home, as speaking almost exclusively Spanish and living on "scattered Mexican ranches," though it was located just outside Albuquerque.[80] Numerous officials from Socorro, located about 78 miles south of Albuquerque and about 147 miles north of Las Cruces, testified that of the approximately 17,500 people who lived in the rural portion of the county, around two-thirds could be described as Spanish speaking.[81] Probate clerk H.G. Baca emphasized that most of Socorro County's Mexican residents could speak English and that he "generally" conducted "all the business" in English.[82] The president of the University of New Mexico, William George Tight, who encountered both Anglos and Mexicans on ranches while conducting anthropological fieldwork, contrasted the ranch population with that of the mountains, where he found that "most of them speak Spanish."[83] The Senate hearings confirmed that Spanish remained an asset for individuals traversing New Mexico's rural roads. Outside of concentrated urban pockets, New Mexico was Spanish speaking.

RETURN TO NEW MEXICO: LAS CRUCES AND EDDY COUNTY

The senators arrived in Las Cruces on November 20, 1902, after a four-day visit to Arizona. There they had confirmed through observation and brief questioning that Spanish was a marginalized language in Arizona. Their conclusions would have been different had they visited places like Tucson, where more Spanish speakers resided. The people of Las Cruces welcomed the senators' train from Bisbee, with "several hundred school children" cheering their arrival. Carriages toured the senators around town and to the New Mexico College of Agriculture and Mechanic Arts. After a lunch at "Mrs. Carroll's," the senators began their work. Despite reports among the locals that "the members appeared to be well pleased with their reception," the senators continued their sharp-eared observations.[84]

As elsewhere in New Mexico, the senators encountered more Spanish than they had originally anticipated. As they passed a schoolyard at recess, they heard the children "using the Spanish language among themselves at play."[85] They found they could buy newspapers in either language, as two of the town's five newspapers published exclusively in Spanish. Of the three remaining papers, two were published in English and one was bilingual.[86]

Once again, witness testimony uncovered the extent to which New Mexicans lived and worked in Spanish, even as they increasingly encountered

English. Martin Lohman, the bilingual postmaster and owner of a large store, employed six bilingual clerks and one monolingual Spanish-speaking clerk. Spanish remained the language of two-thirds of his business. "It is a surprise even to me the amount of English used by the Mexicans here," he marveled.[87] The third district judge, Frank W. Parker, and the bilingual census taker Eugene Van Patten corroborated Lohman's statement by describing Doña Ana County as being two-thirds Mexican. Even so, Isidor Armijo suggested that parents with any financial means preferred that their children use English, as "progressive people here will insist upon them speaking English, and they all speak English when you address them in English."[88]

The senators did not remain long in Las Cruces, because their opinions had already solidified after the first three New Mexico stops. They ate dinner at Martín Amador's hotel. Amador held the distinction of being the only person the hearings identified as having "voluntarily appeared as witness."[89] He expressed his opposition to statehood, largely because of the people's lack of education. Amador offered a ten-year timetable for statehood to allow children to come of age in a stronger educational system.[90] His outspokenness as the sole witness to oppose statehood—boosters had convinced the general public that statehood was the best option for the territory—created a backlash.[91] His wife and children claimed that the negative reactions to his testimony contributed to his death just three months later.[92]

From Las Cruces, the senators traveled to El Paso, Texas, and questioned a few individuals that evening. They interviewed no census takers but instead spoke to Judge Daniel H. McMillan. The judge confirmed that students in New Mexico often learned English in the schools but chose not to "hold to it" during vacation periods.[93] He editorialized on the senators' interest in Spanish use in the territory by saying that the federal government placed "no limitation upon them [monolingual Spanish speakers] as to the right to hold office or serve on juries." New Mexico's language use could not change in one day, and those restrictions, he argued, "can not be done . . . now."[94] The next evening, people interviewed near Carlsbad, in Eddy County, explained that the settlement in their county was about a dozen years old and contained hardly "over six Mexican taxpayers."[95] After three confirmations that the population was almost exclusively Anglo, the senators were appeased. They did not ask the census enumerator, William C. Reiff, to state the language he used when collecting the census.[96] The brief visit—the senators interviewed Carlsbad residents on the train—and their tendency to take this testimony on face value further suggests that the main point of their tour was to unveil the extent of the Spanish language in New Mexico. From Carlsbad, the train continued on to Oklahoma.

TERRITORY? COLONY? STATE?

On November 27, 1902, just one week after the senators left Las Cruces, Enrique H. Salazar, editor of Las Vegas's *El Independiente* (The Independent) anticipated "un informe desfavorable" (an unfavorable report) from the committee, after all, "que hay hostilidad latente y marcada en contra de Nuevo México entre ciertos senadores influyentes de la mayoría está fuera de toda duda" (that there is latent and marked hostility against New Mexico from certain influential majority senators is beyond doubt).[97] The locals read the senators' probing questions, presumptions, and conclusions correctly, understanding that the findings would fuel debate about New Mexico's future both at home and across the country. Spanish-speaking locals, particularly those who endorsed statehood, recognized that in Beveridge they had encountered their "enemigo mas acerrimo" (biggest archenemy).[98] A *junta de indignación* also broadcasted *nuevomexicano* lack of support for Beveridge.[99]

On New Year's Day, *El Independiente* observed that "el negocio del estado se ha convertido en una materia de importancia nacional" (statehood business has become a matter of national importance).[100] Spanish-language newspapers kept track of and commented on congressional proceedings and newspaper articles that spoke negatively of the territory. Readers in New Mexico could not help but notice the senators' fixation on language, on the idea that "New Mexico is too much Mexico and not enough new."[101] Local boosters began to realize that by retaining Spanish in official settings they had created a political and social system that appeared "foreign," either "Spanish" or "Mexican," and it was this very foreignness that had elicited opposition from national politicians. The question entertained in the local press following the Senate subcommittee visit was whether the presence of Spanish would be enough to drive off statehood.

The senators remained largely quiet on the matter until Beveridge released the subcommittee's report in mid-December.[102] Even before then, however, they leaked some of the Spanish-language findings to the press. Newspapers especially reported on the use of Spanish in the courts and by children. The subcommittee released several photos of individuals with captions saying they spoke no English. One photo was of a nineteen-year-old man who was "born and reared in that territory, who cannot speak a word of English."[103] The subcommittee members intimated that because of the presence of Spanish-language businesses and political institutions "in parts of both [Arizona and New Mexico], the native American citizen sometimes feels that he is in a foreign country."[104] The idea that native-born citizens (even in a territory) did not speak English had previously escaped notice and calculation on the national level.[105]

As the Senate testimony confirmed, Anglos continued to be a minority population within New Mexico and *nuevomexicanos* could not be relegated just to its past. The question remained: Could *nuevomexicanos'* loyalty to the Spanish language exclude them from full citizenship? Long before Beveridge's visit, New Mexicans recognized the uncertainty of their status and the distinct treatment they received compared to other western continental territories.[106] New Mexicans felt an acute sense of federal neglect, particularly after the Spanish-American War led to the United States acquiring more territories. Martin Lohman of Las Cruces took pride in what New Mexico had accomplished "without any aid from the National Government." He contrasted the government's neglect of New Mexico to its support for its new insular territories: "The Government has done more for the Porto Ricans in the last two years than they have for the New Mexicans in the past fifty years."[107] Superintendent of Public Instruction J. Francisco Chaves echoed the charge in a letter to the subcommittee. "If, half a century ago, as by every moral and humane right they should have done, the United States had thus sent train loads of teachers into New Mexico, this population would rank to-day with the most enlightened communities," he wrote, after noting the teachers sent to Cuba, Puerto Rico, and the Philippines.[108] He continued his complaint, writing that "the Federal Government has persistently ignored the true citizenship of the territory" and that New Mexico's taxes now supported the education of "long haired, blanketed Indians."[109] New Mexicans kept tabs on the specific level of aid in the noncontinental territories: "Hay actualmente 150,000 Filipinos asistiendo á las escuelas públicas, con 800 maestros americanos y cerca 4,000 maestros nativos" (There are currently 150,000 Filipinos attending the public schools, with 800 American teachers and around 4,000 native teachers).[110]

Critics like Chaves and Lohman were playing into a federal desire to create hierarchies and division. Other New Mexicans followed suit. Jon L. Gay, Esq., of the Railway Mail Service, suggested an imperial hierarchy in which "the average New Mexican is far ahead of the average Porto Rican to-day in point of intelligence and in point of being capable of self-government."[111] Representative Rodey expressed a similar sentiment when he told those visiting New Mexico, "We regret that we are not being as well treated as the Philippines and Porto Rico."[112] Each of these New Mexicans saw statehood as the best remedy for federal neglect, yet their insistence on making this claim by comparing the situation to that of American Indians or the noncontiguous territories reinforced New Mexico's distinctness.

As some New Mexicans complained that its citizens did not receive as much federal support as residents of territories, others continued to argue that they would never be treated as true citizens until New Mexico was granted statehood. Supporters reminded Congress of the Treaty of Guadalupe Hidalgo, which "promised to give the inhabitants of the territory acquired by that treaty the full rights of American citizenship." A *Denver Republican* article expressed a western regional pride by praising *nuevomexicanos* as "some of the best and most loyal citizens." The article reminded its readers that even if an American citizen "habitually speaks the Spanish language," that was "no valid ground for denying him full rights."[113] Statehood was a marker of full citizenship; the *Denver Republican* did not see language as posing a barrier to statehood.

By inserting race and language in the subcommittee's investigation, Beveridge had succeeded in sensationalizing New Mexico's cultural differences, which lengthened the debate over statehood.[114] New Mexicans' use of Spanish gave many national supporters pause and brought down a rain of negative press on the territory. The *Muskogee Daily Phoenix* used English-language deficiency to support Oklahoma's statehood bid as *nuevomexicanos* "are less fitted for statehood than the . . . Indians who . . . all . . . speak the English language and are familiar with American institutions."[115] A *New York Times* editorial urged caution against statehood for Arizona and New Mexico: "Clearly there is an immense risk in admission; there is none in waiting."[116] Senate informants contributed to the most damaging articles, leaking that the use of Spanish had cost the territory its presidential ally for statehood, Theodore Roosevelt. The president reportedly saw the territory as "backward" both "in learning the English language and in active participation in political life"; the use of Spanish in the courts especially shocked him.[117] The *Arizona Republican* blamed Beveridge's focus on Spanish for "caus[ing] to be printed in every paper in the United States an indictment against the people of New Mexico and Arizona."[118] Beveridge likely reveled in the condemnation.

When Beveridge's long-awaited majority report for the Committee on Territories finally appeared in December 1902, it asserted that statehood required Anglo territorial dominance and *nuevomexicano* conformity to dominant cultural practices: "When the immigration of English-speaking people who have been citizens of other States does its modifying work with the 'Mexican' element—when all these things have come to pass, the committee hopes and believes that this mass of people, unlike us in race, language, and social customs, will finally come to form a creditable portion of American citizenship."[119] As one example, Beveridge cited the broken English used by interviewees, which made it "frequently impossible to subpoena witnesses except by the aid of the committee's official interpreter."[120] The majority report withheld credit for the New Mexicans' obvious facility with U.S. political systems. The senators had interviewed almost exclusively those in public positions, including census takers, justices of the peace, court interpreters, court clerks, school administrators, teachers, sheriffs, and mayors, and yet Beveridge could not fathom monoglot Spanish-speaking officeholders fulfilling any role in U.S. institutions. His nativism blinded him to the U.S. political system in practice in New Mexico and focused his attention on an English future.

With the committee's vote on statehood attempted numerous times before the Senate adjourned on March 4, *nuevomexicano* newspapers placed their hope in the prestige and influence of the minority report authors, who downplayed the political importance of language.[121] "'The future of the Mexican element' may be safely left to the spirit of Americanism, which has assimilated Swedes, Poles, Germans, and Scandinavians," wrote William Bate of Tennessee. Bate questioned Congress's right to make a moral judgment or to "inquire into the character of the population."[122]

Both Bate and Matthew Quay of Pennsylvania claimed that New Mexico's long endurance as a territory made its citizens more than deserving of statehood. Recognizing the promises of the Treaty of Guadalupe Hidalgo to make treaty citizens full citizens, Bate argued, "The lapse of time has converted the 'proper time' (to be judged by the Congress of the United States) into the present if the provision of the treaty is ever to have significance."[123] Most of the treaty citizen generation had died without ever seeing this promise fulfilled. Quay rejected comparisons of New Mexico to imperial territories like Puerto Rico, Hawaii, and the Philippines, as he saw New Mexicans as fully

American; indeed, as the "pioneers of American civilization in the great West, those who were born under the flag, and have lived under it, fought for it." He viewed the territory as a state in all but name.[124]

In support of the minority report, an editorial in the *Washington Post* argued that "the Constitution of the United States does not put the Spanish language among the disqualifications for Statehood, nor the English language among the qualifications." Further, the Constitution did not require high literacy rates (29 percent of New Mexicans were reportedly illiterate in any language). The editorial explained New Mexico's cultural differences not by infantilizing its residents but by pointing to the consistent lack of federal funding to the territory and its schools. New Mexico was, effectively, an under-funded colony. The federal government could best remedy the situation "by bestowal of the American birthright of self-government."[125] While supportive of statehood, the *Post* nevertheless viewed New Mexico's use of Spanish as temporary. With increased "American" migration, which statehood would encourage, Spanish would fade away naturally.

Other newspapers conflated *nuevomexicanos* with recent immigrants from Italy. An article published in Philadelphia after the release of Beveridge's report explained that New Mexico's "Spanish-Mexican origin" individuals, "speaking a Spanish dialect," were as "thoroughly foreign in life, manners, habits, and conditions as the latest contingent of immigrants now arriving fresh from Sicily."[126] The rise of xenophobia among Anglos had increased national incredulity that anyone who did not speak English could ever have access to the rights of U.S. citizens.

New Mexican newspapers followed these national discussions closely, publishing excerpts with commentary. The *Alamogordo News* talked about the "score" the *El Paso Times* made when it argued that Beveridge should learn "that a large percentage of the men who voted the Republican ticket in Penn-sylvania last week cannot speak English."[127] New Mexican journalists—both English and Spanish speaking—rallied behind Spanish speakers to counter-act the negative portrayals in the national press. Their responses could be direct, like the one targeted at the *Des Moines State Capital* after it published an editorial against statehood: "It is doubtful if any citizen of New Mexico, even if he does not understand the English language . . . is ignorant and stupid enough to [believe] such foolish, false and ignorant statements."[128]

In the months that followed, Spanish-language newspapers carefully reported the back-and-forth of congressional politics in anticipation of learning their fate. Exemplifying the degree of attention the papers devoted to the topic, the editor of La Voz del Pueblo translated longtime New Mexican resident and then Indiana senator Stephen B. Elkins's speech before the Senate into Spanish. Point by point, he struck down cultural differences between *nuevomexicanos* and Anglos as a reason for denying statehood and held up the Treaty of Guadalupe Hidalgo as proof of the country's obligation to the population. Elkins reminded the Senate of the original pact General Kearney proposed in 1846 and asserted that *nuevomexicanos* had fulfilled their end of the bargain by becoming good U.S. citizens. "El uso del idioma español no debiera de ser obstáculo para que hiciéramos justicia al pueblo de Nuevo México admitiéndolo como un estado / Speaking the Spanish language should be no bar to doing the people of New Mexico justice, and admitting it as a State," Elkins asserted. He pointed to California as another example. After all, "lenguaje no determinan el carácter, lealtad, y lo que vale un pueblo, ó sus calificaciones para ciudadanía / language does not determine the character, loyalty, and worth of a people, or their qualifications for citizenship," particularly those "que han [sido] conquistado y anexado ... contra de su voluntad / that have been been conquered and annexed . . . without their consent."[129] Elkins's comments echoed *nuevomexicano* beliefs and likely helped them heal from the senatorial visit.

———

As Congress and the rest of the nation shifted to other interests after the winter of 1902–3, national coverage of New Mexico's use of the Spanish language tapered off. The wounds in New Mexico remained. "Refutación categórica" (Categorical Refutation), a poem published in March 1903, details the insult felt by Spanish speakers: "La principal objecion / repitenla con disfraz / diciendo que el ingles / nuestro pueblo es muy chambón" (The main objection / masked repeatedly / said that in English / our people are very unskilled).[130] It rebukes the senators in their preferred language, inviting them to "go to hell!"[131] English had uses, the poem continues; after all, words such as "liar" are used "si un embustero hay" (if there is a liar) prior to saying "goodbye."[132] The poem's palpable anger at the senators contrasted with its unwavering pride in New Mexico and a preference for Spanish: "tienen ideas pocas / de lo que somos capaces" (they have little understanding / of what we are capable).[133] Written almost entirely in Spanish, the poem plays with language, making light of the crushing blow that members of the Senate subcommittee dealt by discrediting a large part of *nuevomexicanos'* lives—use of their native tongue. Even so, the poem's author desired statehood: the penultimate stanza made this apparent with the positive use of English, describing the Union as "great," followed by a request to Congress to grant full inclusion.[134]

This plea and the more traditional political appeals were unsuccessful.[135] Beveridge almost single-handedly halted New Mexico's bid for statehood in 1903 by successfully thwarting a vote before the end of the session.[136] This procedural act was his only option: even after his damaging visit, the loss of President Roosevelt, and the publication of his findings, Republican statehood allies had the required votes. New Mexico would have to wait another decade for statehood.

Language was not the only reason that New Mexico's bid for statehood was defeated in 1903, but Beveridge's opposition on these grounds thrust language to the forefront of the territorial debates. The experience led New Mexicans to embrace politics that ultimately ousted Spanish from its place of supremacy across the territory in the decade that followed. When English acquisition increased in New Mexico in the years following the state's admittance into the Union in 1912, it did so not just because of a federal preference or mandate, but through state and local policy.

PART TWO

A Political Language

1902–1945

CHAPTER 6

A Language of Identity

El Proyecto de Estado para admitir Arizona y Nuevo México á la Unión pasó la Cámara
hoy á las tres de la tarde. Ahora requiere la firma del Presidente para que sea ley. La
*Cámara concurrió por Voto á Viva Voz en las enmendaciones del Senado al proyecto.**

—*El Independiente*, June 23, 1910

In 1911, Aurora Lucero, a teenager from Las Vegas, New Mexico, won an oratory contest in English about the cultural and economic benefits of retaining
the Spanish language in New Mexico's public schools. The teen argued that
the territory was the "meeting ground" for the descendants of the "Spanish
conquistadores" and those of "Anglo Saxon blood," which would likely enable
the development of a "new race" that "will far surpass either." Lucero pushed
for these populations to learn one another's language; she described English
as the language of government and business and Spanish as the "home language of the territory." She spoke of the "richness" of the Spanish language, a
language that is "as cultured and refined as any of the modern languages and
far surpasses them in dignity, beauty and majesty" and offers "an unlimited
field" for Latin American commercial and investment opportunities.[1]

This was not a spontaneous defense of the Spanish language: Lucero's
speech railed against the Enabling Act of 1910, which laid out Congress's terms
for New Mexico's admission to statehood and required that New Mexican
territorial officeholders speak English. Lucero viewed this prerequisite as
"unwarranted interference . . . with his [the *nuevomexicano's*] natural rights."

---

* "The statehood project to admit Arizona and New Mexico to the Union passed the House
today at three in the afternoon. Now it requires the signature of the president to become law.
The House concurred with the Senate amendments in a voice vote."

Lucero saw "the right of language" as a "God-given right" supported by the "federal constitution." She pointed to the restrictive provision as "unprecedented treatment" for New Mexico "at the very moment that she is welcomed into sisterhood," a "gratuitous insult to the intelligence of her people" and "outrageous in its intent." Her speech ended "in the name of" all the possible beneficiaries of Spanish-language instruction and "in the name of its [this great republic's] duty to them, as contracted most solemnly before the world at Guadalupe Hidalgo."[2]

Lucero's speech combined the two major political arguments that *nuevomexicanos* made for retaining an official place for the Spanish language in New Mexico's social and political institutions: its long cultural legacy in New Mexico and its economic importance for building relationships with Latin America. She also acknowledged the more obvious reason that Spanish should be taught in New Mexican schools, namely, to continue its place as the "home language of the territory." She did not diminish the importance of learning English in school, but neither did she accept an English-only policy, which would deny *nuevomexicanos'* "origin[,] . . . race[,] . . . language[,] . . . traditions[,] . . . history [and] . . . ancestry."[3] Her argument to retain Spanish as a subject of instruction tied the new state's cultural legacy to a language—Spanish—rather than a place—Mexico. Reprinted in English- and Spanish-language newspapers throughout New Mexico, Lucero's speech appealed to *nuevomexicanos* who hoped to retain Spanish as cultural affirmation rather than as political necessity.

This chapter explores the changing political meanings of the Spanish language in the U.S. Southwest in the first decades of the twentieth century. Both Arizona and New Mexico finally attained statehood in 1912, the last territories within the continental United States to do so. New Mexico's constitution enshrined some rights to Spanish-language use; the Senate's earlier threats to once again deny statehood to a largely Spanish-speaking territory turned out to have been empty. But just as New Mexico gained statehood, the demography of Spanish speakers in the United States began to shift. The Mexican-born population in the United States grew to 651,596 in 1920.[4] These Mexican immigrants worked in Arizona mines, on Kansas railroads, in Colorado beet fields, in Chicago slaughterhouses, and in fields all across the country but especially in Texas and California. The language rights guaranteed New Mexico's citizens stood in stark contrast to the lack of language protections afforded the new immigrants.

Both in New Mexico and beyond, Mexican immigrants' use of Spanish was changing the political meanings of Spanish in the United States. These meanings and their interpretations were as varied as the rhetoric surrounding Mexican immigrants. Anglo citizens saw them as subservient and compliant workers, as lazy and unintelligent, or as radical and subversive elements. Residents' decision to retain and use the Spanish language played a role in bolstering each of these images. In what follows, I begin by looking at the ways that the presence and actions of ethnic Mexican immigrants transformed the rhetoric surrounding the politics of the Spanish language throughout the Southwest and then turn to what was at stake for *nuevomexicanos*.

The decade leading up to statehood offers an abundance of New Mexican sources that permit a reconstruction of what Spanish-language partisan politics looked like on the ground, in villages, at the county level, and among territorial officials. Following statehood—which in New Mexico included constitutional protections for Spanish—the sources that explicitly discuss language rights or the Treaty of Guadalupe Hidalgo become increasingly sparse. The importance of Spanish-language newspapers declined, as their editors died or ceased circulating them. Within a dozen years after statehood, the state legislature no longer required a translator on the floor. Spanish experienced an incremental decline in official recognition, a process that included some pushback against restrictive policies. The chapter closes with an exploration of how the Great Depression and the arrival of the New Deal finished this process. In New Mexico, Spanish lost its place among the young even at the village level, though hints remained of the legacy that linked politically permissible uses of Spanish to U.S. citizenship.

A CHAMELEON LANGUAGE

During the first few decades of the twentieth century, racial categories in the United States solidified in unexpected and uneven ways. Jim Crow policies, a race war in Texas that led to an unknown number of lynchings of ethnic Mexicans, and Americanization projects that sought to introduce immigrants and long-standing ethnic residents to Anglos' preferred cultural practices encouraged the nation to view those deemed nonwhite as "other" and often as unassimilable.[5] Increasingly, those rejected as "un-American" included those who could not speak English.

In 1906, Congress made the connection between citizenship and the English language explicit while also singling out New Mexico for special language concessions. In Section 8 of the 1906 Act to Establish a Bureau of Immigration and Naturalization, Congress stated, "No alien shall hereafter be naturalized or admitted as a citizen of the United States who can not speak the English language."[6] Congressional concessions for New Mexico four days before the act passed further highlight the variability of policies regarding the Spanish language in New Mexico in a period of increasingly heated views about immigrants who did not speak English. Congress moved to outlaw the use of Spanish in territorial courts, but then its members learned that the judicial system in New Mexico could not function in English. Congress therefore backtracked and continued to permit Spanish-speaking citizens in New Mexico to conduct their legal affairs in a "foreign" language.[7] *Nuevomexicanos* remained outliers even at a moment when a nativist tide throughout the United States was pushing xenophobic rhetoric that depicted Spanish as a language of immigrants.

Recovering discussions of local or state policies related to the Spanish language outside of New Mexico is difficult, because very few existed. For example, Spanish-language concessions or official policies did not arise in California's legislature in the early twentieth century. In California, where few if any *californio* families remained in positions of power, legislators encountered little organized opposition to the absence of policies that aided Spanish speakers. Elite *californios* had largely intermarried, and nonelite citizens—including the children and grandchildren of early Mexican immigrants who lived clustered in communities in Southern California—focused their organizing efforts on making a livelihood and improving the lives of their neighbors in the barrios.[8] Without a solid geographic base (Latinos made up only approximately 3.3 percent of the state's residents in 1900), existing ethnic Mexican families had little political clout to support the newly arrived Spanish-speaking immigrant community.[9] The use of Spanish in the California legislature and schools became largely a moot political point, aside from some use of Spanish in discussions of the founding settlers where it became a symbol in pageants and historical displays that largely ignored the current "Mexican" community's role in this history.[10]

Even while treaty citizen families continued to perceive and describe Spanish as a regional language, Anglos increasingly saw it as foreign and possibly threatening. Spanish-language networks grew far beyond treaty citizen families during this time. The violence of the Mexican Revolution and earlier government policies in agrarian Mexico under the decades-long dictatorship of Porfirio Díaz led unprecedented numbers of Mexicans to migrate to the United States, dwarfing the previously dominant population of treaty citizen families throughout most of the Southwest.[11] The passage of the Newlands Reclamation Act (1902) and other federal water projects transformed the West. Large-scale agriculture became possible in regions formerly too arid to farm and irrigation created new jobs for migrants just as larger numbers of Mexican immigrants were arriving.[12] These agricultural jobs, usually confined to the harvest, provided immigrants with little stability. Growers saw the Mexican laborers as impermanent and therefore not a threat to U.S. social or political institutions, and they typically used just enough Spanish to get their goods to market.[13]

Growers used a broad network to recruit Mexican laborers, whom they saw as the ideal replacement for the limited numbers of Chinese and Japanese immigrant laborers who previously worked in agriculture but had been targeted by federal and state immigration restrictions.[14] Advertisements in Los Angeles's Spanish-language press and *enganchadoras* (agricultural recruiters) in Los Angeles's *colonias* ensured that workers learned about available employment in the Inland and Central Valleys.[15] Cheap transportation, either automobiles or grower-supplied vehicles, relocated workers to these communities. Ever in search of cheap labor, recruiters also traveled to Mexico's northern states to encourage migration.[16] Recruiters, growers, and foremen often used Spanish to interact with the monoglot workers.[17]

From 1910 to 1940, Mexican immigrants faced various competing Anglo views of what their presence in the United States meant. They became a major part of Anglo discussions throughout the Southwest about how to obtain the cheapest, most compliant labor without encouraging the settlement of a permanent population of "undesirables." Mexican immigrants overwhelmingly worked in low-end and low-skill jobs and found few opportunities for advancement.[18] Their inability to understand or use the English language exacerbated their situation. They could not read labor contracts or laws protecting workers.[19] In 1928, José Solís explained to Paul Taylor, an economist who was conducting a three-year study of Mexican employment patterns in the United States, how his reliance on Spanish harmed his ability to navigate in an English-language world. As Solís explained, "Lack of the English language has cost me a lot of money." He required an interpreter to deposit his hard-earned money at the bank. He spoke of how he entered an employment agency with an interpreter but was left with no options when his interpreter left before his turn. He also said he was "roughly handled" by the police because he was unable to answer questions posed in English.[20]

Retaining Spanish had its benefits, though, particularly in building tight communities far from home. With few connections to the broader English-speaking population, Mexican immigrants had a heightened sense of being Mexican. In a 1930 study of Mexicans living in the United States, the Mexican anthropologist and sociologist Manuel Gamio wrote that Mexican villagers from different parts of their home country found a way to come together and "forjar patría" (forge a homeland).[21] Racially restrictive housing covenants and mistreatment of Mexicans by Anglo locals encouraged Mexican immigrants to create separate communities to survive in a foreign and unfriendly environment, which led to strong and vibrant Mexican immigrant communities across the Southwest. Groups of Mexican immigrants formed mutual aid organizations with patriotically inspired Spanish-language names like Santa Barbara's Club Mexicano Independencia (Mexican Independence Club) and La Unión Patriótica Benéfica Mexicana Independiente (Independent Mexican Benevolent Patriotic Union).[22] As twenty-two-year-old Miguel Chávez, originally from Mocorito, Sinaloa, told Gamio, he planned someday to return to Mexico. Even though he attended school in the United States, "he weeps when he hears the Mexican National Hymn" and "knows more Mexican history than American because the latter doesn't interest him." He spoke Spanish and formed his view of Mexico from Spanish-language newspapers in Los Angeles and at Zaragoza, the patriotic society he joined.[23] Mexican immigrants heeded the calls of Mexican officials to create a "México de afuera" (Mexico outside the nation) that kept them in a world where they identified and communicated with one another in Spanish.[24]

The very nature of migrant labor meant that few Mexican immigrant workers had permanent or stable occupations. The reality of this situation helped solidify in many Anglo minds a view of Spanish speakers as noncitizens, transient, foreign, and unassimilable. This view of Mexican immigrants in the West folded into a national xenophobia that made itself known in the halls of Congress, in national and regional newspapers, and in Anglos' daily interactions with immigrants.[25] In 1924, Congress passed the Naturalization and Immigration Act creating a national origins quota. While the original law did not apply to persons arriving from the Americas, that same year the U.S. Border Patrol was established, beginning federal regulation of the U.S.-

Mexico border.[26] Newspapers, lobbyists, and sociologists across the Southwest collectively discussed the "Mexican problem."[27] While growers advocated for Mexicans as compliant and trustworthy workers uniquely suited to agricultural work, opponents of Mexican immigration had other opinions.[28] Among the latter was the opinion that Mexican workers lacked "thrift, ambition, intelligence, and strong moral fiber." That they did not remain in any place long enough to learn English and become a part of the community was likely another strike against them, leading to the view that they were "unprogressive."[29]

These stereotypes of subservience and indolence stood in sharp contrast to the organizational prowess of many Mexican immigrants. Mexicans brought with them to the United States labor experience and radical politics that threatened to upset the dynamics of power in California.[30] They used labor activism to attempt to draw the support of politically influential union leaders. For example, as early as 1903, in Oxnard, California, Japanese and Mexican immigrants formed a union with slogans in Spanish and Japanese. Farm laborers created a successful union movement that led the American Federation of Labor (AFL) to consider permitting them to join.[31] The AFL eventually declined to admit this union, opposing the inclusion of Japanese (but not the Mexican) members. Just half a dozen years later, writing in *Regeneración*, Praxedis Guerrero encouraged Spanish-speaking immigrants and workers to "dedican á la lucha contra los tiranos y los explotadores" (dedicate themselves to the fight against tyranny and exploiters).[32]

At times, opposition to Mexican immigrants reached a breaking point, leading to deportations. In many mining communities, such as Bisbee in Cochise County, Arizona, local authorities began to paint Spanish as a foreign language whose speakers were expendable. As was common practice throughout the Southwest, Cochise County mines paid immigrant workers significantly less than Anglo U.S. citizen workers. As Anglo union organizers became more radical, they began to reach out to and organize the Spanish-speaking population (including workers from Mexico, Spain, New Mexico, and Arizona) into a more formal union along with other immigrant groups.[33] Anglo labor organizers used the Spanish language, including a regular feature in the *Arizona Labor Journal*, to organize Spanish-speaking miners.[34] In 1917, the Industrial Workers of the World (IWW)—a union that did not discriminate against workers based on skills, sex, or race—held a general strike in the copper mines of Bisbee. Participation in the strike was estimated at as high as 90 percent of mine workers.[35] The authorities did not tolerate the strike for long. On July 12, over two thousand county deputies entered Bisbee and rounded up over a thousand workers, including some U.S. citizens and immigrants from thirty-four countries, of whom half "were either Mexican or Eastern European." After collecting them in the town's baseball field, the authorities forced the striking miners into boxcars and shipped them to a deportee camp in New Mexico.[36] The deportations separated at least 174 Mexican families.[37]

This brazen antiunion and anti-immigrant police action sent a message to union organizers that attempts to upend the wage differential would not be tolerated. Occurring at the height of hysteria over World War I and the Mexican Revolution, the Bisbee Deportation discouraged Anglo labor organizers from recruiting Spanish-speaking workers in Arizona. The *Arizona Labor Journal* stopped publishing its Spanish-language column two years later. Radicalized or, at the very least, union-supporting immigrants diverged from employers' expectations of ethnic Mexican workers as docile, compliant, and willing to settle for the dual-wage system. Worker activism changed employers' views, so that they now saw Mexican immigrants as potential leftist organizers united with other immigrants by their working-class identity.[38] Nor was this view confined to Arizona. In 1928, in San José, California, Fred Marvin agitated a crowd when he stated that Mexicans were agents of the IWW and were in the community "to transmit the socialistic theories," not to work.[39] In such an alarmist environment, some Anglo community members read the presence of workers speaking a language they could not understand as proof of their subversive intentions and as evidence that their presence should be discouraged.

An increase in union organizing occurred after passage of the National Industrial Recovery Act in 1933. Unions like the IWW worked to organize unskilled laborers across the United States in various immigrant languages, including Spanish.[40] Other unions followed suit, especially during the 1930s, when dozens of major agricultural strikes rocked California, including thirty-seven during 1933 alone.[41] For example, the International Ladies' Garment Workers Union (ILGWU) used Spanish in meeting announcements and produced *El Organizador,* a Spanish-language newsletter, for the ILGWU chapters in Los Angeles.[42] The Needle Trades Workers Industrial Union, which competed with the ILGWU, posted Spanish- and English-language flyers that announced "A Todas Las Costureras NO SE DEJEN VENDER!"

(To All Dressmakers! SMASH THE SELLOUT!) during the 1933 Dressmakers' strike and also published a Spanish-language newsletter, *La Costurera de Los Angeles*.[43] Spanish-speaking workers felt comfortable using Spanish in labor negotiations, as Dolores Nuno's letter to her employer, Lou Kornhandler, Inc., demonstrates. After the strike, she wrote asking for work: "Sostengo á cinco de familia [y] . . . tengo que pedir ayuda del condado porque no tengo nada de dinero" (I support a family of five [and] . . . I have to ask for help from the county because I do not have any money).[44] By the late 1930s, the CIO-affiliated United Cannery, Agricultural, Packing, and Allied Workers of America (UCAPAWA) also showed great interest in organizing Spanish speakers.[45] Although Mexican immigrant workers risked their jobs and their place in the United States if they joined strikes, tens of thousands nevertheless did in the 1930s.[46]

Amid the strikes, workers and politicians looking for scapegoats for the growing unemployment crisis of the Great Depression pushed anti-Mexican sentiment to a fever pitch—not just in the Southwest, but nationally. Late in 1930, President Herbert Hoover singled out Mexicans for taking jobs from citizens and appointed William N. Doak secretary of labor to deal with the problem. Doak set his sights on deporting a quarter of the 400,000 undocumented foreigners in the United States. Sweeps by the Immigration and Naturalization Service (INS) began, largely in urban areas, in 1931.[47] A Los Angeles Spanish-language daily, *La Opinión*, increased immigrants' fear and uncertainty by publicizing raids in advance and sharing accounts of agents going door to door without warrants and arresting individuals. Residents of different *colonias* had little opportunity to confirm or dispel the rampant rumors.[48]

The federal strategy of rounding up and deporting Mexican immigrants proved inefficient: the INS deported fewer than 20,000 undocumented Mexicans. Local governments, however, did a much better job.[49] The campaign in Los Angeles was particularly effective. Local officials excluded Mexicans from lists for county aid, offered to pay for their return to Mexico, and encouraged businesses to hire "Americans." Businesses complied by replacing Mexican workers, who often could not find another way to support their families.[50] Organizations paid to send over 12,500 people from Los Angeles to the border, and one newspaper claimed a total of 75,000 Mexicans left the city.[51] Technically, these were "voluntary" repatriations, but under the circumstances, they must be considered coercive. Between 1930 and 1934, Mexico documented the entry of 350,000 returning citizens, an estimated 40 percent of whom were children (many likely born in the United States and therefore U.S. citizens). The devastating result of the repatriation campaign is visible in the federal census. For the first time in eighty years, the 1940 U.S. census documented a decrease in the number of Mexican-born individuals in the United States (from 641,462 in 1930 to 454,417).[52]

With the rising rhetoric surrounding the "Mexican problem," some treaty citizen families sought to distance themselves from Mexican immigrants. Spanish-speaking descendants of treaty citizens joined the growing migrant agricultural workforce, but they resisted calls to band together on the basis of language. In places like Colorado, where treaty citizen families and Mexican immigrants sometimes worked together, the split was noticeable to community members.[53] Taylor recorded that T. Aragon, a Fort Collins store clerk, told his research team that "S[panish] A[mericans]" preferred that he address them in English. Once it was established that they could speak English, then "one may speak Spanish to them and they will appreciate it."[54] Fred Holmes, a labor superintendent in Colorado, elaborated on the differences in the community by saying that "Colorado and New Mexico Mexicans" were at times preferred to those from "Old Mexico."[55] A teacher, "Gutiérrez," in the Hudson community, stated that Mexican immigrants "gave S[panish] A[mericans] a bad reputation." He even claimed that Mexican immigrants, had they been offered the option, would prefer a separate school (presumably conducted in Spanish) from both the "S[panish] A[mericans]" and the "Americans," whereas Spanish Americans wanted to attend with Anglos.[56] The Spanish heard in work camps, on ranches, or in cities across the Southwest was spoken using different vocabularies and accents by a broad and varied population that experienced distinct social realities and held different views about politics, class, and national identity.

At the same time that immigrant and working-class Spanish speakers used Spanish as a language of activism, treaty citizen families were abandoning their defense of Spanish-language concessions in formal political institutions. The bilingual elite did not need access to Spanish to conduct their affairs, and increasingly neither did their base. Outside of New Mexico, the most powerful advocates for Spanish-language concessions were dying out. In Colorado, for example, language concessions for jurors and ballots persisted as long as state senator Casimiro Barela remained in office, but his death in 1920 after forty years of service left an unbridgeable gap in ethnic Mexican political power in the state. Attacks against the Spanish language began in earnest just one year after Barela's death. *El Anunciador* learned of two English-only bills proposed by the legislature. The first was a law that would require all jurors to speak English. The newspaper's editor saw the English-only legislation as being "en violación de el tratado de Guadalupe Hidalgo" (in violation of the Treaty of Guadalupe Hidalgo). He warned that if the bill passed, "debía de ser resentida por toda nuestra gente" (it will be resented by all of our people), who numbered in the thousands in the state, as it would be "un guantón bien dado a nuestra populación de viejos pobladores" (a hard hit for this old settler population). The second bill proposed by Representative Minnie C. T. Love sought to allow "ninguna publicación de periódico, magazine, folleto o circular en Colorado" (no newspaper, magazine, brochure, or circular to be published in Colorado) in any language other than English. *El Anunciador* encouraged Spanish speakers to work against the Republican Party on these two proposed bills, saying, "No es el partido de nosotros" (It is not our party).[57] In 1925, English-language requirements for jury members became law in Colorado.[58] *El Anunciador*'s focus on protecting language concessions by means of partisan politics stands in stark contrast to the labor and grassroots immigrant activism happening in the fields and the mines.

As a rights-based approach to language declined in the U.S. Southwest, ethnic Mexican citizens of long standing increasingly distanced themselves from Mexican immigrants and Spanish. This was a defensive move intended to protect their waning political power and way of life. Mexican immigrants often distanced themselves from ethnic Mexican citizens, too, because of cultural differences. Gamio reported that Mexicans judged Spanish-speaking Americans' "imperfect Spanish" and different cultural behaviors. Concha Urzaiz explained to Gamio that Spanish was not taught in the public schools, with the result that students "get to using very insulting or incorrect words without knowing it" and that the "Mexican woman is generally overcritical and offends the Texan women by making fun of their language."[59] These Mexican immigrants hoped to retain their Mexican culture—including language—and saw Spanish-speaking citizens as too American.[60] Elías Sepulveda, a twenty-three-year-old native of Nogales, Arizona, said he knew how to read and write in Spanish because his parents had taught him at home, but, he continued, "[I am] ashamed when I meet a well educated Mexican . . . for I speak Spanish very brokenly."[61] Sepulveda's experience, however, differed from that of other native-born individuals from New Mexico and Arizona whom Gamio praised for speaking Spanish like *mexicanos*.[62]

Language use among ethnic Mexicans was completely dependent on their opportunities to learn either English or Spanish, just as it was in the nineteenth century. The ability of a community of Mexican immigrants or long-standing Spanish-speaking citizens to use Spanish depended on local conditions. For example, one Mexican immigrant saw learning English as a prerequisite for coming to the United States. J. M. Guajardo, who lived at the time in Gary, Indiana, told Taylor in 1929, "I would not let the Mexicans come to the United States until they knew English. The American people dislike the people who come here . . . but stick to Mexican societies, criticize Americans, and don't know English." He went on to say that some of those who do learn English "deny their nationality. They don't help out or associate with other Mexicans."[63] Guajardo likely would have had a different perspective if he had migrated to New Mexico instead of Indiana.

In the midst of all these competing attitudes toward Spanish speakers across the Southwest, and in other parts of the nation, New Mexico's residents enjoyed a more positive political climate surrounding the use of the Spanish language. New Mexico was not insulated from the broader national mood that favored Anglo rhetoric, but its long-standing demographic majority of *nuevomexicanos* meant that the state's language politics diverged from the rest of the nation. But as new Mexican immigrants entered the United States in the twentieth century, New Mexico became an exception, rather than the model, for the rest of the Southwest.

A PARTISAN REDOUBT IN NEW MEXICO

Spanish-language rights persisted longer in New Mexico than anywhere else in the Southwest. Beyond demography, more *nuevomexicanos* were involved in public life in New Mexico than in any of the other former Mexican territories. But their involvement in public life cannot be separated from a second factor that led to their continued influence: the political power *nuevomexicanos* exerted in the Republican Party.

The Republican Party made significant inroads into the Spanish-speaking vote over the second half of the nineteenth century; it required their continued allegiance as a bulwark against the increasing numbers of Texas and Midwest Democrats who came to the state.[64] At statehood, *nuevomexicanos* continued to outnumber Anglos in the local Republican Party.[65] The Republican Party courted *nuevomexicano* votes with favors and patronage positions. By this time, literate party members in even the most remote regions of the state demonstrated a solid understanding of the general political calendar; they wrote to their leaders when their letters would carry the most political weight.

Letters written to Secundino Romero, a Republican Party official, provide a glimpse of Spanish as an important political language in San Miguel County, one of six northern counties where *nuevomexicanos* made up over 75 percent of voters in 1915. As chairman of the county's Republican Central Committee from 1896 to 1911, Romero doled out patronage appointments.[66] The mostly rural population of 23,000 looked to its largest town, Las Vegas (pop. 3,755), as the county's political headquarters.[67] Of fifty-three county precincts, just six comprised populations greater than 1,000. The smallest precinct—Los Torres—had just 105 residents.[68] With so many small precincts vying for political handouts, county party leaders held significant power.

While insignificant in the grand scheme of the state's political structure or economy, literate villagers were the cogs that turned the wheel of the larger political machine. They appealed to Romero to receive the rewards for their loyalty. Spanish-speaking party members made up a large percentage of the political representatives at county conventions. A small group of individuals held most of the territory's elected political positions.[69] Village delegates like Antonio Archuleta y Flores, from the small village of Rowe, recognized the importance of attending party functions; he missed a party meeting with much regret: "Pues segun yo estoy informado anoche dicen que estavan teniendo una Junto; para nombrar delegados. . . . Y con mucho gusto hubiera yo ido" (Well, I was informed last night that there was a meeting to name delegates. . . . And I would have gone with great pleasure).[70] One *nuevomexicano* correspondent proclaimed his party loyalty in his signature: "Puro Republicano" (Republican through and through).[71] A young man, Balentín Sena, wrote of his desire to participate as soon as possible: "Yo deseaba llegar a la edad de 21 años. . . . [H]e tenido deseos de ayudar con mi opinion a fomenter con mi humilde voto los prinsipios del grande y glorioso partido Republicano" (I wanted to reach the age of twenty-one . . . . I wished to use my voice to help foster, through my humble vote, the principles of the grand and glorious Republican Party). Sena could recite the party's slogan and knew it was something he must join but as a newcomer had yet to grasp the details of the larger party apparatus (he addressed his letter generically).[72]

New Mexico's political structure functioned as a "patronage machine," a fact that quickly becomes apparent in Romero's correspondence.[73] Most of the letters he received clustered around two central themes: requests for patronage positions and discussions about elections. The writers pledged support for the current Republican candidates and/or requested that they, their friends, or their family members be placed in vacant or anticipated positions.[74] A large number of letters sent from the villages were written in Spanish. Romero replied in kind and initiated correspondence with delegates in Spanish as well.[75]

No position was too small or seemingly undesirable for a patronage request.[76] For example, a number of villagers wrote to request membership on a petit jury, which required absence from work and often a long trip to where the justices held court.[77] With the cash economy increasingly affecting village life in the form of country stores and taxes on their land, the per diem jury duty payment could help the recipient make ends meet.[78] Other popular requests included serving as interpreters for the district court or justice of the peace.[79] Beyond court-related positions, patronage requests included appointments as precinct delegates, county delegates, and representatives for territorial and then state conventions and elections. An additional position that received a lot of interest—unique to New Mexico by the twentieth century— was legislative interpreter.[80]

Village party leaders eagerly wrote to Romero about local precinct nominations and Republican Party votes. At times, they expressed concerns that precinct officeholders were undermining the Republican cause by not adequately performing their jobs.[81] They also warned Romero of the inroads that Democrats were making in county politics.[82] Some loyal party members claimed victory as they shared news about the successful political conversion of an individual family (sometimes seeking a patronage position or even money in return).[83] The letters demonstrate a broad and geographically far-reaching network of party connections and knowledge about who served in leadership roles and who could distribute or influence the vast—though competitive and never sufficient—number of patronage positions available.

The letters suggest a vibrant and active political party life at the village level. Correspondents requested financial assistance to host local party-sponsored festivities. In addition to requesting funds for a party in Las Colonias, Abenicio Rodríguez asked county Republican officials to provide a gallon of a beverage to reassert the party's interest in the village.[84] Another letter requested that Romero support a Republican-themed village dance. Campaign festivities, in turn, produced more patronage positions. Romero

received requests for patronage posts as musicians, a prestigious position lasting the entirety of the campaign.[85] The political party system was an accepted
part of the everyday lives of villagers and infiltrated even their leisure and
celebratory activities.

Village party members understood that their actions counted in the party's
eyes. José Chávez from Lemitar in Soccoro County apologized for not comply-
ing with H. O. Bursum's requests to assist with the 1904 election. Chávez's
letter described his poverty and large family, explaining that he had to become
a migrant worker—an increasing reality for villagers in the northern counties—leaving him unable to campaign locally. "Si estoi en mi caza para la
Elecion, puede que los allude, si no puedo con mi trabajo, con mi Voto puede
que sí" (If I am in my house for the election, I can help the party, if I cannot
due to my work, then with my vote I will), he wrote.[86] Others threatened to
defect if the party refused their request. For example, Cecilio Valverde asked
that his friend Nasario Martínez receive a juror position, or he and all his sons
would leave the party. Martínez complained to Valverde "que él asido un
republicano toda la bida y que jamas a resebido ningun benefisio de su partido"
(that he had been a Republican his whole life and had never received any
benefit from his party).[87]

The number of Spanish-language letters in the Republican Party files never
approached the number of those in English. Many *nuevomexicanos* could write
in English; it is possible that they chose to write to the disproportionately
Anglo party leadership in the language they were more likely to understand.
Spanish-language letters increased during elections, when writers pledged
their support, and immediately afterward, to capitalize on new patronage
appointments.[88] The letter writers were not necessarily members of the true
territorial elite or *ricos* (rich), but they had the skills by virtue of their literacy
or political contacts to obtain patronage positions and leave a mark in the
historical record. At statehood, Spanish-language letters to party officials
followed the same pattern they had since the late nineteenth century and
would continue, albeit in smaller numbers, through the 1930s.

Nuevomexicanos' crucial votes meant that they retained the ear of party
officials. The Republican Party's geographic Spanish-language strongholds are
detailed in a letter from Mariano Larragoite, a Spanish-speaking political ora-
tor, on the most strategic uses of his talents. He explained to Bursum, chairman
of the party's territorial central committee, that Taos and Rio Arriba Counties
did not need his services because local leaders controlled the situation. He

FIGURE 7. Spanish-language interpreter Luis Armijo working on stage with L. Bradford Prince in Las Vegas, New Mexico, 1910. Courtesy Palace of the Governors Photo Archives (NMHM/DCA), 158257.

suggested that the party send him north to Mora, Union, and Colfax Counties but emphasized that the southern counties needed him most.[89] W. W. H. Llewellyn, a lawyer, provided Bursum with a list of individuals in Doña Ana and Otero Counties who could read Spanish, suggesting that he ask them to inform their neighbors about news of the party and the election.[90]

Republican Party officials understood that their Spanish-speaking supporters had to be cultivated in Spanish. Their efforts to reach these voters ensured that Spanish-speaking voters retained access to New Mexico's elections. The party paid for speeches in both English and Spanish.[91] Albuquerque's Ed Lavelle, for example, planned to travel with a "horse and buggy" and a "Mr. Sandovol" to campaign in both English and Spanish.[92] (See figure 7.) Spanish-language campaigning was pragmatic. During the 1904 campaign, San Miguel County's E. H. Biernbaum requested 4,500 "county tickets," 3,500 of them in Spanish.[93] And Bursum ensured that the party had a presence in rural villages by distributing buttons to local voters featuring the territorial candidate, the president, and the vice president.[94]

The Republican Party supplemented its Spanish-language campaign efforts with the party-subsidized Spanish-language weekly, *El Nuevo Mexicano*.

Shipping the paper proved a better use of funds than attempting to get speakers to each of the small villages.[95] During the 1906 campaign, the party paid to distribute five thousand copies to select individuals for the three months surrounding election season.[96] The $3,000 spent on circulars was a good investment given voters' dispersed residences.[97] Party leaders saw reaching out to Spanish-speaking readers as "the best investment that can be made."[98] Only 20 percent of voters lived in cities reached by speakers or local papers. Four-fifths of Republican voters lived "in the country districts and small settlements" that could only be served by print media. Sending newspapers to individuals, which included "names of voters getting mail at post offices," kept rural residents informed about the candidates and, by extension, elections in general.[99] In exchange for their financial support, the party ordered the editors to run weekly editorials on the preferred candidate and positive editorials on statehood. The Democrats used similar tactics to reach Spanish-speaking *nuevomexicanos*, distributing six thousand copies of the weekly *La Voz del Pueblo* in favor of Octaviano Larrazolo, the Democratic candidate for territorial congressional delegate.[100]

The correspondence and actions of New Mexico's Republican Party clearly demonstrate that Spanish remained an accepted part of partisan politics in the decade preceding statehood. The patronage system provided a channel for Spanish-speaking villagers to gain status and resources in exchange for their electoral support. While towns and the highest echelon of both parties operated in English, the system would have collapsed without the use of some Spanish.

STATE PROTECTIONS OF SPANISH

The New Mexican Republican Party's pragmatic embrace of Spanish survived into statehood, but the debates surrounding the role of language at the moment of transition revealed developing fissures. The 1910 Enabling Act permitted the creation of the states of Arizona and New Mexico and required all elected state officials to speak English. It also limited the degree to which the Spanish language could be used in the schools (it could not serve as the language of instruction). The House stipulated that the "ability to read, write, speak, and understand the English language sufficiently well to conduct the duties of the office without the aid of an interpreter shall be a necessary qualification for all state officers." The Senate expanded the requirement to include the state legislature, theoretically blocking monolingual *nuevomexicanos* from political positions in the new state.[101] Nevertheless, New Mexico's first state constitution maintained Spanish-language concessions and a mode of operation that would continue to privilege the use of Spanish. With the passage of time, the situation in New Mexico proved increasingly divergent from that of its neighbors.

The 1911 state constitutional convention met in Santa Fe with delegates from all over the territory. While underrepresented compared to their population, the *nuevomexicano* delegates made up nearly half of the dominant Republican Party delegates (32 of 71) and a significant minority among the 100 elected delegates. Together with Anglo allies, these Spanish-speaking delegates safeguarded the place of Spanish in the state's constitution.[102] The constitutional protections ensured that New Mexicans could vote and serve on juries regardless of whether they spoke, read, or wrote English or Spanish.[103] The constitutional provisions had the effect of protecting Spanish-language use during a time when national opinion was turning against "foreign" languages. The constitution notably also protected the rights of English speakers in parts of the state that operated almost exclusively in Spanish but omitted mention of other language speakers. The delegates authorized Spanish-language translations at the convention, in the constitution, and in state governance. They required all convention reports, the constitutional ballot, the constitution itself, and the convention proceedings to be published in both English and Spanish.[104]

New Mexicans needed look no further than their western neighbors in Arizona to understand the threat posed by the absence of language protections. Much as California had done in 1896, in 1910, Arizona passed a law requiring that voters be able to write in English. "Hundreds of taxpayers will be disfranchised by the proposed law, citizens of the Spanish, German, Scandinavian, and other national descent, for no sufficient reason," wrote Governor Joseph H. Kibbey in his second veto of the law and before leaving office in 1910.[105] The Arizona legislature passed the bill over the second veto.[106] This was too much, even for Congress. The Senate's Committee on Territories, dominated by Republicans, deemed it discriminatory (not coincidentally, the disenfranchised largely voted Republican). The Senate refused Arizona's bid for statehood until its legislature repealed the law. Its repeal guaranteed the voting rights of Arizona's ethnic Mexicans who continued to speak only Spanish—a sizable minority, estimated at 10 percent of the population, and largely concentrated in the border counties.[107] *Nuevomexicanos* firmly criticized the law as "el desfranquisio de los hispano americanos en ese desgraciado país lleno de entrañas, nopales, tunas y tunantes, que ya se aprovecharon de los nativos" (the disfranchisement of Spanish Americans in that unfortunate country full of viscera, cactus, prickly pears, and rascals, who already took advantage of the natives).[108]

While New Mexico's constitution protected Spanish speakers' access to the political process, it also included provisions that prioritized an English-speaking future. The constitution made English the official language of the legislature and schools by not explicitly including Spanish or becoming officially bilingual. It required printed versions of all state laws to appear in Spanish for twenty years after statehood—not indefinitely.[109] The constitution promised to train bilingual teachers to work with monolingual Spanish-speaking students but did so largely as a pedagogical aid to teaching monolingual Spanish-speaking children English, not to maintain Spanish.[110] Even with these restrictions, however, Spanish-language protections remained through the absence of English-only restrictions in other areas of civic life. The constitution requires a super majority, "an election at which at least three-quarters of the electors voting in the whole state and at least two-thirds of those voting in each county" must agree in order to overturn any of the language provisions.[111] By imposing almost insurmountable requirements, the delegates guaranteed that its long-standing Spanish-speaking citizens would retain a minority vote.

Few treaty citizens lived to see statehood, but the constitution ensured their legacy. "The rights, privileges and immunities, civil, political and religious, guaranteed to the people of New Mexico by the treaty of Guadalupe Hidalgo shall be preserved inviolate," promised the constitution.[112] This specific mention of treaty rights is unique. Arizona's constitution (drafted concurrently) includes no mention of Spanish and not a single Spanish-surnamed delegate.[113] Once Arizona was a state and free from the oversight of Congress, the Arizona legislature further alienated ethnic Mexicans when, in 1912, it again passed an English literacy requirement that disenfranchised all monolingual Spanish speakers. The requirement crippled the voting system in the counties of Pima (where Tucson is located) and Cochise, where so few eligible voters remained that many precincts could not hold a primary.[114] A joint resolution from the New Mexico legislature condemned its neighbor's action, deeming it "an outrage upon the loyal public spirited and intelligent

Spanish-American population of the State," as well as a "contravention of the sacred rights guaranteed by treaty to the native people of Arizona."[115]

The New Mexico constitution's concessions to Spanish speakers are all the more remarkable given the state's conservatism.[116] Advocates of progressive measures including direct democracy were gaining ground across the country in the 1910s. Supporters of progressive policies in New Mexico were led by delegate Harvey Ferguson, whose efforts to implement direct legislation through propositions failed, as did attempts to provide for referendums and recall.[117] New Mexico did not grant women suffrage, though many other western states, including Colorado (1893), California (1911), and Arizona (1912), were at the forefront of this fight.[118] Nor did New Mexico's constitution safeguard African American children from segregated schools, even as it banned de jure segregation of *nuevomexicano* children.[119] In this way, the constitution mirrored larger trends concerning race and citizenship rights in the United States during the 1910s, making its language protections striking.

The constitution gave political protections to Spanish speakers but left the legislature to decide the particulars of bilingual governance. Early laws passed by the legislature suggested continued support for Spanish-speaking office-holders and constituents. For example, in its first legislative session, the state of New Mexico went against Congress's wishes and amended the constitution so that individuals did not have to understand, speak, or write English to hold office.[120] The many explicit mentions of Spanish in New Mexico's Session Laws show that the new state was not truly bilingual, for if it truly was, specifications for bilingual printing of this or that document would be redundant. State law routinely invoked specific protections for Spanish speakers, but each came about through the active mobilization of constituents and legislators, and each was negotiated and impermanent.

Consider, for instance, the issue of translation. During the 1910s, the legislature expanded the role of legislative translators and interpreters by requiring sessions to employ two of each.[121] The legislature also clarified the promise of bilingual publication by specifying which reports and county notices would be printed in Spanish. The translated documents centered on two issues of utmost concern to treaty citizen families—land and elections. The legislature required that land grant commissions, reclamation and water-related boards, and election boards publish their materials in Spanish.[122] The victories for translations of the state laws and business came about through the continued support and strength of *nuevomexicano* legislators and voters.

The new state legislature's support for the Spanish language had limits. New Mexico's system of translation and printing of notices in 1919 required communities where 75 percent of the population spoke a specific language to publish notices in that language. Those regions where 25 to 75 percent of the population spoke one language would be required to publish notices in both English and Spanish.[123] The law did not privilege either Spanish or English, allowing communities to publish only in Spanish if it made fiscal and linguistic sense to do so. The state never adopted the same sort of English-only or English-as-supreme-language restrictions as did California and Arizona, but neither did it do much to cement the place of official Spanish-language protections statewide.

The use of Spanish remained a potentially potent political symbol for at least a few years after statehood, as an incident at the Democratic Party County Convention in September 1918 makes clear. E. Barber, a new settler originally from Mississippi, took the stage and began speaking. The interpreter on stage listened and at the seventh word began to interpret. Barber cut him off. This dance continued three times, with Barber beginning and then stopping the interpreter until Barber finally burst out, "I don't want to talk to anybody but Americans." The *Santa Fe New Mexican* describes the gasp that escaped the crowd and explains that not even "a group of Bolsheviki [that] had thrown a bomb" could have caused more commotion. Barber apologized for his error, but the newspaper suggests the negative political ramifications coming to Barber due to his outburst. Next up was Antonio Lucero, a newspaperman. The convention greeted him with cheers and cries to speak in Spanish (an estimated 40 percent of the crowd was *nuevomexicano*). Lucero declined, but promised to speak in Spanish later. Instead, he began with a scathing critique of Barber's statements, describing "Spanish-American" New Mexicans as "100 percent loyal Americans" who fought and died on the battlefields of Europe at a higher rate than Anglos. The crowd "went wild."[124]

Lucero used English to criticize Barber. He made a calculated choice to ensure that Anglos fully understood the patriotism of his people. In the process, however, he relegated Spanish to a secondary language. It was a language he chose to speak at a later time. Lucero used English to remind individuals of "Spanish American" history and *nuevomexicanos'* continued legacy in the state rather than asserting the continued relevance of Spanish as a major language of political communication. By focusing on military service, Lucero criticized Barber's refusal to see *nuevomexicanos* as "American" more than his attitude toward the interpreter's use of Spanish. Elite, bilingual *nuevomexicanos* like Lucero increasingly chose when to use Spanish in political settings.[125] The discrepancies in language skill between those on governing bodies at the state level and their monolingual constituents continued to grow, yet Spanish concessions and patronage positions persisted as a major link to retain votes.

Nuevomexicanos constituted the majority in the New Mexico Assembly through the 1920s.[126] The fits and starts of bilingual policies are starkly apparent in the level of detail required to safeguard Spanish speakers in the voting booths. While the session laws were translated by law until 1931 (a concession renewed for ten years) and law translators received their own offices in 1921, local notices about laws of importance to *nuevomexicanos* required a clause explicitly stating that there be a Spanish-language version. The legislature depended on the Spanish-language press to get the notices out. These newspapers declined during the 1920s, which opened the possibility that Spanish-language voters would not receive Spanish-language notices.[127]

Because specific translation initiatives required individual bills in the legislature, their stipulations provide clues as to what kinds of rights were eroding for Spanish speakers. The 1927 election law, for instance, included a long list of required bilingual notices or printings, suggesting that local English-only practices had likely hindered *nuevomexicanos*' access to the polls. For example, the printed oath for the board of registration, poll books, ballots, instructions to voters, and proposed constitutional amendments, along with resolutions proposing constitutional amendments were all to be printed with a Spanish-language version accompanying the English one.[128] Additional language securities promised defendants the right to a court-subsidized interpreter and required the secretary of state—a position almost exclusively held by *nuevomexicanas*—to print and distribute election laws in both languages.[129] The law concerning the secretary of state's translation duties further specified that the materials be distributed to all county clerks for use in their election office, suggesting that, prior to this, some communities may not have received these materials. Maintaining access to constitutionally supported language rights in New Mexico was a constant fight that required the attention of *nuevomexicano* legislators and their supporters.

Election provisions persisted into the 1930s. The 1938 state election law explicitly promised Spanish announcements and ballots for party primaries. (See figure 8.) Recognizing the dwindling number of Spanish-language newspapers by 1938, the law required county officials to post notifications of primary

Sample Direct Primary Election Ballot

DEMOCRATIC   **SEPTEMBER 14, 1940**

SANTA FE COUNTY

To vote for a person make a cross [X] in the square at the right of the name of each person for whom you desire to vote.

Boleta de Muestra, Eleccion Primaria Directa

DEMOCRATA   **SEPTIEMBRE 14, 1940**

CONDADO DE SANTA FE

Para votar por una persona, haga una cruz [X] en el cuadro a la derecha del nombre de cada persona por quien Ud. desea votar.

FOR UNITED STATES SENATOR PARA SENADOR DE LOS ESTADOS UNIDOS	(Vote for One) (Vote por Uno)
DENNIS CHAVEZ	☒
JOHN J. DEMPSEY	☐
FOR REPRESENTATIVE IN CONGRESS PARA REPRESENTANTE AL CONGRESO	(Vote for One) (Vote por Uno)
LAKE J. FRAZIER	☐
FLOYD T. KENNEDY	☐
CLINTON P. ANDERSON	☐
SOLOMON L. BURTON, M.D.	☐
ROBERT HOATH LaFOLLETTE	☐
FRED E. WILSON	☐
G. L. GIBBONS	☐
FRANK H. PATTON	☐
LOUISE H. COE	☐
FOR PRESIDENTIAL ELECTORS PARA ELECTORES PRESIDENCIALES	(Vote for Three) (Vote por Tres)
HENRY H. KRAMER	☒
PROCOPIO TORRES	☐
MRS. HORACE B. OWENS	☒
FOR GOVERNOR PARA GOBERNADOR	(Vote for One) (Vote por Uno)

FIGURE 8. In 1940 Santa Fe County's Democratic sample ballots were bilingual. Sample Ballot, 1940, box 71, folder 22, Dennis Chávez Papers, MSS 394BC, Center for Southwest Research, University Libraries, University of New Mexico.

elections in prominent county locations. At the same time, the law supported these publications only "as shall be necessary," exempting certain counties.[130] State law also required registration officers to assist voters who could read neither English nor Spanish. The law stipulated that the occupation and mailing address of each candidate accompany election materials in both languages.[131] While language rights remained secure at the voting booths, state law increasingly provided loopholes for informing residents about new laws by explicitly requiring Spanish on fewer and fewer notices—particularly school bonds, delinquent taxes (when Spanish-surnamed individuals appeared on the list), notifications for recording sheep brands, and instructions related to conservancy.[132] Each of these Spanish-language provisions appeared in a different set of state laws during the 1930s, though none received explicit instructions by the 1940s.

The rapidly diminishing Spanish-language concessions did not correspond to loss of *nuevomexicano* votes or the number of mentions of Spanish election laws. *Nuevomexicano* strongholds in the northern counties voted at higher rates than Anglo-majority counties in 1948. In that election, *nuevomexicano* voter turnout resulted in a disproportionately larger impact on the election, which demonstrated their continued commitment to electoral politics and suggests county language policies may look significantly different from state policies.[133]

By 1940, a new stipulation exempted counties with less than 30 percent of their newspaper "reading matter" published in Spanish entirely from publishing delinquent taxpayer lists in Spanish.[134] By this time, the split in language abilities had likely become generational, as increased access to English classes, the army, and other English-language immersion opportunities arose for New Mexico's youth. While Spanish persisted as the preferred language of many village families in the home, increasing numbers of village residents understood English. But English also found its way into previous Spanish strongholds in New Mexico through the rise of New Deal programs that sought to provide economic relief and teach new skills.

PUTTING CITIZENSHIP TO WORK IN THE NEW DEAL

Over four-fifths of New Mexico's population lived in rural areas in the 1930s, and the state lacked almshouses and had few state-level relief programs.[135] The vast majority of residents relied on family, friends, and neighbors when in need, since the state's sheer size and poor roads made it difficult for the government to get aid to them.[136] When the Great Depression hit the villages of northern New Mexico, which for decades had not been self-sustaining, its *nuevomexicano* residents were already in great need of help. Most able-bodied workers already had to leave their villages to find jobs, and these jobs largely disappeared with the start of the depression.[137] New Mexican officials at first did not concern themselves with rural districts, thinking they were self-sustaining. In 1935, after fact-finding studies revealed the extent of the crisis in *nuevomexicano* strongholds and state officials prioritized the forms of aid, the New Deal finally began to reach them.[138]

New Mexico's elected officials, along with federal officials, introduced a slew of federal programs to New Mexico's small villages and towns. In some locales, villagers were given the opportunity to take English courses near their homes or from coworkers.[139] Wage labor provided relief to families but also drew men away from the villages into programs like the National Youth Administration (NYA) or the Civilian Conservation Corps (CCC). In contrast to the predominantly Spanish-language world of migrant agricultural labor, New Deal work camps offered *nuevomexicanos* an often jolting experience in an English-dominated setting. The programs exposed workers to the English language, a more regimented work schedule, Anglos' racist attitudes, and life away from Spanish-speaking parents and villages.[140] Camp courses emphasized "English, American politics, and good citizenship," filling in for many rural schools that lacked access to teachers with knowledge of these subjects.[141]

While New Deal programs challenged the supremacy of Spanish in the villages, Spanish-speaking family members continued to use it in the home. Moreover, some government assistance programs, including those that provided villagers with instructions on effective irrigation techniques and restoration projects, were conducted in Spanish, sometimes by native Spanish speakers.[142] Federal programs reached villages unevenly, meaning exposure and introduction to English and federal workers varied.

The increasing presence of the federal government, as well as villagers' need to travel to find work, broke up the patronage system in New Mexico.[143] While *nuevomexicanos* already migrated to places like northern Colorado to work in the beet fields in the early part of the century, the sheer number of programs and amount of federal contact in the 1930s forever decentered the place of the patronage system and, with it, the need for political parties to count on the Spanish-language vote. As more and more villagers left home to participate in the market economy or federal work projects, the language gap between villagers and the state's Spanish-speaking elite narrowed.[144] Elite officeholders already spoke English, and after 1923 the legislative senate or assembly had no need for interpreters.[145] The census asked only a 5 percent sample of the population about their language use in 1940, so it is impossible to know how closely constituents followed their elite officeholders in using English.[146]

Spanish nevertheless retained some of its political uses in New Mexico. Federal officials working in the villages and in Washington, DC, were reminded of the long legacy of Spanish politics through their interactions with Spanish-speaking citizens and their receipt of letters written in Spanish.[147] Nuevomexicanos reasserted their place as citizens, which included demanding fair and nondiscriminatory treatment in the workplace. When they encountered racism or discrimination, sometimes because of their use of Spanish, they filed petitions and sent letters to their elected officials.[148] Many wrote in English, but they also composed letters to Washington in Spanish, confident that they would receive justice.

With their long participation in partisan politics, many villagers understood the channels through which to contact their political superiors, but the small number of letters suggests that not all nuevomexicanos were aware of their rights. Prior to the 1930s, Spanish speakers had limited access to relief services, due to discriminatory policies as well as to the fact that little aid existed where they lived. The New Deal extended aid to some rural non-English speakers. Still, nuevomexicano access to New Deal resources was limited compared to that of European immigrants.[149] Local social workers and aid distributors pursued distinct policies that provided less aid to nuevomexicanos. Translations at the federal level did not exist for most New Deal procedures, requiring counties like San Miguel to print federal relief rules in Spanish at their own expense.[150] Limited evidence of broadly employed translations or interpreters meant that many monolingual Spanish speakers likely never heard about the aid available to citizens from the federal government.

Nuevomexicanos continued to elect state officials with Spanish surnames, but by World War II, they overwhelmingly operated in English. The federal government's efforts to preserve Spanish as a language of folklore reflected this broader shift toward using Spanish as a marker of cultural identity. Nuevomexicanos employed by New Deal programs translated historical Spanish documents and began to collect various written and oral forms of northern nuevomexicano culture. The now-married Aurora Lucero-White Lea diligently worked to preserve dichos, corridos, poems, stories, and plays. Originally intended as a classroom supplement, by the 1940s the project had blossomed into two books on northern New Mexico's Spanish-language folklore.[151] Even though Lucero-White Lea (and other *nuevomexicano* workers) actively participated in this culture—she began the project by collecting material from her native San Miguel County—the act of collecting folk culture as a federal preservation project suggested that Spanish had made its greatest contributions to the nation's culture in the past. The translation project focused on official documents issued between 1682 and 1844, a periodization that, by definition, neglected the contributions of Spanish-speaking treaty citizens to the history of the United States.[152] In this telling, Spanish-language sources contributed only to the early founding of the region by Spain and Mexico.

While the Federal Writers' Project—a program under the New Deal's Works Progress Administration—and *nuevomexicanos* preserved Spanish as a language of culture, Spanish speakers outside of New Mexico used it as a political language to further class struggle and workers' rights. Spanish-language political activism became more palpable in grassroots, labor, and community activism among more recent immigrants in the interwar years.[153] Migrant laborers in California pledged their support for unionization in the fields in the form of handmade signs and placards. One sign written from the "oficina del Campo de la Union" (Field Union office), which represented the Cannery and Agricultural Workers Industrial Union (CAWIU), expressed full support for the National Recovery Administration (NRA), a controversial agency that raised prices and wages: "Todos los trabajadores . . . autoriza NRA 100%" (All of the workers . . . authorize the NRA 100%).[154] Drawing on their long history of organization and advocating for their rights as workers, these Mexican migrant laborers, while not citizens, discussed and understood the ways in which New Deal programs protected them. Spanish speakers—both Mexican immigrants and treaty citizen families—exhibited their resourcefulness by learning about New Deal supports for labor. This community knowledge suggests an informed network and a certain level of understanding of the changing nature of national politics.

One of the best known union organizers was Luisa Moreno, who entered the United States from Guatemala in 1928. She first settled in Spanish Harlem, where she had a radical "political awakening" and joined the Communist Party in 1930. She spoke English, French, and Spanish. Before becoming the editor of *Noticias de UCAPAWA*, the Spanish-language version of *UCAPAWA News*, she created a labor school that taught organizing tactics in Spanish.[155]

Moreno led a new organization called the Spanish-Speaking People's Congress (best known as El Congreso), which first met in December 1938. The founding convention, held in late April 1939 at the New Mexico & Arizona Social Club on Spring Street in Los Angeles, drew approximately 1,500 attendees from California, New Mexico, Arizona, Colorado, and Texas. Convention delegates, some of whom were not citizens, displayed binational allegiances as they sang the national anthems of Mexico and the United States gathered under both flags. The new organization adopted a broad platform that touched on civil rights and righting injustices against the Spanish-speaking community across the Southwest. Delegates read reports from the various committees in both Spanish and English. The second objective listed on a draft of the organization's program concerned language. It began by encouraging the preservation of Spanish but went on to advocate for Spanish to receive official status in communities with large numbers of Spanish-speaking people.[156] This stance was a clear affront to English-only Americanization efforts.[157] Later, a "special bulletin" explained this goal could be accomplished through a "real fight for BI-LINGUAL classes." The goal for El Congreso was not to preserve Spanish for the sake of retaining Spanish but to address illiteracy rates and encourage true bilingualism.[158]

El Congreso splintered soon after this rosy and optimistic first meeting over Los Angeles organizers' purported ties to the Popular Front. The Popular Front united various leftist organizations in a movement that spanned the globe and focused on class and labor issues over national allegiances. In 1940, the prominent scholars Arturo L. Campa of the University of New Mexico and George I. Sánchez of the University of Texas withdrew their membership because they viewed El Congreso as a "communist sponsored affair."[159] Hints of earlier divisions can be seen in the way the delegates chose to identify themselves. There were the "Mexican" and the "Spanish American elements" in El Congreso.[160] The more radical direction that the "Mexicans" in Los Angeles took looked back to their experiences as immigrants, whereas the New Mexico–born Sánchez claimed deep roots in the Southwest and distanced himself from any perceived radicalism. Sánchez's 1940 book on New Mexican schools, *Forgotten People*, spoke of New Mexico's geographic and cultural isolation and advocated for strong Spanish-language instruction, but he preferred to advocate for civil rights within the U.S. political system.[161] Campa was born in Sonora, Mexico, and studied the use of Spanish in the United States as folklore, not activism; most of his studies focused on Colorado and New Mexico.[162] El Congreso offered the promise of a brotherhood among Spanish-heritage speakers with such different histories, but the political gulf between radicalism and respectability remained wide.

These incidents of Spanish language use cannot make up for the fact that the Southwest's language of government was almost exclusively English during the Great Depression. Civic action organizations, like the League of United Latin American Citizens (LULAC), which began in the late 1920s in Texas but expanded into New Mexico and other parts of the Southwest, excluded noncitizens, made English the official language of its organizational functions, and by 1940 encouraged its membership to speak in English. LULAC and La Alianza Hispano-Americana chose to support ideas of Americanization that included teaching English in order to retain their political power. In doing so, they hoped to avoid the racialization that Mexican immigrants faced.[163] Adopting English served as a strategy for ethnic Mexicans to retain political relevance. This insistence on operating in the English language coincided with the decreasing use of Spanish in partisan politics by the late 1930s and 1940s.

The 1930s marked the great transition from Spanish as a powerful political language of treaty citizen families to an immigrant language used for distinct causes and purposes. After almost nine decades, the United States had successfully integrated almost all treaty citizen families into an English-language political system. In the minds of many Anglos, employers, and even ethnic Mexican citizens, Spanish became a language of immigrants. The shift in their perception began when federal legislation, starting with the Newlands Reclamation Act of 1902, allowed access to water across the West—the same year Beveridge and his committee of senators successfully turned New Mexico on a path away from using Spanish as a language of politics. This new funding changed the demography of the Southwest as growers recruited and employed more migrants from Mexico.

The Spanish language subsequently became racialized along with Spanish speakers. Local officials who excluded Mexican immigrants from the relief rolls in Los Angeles and efforts to halt labor activism could target groups by their use of language. This helps explain LULAC's and La Alianza Hispano-Americana's choice to distance themselves from Spanish in order to appear more respectable to employers and politicians. For these ethnic Mexican citizens, Spanish was a language of heritage, home, and culture, a language to respect through folklore but not really appropriate for situations involving U.S. political power or civic engagement.

Without continuing migration, the story of Spanish-language politics would have ended here, a story of decline or loss that would mirror those of so many other languages used in the United States. Instead, the decades after the 1930s saw the arrival of ever-increasing numbers of Spanish-speaking migrants (even after the repatriation of ethnic Mexicans). Many of these migrants arrived as temporary laborers who fully intended to return home but ultimately chose to remain in the United States when faced with restrictive immigration laws that limited their movement across the border. Their struggle for language rights lies outside the scope of this book, but the politics of their language choices deserves a closer look.

U.S. citizens of Spanish-speaking descent shifted course during this period. Instead of requesting translations and bilingual ballots, they attempted to protect and encourage the teaching of Spanish in the schools—not instruction *in* Spanish but instruction *of* Spanish, for Anglos as well as their own children. They were not alone in their focus. Political leaders, state legislatures, school boards, and the Spanish-language press all entered the fray as local and state policies determined the language of instruction policies for students throughout the Southwest. Lack of access to Spanish in the schools further relegated it to a language of the home rather than one of society. Advocates and detractors fought over the relative merits of Americanization, which demanded English-only instruction, and Pan-Americanism, which highlighted the importance of Spanish for U.S. hemispheric ambitions. In this new context, schools became the major site of struggle over language politics in the United States.

CHAPTER 7

The Limits of Americanization

*Residentes de habla Español . . . haber construido una escuela . . . en orden de permitir su atendencia á una escuela donde se enseñe español[.] Todo eso es un equivoco. Los niños de padres de habla Española deben mezclarse libremente con los niños de padres de habla Inglesa.**

—*El Nuevo Mexicano*, April 21, 1906

The absence of a uniform school system in the U.S. Southwest opened the door for competing and often inadequate schooling options that contributed to the persistence of Spanish in the new U.S. territories. With some elite exceptions, treaty citizens almost universally spoke Spanish, rather than English, at the time of their incorporation into the United States. Strong federal educational policies could have ensured that these new citizens—or at least their children—learned English quickly, but in their absence, children's language abilities followed the preferences and opportunities of their parents. Unfortunately, it is nearly impossible for the historian to reconstruct individual family choices. It is conceivable that parents might have supported the sentiments expressed in the epigraph, which advocated for English-language learning as a step toward integration, or they might have agreed instead with Benjamin Read, who encouraged *nuevomexicanos* to develop pride in their mother tongue. Read explained that there was a pervasive indifference to learning Spanish and many Spanish-speaking *nuevomexicanos* "que aun de hablarlo se averguenzan" (who are ashamed of speaking it). Read saw this

---

* "Spanish-speaking residents . . . have constructed a school . . . in order to attend a school where they teach Spanish. All of that is an error. The children of Spanish-speaking parents have to mix freely with the children of English-speaking parents."

distancing from the language as providing fuel to opponents who held discriminatory views of *nuestra raza* (our people).[1]

Parents—as informal educators, as members of communities, and in their role as elected officials—shaped the development of educational systems, including their language of instruction, in the Southwest. Their views and preferences were sometimes supported, and sometimes opposed, by state and national officials who increasingly viewed an English-language education as part of the American experience. No single monolithic Americanization educational campaign existed, and the goals and methods varied among regional and individual instructors. The basic premise of Americanization involved civic and U.S. citizenship instruction. A core teaching area of this effort focused on mastering the English language.[2] Americanization policies in the Southwest and the new insular territories proceeded unevenly, with distinct strategies for immigrants, territorial residents, and treaty citizen families.

This chapter—the first of four that address the politics of language in education in the first four decades of the twentieth century—considers the particular ways that both parents and educators supported Americanization policies in the Southwest. It begins with some necessary national context on how schools became a central site for creating citizens in the late nineteenth and early twentieth century. As the second section shows, these ideas about citizenship were complicated in the Southwest by the presence of Spanish-speaking descendants of treaty citizens whose Anglo-perceived loyalty and worth sometimes protected them from the segregation and hostility encountered by newer arrivals from Mexico. The chapter then examines New Mexico as a case study of how treaty citizen families' personal preferences and citizenship claims allowed supporters to initially retain Spanish-language instruction even as the country at large turned to English-only instruction.

Educational policy is arguably the most important arbiter of citizenship and language because it sets up an understanding of these concepts for the next generation. In the first three decades of the twentieth century, legislators and educators in the Southwest successfully enforced English-language instruction over Spanish. Between 1910 and 1940, older systems of Spanish instruction were abandoned in all but the poorest and most isolated regions. For example, growing opportunities for English acquisition after 1891 for youth in New Mexico enabled its legislature to no longer require an interpreter by the 1925 legislative session. New Spanish-language policies lacked the urgency of community survival by the 1920s, since legislators could increasingly chart a future end date for language concessions for monolingual Spanish-speaking citizens due to increasing educational opportunities for New Mexico's youth.

A CHANGING EDUCATIONAL SYSTEM

The Spanish-speaking territories included in the Treaty of Guadalupe Hidalgo entered the United States before the country at large had reached consensus about what a proper education looked like, or who should pay for it. While some cities began offering comprehensive schools in the 1820s, the country's most famous advocate of common schools, Massachusetts's Horace Mann, was still arguing for their creation as late as 1846, as the U.S.-Mexican War began.[3] The development of the U.S. educational system was therefore maturing at the same time as new state and territorial governments. This parallel development and nonstandardized national system of education created an extremely fluid situation with a lot of local control and a variety of educational approaches.

States increasingly adopted common schools in the decades surrounding the Civil War. By 1900, thirty-three states and territories had passed compulsory attendance laws, including California (1874), Colorado (1879), New Mexico (1891), and Arizona (1899). These laws varied in terms of penalties for truants and even in the number of months a year that students were required to attend school.[4] Universal and compulsory modern education began under a system with vast national disparities. For example, in 1890, the average length of the school year in New Mexico was 77 days, which placed it 53 days below the U.S. average. By comparison, in the North Atlantic region the average was 160 days, and the western states averaged 120 days.[5]

Students entered schools that looked very different from one another. For instance, in New Mexico, the plurality of schools in 1914 were constructed of adobe and were located in rural communities. Around two-thirds of the students eligible for school were enrolled. The vast majority of students attended one-room schools with few resources, and enrollment numbers decreased by grade. For example, 19,872 students were enrolled in first grade but only 2,270 in eighth grade. Alvan White, state superintendent of public instruction, encouraged the New Mexico legislature to consider a law that would provide textbooks in classrooms across the state. He requested an increase in the school year from the required five months to seven months. White also hoped to change the compulsory law to sixteen years old for students who did not reach the eighth grade by age fourteen.[6] These realities would be unrecognizable to students in Los Angeles who attended neighborhood schools with multiple classrooms. These schools could be multiethnic and their students had a greater opportunity to attend high school.[7] Material and educational disparities meant "school" looked very different for students across the Southwest and, more broadly, across the country.

The imbalance in material resources and funding was not entirely unintentional, as educators meant for schools in different places with different subjects of study to fulfill different functions. A sharp split existed between schools that worked to form citizens (in both the social and political meanings of the term) and schools that produced second-class citizens (largely rural, Black, Indian, and immigrant students). The split could occur between urban and rural schools due to the availability of highly trained teachers. Or it could arise based on where districts chose to send the better-trained and more effective teachers.[8] At their best, public schools offered academic subjects that increasingly encouraged students to complete secondary school and enroll in college. By comparison, schools for "second-class citizens" often focused on vocational and agricultural training. Education advocates intended public education for these students to instill the particular moral values (i.e. work ethic, punctuality, respect for authority, silence) that would increase profits by producing better industrial and agricultural workers.[9]

As the national educational system moved toward the modern system, preparing and training students to be U.S. citizens became an overarching mission of public schools.[10] Textbook publishers who commanded large markets by the twentieth century took on the task of producing good citizens and supporting the current economic structure.[11] When the United States acquired four new Spanish colonies in 1898 (the Philippines, Guam, Cuba, and Puerto Rico), military officials in the territories saw an opportunity to test this curriculum on a student population they deemed profoundly in need of Americanization. One year after acquiring the islands from Spain, the federal government began using federal funds to build an educational system in territories whose military overseers believed few educational opportunities had existed. Congress and the U.S. military created educational systems for these Spanish-speaking residents that conveyed mainstream American values, including multiple different language strategies that ranged from difficult to enforce English-only to Spanish allowed as the language of instruction in the primary grades. The expanding market interests of the United States in the Pacific and the Caribbean justified the investment in education, as lawmakers hoped to capitalize on human labor.[12]

Spanish-speaking treaty citizen families living in the remaining territories in the United States—Arizona and New Mexico—did not receive the same federal attention. The distinction in their treatment from either residents of the new insular territories or the region's American Indians is striking. Federally funded American Indian schools—there were twenty-six in New Mexico in 1914—were instituted in the 1880s with the purpose of "civilizing" the American Indian population by depriving them of their culture and "Americanizing" them. One of the first goals of these schools was to strip indigenous children of their native languages and impose the English language.[13] Given the region's few entrepreneurial opportunities, the federal government saw little reason to build an educational infrastructure.

Federal authorities' neglect upset New Mexican politicians, who watched the mounting federal educational funding in Puerto Rico, Cuba, and the Philippines with dismay. The government's efforts included sending large numbers of English-speaking teachers to Americanize and teach English to students in the Philippines and Puerto Rico. One thousand English-speaking teachers, called Thomasites because half of them arrived in the Philippines on the USS *Thomas* in 1901, taught in Filipino schools.[14] For comparison, in 1898 the territory of New Mexico had 846 teachers; that number would grow to 1,474 teachers in 1910. New Mexico's teachers included many *nuevomexicanos* who were not native English speakers or who could not speak English.[15]

Elite New Mexicans objected more to their lack of financial resources than to the specific curriculum, but the details of educational policy in the new territories deserve closer examination. The curriculum in the new territories often centered on English as a language of instruction, especially for the elite. Voting privileges extended only to literate individuals in Puerto Rico and the Philippines, reinforcing the position of elites in territorial administrative positions.[16] Even so, the language of instruction varied both within and across the new territories. Most educational policy makers promoted English-only policies in Puerto Rico, the Philippines, Cuba, and the Dominican Republic during their terms of service. Others encouraged the use of Spanish to aid with Americanization. Vocational and agricultural education often took precedent over language instruction, since U.S. companies preferred cheap and willing workers with transferable labor skills. Still, language of instruction debates in the territories sometimes hinged on the expectations for territorial residents. For example, U.S. Commissioner of Education William T. Harris preferred a heavy focus on English lessons in Cuba "to bring about 'civilization' to the island," in preparation for self-government. Opposing Harris's vision and language focus, the short-lived superintendent of Cuban schools, Alexis Everett Frye, altered pedagogical protocol to include more Spanish instruction and hired "native" teachers.[17]

Puerto Rico's struggle for local control of its schools followed a similar pattern. The second superintendent of public instruction, Samuel McCane Lindsay, a sociology professor at the University of Pennsylvania, believed Puerto Ricans required specific preparation prior to annexation. He therefore prioritized U.S.-centered patriotic displays and citizenship instruction (in Spanish) over mandatory language acquisition.[18] He, like Frye, proved exceptional; the island's ever-changing superintendent-directed school policy decisions largely encouraged a more comprehensive and English-language-focused academic learning environment.[19] In 1902, the Official Languages Act made both Spanish and English acceptable in public and in government, but harsh English instruction policies in the schools still prevailed from 1903 to 1914. Like the treaty citizens who were granted U.S. citizenship without having to learn English, Puerto Ricans received citizenship regardless of whether they had acquired proficiency in English. Puerto Ricans' use of Spanish did not dissuade Congress from imposing U.S. citizenship in 1917, which led to renewed Americanization tactics in schools.[20] The realities of territorial policies did not always match up with the professed ideals of creating U.S. citizens.

These opposing approaches to educational policy in the contiguous and noncontiguous Spanish-speaking territories showcase larger national academic debates that emerged during a period filled with progressive educational efforts. John Dewey, the most prominent U.S. educator, saw schools as "incubating the democratic way of life," as two historians have summarized.[21] School districts with significant local control over how they chose to teach students gave way to more centralized county and state oversight of teacher certification and superintendent-driven instructional material in the first decades of the twentieth century. The process also provided a channel for new national professional organizations to develop a more standardized curriculum and instructional approach over the first decades of the twentieth century.[22] These new practices included English-only policies that imposed English on colonial subjects, immigrants, and American Indians.[23]

The role of the federal government in education changed drastically during the twentieth century. Federal support of land grant colleges, research universities, and military schools broadened federal financial involvement in schools. New Mexicans continued to complain that they were not receiving their share of these funds, even following statehood. In 1929, Senator Octaviano Larrazolo prepared a speech for Congress in a bid to create a military school. He hoped federal funding would raise residents' earning potential and create more opportunities for them. Comparing the situation of his state to the insular territories, Larrazolo explained how "New Mexico, like the Philippine Islands, Porto Rico and Guam and Hawaii, by the fortune of war in 1847 came to be a portion of this great nation." After boasting about New Mexicans' eighty-two years of military service as U.S. citizens, Larrazolo asked his colleagues to consider that "as far as common education goes, this government has not spent one penny in supporting and maintaining the schools in New Mexico." He argued the omission remained "absolutely contrary to our views and system of government."[24]

Larrazolo drew his colleagues' attention to *nuevomexicanos'* lack of English skills. Prior to 1916, he claimed, "you could hardly find" children "from the country districts" who spoke English; he estimated that few citizens over the age of forty in 1929 could. Larrazolo blamed the territory's isolation from both the United States and Mexico, its small and dispersed population, and four hundred years of "relentless and uncompromising war" with "savage Indians" for the lack of universal educational opportunities. Larrazolo encouraged the Senate to turn its attention to a previously neglected territorial population with its own English-language deficiencies.[25]

States, unlike territories, had the power to tax and create their own school policy; this left little justification for funding from the federal government. The condition of statehood meant that Larrazolo could only urge the Senate to fund a single military school rather than its entire schooling system. Having entered the country at a moment when the federal government's interest in funding education was minimal, New Mexico's rural and Spanish-speaking communities never received the same educational attention as the newer territories. More than sixty years later, statehood provided autonomy that set New Mexico on a divergent educational path from Puerto Rico, in the same way that New Mexico's and California's educational systems had diverged in the nineteenth century. The heated debates over language policies for schools in the Southwest make explicit the usually unspoken connections between language and the ideals of citizenship.

AMERICANIZATION THROUGH ENGLISH

Language policy debates in the Southwest paralleled national discussions about Americanization during the first decades of the twentieth century. An unprecedented influx of immigrants raised the stakes for defining who could be classified as "American"; those who could not fit into this increasingly narrow and nativist definition could be cast out.[26] World War I heightened this nativism. State and local policies that targeted the German language during this period are a good example of mainstream Americans' restricted views of language.[27] As one historian explained, "Americanization became an all-consuming passion in the United States from about 1914 to the early 1920s."[28] The Americanization campaign encouraged English as a common national language, as many nativists believed "the strength of a Republic ... [was] dependent upon the unification of all nationalities."[29] Nativists' tactics and approaches nevertheless differed substantially, and their efforts in the Southwest exemplified the diversity of opinion.

Nativist efforts to Americanize the country ranged from the extreme to the optimistic. On one end, thousands marched at Ku Klux Klan–sponsored "patriotic" festivals in Colorado, and their anti-immigrant, anti-Catholic rhetoric largely targeted the recently arrived Mexicans in the sugar beet towns. The Klan did not distinguish between treaty citizen families who migrated for work and immigrants: both were viewed as nonwhite and undesirable. Alvin Garcia of Greeley, Colorado, remembered the Klan's intimidation tactics as they marched through the Spanish-speaking neighborhoods and burned a cross in front of his home.[30] On the other end, state governments in Arizona and California supported Americanization educational efforts through adult night courses and other educational endeavors.[31] Centered on teaching immigrants the basics of U.S. government and the rights and freedoms of citizens, the programs in Arizona used English-language instruction as a strategy for incorporating immigrants into their communities. The legislature backed these efforts because its members agreed that, without them, immigrants only had "haphazard opportunities for acquiring a knowledge of the English language, and of the customs of our Country."[32] In California, courses for adults, mothers, and youth sponsored by the California Commission of Immigration and Housing taught the English language and mainstream American values that extended to ideas of hygiene and proper social behavior—essentially Anglo-Saxon and Protestant views of culture, which racialized and demeaned ethnic Mexican culture.[33] In 1915, the Home Teacher Act, for instance, placed Americanization instructors in Mexican immigrant homes to target mothers. These instructors believed that by stripping women of their culture they would reach their children too. Teaching Mexican immigrant women the English language was viewed as one of the most basic requirements for them and for creating a homogeneous workforce. This strategy largely failed. Americanization advocates moved next to U.S.-born female youth.[34]

Americanization efforts, too, fell between these two extremes as states carefully cataloged and attempted to understand the new immigrants. Colorado legislators were particularly interested in understanding the motivations of non-English-speaking union organizers and activists after the Coal Strike of 1913–14. For example, in 1914, Colorado passed a law creating a joint legislative committee to compile information on individual strikers, including their country of origin and language.[35] At the same time, Colorado legislators required that laws concerning mine safety be translated and distributed to non-English-speaking workers, and they insisted that danger signals be translated.[36] As progressive politicians secured the passage of state and federal regulations on labor safety, work hours, and education, the nation at large had to come to terms with the fact that many of its workers did not speak English.

The rising fear of un-American radicals reached its peak during and shortly after World War I, with the passage of the Sedition Act in 1918 and in postwar incidents like the Palmer Raids and the Sacco and Vanzetti case. State legislators and educators throughout the country successfully curbed "foreign"-language instruction.[37] During the war many of these campaigns were directed at German, the most common non-English language taught nationwide before the war. For example, 70 percent of New York state students who took a modern language studied German, the language of science.[38] Even the *New Mexico Journal of Education* (*NMJE*) linked language and Americanization when it concerned German: "We believe that the English language should be the first means of Americanization and should be the medium of communication between all citizens. We favor the suspension of instruction in the German language during the war."[39] In Hawaii, Americanization efforts discouraged learning Asian languages—especially Japanese.[40]

Local control of schools across the country had resulted in some districts and schools choosing to teach all subjects in a language other than English in elementary school. States varied regarding their adoption of English-only policies in these early grades. California and Arizona, for example, had required schools to be taught in the English language since 1870 and 1883, respectively.[41] Between 1897 and 1915, at least thirteen states made English the language of instruction.[42] Twenty-six states restricted "foreign"-language instruction in the primary grades between 1919 and 1921. Colorado joined the wave by placing language restrictions at both public and private schools after 1919. In 1921 California extended its English-only law to include private schools.[43] New Mexico's legislators also mandated instruction in English but in 1919 also required Spanish-language instruction in rural and high schools.[44]

The Supreme Court reclaimed parents' rights to choose their children's language of instruction in *Meyer v. Nebraska* (1923). In 1920, the district attorney for Hamilton County charged primary teacher Robert Meyer with violating a newly passed English-only state constitutional provision.[45] Meyer, with the support of parents, persisted in teaching German despite broader complaints and animosity. In its decision, the Supreme Court determined that individual states lacked the authority to ban language instruction, which invalidated Americanization arguments that teaching "foreign" languages exhibited national disloyalty.[46] The Supreme Court also overturned laws dictating the use of English in private and parochial schools, although states retained a number of educational language restrictions already in place in public schools that drastically reduced the number of German speakers in the United States.[47] German-speaking children entered elementary schools where they largely learned to speak English after the Americanization efforts that targeted them.

In California, decisions regarding the instruction of English in the 1910s grew from larger concerns about the best way to educate immigrants. The rise in Americanization policies coincided with the creation of segregated schools for ethnic Mexicans. The proponents of segregation worked remarkably fast; by the mid-1930s upwards of 85 percent of Mexican-origin children in the Southwest attended segregated schools that were taught in English.[48] Pasadena created the first segregated Mexican school in California in 1913 in response to pressure from Anglo parents. Increasing numbers of Anglo parents in Southern California desired separate schools as tens of thousands of Mexican students entered their communities. Between 1913 and 1928, Mexican schools dotted Southern California, appearing in Riverside, Orange, and Los Angeles Counties.[49] In contrast to the situation in the South, where Jim Crow practices solidified with the help of de jure segregation, these segregated schools violated California law that allowed segregation of "Indian, Mongolian, or Chinese children" but made no provisions for separating ethnic Mexican children.[50]

Those who backed segregated schools in California attempted to justify their existence using language rather than racial arguments. Educators across the Southwest pointed to Mexican immigrants' expected English-language deficiency, claiming that the students' lack of English required different instruction techniques. Districts also drew school boundaries based on racially segregated residential patterns.[51] Prior to these changes, ethnic Mexican children had attended public schools alongside Anglo students. The presence or absence of complaints from local parents could determine whether or not a district would establish segregated schools, but districts segregated students on their own too. Yet in urban areas some students remained in integrated settings.[52]

School districts also sometimes accommodated long-standing Mexican American citizens. The famous *Mendez v. Westminster* (1947) desegregation case in Orange County provides evidence of how this worked. When school administrators released the district's student demographics, it included twenty-six Mexican American children who attended the otherwise Anglo Franklin School, "because their families had always gone there."[53] Subsequent interviews with the Méndez children suggest these exceptions correlated to lighter skin color.[54] Both Gonzalo and Silvia Méndez spoke English with their children and were able to hire a lawyer to support their case and advocate for all ethnic Mexican children in the district. Being bilingual helped them mobilize the community.

The creation of parallel segregated schools meant that members of the same communities in Southern California learned about citizenship—and about one another—in separated settings from childhood up. This division helped to make ethnic Mexicans perpetually foreign and racialized ethnic Mexican children while allowing Anglo prejudices to fester. A consideration of the alternative, an integrated school system, makes this readily apparent. If monolingual Spanish-speaking students were a regular presence in school, all students in attendance would gain a familiarity with the Spanish language, even if the classroom remained English-only. Students would learn English and the values of U.S. citizenship together. In integrated schools, Anglo students could pick up or adopt certain Spanish-language phrases, slang, or words that they heard on the playground or after school. Segregation had the effect of magnifying both Anglo and ethnic Mexican perceptions of Spanish as a language of immigrants rather than the language of U.S. citizens of a different cultural background.[55]

Educational policies in California treated Spanish as an immigrant language rather than as a language of the region. With the ethnic Mexican population increasing tenfold between 1900 and 1930, this approach made some sense.[56] In California, where the school system was founded by local English-speaking community members rather than Spanish-speaking parents, there was no history of Spanish-language instruction in most schools, though the Mexican consulate did support some Mexican schools in the 1920s in Los Angeles.[57] The absence of Spanish speakers among community leaders and elected officials permitted the schools to see Spanish as an immigrant problem to be ameliorated. The resulting segregation, often justified based on language, inevitably accompanied by inadequate materials and poorly trained teachers, contributed to poor English proficiency among native Spanish speakers. The confluence of these conditions resulted in poor intelligence test results, which social scientists interpreted as scientific proof of the biological inferiority of Mexican students in comparison to white students. Those test results, in turn, further validated segregation policies.[58]

No state in the Southwest attempted to create a bilingual educational system in the first decades of the twentieth century. Instead, ethnic Mexican parents worked to desegregate schools at a district level. These cases appeared in Texas, California, and Colorado. *Maestas v. Shone* (1914), in Colorado's San Luis Valley, is the earliest known challenge. After the Alamosa school district created a separate Mexican school, the treaty citizen families formed a group called the Spanish American Union to organize against the school district's discriminatory practices. The union circulated a petition that garnered 180 head-of-household signatures, complained to the school board, and even staged a school boycott. Those students attending the Mexican School largely hailed from New Mexican settler families who came to Colorado to build the railroad in the late nineteenth century. Their citizenship was never in question during the dispute; their rapid organizing and escalation tactics demonstrated a solid grounding in U.S. political systems. Francisco Maestas filed a lawsuit in 1913 to permit his son to attend a neighborhood school rather than the Mexican School. After determining that over half of the students at the

Mexican School could understand English and that Maestas was a tax-paying U.S. citizen, Judge Charles Holbrook ruled that children with adequate English be enrolled in the other district schools. Though some reports claimed race was at the center of the controversy, the court acknowledged language skills served as a valid pedagogical reason for separation. According to Holbrook's ruling, if schools determined that students were unable to keep up with grade-level English-language schoolwork, they could be placed in Mexican schools.[59] Attorney Raymond Sullivan was not satisfied with the ruling, writing that "you are getting perilously close to separation on account of race" if you use language as the criterion for separation.[60] The *Maestas* case was followed by the unsuccessful *Del Rio ISD v. Salvatierra* case (1930) in Texas and, most famously, by *Alvarez v. Lemon Grove* (1931) in San Diego County, where Mexican American parents successfully challenged attempts to segregate their children into Mexican schools.[61]

Other parents made individual efforts to register their children in white schools. These victories paled in comparison to the overwhelming reality of segregated schooling for most ethnic Mexican children in the Southwest. Although Colorado's constitution forbade segregation based on race, as late as the 1930s Spanish-speaking children there largely attended rural schools that segregated Anglo and Mexican-origin students on the basis of language.[62] Language-based segregation became the norm in Colorado, especially in northern beet towns where Mexican immigrants resided. Segregation, the dearth of trained teachers, and inadequate supplies contributed to low achievement rates and increased the likelihood that ethnic Mexican students would be categorized as "retarded" or "morons."[63] These challenges were compounded by high absenteeism as students worked during the beet harvest.

In Arizona, too, the de facto segregation of ethnic Mexican students solidified during this same period. In many towns, segregation had as much to do with the rising number of Anglo settlers who wanted their children to attend public schools as it did with the entering Mexican immigrants.[64] Ethnic Mexicans comprised the vast majority of students in Arizona schools when the school system was first created in the late nineteenth century. Early settlers did not bring families, and Spanish-speaking parents built much of the territory's educational system. Given this demographic reality, educators in Arizona counties with large numbers of monolingual Spanish-speaking students encouraged schools to train and hire bilingual teachers to support their students' ability to acquire English.[65] But while educators at times expressed a preference for bilingual instructors, no state law provided the funds necessary to train them or required their presence in schools with significant numbers of English-language learners.[66]

New Mexico's neighbor to the east, Texas, in contrast to Arizona, Colorado, and California, embraced Spanish-language instruction as a subject in the 1930s but rejected bilingual education, which remained illegal until the 1960s. The implementation of Spanish-language instruction was scattered, but Corpus Christi schools enrolled 16,000 students in grades 3 to 6 in Spanish courses.[67] While Texas legislators permitted Spanish-language instruction in the primary grades, their efforts still neglected monoglot Spanish-speaking childrens' experience when they first entered the classroom.

As the exceptions in southern Colorado and parts of Arizona suggest, local control of schools established prior to the arrival of Mexican immigrants made a difference. But school law in California, Colorado, and Arizona did little to protect monolingual Spanish-speaking citizens beyond permitting local variation. New Mexico's state legislature, by contrast, initially encouraged students to retain their Spanish while still privileging English-language instruction in public schools. This disparity in state policies depended both on the continued political strength of *nuevomexicanos* and the demographic realities of the state. State education officials' limited ability to regulate the use of language in these remote areas resulted in more Spanish-language instruction, which meant that many rural communities in New Mexico escaped the most virulent forms of Americanization—though this result limited their opportunities for economic mobility.

BILINGUAL EDUCATION IN NEW MEXICO

From the moment of statehood, provisions in New Mexico's school code required teachers to recognize and respond to a given community's language needs. In 1916, newly trained teachers began their New Mexico careers under state laws that demanded that they print all school forms and notifications of delinquent children in English and Spanish. At the state level, in 1907, the assistant state superintendent of instruction's job qualifications expanded to include fluency in both English and Spanish. The state paid to publish the state's school laws equally in both languages (two thousand copies of each). All of these actions recognized and respected the language situation of both Spanish- and English-speaking parents and students.[68] This legislative recognition of Spanish did not mean that Spanish-language instruction was encouraged for all of New Mexico's students. Legislators viewed Spanish as a tool to teach English to monoglot Spanish-speaking students and English was expected as the language of instruction.

Administrators faced the problem of disseminating effective English-language instructional techniques to rural schools. In 1914, 82 percent of the student population attended small rural schools in remote areas where they often only heard Spanish.[69] Due to the short school year, students in rural schools regularly spent two years in a single grade, meaning that fourteen-year-old students often only made it to fourth grade before compulsory laws stopped requiring their attendance in schools, leaving them with an inadequate English-language education.[70] The state constitution anticipated the need for bilingual teachers to aid in English-language acquisition and supported their use in the schools.[71] Training teachers in English-language instruction was a problem New Mexico had faced since the territorial era. In 1909, the legislature created and funded the El Rito Spanish-American Normal School to prepare promising native Spanish-speaking students to work in schools with monolingual Spanish speakers—nine years after a normal school was created in Puerto Rico.[72] Superintendent of Public Instruction Alvan White recognized that most of the potential teachers for the rural districts were "Spanish-American young men and women," and he hoped to train them beyond just English "in order that teaching of our two languages may be effectively accomplished beginning with the primary grade."[73] In 1912, for example, White requested an additional $12,000 to train Spanish-speaking teachers.[74] As Frank H. Roberts explained at the New Mexico Education Association's (NMEA) conference in 1914, "cuando un niño de habla española entra a la escuela" (when a child who speaks Spanish enters school), they encounter teachers who teach the "desconocido a lo desconocido por el camino de lo desconocido" (unknown to the unknown by way of the unknown). He argued that the constitution's priority on teaching English would result in poor instruction and worse outcomes—a large price to pay for Americanization. As a professional advocate for monolingual Spanish speakers, Roberts explained that the vast language gulf left monolingual Spanish speakers at a disadvantage in an English-only system. English-speaking students, after all, learned to read in their home language, while Spanish-speaking students could not understand the words used to teach.[75]

School critics denounced the inadequacy of rural teachers, noting how "los convierten en papagallos que repiten palabras sin comprender su significado" (they turn [students] into parrots who repeat words without understanding their meaning).[76] These rural students had little chance of learning to speak English "si no hay quien se los explique en Español" (if they do not have anyone who can explain things in Spanish).[77] A former administrator chastised teachers by claiming that if a student could not carry on a conversation in English at year's end, "Vd. ha fracasado en el objecto mas importante de su trabajo" (You have failed in the most important objective of your work).[78]

In 1915, state legislators responded to English-only complaints by legalizing a transitional bilingual system in the primary grades. The Board of Directors backed up the law by voting to add Spanish as a subject in the primary grades. The new law encouraged teachers to speak as much Spanish as students required to properly learn English. The legislature made the act effective on passage since it was "necessary for the preservation of the public peace and safety of the inhabitants of the State of New Mexico"—language that suggested a dire educational problem that required immediate attention.[79] The 1915 legislature delegated funds to create a training program for fifty student teachers to help alleviate the situation. This program required student teachers who could speak, read, and write fluently in both English and Spanish. They took a course that focused on "Spanish grammar, Spanish reading, Spanish orthography, Spanish composition and translating from English to Spanish and from Spanish to English." After graduating, student teachers taught for a required two years in a rural district in designated "Spanish-American communities of the state."[80]

New Mexico's educational journal reinforced and supported the implementation of state law in individual classrooms. In 1916, the NMJE instituted a regular column titled "Teaching Spanish," written by the assistant superintendent of public instruction, Filadelío Baca. The articles provided teachers with proper Spanish pronunciations, though only a minority of readers would need this information, since, as the NMJE explained, in "all except a very few of the Spanish-American districts in the state the teachers themselves are Spanish-American."[81] This observation on the native language of New Mexico's teachers helps explain why the state would simultaneously pass laws that required teachers to use Spanish as a means to teach English but also complain of teachers' inadequate understanding of English.

Other articles in the NMJE provided suggestions on how to teach English while using Spanish words for directions and understanding. Some articles ridiculed those who argued for a "direct method" of teaching English without the use of Spanish—a method that went against the 1915 state law.[82] As D. B. Morrill asserted, "You are not qualified to teach the native child until you know his language. And he will be robbed of his opportunity for an education until his problem is regarded as a special one, and definite effort is made to reach his case."[83] Morrill believed that teaching with the direct method was inefficient, ignored children's knowledge base, and was the main reason that an estimated 90 percent of students did not continue past the fourth grade.[84] *NMJE*'s articles suggest its editors agreed with state legislators that students required Spanish to adequately learn English.

New Mexican schools' poor performance resulted from unrealistic expectations, not their students' inherent lack of intelligence. Short school years, inadequate resources, and poorly trained instructors all resulted in an adult population that was not fully literate in either English or Spanish. In 1917, only one of every three thousand native Spanish-speaking students in New Mexico earned an eighth-grade diploma.[85]

State legislators adopted a hands-off and decentralized approach to language instruction in the years before World War I that left local districts in charge of deciding their policy. In 1914, New Mexico counted 983 rural districts in the state, with the vast majority having one-room schools.[86] The 1915 school code permitted local boards of directors to choose Spanish as a language of instruction. The 1917 law shifted the balance of power to parents, allowing Spanish "whenever the majority of the patrons of the school shall demand it by written petition to the County Superintendent," which revoked board members' ability to make choices antithetical to community preference. The bill instructed that each school that hired a bilingual teacher offer bilingual instruction in the first three grades and withheld teacher pay for those who could not meet the community's language preferences.[87] The 1917 legislature included a majority of native Spanish speakers in the House and a significant minority of Spanish speakers in the Senate (almost a third) who refused to vote on any items until everything was translated into Spanish—modeling the bilingual method daily in practice.[88] Anglo senators who voted for these provisions may have done so pragmatically, recognizing both their Spanish-speaking colleagues' legislative power and the state's demographic realities, or they may have placed cultural relevance on Spanish.

New Mexicans continued to accept Spanish as a permanent part of the state's culture at the same time that the fervor for Americanization spread nationally. Many New Mexicans recognized Spanish as the reigning imperial language of the state and a symbol of its illustrious history—not as an immigrant language that needed to be eradicated to meet the needs of Americanization. New Mexicans took pride in Spanish's long-term presence in the state, peppering their language with Spanish words and phrases.[89]

Nuevomexicanos retained their own unique form of cultural citizenship that unabashedly included Spanish. Aggrippina Carreras linked Spanish speakers and U.S. patriotism in an article supporting "Francisco" Hubbell's candidacy for the U.S. Senate in 1916:

> Porque respeto a los colores azul, blanco, y colorado de nuestra bandera amada, deseo que los Hispano-Americanos sean mejores ciudadanos. Porque amo a esos rostros morenos de ojos y cabello negros, deseo que su lengua que es también la mia, sea respetada.

> (Because I respect the red, white, and blue colors of our beloved flag, I want Spanish Americans to be better citizens. Because I love the faces with brown eyes and black hair, I want their language that is also mine to be respected.)[90]

Carreras supported learning Spanish as a right of her U.S. citizenship. In fact, she praised her community for successfully becoming bilingual while she challenged, "Si los Anglo-Sajones se dedicaran a estudiar nuestro rico y dulce idioma, no nos competirian" (If the Anglo-Saxons were devoted to studying our rich and sweet language, they could not compete with us).[91] This divergent perspective on language, so deeply held, persisted in large part because so few immigrants came to New Mexico during the most fervent decades of Americanization efforts. In 1920, just over 8.5 percent of the state's white population was foreign born, with just over two-thirds of these immigrants coming from Mexico, which meant that Spanish-speaking *nuevomexicanos* dwarfed the entering Mexican immigrant population.[92]

Other New Mexicans, including some *nuevomexicanos*, argued that the state's citizens required English if they were to succeed in the United States. One advocate for English spoke of bilingual classrooms where students were left ignorant of the English language, which was unacceptable because while "Spanish is our native tongue . . . and . . . it is an honor, indeed, to be able to speak both languages, it is a calamity to know only the Spanish." He explained that Spanish speakers could not expect to become "efficient citizens" or "hold any position of responsibility and honor" without mastery of English.[93] Unlike his nineteenth-century predecessors, this author placed little social or economic value on fluency in Spanish. Local administrators and teachers had a lot of power to shape their students' understanding of the language as a source of pride or shame.

In 1919, supporters of bilingual education methods received a strong advocate in the new governor, Octaviano Larrazolo—a native Spanish speaker, former schoolteacher, and Mexican immigrant. Speaking at an educators' conference during one of his first gubernatorial appearances, he staked his claim on the "language question": "If I had my way there would not be a Spanish-speaking child who did not also speak English. But wouldn't it be well for every English-speaking child to also know Spanish?" Larrazolo "never permitted a pupil to speak a word of English that he did not understand in Spanish; never to recite a lesson in English that he did not also know in Spanish." He viewed the bilingual method as the "one method to teach English to Spanish-speaking communities." Larrazolo proclaimed that teachers without Spanish-language skills could not effectively teach English to native Spanish speakers.[94] In a speech before the legislature Larrazolo continued his discussion on language instruction. "I confidently believe that the money spent in such schools is absolutely wasted to no purpose," he explained. The governor recommended that, despite the state's shortage of teachers, all rural districts employ teachers able to read, write, and speak both languages.[95]

Larrazolo's position on language implicitly endorsed a bilingual future for New Mexico. New Mexicans wrote to him to chime in. A school board member from the Anglo-dominated town of Roswell praised the governor's stance on language. She had hired and paid for Spanish lessons for her own children and believed "Spanish learning . . . is essential to our young people growing up in the West."[96] Another supportive educator lamented the difficulty of teaching in an English-only setting, writing that Spanish in the classroom provided a true education to students.[97] Spanish speakers wrote to Larrazolo in English and Spanish expressing their desire for bilingual schooling, especially a system that included better Spanish-language instruction, suggesting their goal was to maintain Spanish and not transition entirely to English.[98]

Other letter writers viewed Spanish as an immigrant or foreign language rather than a legacy of the American West. "Governor, we must Americanize all peoples coming into the United States, and this we cannot do to the best advantage, unless we see all persons learn the English language," wrote one opponent who failed to see *nuevomexicanos* as citizens but only as newcomers.[99] Another supporter of Americanization intimated that the nation as a whole demanded that students be taught only in English and that doing otherwise was "trying to foster a Mexican state in a Community of American states." He further explained that the use of Spanish placed the state's schools a century behind the rest of the country, fostered animosity between native Spanish speakers and Anglos, and harmed "American Teachers" who did not know Spanish.[100]

Many Spanish speakers supported English-language education efforts because they believed that familiarity with the language would increase their children's economic and political success. An editorial in the Spanish-language newspaper *El Independiente* supported the bilingual method but saw Spanish as a means to an end: "El inglés debe siempre llevar lugar preferente, primero por ser el idioma del gobierno y segundo por ser ya una necesidad absoluta para todo el que quiera adelantar en sus negocios" (English should always take the preferred place, first because it is the language of government and second because it is absolutely necessary for anyone who wants to advance in business).[101] Spanish-language newspapers published differing perspectives on the controversy over language of instruction. Editorial disagreements could be generational, partisan, or geographic.

The debate in New Mexico reached a head in March 1919, when the legislature accepted Larrazolo's proposal and required that teachers in rural school districts with a majority native Spanish-speaking student body be able to speak, write, and read both Spanish and English.[102] The law required "all branches of study" in English but permitted the use of Spanish translation for understanding and as a separate subject of reading. The State Board of Education in return clarified its stance on language in late April by explaining that aside from language as a subject of instruction, limited use of "foreign" languages (including Spanish) was allowed in New Mexican classrooms— casting all non-English languages as unwelcome. Ultimately, this decision supported the unenforced school code that had been in place since 1891 that required "all branches of learning taught in our schools be so taught in the English language." The board additionally declared that any child attending a private or boarding school conducted in a "foreign" language (including Spanish) where there was a possibility to attend a local school conducted in English would now be considered truant and their parents held accountable— a position analogous to what later occurred in Nebraska.[103]

As the state board released the new language resolutions in April 1919, it closed at least one private one-room school in Mesilla for teaching solely in Spanish. The board used clear arguments for Americanization when it praised the public school across the street from the "alien institution" that had been closed: "The Public School is standard. . . . The boys and girls . . . are being trained to become efficient citizens of the United States. In direct contrast to this is the other school which pays no attention whatever to courses, standards, etc., [and] leads away from rather than toward American citizenship."[104] The reasons for closure reflected nativist standards of citizenship and cleanliness that also precluded instruction in Spanish. Instead of creating segregated schools, complaints about insufficient Americanization in New Mexico resulted in integrated schools. The closure signaled the state's growing commitment to regulation and Americanization, though it did so in an altered form by continuing to permit Spanish as a subject for reading and to aid English-language reading. By November, the NMEA followed the board's view, pledging "one flag and one language for America."[105]

Even after these changes, however, geographic and fiduciary constraints limited the state's ability to enforce its English-only policies. State reports on classroom visits suggest that New Mexico's teachers continued to teach in Spanish as well as English and that the state had little capacity to prohibit the use of Spanish in the classroom. For example, L. Bell Reed, a truant officer and rural school supervisor, visited San Miguel County schools in 1920. Of the 109 public schools operating in the county, 101 had predominantly Spanish-speaking students. Reed primarily blamed teachers for the language gap between rural and urban students, commenting that "seventh grade Spanish-speaking children in the rural schools do not know as much spoken English as second grade Spanish-speaking children in the town schools where the teachers are required to use the English language while in the class room." She attacked the professionalism of older teachers and recommended that many rural teachers, whom she viewed as working with outdated and undeserved credentials, be dismissed. Even so, she recognized the difficulty of recruiting more adequately trained teachers in remote posts.[106] The state's regulatory board could only make recommendations after these sorts of visits; in practice, it very rarely shut down schools or replaced rural teachers.

In 1923, the state legislature centralized its school laws and moved away from local control. The 1923 school code strengthened teacher qualifications and adopted policies that allowed for a more universal statewide curriculum.[107] New Mexico's superintendent of public instruction explained that prior to 1923 "little attention was paid to the inspection and accrediting of state schools." It is not clear how effective the new system was for Spanish speakers.[108] After 1923, references to the Spanish language largely disappear from legislative accounts, not appearing again until the late 1930s. New Mexico continued to require that the assistant superintendent of public instruction be bilingual and that school laws be translated and printed in Spanish. In 1927, English became the only required language for publications and advertisements written by schools, but Spanish translations persisted in the requirement for "bonos de escuela" (school bonds).[109] The different requirements for translation may have stemmed from a generational gap in language acquisition: Most parents by this point could be expected to understand announcements in English, but older voters—taxpayers—still may have required voting announcements in Spanish. Local choice and necessity became the only criteria for providing parents with bilingual announcements.

These changes to state law suggest a larger shift in New Mexico that ignored the fact that rural students and teachers continued to enter school without English-language skills. Superintendents' reports from Taos and Bernalillo Counties in the 1930s described their student population as remaining overwhelmingly Spanish speaking.[110] Local variations in the curriculum continued to encourage teachers to use some Spanish in reaching these students. Teachers in these schools needed financial and curricular support to teach students English; in the absence of that support, schools would continue with ineffective English-language instruction. Advocates for the bilingual method like Adelina Otero-Warren (better known as Nina Otero-Warren), county superintendent of Santa Fe's public schools, found ways to incorporate some bilingual instruction in their programs during the late 1920s.[111]

Those New Mexican schools with the ability and resources to do so generally followed state policy and adopted English as the language of instruction in the lower grades. In New Mexico, the use of Spanish shifted in cultural value, as young students in English-only schools had little opportunity to learn their home language in school. Beginning in the 1920s, many students reported bans on Spanish even in the playgrounds, echoing the message heard throughout the rest of the Southwest that there was something wrong with their native language. Otero-Warren lamented the shift after a 1929 visit to a rural school. She wrote that when the students sang one song in Spanish, "their voices rang out with real feeling." She advocated for restoring pride in Spanish language and culture by using Spanish in the schools.[112]

New Mexico's approach to more stringent Americanization policies during the 1920s recognized the cultural capital that Spanish provided to the state's heritage, but only if students adopted English. Still, the rhetoric surrounding

Spanish differed from other parts of the Southwest. For example, a report that created a vocational education school within the Spanish-American Normal School noted "that the fact that they [students] speak Spanish is an asset for the Nation rather than a liability."[113] Concessions to the usefulness of Spanish by New Mexico's educators could not have come about without the lasting presence of *nuevomexicanos* who remained a political powerhouse in the counties of traditional Spanish-language settlement and advocated for less stringent English-only policies that incorporated Spanish at least as the language of students' culture. Many of the local, county, and state officeholders—including those who determined state educational policies—owed their positions to these rural monolingual Spanish-speaking voters. These elected officials could not survive politically if they were to paint Spanish as new to the region or as an immigrant language.

————————

School language policy in all four southwestern states mirrored the national mood of xenophobia and Americanization that rejected the presence of languages other than English in primary school education. Yet the degree to which these states adopted and implemented Americanization policies depended on local conditions. When a large immigrant community prevailed, Anglos perceived the language as radicalized, foreign, and other, giving them an excuse to segregate students or to monitor the behavior of Spanish-speaking laborers and unions. That was the case in California and in the mining regions of Arizona and Colorado but not in New Mexico or the predominantly Spanish-speaking areas of southern Arizona and Colorado, where fewer Mexican immigrants settled in the first decades of the twentieth century. With landowners and political leaders who spoke Spanish, these communities had a different understanding of the language's social and political worth. Not coincidentally, these same communities often possessed fewer financial resources to demand bilingual educational services.

New Mexicans followed a different path from the rest of the Southwest, as its leading citizens carefully sidestepped Americanization efforts by arguing for bilingual instruction. Despite these efforts, over time an increasing number of Anglo migrants led to the replacement of Spanish by English, particularly in urban communities. While state policy embraced more regulation by the 1920s, local conditions and individual preferences meant that many rural schools continued to retain Spanish as a reading subject.

Nuevomexicanos and supporters of their culture found a strong argument for retaining their linguistic heritage by looking beyond the borders of the United States. While not a new idea, the desire to link knowledge of the Spanish language to U.S. power in the western hemisphere increased in tandem with Americanization policies. New Mexicans argued their linguistic heritage and citizenship uniquely positioned them to help the nation realize its political and economic ambitions.

CHAPTER 8

Strategic Pan-Americanism

*Algun dia Nuevo México será honrado por no haber abandonado enteramente el idioma español.**

—*El Independiente,* October 27, 1910

Aprendase español . . . [e]n vez de tomar la actitud de que nuestro país es el maestro de este hemisferio y que los paises de la America del sur están inutilizados sin nuestra ayuda.†

—Bainbridge Colby, former secretary of state, quoted in *El Anunciador,* March 5, 1921

As much as advocates for Americanization argued that English opened the door to economic opportunity in the United States, they recognized that Spanish offered a tool necessary for infiltrating and establishing entrepreneurial projects in Latin America. The Americas held great economic potential for the United States—an argument in favor of fostering knowledge of Spanish. Some Californians recognized Latin America's economic promise as early as the late nineteenth century. "In the future it will be a popular question in this State to control the commerce of the vast populations which are to the south of us," a delegate at the 1879 California Constitutional Convention accurately predicted.[1]

This desire to foster friendly relations among American nations—particularly the kinds of relations that could bring economic and political benefits to

---

* "One day New Mexico will be honored for not having entirely abandoned the Spanish language."

† "Learn Spanish . . . [i]nstead of taking the attitude that our nation is the master of the hemisphere and that the South American countries are useless without our help."

the United States—came to be known as Pan-Americanism. Over the course of the twentieth century, the term also came to be associated with larger projects of hemispheric unification, from the Pan-American Conference and the Pan-American Union to the federally recognized Pan-American Day.[2] Celebrated on April 14 since 1931, Pan-American Day began with celebrations sponsored by Pan-American organizations in large cities like New York, Miami, Atlanta, and Los Angeles. The day united otherwise disparate groups interested in hemispheric relations.[3]

The scattershot focus of these different organizations meant advocates for Pan-Americanism held few goals in common aside from a commitment to furthering better relations with Latin America. Practically everyone involved, however, recognized the importance of proficiency in Spanish (and sometimes Portuguese) as a precondition for building relationships with Latin Americans, whatever the particular objectives. A focus on promoting and acquiring the Spanish language provided a major way to unify otherwise disparate groups that splintered around distinct economic, social, cultural, and political concerns. Pan-Americanism, with its obvious benefits to U.S. national goals, offered a strategy for Spanish speakers to push back against the forces of Americanization that often advocated English-only or English-language acquisition at the expense of Spanish-language knowledge. One would think that the nation's pundits and political leaders could not simultaneously praise Spanish for its benefits for hemispheric expansion and deride native Spanish-speaking citizens in the United States. And yet they did, thereby derailing their overall message of hemispheric unity and opening the door for stronger advocacy for Spanish-language instruction in the United States.[4]

Pan-Americanism increased the cultural capital of Spanish in the United States. The language had viable capital-producing power and promise. The new hemispheric interests of the United States catapulted Spanish beyond its long-standing importance to a single region's electoral and cultural politics. Familiarity with Spanish offered its speakers the possibility of increased global influence; it became impossible to achieve one's political and economic goals in Latin America without it. But the cultural meanings of Spanish changed only for those with the financial capital to take advantage of the opportunities. Acquiring Spanish for the purpose of Pan-Americanism was almost entirely a middle-class strategy.

Well-educated ethnic Mexicans capitalized on Spanish's new perceived worth by seeking opportunities for middle-class members of their own community in the form of patronage positions, cultural affirmations, or the establishment of U.S.-based cultural centers. Privy to the discussions in both Latin America and the United States concerning Pan-Americanism, they presented members of their communities as either U.S. citizens or Latin American citizens, depending on which strategy aided their cause. In the process, some distanced themselves from their U.S. citizenship and adopted a broader hemispheric outlook that they hoped would allow them to retain their linguistic cultural legacy. This chapter explores this ingenious strategy to use Pan-Americanism to extend Spanish-language use and instruction for Spanish speakers in the United States.

THE EMERGENCE OF PAN-AMERICANISM

The desire to forge unity across the American continent has a long history that predates Pan-Americanism or the Good Neighbor Policy. U.S. politicians' hemispheric ambitions stemmed from a combination of geopolitical fears of European influence in the Americas and economic interest in gaining access to natural resources and exploiting markets. The lofty proclamations of the budding nation in 1812—as stated in the ineffective Monroe Doctrine— exemplified this impulse. Portions of Latin America remained tantalizingly close to the nation's borders; as early as the mid-nineteenth century, the region drew the interest of Southern slaveholders and filibusterers who hoped to expand their domain.[5] With the U.S.-Mexican War exposing the military's inadequate language preparation, West Point cadets studied Spanish (in addition to French) during the period 1856–1914.[6] U.S.-led efforts in the 1880s to create a Pan-American conference led by the United States followed Latin American attempts, which began as early as the 1840s, to do the same. U.S.-led Pan-Americanism took root only after major Latin American nations affirmed the place of the United States in the discussion.[7]

U.S. hemispheric desires remained on the back burner for most of the second half of the nineteenth century, until 1898, when the end of the Spanish-American War presented the country with a major noncontiguous land grab. U.S. economic interests throughout Latin America grew exponentially; as one historian summarized the situation: "Americans had invested overseas $0.7 billion in 1897, $2.5 billion in 1908, and, by 1914, $3.5 billion. Nearly half of those amounts went into Latin America."[8] Ethnic Mexicans joined the larger national movement that, at the turn of the twentieth century, looked to Latin

America for resources and cheap labor opportunities. The United States could not dominate other countries' economies without understanding their language, politics, and business culture, creating further opportunities for exchange between the nations. Anglos increasingly traveled to Latin America for pleasure, business, or exchange, more often than not returning as converts to the idealism of Pan-Americanism.[9]

The 1916 Pan-American Congress, held in Washington, DC, fueled national interest in learning Spanish, primarily for economic gain. "Appreciating the practical profit that may be derived from a knowledge of Spanish," supporters encouraged universities to offer instruction in the language. As the *NMJE* reported, "Engineering schools are regularly insisting upon Spanish as an essential part of their curriculum." The University of New Mexico, for example, mandated that all engineering majors take Spanish as an entrance subject and then required an additional two years.[10] Spanish, characterized as a "weapon of commerce for Americans," aided the U.S. relationship with Latin America and was, as such, a "patriotic thing."[11]

The interest in learning Spanish as a language of opportunity led prominent private and public high schools and colleges to add it to the curriculum. By 1921 New York City's public schools taught more students Spanish than any other non-English language.[12] Spanish had a distinct advantage in this competition among the modern languages, since it was "the language of that part of the world in which our Government claims a traditional and exclusive political interest."[13] Universities and schools placed the importance of learning Spanish on a par with or above the other traditional language choices, French, German, Greek, and Latin. Spanish rose in national popularity while other languages—most prominently German—declined in the aftermath of World War I and its associated Americanization policies. In Los Angeles, the high schools offered many innovative programs in Spanish-language instruction to their largely Anglo students. For example, in 1911 the Los Angeles Polytechnic High School offered courses in traditional and commercial Spanish. The commercial class taught students to write and translate business forms and letters—presumably as preparation for jobs in Latin America.[14] With an estimated 29,000 ethnic Mexicans in the region in 1910, Los Angeles businesses had little need for Spanish until the huge wave of immigrants entered the city during the Mexican Revolution, though increasing numbers of Mexican immigrants did lead to segregated schools just a few years later.[15]

As one New Mexican wrote in 1921, the national interest in learning to speak Spanish was entirely new. Previously, Anglos had very little interest in "nuestra lengua" (our tongue); now the language was the preferred choice for preparing for careers.[16] High schools formed World Friendship Clubs, Spanish Clubs, and, later, Pan-American Clubs that sponsored events exposing students to Latin American culture.[17] Spanish American Clubs popped up in cities as unlikely as Birmingham, Alabama. According to an editorial in the *Southwestern Catholic*, the purpose of these clubs was "el estudio del idioma, costumbres y literatura española y además el cuidadoso estudio práctico de las relaciones comerciales e industrial" (the study of Spanish language, customs, and literature as well as the careful practical study of commercial and industrial relations). More pointedly, the editorial linked these efforts to "la formación de un sentimiento más amistoso entre los países sud americanos" (the formation of friendlier relations among South American countries).[18] Commercial opportunities and interest in Latin American politics and culture greatly expanded Spanish's profile in the United States.

The Pan-American movement increased the U.S. public's awareness of Latin American social and political issues in a way that had previously been unimaginable. For example, in California, Anglo allies of the Partido Liberal Mexicano (PLM) worked closely with party leaders to expose the Yucatan's slave conditions to English-speaking readers and advocated for the release of PLM leaders from prison.[19] The national press did not pick up PLM members' coverage of labor injustices in the United States, however.

New Mexico's Spanish-speaking citizens observed Pan-Americanism with interest, spotting an opportunity for leadership. After all, with its large native Spanish-speaking population and many bilingual Anglos who understood not only the language but also the culture, what better place than New Mexico to model larger hemispheric projects initiated in the United States?

NEW MEXICO'S PAN-AMERICANISM

The month after New Mexico's ratification as a state, the president of the University of New Mexico published an article extolling the Spanish language as an undervalued national resource. E. D. McQueen Gray argued that the majority of New Mexico's residents "have . . . an endowment the value of which has never been fully estimated." He regretted that Spanish speakers often underestimated this "valuable inheritance," as they held it in "small esteem" because of the condemnation of others. Gray criticized the United States more generally for its "indifference . . . to the importance of the gift of tongues," especially of Spanish, since "there is no foreign language which possesses so great a practical value for the American citizen as Spanish does." He connected Spanish with larger Pan-American interests by extolling "the connection between the Spanish-American citizen of New Mexico and his neighbors to the south."[20]

Between 1904 and 1910, U.S. trade with Latin America expanded to more than twelve times its previous rate, creating new economic markets that required individuals well versed in the hemisphere's major cultures and languages.[21] With the opening of the Panama Canal in 1914, one newspaper wrote of "un sin numero de oportunidades, de que se aprovecharán preferentemente los que hablen el idioma de los paises situados en el Pacífico y el Caribe" (innumerable opportunities, of which those who speak the language of the countries of the Pacific and the Caribbean will primarily reap the benefits).[22] Gray saw New Mexican citizens as the ideal candidates for these new jobs. The state had to "arouse herself and awaken to a realization of the advantage of her position." Like many citizens, he saw university instruction as the primary means to train state residents for new jobs in Latin America. He sought federal support by calling for a national endowment to fund a state "Spanish American College" that would teach Latin American language(s), culture, and history.[23]

Other prominent New Mexican citizens saw similar opportunities in Pan-Americanism for the state's native Spanish speakers. In 1915, New Mexico became a leader in Pan-American instruction when New Mexico State University (NMSU) established a school to prepare "young men for official and commercial employment in the southern republics." It planned to build on the linguistic skills that half of the matriculating students already had. Hoping to secure federal funding for the school, New Mexican educators appealed to the U.S. commissioner of education and attended a conference on "educational preparation for foreign service."[24] An article in the *NMJE* apprised readers of Spanish's new national status and commented on the demand for Spanish-language classes across the country, which could lead to job opportunities for competent Spanish teachers from New Mexico.[25]

Nuevomexicanos joined the call and spun their language capabilities as real national assets. New Mexicans should be skilled in both languages; after all, "en la América Latina no se dan buenos puestos al que DICE hablar inglés y español, sino al que EFECTIVAMENTE los habla" (In Latin America they do not give good posts to those who SAY they can speak English and Spanish but to those who can EFFECTIVELY speak both).[26] Others placed Spanish's usefulness firmly in the United States: "Ustedes tan bien como yo, saben que la lengua Española y la Inglesa son las más importantes en nuestro país y por lo tanto ambas debemos estudiar" (You know as well as I that Spanish and English are the most important languages in our country and therefore we must study both).[27] Promoters of Spanish instruction and use built programs based on both local and national desires.

Other educators hoped to use New Mexico's unique language environment to aid the nation by encouraging bilingualism for Anglo students. "Is there, for New Mexicans, anything of greater value than a knowledge of both Spanish and English?," asked former state superintendent Hiram Hadley. His 1918 article continued that New Mexico had two common languages; individuals would "possess greater commercial value" if they could respond to ads seeking bilingual employees. Hadley regretted not learning Spanish himself and felt that all Anglo students should be asked to learn the language, since increased bilingualism would greatly benefit New Mexico and aid the country's relations with Mexico.[28]

Nuevomexicanos rejected the notion of compulsory Spanish instruction for all New Mexicans as unrealistic and unwanted. Most parents preferred to choose their children's language instruction practices. As one person explained, "Eso de querer generalizar la enseñanza del idioma español en todo el estado no es sino una ridiculeza que traería inevitablemente el fracaso de todo el proyecto" (The desire to generalize that it is inevitable to teach the Spanish language to the whole state is not only ridiculous, but inevitably would bring failure to the whole project), which suggests a desire to protect bilingual instruction for native Spanish speakers at all costs.[29] While Anglo New Mexicans' interest in Spanish-language instruction increased during the late teens, they prioritized compulsory instruction in English. When the state board of education doubled down on English instruction in 1919, the action did not inspire public outcry from Anglos.

New Mexico was caught between dueling arguments for Americanization and Pan-Americanism that ultimately expected Americans to speak English, without an accent, before acquiring a language that would be useful to the nation's hemispheric goals. Spanish-language use symbolized global citizenship available to Anglos at the expense of native Spanish-speaking students. Despite the nation's acceptance of Spanish as an important "foreign" language to learn, few national commentators acknowledged the language's regional legacy in the Southwest. One editorial in New Mexico described states' new-found interest in promoting Spanish as embarrassing, given that New Mexico's own educational policies thwarted the retention of Spanish among those who could benefit from it the most, "la raza hispano-americana" (the Spanish American people).[30] Native Spanish speakers rarely questioned the importance of English but argued "que se enseñe el ídioma español en las escuelas públicas á la par que se enseñe el gran idioma del país el idioma Ingles" (that public schools teach Spanish on par with teaching the great language of this nation, the English language).[31]

Throughout the Southwest, language of instruction policies that separated English-language learners from native English speakers produced segregated classrooms. The Spanish-speaking students almost always ended up with inadequately trained teachers and inferior resources.[32] As the United States increasingly viewed Spanish as a language of Latin America rather than a language with roots in the U.S. Southwest, they ignored the presence of a growing number of Mexican immigrants who spoke the language on U.S. soil. Spanish continued to play a role in the contemporary United States, even within its borders, but Americanization campaigns and English-only education policies had distorted the language's larger history in the politics of place. This rejection of Spanish as part of the present-day reality of the country also ignored the acquisition of territories like Puerto Rico. "¿Es el español la lengua de los pocos, si tomamos en consideracion nuestras posesiones americanas?" (Is Spanish the language of the few, if we take into consideration our American possessions [territories]?), opined one writer.[33]

U.S. language policies in Puerto Rico laid bare the contradictions between Pan-Americans' desire to learn Spanish for use in Latin America and their resistance to non-English languages within the United States. Federal administrators in Puerto Rico sought to eradicate the Spanish language by implementing draconian school language policies that did not work because of insufficient instruction time and because Puerto Rican teachers pushed back against English-language instruction (though not the U.S. goal of creating literate and productive citizens).[34] The language of instruction policies changed according to the whims of each new superintendent of public instruction. Puerto Rican students attended schools that flip-flopped in their approach to language, never permitting a stable system of language instruction to take hold.[35] For most people in the United States, the Spanish language remained tied to Latin America and to some Latin American immigrants and visitors rather than to *puertorriqueños* or *nuevomexicanos*.

FORGING LINKS THROUGH THE SPANISH-LANGUAGE PRESS

The Southwest's Spanish-language newspapers provided a link between Spanish speakers in the United States and Latin America. As early as 1891, La Prensa Asociada Hispano-Americana (the Spanish American Associated Press) created a professional network of Spanish-language journalists across New Mexico, southern Colorado, and West Texas. These journalists often had long histories in the Southwest and covered local and national politics, among other topics of interest. The editors formed a strong organization that shared articles among themselves and worked with journalists in northern Mexico. These relationships permitted them greater access to both Mexican and Latin American articles.[36] La Prensa Asociada members then republished these articles for Spanish-language readers based in the United States.

In California, the Spanish-language press grew along with the population of Mexican immigrants. In the first decades of the twentieth century, political enemies of Porfirio Díaz's dictatorship relocated to the United States, as did other Mexicans searching for work in Arizona and California (Díaz's policies in the countryside had created widespread famine). Newspaper articles written by these exiles and immigrants reached an audience that preferred articles on Mexican affairs to those on U.S. elections or the local concerns of the native-born. Some of the newspapers, most famously the weekly *La Regeneración*, expressed sympathy for larger class conflicts, immigrant rights, and anarchism. The first major Los Angeles–based Spanish-language daily, *El Heraldo de México* (the Mexican Herald), which was first published in 1915 under the banner "Defensor de los mexicanos en E.U." (Defender of Mexicans in the United States), served Los Angeles's growing community of Mexican immigrants.[37]

Spanish-language newspapers from California to Texas encouraged greater communion between residents of the United States and Latin America, regardless of whether editors wrote for an immigrant or U.S. citizen reader. Both audiences used the newspapers to learn about Latin American culture and politics, which left them in a good position to claim stronger ties with Latin Americans. Conversely, the Spanish-language newspapers published in the United States provided an opportunity for Latin Americans to learn how the United States treated newly arriving Mexican immigrants and its Spanish-speaking citizens of long standing. For example, *Regeneración* included critiques of Porfirio Díaz and later about the revolution while also publishing articles that commented (often negatively) on the United States and its citizens' beliefs and discriminatory practices.[38]

There is other evidence that the Spanish-language press facilitated exchanges between Latin America and the Spanish-speaking population in the United States. *El Heraldo de México* announced the first meeting of El Congreso Panamericano de Periodistas (the Pan-American Congress of Journalists), to be held in Washington, DC, in April 1926.[39] Perhaps inspired by the unity among Spanish-speaking journalists, Los Angeles's Spanish-language journalists founded the Asociación de la Prensa Mexicana de California (California Mexican Press Association) a year later. Meeting in the offices of *El Malcriado* (the Ill-Mannered), seventeen journalists unanimously agreed to create the organization. After all, they argued, Spanish-language news was large enough to warrant an organization as the city now boasted "tres grandes diarios mexicanos" (three large Mexican dailies).[40] By reporting on the decision to form this organization, *El Heraldo de México* unmasked the "fatiga" (fatigue), "desvelos" (sleepless nights) and "cansancios apostólicos" (apostolic tiredness) that perpetually plagued journalists and that, it claimed, readers never considered when reading a newspaper. Together, the journalists created a mutual aid organization where they could share the difficulties of their work and specify improvements in working conditions they hoped to attain (e.g., life insurance, medical benefits, sick leave, and unemployment benefits).[41] Rather than claiming to be Californians, they saw themselves as Mexicans in "nuestra extensa colonia en el Estado de California" (our extensive colony in the state of California). In other words, they saw their communities as part of *México de afuera*.[42] (See figure 9.)

Ethnic Mexican journalists drew inspiration and support from an imagined international community of writers in Spanish. Future movie director and writer Armando Vargas de la Maza, president of the Asociación de la Prensa Mexicana de California, spoke of previously unsuccessful attempts to organize journalists in Mexico, but he believed that this union would succeed through international support. He quoted *La Prensa* (the Press) in Buenos Aires, which had called for Spanish-language journalists to "unificar el criterio de toda la prensa latino americana" (unify the entire Latin American press's canon), and he hoped to extend the campaign to Spanish-language journalists in the

FIGURE 9. *México de afuera*. A man walks past El Mundo Nuevo Café's bilingual signs on Main Street in Los Angeles, California [ca. 1937]. Herman Schultheis, Herman J. Schultheis Collection, Los Angeles Public Library.

United States "de una campaña en favor de nuestra América Española" (in a campaign in favor of our Spanish America). Their aims included destroying "montañas de prejuicios" (mountains of prejudice) to create "una visión perfecta de nuestra raza, aquí, en [los] Estados Unidos" (a perfect vision of our people, here, in the United States).[43] In essence, the journalists wanted to extend Pan-Americanism into the United States itself, thereby generating more respect and justice for its Latin American residents. By remaining tied to the Latin American press, California's Spanish-speaking journalists bridged the gap between the greater Mexican immigrant community and Pan-American efforts in the United States that often focused on the Latin American elite or U.S. elite concerns in Latin America.

The journalists' transparency about their working conditions served as a primer on labor activism for California's Spanish-speaking population. Readers likely already saw journalists as allies for their own labor struggles, since *El Heraldo de México* previously helped organize an association for workers.[44] With the help of the Spanish-language press, labor organization and activism grew throughout the U.S. Southwest during the late 1920s and early 1930s.[45] Literacy, specifically promoted in the Spanish-language press, served as a strategy to address larger systemic concerns in the Mexican American and Mexican immigrant community and, most important for my purpose here, opened a door to Latin America. These newspapers helped remind immigrants that their language provided a link to a larger *América española*.

As support for Pan-Americanism grew among Anglos, Spanish-speaking journalists sought to cultivate a more expansive view of the worth of Latin America and Latin Americans in the United States. Their efforts never reached fruition, however, because of the devastating effects of repatriation programs on Spanish-speaking communities. Between 1929 and 1934, local and federal agencies encouraged the repatriation of at least 350,000 Mexican immigrants and Americans of Mexican descent, destroying communities and generating a climate of fear. City officials in Los Angeles repatriated Mexican immigrants at a level far greater than that of other cities in the country.[46] By the late 1930s, the city's immigrant community had become a minority of the ethnic Mexican population. With a young population that was disproportionately targeted and arrested by the police in Los Angeles, leading to a perceived problem with juvenile delinquency, Mexican American community organizers once again turned strategically to Pan-Americanism in hopes of reversing the tide of negative perceptions of the ethnic Mexican community.[47]

CULTURA PANAMERICANA, INC.

¿Qué onda? Vamos a chanclear, ruca. ¡Orale pues, carnal! (What's happening? Let's dance, chick. Right on, brother!) Los Angeles's ethnic Mexican community had a new face in the early 1940s. As a result of repatriation, the rising second generation of ethnic Mexicans held a demographic majority for the first time since the nineteenth century.[48] Many of these ethnic Mexican teens embraced both a Mexican and an American identity and created a street culture, language, and way of dress that differed from the American or Mexican norm.[49] Between 1942 and 1943, Los Angeles newspapers—including the Spanish-language newspaper *La Opinión*—sensationalized the teens and their culture to such an extent that they directly contributed to the escalating tensions that led to the so-called Zoot Suit Riots in the summer of 1943.[50]

The parents of these young people criticized this emerging culture, including its use of language. Caló, the preferred dialect among these Mexican American youth, was a distinct "linguistic variety" that these self-identified *pachucos / pachucas* spoke in Southern California and across the Southwest.[51] The new *pochismos*—or borrowed words and slang from both Spanish and English—drew negative press both in the United States and in Mexico. Instead of recognizing that these young people had created a new and uniquely Mexican American culture, the acclaimed Mexican poet Octavio Paz criticized them as "instinctive rebels." He accused them of using a name of "uncertain derivation, saying nothing and saying everything. It is a strange word with no definitive meaning: or, to be more exact, it is charged like all popular creations with a diversity of meanings." He saw *pachucos* as "one of the extremes at which Mexicans can arrive."[52] Paz and Mexican American community activists blamed larger societal inequalities for *pachucos'* "deviant" culture. For example, the educator and community activist Victor M. Egas spoke of juvenile delinquency in the community as "the social evil we intend to cure." He explained that youth did not "try for a higher-up level of living" because they saw their situation as "irremediable," since they believed "North Americans are determined to keep them down in such a condition."[53] The anti-Mexican hysteria that grew in the years surrounding the war led middle-class Mexican Americans to come up with strategies that encouraged respectability rather than defiance.

Middle-class Mexican American activists searched for funding to support educational and recreational activities to benefit Mexican American youth, which they believed would alleviate the juvenile delinquent "problem."[54] In 1940, three U.S. citizens, Egas, Manuel Ruiz, an attorney, and Reynaldo Carreon, a physician, created a new organization, Cultura Panamericana, Inc. to draw Pan-American interests in Los Angeles toward the city's Mexican American community. They recruited other prominent middle-class native

Spanish-speaking community members and individuals connected to the Latin American consuls to join the organization.[55]

Egas, Ruiz, and Carreon immediately set about canvassing the country for donations and other forms of support.[56] They appealed specifically to the Los Angeles Chamber of Commerce, an organization supporting businessmen throughout the county. They expected to gain the support of national politicians and Latin American consuls, along with government agencies like the Office of the Coordinator of Inter-American Affairs (OCIAA), because of the national emphasis on hemispheric goals.[57] Their decision to use the word *Cultura* in the organization's name dovetailed nicely with larger federal and local inter-American interests. As Charles A. Thomson of the Division of Cultural Relations in the State Department explained to Egas, now Cultura Panamericana's president, his department sought "serious initiatives" that highlighted the "cultural achievements" of people from Latin America and the United States.[58] The organization, founded by politically involved and savvy Mexican American leaders, tailored its purpose and goals to align with the larger national impulse just as war loomed and Pan-Americanism took on new meaning.

Cultura Panamericana's proposals encouraged Spanish-language instruction for Mexican American youth and Pan-American supporters alike. Instead of incorporating language instruction into the formal classroom curriculum, the organization sought to initiate an after-school program to teach the Spanish language and Latin American culture to students. It also hoped to create a free circulating library to expose Spanish speakers to Spanish-language material. Planned as part of a "center of intellectual activity," the library would include books dealing with literature, politics, and economy. The center would also provide a space for Spanish speakers to come together, share their culture, and speak in Spanish.[59] The center's advocates believed it would instill cultural pride and broker a relationship between youth and educated professionals.[60] Using such politically relevant phrases in its incorporation documents as "American Continental solidarity" and the desire to "promote and stimulate interest in Inter-American culture," supporters of Cultura Panamericana bragged that their organization would help to "encourage and foster an interchange between the Republics of the Western Hemisphere."[61]

Cultura Panamericana attempted a new strategy to obtain support that painted Mexican American youth as Latin Americans rather than U.S. citizens. Unlike advocates for Spanish in New Mexico, the Los Angeles activists did not mention the positive role Spanish-speaking citizens would play in the growth of the nation. Instead, they spoke of these young people as Latin Americans whose lack of Spanish skills rendered their citizenship incomplete. Cultura Panamericana, Inc. appealed to Clarence H. Matson, a member of the Los Angeles Chamber of Commerce, for support. Matson, who had a long history of working with Mexican businessmen, received a letter from the organization written entirely in Spanish (even though its authors could write in English).[62] Carreon, Egas, and Ruiz spoke of how youth from "Hispano America" chose Los Angeles over Europe as the place to receive "la educación moderna" (modern education) but feared the return "a su tierra" (to their land) after years of living in the United States. Without Spanish-language skills, these youth could be branded as "hombres extraños" (foreign men)—putting them at a distinct disadvantage. Los Angeles's lack of a space for these youth to converse in Spanish set them up for failure in Latin America.[63] This appeal succeeded: in its letter of support, the chamber distinctly spoke of "an actual blood tie between citizenry of the Americas."[64] Cultura Panamericana gained some supporters by reassigning the youths' citizenship to Latin America, but the choice obscured the rightful identity of many of them as U.S. citizens. Activists appealed for funds by describing what amounted to a small percentage of the population, namely, the foreign-born youth of some financial means.

One strength of Cultura Panamericana's appeal was its focus on a concrete population in Los Angeles. With so much of the discussion on Pan-Americanism focusing on abstract values of fraternity and capitalism, the emphasis on Spanish speakers in Los Angeles captured the interest of the greater Pan-American community. The founder and president of the Beverly Hills Women's Democratic Club, Ila Dixon Buntz, wrote to Eleanor Roosevelt in early 1941 about her frustrations with traditional Pan-American groups. She criticized them as largely academic, providing only a "superficial exchange of courtesies by diplomatic specialists, social intercourse by academic intelligencia [sic], and the compiling of data by visiting researchists." Buntz concluded these tactics "lacked substance," but she held up Cultura Panamericana as a model for its "Latin-American" activists.[65]

Buntz supported the founders' efforts to create a Pan-American center in Los Angeles. She highlighted the dearth of Spanish-language material in a city with more Spanish speakers than the second-largest city in Mexico. She argued that disseminating Spanish-language material and radio broadcasts in Spanish would produce direct benefits for Pan-American relations locally, in contrast to the broader Pan-American movement's focus on conferences and reports for an abstract population. Buntz viewed the center's potential beneficiaries as citizens of both the United States and Latin America. She placed her confidence in Cultura Panamericana because its membership, and in particular its leadership, consisted of Latin Americans, a factor she believed explained its general appeal.[66]

As Buntz's letter suggested, Cultural Panamericana rapidly attracted members. In the months after its founding, it claimed 500 members; by March 1941, when Buntz wrote to Roosevelt, the organization could claim more than 1,000 members regularly attended its meetings. The organization boasted that prominent group members included all of the major Latin American consuls. Beyond meetings, the group reported upwards of 800 participants at its earliest cultural events.[67] In August 1940, Cultura Panamericana hosted an event featuring high-profile speakers that boasted 1,500 attendees. The solid turnout demonstrated the significant interest in the organization's efforts and the pull of its leaders (speakers included Manuel Muñoz, Colombian consul; Spanish writer Luis Careaga; and Juan B. Sacasa, former president of Nicaragua; and various cultural acts performed). Cultura Panamericana specifically encouraged local youth to attend its events. In a letter to the Los Angeles Board of Education, President Egas extended an invitation to students taking Spanish in public schools, along with prominent local families of Spanish-speaking origin.[68] The height of Cultura Panamericana's public exposure occurred in April 1941 when the organization sponsored a Pan-American celebration, which included a Spanish-language dialogue on *cultura* and high-profile attendees like Governor Culbert Olson and the Venezuelan consul, A. Posse Rivas.[69] The printed materials describing the performances and speeches delivered at Cultura Panamericana events all focus on linkages with Latin America itself. None of the surviving evidence suggests that the group ever referenced the place of Spanish or Mexican settlers in the U.S. Southwest's past, a strategy that contributed to the broader perception of Spanish speakers as tied to Latin America.

Cultura Panamericana's founders hoped to use national political and economic enthusiasm for Pan-Americanism to obtain support for the "Spanish-American element in Southern California."[70] Specifically, they hoped to change an international effort into a program that would benefit children who might have had no interest in Pan-American ideals. And, in fact, their strategy yielded some results. Their calls for a library, for instance, collected several

thousand books and magazines; the organization had to refuse further donations due to insufficient storage space. Each of the Latin American consuls
supported the effort and promised to collect books for the library from their
own governments.[71] Other potential supporters, however, pushed back at this
more community-oriented version of Pan-Americanism. One of the members
of the proposed library's board of directors—who was president of an unnamed
university library—agreed to support its creation if the books remained a part
of his university's private collection. Cultura Panamericana's organizers found
this stipulation discouraging, as they had hoped that the library would serve
the entire Spanish-speaking community regardless of educational attain-
ment.[72]

Faced with one potential roadblock, Cultura Panamericana's backers mar-
shaled different arguments on behalf of the cultural center. Egas contacted
Robert Neeb in the District Attorney's Office who was charged with coming
up with plans for crime prevention in Los Angeles. Cultura Panamericana
believed their cultural center deserved financial support because it could end
juvenile delinquency by offering a place where Mexican American youth could
be introduced to more educated Spanish speakers and lead to more "ambitions,
self-confidence, [and] self-respect." With the onset of war, they suggested that
a Pan-American cultural center would thwart the formation of Latin American fifth-column elements; they explained that taking care of Los Angeles's
Spanish-speaking community would demonstrate the nation's goodwill
toward Latin America.[73] These larger plans never materialized because of
constraints imposed by the war.

Cultura Panamericana's more limited programming focused on Spanish-
language instruction and Latin American culture. The organization recruited
and created the course list for a "Pan-American School" that hoped to teach
formal written Spanish to students who might have only known the vernacu-
lar at home.[74] Similar to language schools that Japanese immigrants created as
early as the 1890s in Hawaii, the school started off as an after-school program.[75]
Its initial curriculum focused on language learning and cultural subjects. The
listed language courses employed classrooms separated by ability. There
were separate afternoon courses for "North American Cadets" and "South
American Cadets," in addition to "adult" evening courses.[76] Prominent Latin
Americans—including Sacasa, former president of Nicaragua; Alejandro
Pardiñas, a Spanish modern painter; and Manuel Arrellano, a former professor
in Chile—joined Ruiz, Carreon, and Egas in proposing courses taught in

Spanish and Portuguese on Latin American art, literature, history, and language for adults.[77] Presumably, if those Ruiz and others hoped to serve, namely Mexican American youth, registered for these courses, exposure to these prominent individuals would prove inspirational for students who had few positive role models in local schools. Cultura Panamericana planned to host courses at the Black-Foxe Military Institute in Hollywood, but pressing war needs reallocated the space for war training courses instead.[78] Low enrollment for the proposed classes likely disappointed organizers more than lack of space. The organization received 548 responses to the 1,475 circulars it mailed to schools. Only twenty five people signed up for the courses by mail, though the circular elicited a lot of teachers who hoped to help.[79]

Ruiz's desire to set the record straight (in a 1977 memo) on the organization's original purpose to combat juvenile delinquency suggests that the organization veered far from his original goals.[80] Even if it failed as an intervention for Mexican American youth, Cultura Panamericana nevertheless helped to pool a broader disjointed network of groups interested in Pan-Americanism in Los Angeles. Having Mexican American founders with the cultural and social ability to navigate both American and Latin American business and political organizations made the difference. The organization effectively positioned Los Angeles as a key site of Latin American goodwill. As Cultura Panamericana explained, Los Angeles's large Spanish-speaking population drew visitors and served as "an important front door to the United States."[81] Language proved a safe starting point for uniting those interested in envisioning Los Angeles in this way.

Cultura Panamericana made a lasting mark in Los Angeles's Pan-American community by demonstrating broad support from the city's middle- and upper-class Latin American population for an intellectual center based on language and Pan-American ideals. This emphasis on "culture" and "intellectual activity" exposed the disconnect between how Los Angeles's Mexican community used Spanish in their day-to-day lives and how advocates for Pan-Americanism saw the language.[82] A quick anecdote shows how the use of Spanish had become denigrated in the city. Labor organizer Bert Corona wrote in his memoir about an occasion when while riding a bus he spoke to two Mexicans in Spanish, only to be ignored. Once off the bus, they told him, "Aquí no se habla español. Aquí es mejor que no crean que eres mexicano. Te tratan mejor. / Here it's best not to speak Spanish. It's best if they don't know you're Mexican. They treat you better." The sounds of Spanish pervaded the *colonias,* but bilingual workers code-switched to receive better treatment when they entered greater Los Angeles society. Coming from El Paso, where the use of Spanish was commonplace, Corona likely found this shocking; at the very least, he found it memorable.[83] In Los Angeles, where Spanish had been relegated to the barrios and the immigrant community, Cultura Panamericana offered an opportunity to reclaim Spanish as a language worthy of intellectual inquiry rather than as a marker of difference. By distributing books freely, Ruiz and others sought to promote the cultural and commercial relevance of Spanish to the rest of the city's ethnic Mexican community.

Among the last of Cultura Panamericana's activities were Pan-American Day festivities in 1942 and 1943.[84] The events, held on April 14 in both years, enjoyed a large civic commitment. In 1942 shouts of "Viva! Viva!" followed calls for unity in City Hall, while the University of Southern California hosted a conference sponsored by ninety-one associations and industrial organizations.[85] The 1943 festival had a more pronounced effect on Los Angeles's ethnic Mexican community, as it marked the opening of the Pan-American Trade School in East Los Angeles, where the majority of the city's ethnic Mexican population resided.[86] Rather than linking youth to an intellectual center, this school provided instruction in U.S. citizenship and the skills necessary to obtain blue-collar jobs.[87] Mearl Allen, a candidate for Los Angeles's city council, described the school's purpose as twofold. As the name suggested, one goal was to "promot[e] amity" with Latin America, and the other was to "promote and develop American ideals of democracy and liberty" as a protection against "Fascism."[88]

The Pan-American Trade School, in practice, served more as an extension of California's Americanization programs than as a true Pan-American endeavor. Even while Cultura Panamericana failed to gain the traction its leaders desired, its Pan-American strategy proved resilient. The call for inter-American unity and pressing wartime needs led other groups to use this strategy as an opportunity to benefit the Southwest's ethnic Mexican community.

———

A growing national interest in Pan-Americanism offered Spanish speakers a strategy to counteract discriminatory Americanization policies that had sought to quash seemingly un-American cultural practices, including speaking Spanish. In New Mexico, this meant drawing attention to the state's rich

Spanish-language heritage and what it could offer for the nation's hemispheric efforts. In the Southwest more broadly, ethnic Mexican journalists used their connections to Latin America to remind the Spanish-speaking community that they belonged to a culturally rich heritage that predominated south of the United States. For Mexican immigrants in the 1910s and 1920s, this connection was natural, as they were connected to Latin America by birth. By the early 1940s, Mexican American leaders shifted the focus of these efforts. By deemphasizing their citizenship and reemphasizing their connections to Latin America, the founders of Cultura Panamericana drew the interest of community and business leaders under the aegis of Pan-Americanism. While these leaders hoped above all to help the Mexican American community, particularly its youth, ultimately the language of Pan-Americanism best supported the economic elite and the intelligentsia—a population not originally targeted by the Mexican American activists who founded the organization.

World War II proved a turning point for the strategies that U.S.-based ethnic Mexicans used to obtain services for and opportunities in the Spanish language. During the war, organizations that had previously sought to connect with a broader civilian enthusiasm for Pan Americanism shifted their focus to securing the abundant federal war funds allocated to improve inter-American relations. Throughout the war, Spanish-language advocates in New Mexico and California continued to promote distinct local concerns, but they did so while seeking federal funding. The possibility of increased federal attention to the conditions of ethnic Mexicans in the United States encouraged activists in the Southwest to reclaim their U.S. citizenship, combat racial discrimination, and redouble their community organizing efforts. Meanwhile, many of them hoped that the time had finally come when the federal government would offer financial support for Spanish-language instruction in schools.

CHAPTER 9

The Federal Government Rediscovers Spanish

Que gane en todo lugar
Bandera Estados Unidos,
Emblema de Libertad
*Que nos tiene agradecidos.**

—Luis S. Martínez, "En las Islas filipinas," *corrido* honoring New Mexicans
   of the 200th Coast Artillery (1942)

In February 1944, Manuel Abeyta of Rio Arriba County, New Mexico, wrote to U.S. senator Dennis Chávez for news about his son, Gilbert, a prisoner of war in the Philippine Islands. Discouraged by news releases that called the captors "diablos ó inhumanos" (devils or inhuman), Abeyta informed his senator that he intended to buy $2,000 worth of war bonds "para que le den A McArthur Material para que No los traiga presto" (so that they give material to McArthur in order that he brings him [his son] back soon).[1] Gilbert Abeyta returned from the prison camps, but many other New Mexicans did not. *Nuevomexicanos* sacrificed their sons and limited cash reserves during the war, just like other Americans did, but many of them did so in Spanish. New Mexicans proved their patriotism to the nation in the most dire circumstances, even while they spoke, sang, and wrote in their ancestral tongue. For some of them, that ancestral tongue was Navajo: American Indian code talkers communicated some of the military's most sensitive information. The mountains of Los Alamos guarded the most closely held secret of all, the Manhattan Project.

---

* "Flag of the United States / Emblem of Liberty / May it wave in all places / Over a grateful people."

War can often lead to a criminalization of difference, but World War II had the opposite effect on the federal government's approach to the Spanish language. The federal government's interest in promoting Spanish and supporting Spanish speakers peaked during the war. This chapter discusses two of the most important federal agencies that developed Spanish-language initiatives for audiences in both the United States and Latin America: the Office of War Information (OWI) and the Office of the Coordinator of Inter-American Activities. With an abundance of funding and a varied approach to community outreach, OWI and OCIAA expanded the federal government's influence in the U.S. Southwest, creating new expectations of federal aid among Spanish-speaking communities. In the process, Spanish-speaking individuals in the army or otherwise involved in the war effort found themselves increasingly included under a broader vision of who was American. Native Spanish speakers throughout the Southwest promoted bilingualism as a nationally beneficial way to expand U.S. influence throughout the western hemisphere—a crucial component of the war.[2]

These and other federal agencies relied on ethnic Mexican organizers and educators to reach Spanish-speaking communities. Middle-class activists and educators proactively sought funding, created programs, and encouraged government recognition of the Southwest's assets, which included the Spanish language. The agencies' varied approaches to Spanish-language learning and outreach to the Spanish-speaking community differed depending on location—urban or rural—but also took into consideration whether a given community primarily consisted of treaty citizen families or more recent immigrants. Local activists in New Mexico and California sought federal support—particularly from OCIAA—to advance their own policies and agendas. Their contributions to local and national programs supported the needs of their home states' Spanish-speaking communities.

The war period allowed Spanish speakers in the United States to develop a new approach to civil rights that paralleled the Double V campaign of African Americans. Ethnic Mexican activists sought to fight for a double victory against fascism abroad and discrimination at home. The U.S. government resolved to foster programs that promoted greater understanding, tolerance, and acceptance of all its citizens, including those who spoke Spanish, even as it simultaneously interned more than a hundred thousand Japanese Americans. One of the greatest challenges for federal agencies like OCIAA and OWI was overcoming Anglos' racist views of the Spanish-speaking population. On occasion, these racial tensions broke through the surface, culminating in violence and riots that attracted international coverage and undermined the attempt by the United States to position itself as a beacon of freedom.

THE WARTIME STAKES OF CITIZENSHIP

By December 1941, when the United States entered World War II, years of xenophobia had branded non-English speakers or those with accents as un-American and unassimilated. With the outbreak of war, racism and discrimination against Spanish speakers posed a problem for the U.S. government, both because it needed access to workers' labor and because instances of injustice threatened to alienate potential allies in Latin America. Mexican American activists realized this. Activists both within and beyond U.S. borders highlighted instances of discrimination based on language as well as race.

Discrimination based on auditory cues has a long history but can be difficult for the historian to document. One act of language discrimination, however, became an international incident. In 1943, a diner in Texas refused to serve the daughter of a visiting dignitary from Mexico because she was speaking Spanish with a friend. Mexico's secretary of foreign affairs, Ezequiel Padilla, summed up the incident:

> Not even the families of our official representatives are safe from such persecution, or from unwarrantable molestation. Hardly a week ago, in the heart of an important city of the State of Texas, in a public establishment, they refused to serve the daughter of our Consul, just because they heard her speaking Spanish to another Mexican young lady she was with.[3]

This high-profile incident presumably mirrors the everyday experiences of Spanish speakers whose use of Spanish or English with a non-native accent made them not "sound" American.[4] In this case, Mexico's secretary of foreign affairs shared this story with Texas's governor, Coke Stevenson, to explain the discriminatory treatment experienced daily by Mexican nationals and to account for why Mexico would continue its ban on sending agricultural workers to Texas for the foreseeable future.[5] Mexico continued to send agricultural laborers to other parts of the United States. Soon thereafter, Texas proposed and passed a civil rights bill aimed at eliminating such discrimination.[6]

For help in addressing the situation of immigrant workers, Latin Americans in the United States turned to both private agencies and the U.S. government.

For example, the Pan-American Union had the well-known labor activist Ernesto Galarza check up on braceros throughout the country. Instead of reporting on working conditions and grievances (for which Galarza became famous), his letters on Pan-American Union stationery focused on the need for workers to receive Spanish-language reading and viewing material.[7] A binational agreement between the United States and Mexico in 1942 created the Bracero Program, which brought in Mexican workers at a rate of two hundred thousand per year.[8] Many braceros went to the Southwest, but others found themselves in regions unfamiliar to Mexican workers, where residents had no experience with or knowledge of the Spanish language or Mexican culture.

Employers turned to the federal government to help bridge the language gap. The OCIAA complied by releasing the popular *Guia de Inglés* (English Guide). The guide provided a lifeline for laborers who otherwise could not communicate with employers or the local community. OCIAA distributed upwards of fifty thousand copies of the guide to workers throughout the country and received "an extremely favorable reaction." "I believe [it] will be most useful to farm and railroad workers brought to the United States," claimed the Mexican ambassador, Francisco Castilla Najera.[9] Galarza, in his role as chief of the Pan-American Union's Division of Labor and Social Information, also endorsed the guide and recommended it to those contacting him for advice.[10] The guide proved popular on job sites; numerous companies complained that they ran out of copies. "We received only 400 copies of the Guide. We have about 3,200 Mexican Nationals employed on the lines of this Company, and our inability to furnish each one with a copy of the Guide is causing some disappointment," complained the Chicago, Burlington, & Quincy Railroad Company.[11] OCIAA approved a request for twenty thousand additional copies in 1944.[12] The agency found itself providing new materials for an ethnic worker population that had been present in the United States for decades but only received widespread support because of the war. The Spanish language served as an important tool for interacting with Latin Americans inside and outside the nation, but this realization remained in flux.

Even with these official statements and acts of support for Spanish speakers, the government continued to distrust the presence of "foreign" languages on U.S. soil. In a less extreme version of the double standard faced by Japanese American soldiers and their interned parents, Mexican American soldiers served in the U.S. Armed Forces while other branches of the federal government accused monolingual Spanish speakers of being fifth column elements. Both their inability to speak the English language and their geographic proximity to the border—"a potential breeding ground for disruptive Axis propaganda"—rendered them suspicious.[13] The Office of Strategic Services monitored the political activities of refugees and the response of resident aliens and citizens to their work.[14]

Lacking staff resources, the Office of Strategic Services turned to contacts in New Mexico for help. The organization employed University of New Mexico professor Dorothy Woodward as its Spanish-language eyes and ears in New Mexico. Her readers perused Spanish-language newspapers published in the Southwest for evidence of Spanish Republicans in Mexico City and for reports of activities on the Iberian Peninsula.[15] Woodward's discreet reports came out at the same time that the OCIAA published propaganda pamphlets that praised Spanish-speaking citizens for their loyalty to the United States and their willingness to serve.[16] She found little evidence of antiwar material in Spanish-language newspapers and concluded that the ten Spanish-language newspapers in Texas and New Mexico that she read reported primarily on local concerns and the Catholic Church.[17] The presence of these small community papers—an unlikely source for military intelligence—reminded the Inter-American Centers in the United States that portions of rural northern New Mexico and southern Texas had few bilingual residents and presented them as a minor threat to national security. The nation publicly recognized *nuevomexicanos* as loyal citizens, but internal reports worried that without education and economic opportunities they could easily be tempted by Axis sources.[18]

The Inter-American Centers must have deemed the federal government's educational efforts in the Southwest during this time insufficient. The federal government embarked on a massive cultural and educational project to improve relations nationally between English and Spanish speakers. One aim of the program was to demonstrate the patriotism and capabilities of loyal Spanish speakers by presenting them as equipped to handle more than just menial jobs.[19] Another was to distribute war news (especially positive war news) to what one federal agency referred to as "one of the largest unassimilated minority groups." With several million undocumented immigrants and citizens, the Spanish-speaking population ranked second only to Italians among the nation's residents who did not speak English.[20]

THE OFFICE OF WAR INFORMATION EN ESPAÑOL

"El Tio Samuel me llama al ejercito y me voy" (Uncle Sam Calls Me to the Army and I Go); "Niñas y señoritas, todas, luchan por la nación" (Girls and Misses, All, Fight for the Nation); "En Bataan nuestros muchachos su sangre derramaron" (In Bataan Our Boys Shed Their Blood); "Las orejas de Hitler son muy grandes, silencio" (Hitler's Ears Are Very Big, Silence): These *corrido* titles are some of OWI's lesser-known potential slogans. (See figure 10.) It was hoped that these songs, proposed by OWI's Foreign Language Division, would reach the far-flung Spanish-speaking population.[21] Most active between 1942 and 1943, the division worked to get the war message out in about thirty languages. It strove to boost the morale of foreign-born residents, inform them about available resources and war developments, encourage explicit information on their status in the country, and sell the war to those from Axis nations—especially Germans and Italians.[22] While not the OWI's major foreign-language focus, Spanish ranked among the division's top four targeted languages because of its wide usage in the U.S. Southwest. The OWI also hoped to bolster opinion in the United States against Francisco Franco in Spain and the synarchist movement in Mexico.

The Foreign Language Division delivered its message in feature stories, a weekly column, anecdotes from the home front, editorials, and a question-and-answer column for different language groups. The agency distributed these war updates through more than 150 Spanish-language newspapers and almost fifty Spanish-language radio stations.[23] It provided newspaper copy and encouraged papers to print war coverage specifically provided by the OWI.[24] OWI also sponsored a fifteen-minute weekly radio program released in German, Italian, Polish, and Spanish called *Uncle Sam Speaks*.[25] These regular releases represented only a small portion of the material aimed at Spanish speakers.

Californian Alan Cranston, who led the Foreign Language Division during this period, was particularly interested in Spanish speakers. He hired Ignacio L. López, editor of *El Espectador*, to reach out to the Spanish-speaking community with the nation's war news.[26] López suggested specific strategies tailored to the Spanish-speaking community such as recommending that the office publish patriotic *corridos* and partner with churches. He proactively reached out to various *alianzas* and grassroots organizations for their help in disseminating pamphlets and posters to their members. López also promoted

LUCHAMOS POR LA LIBERTAD DE TODOS

WE FIGHT FOR THE FREEDOM OF ALL.

Publicado por El Coordinador de Asuntos Interamericanos, Washington, E.U.A.

FIGURE 10. "We fight for the freedom of all." A World War II propaganda poster created by the Office of the Coordinator of Inter-American Affairs. Edward McKnight, Coordinador de Asuntos Inter-Americanos, Washington, DC. Photograph. Retrieved from the Library of Congress.

the use of trucks to reach far-flung areas with sound, film, and literature.[27] López kept the rural character of the Spanish-speaking population in mind, devising propaganda techniques that could reach people wherever they lived.[28]

By hiring López, the OWI benefited from the expertise of a Spanish-language media specialist who knew about the distinct approaches needed to serve a heterogeneous community. López developed different strategies for reaching two subgroups of Spanish speakers: those who identified themselves as Spanish and those who saw themselves as ethnic Mexicans. López categorized *nuevomexicanos*, along with those living in rural parts of Arizona, Colorado, and Texas as "Spanish," whereas Californians and urban dwellers in Arizona, Colorado, and Texas he deemed ethnic Mexicans. López explained that the two groups had little in common. Those with long-standing citizenship, the "Spanish," had little connection to Latin America, while those in the cities and California lived transnational lives.[29]

Cranston turned to prominent Los Angeles Mexican Americans like Manuel Ruiz, an attorney and one of the founders of Cultura Panamericana, for information on the situation on the ground. Cranston particularly hoped to use Ruiz to alert Spanish-speaking workers to war industry jobs. Ruiz praised Douglas Aircraft, for instance, for creating Spanish-language billboards but wanted Douglas to use the press and radio too. This relationship provided benefits to both parties, as Ruiz saw wartime work as a key tool for alleviating high unemployment rates in Los Angeles's ethnic Mexican population. He often identified language as the major point of disjunction between ethnic Mexicans and the larger population. For that reason, he did not look beyond language as a reason ethnic Mexicans were not hired for wartime jobs. Ruiz even admitted to Cranston that he chose not to ask about the breakdown of salaries of ethnic Mexican workers, which would have exposed racial or ethnic wage differentials. Ruiz believed it would be "inimical to objectives [of] integration" to interrogate wages.[30] He preferred to focus OWI's efforts on increasing Spanish-language media in Los Angeles in order to recruit more Spanish speakers from East Los Angeles *colonias* to the wartime industry.

OWI's effectiveness in reaching Spanish speakers led Cranston to accuse the other federal agency involved in Spanish-language work, the OCIAA, of abandoning its initial efforts to address the domestic Spanish-speaking population in favor of a hemispheric audience.[31] "It is far more logical," he wrote to Walter H. C. Laves, director of Inter-American Activities in the United States for the OCIAA, "for your office to combat discrimination and to carry out special projects designed to integrate Spanish-Americans more fully into American life." Cranston advocated that the agency carry out its work "in a way designed both to increase American unity and to increase good will between the Americas."[32] Cranston hoped to tap into OCIAA's core hemispheric interests to end discrimination and provide opportunities for Spanish speakers to assimilate, but he had little power to make it happen. OCIAA's sweeping efforts in the United States and Latin America would continue to focus on increasing hemispheric unity and understanding.

THE OFFICE OF THE COORDINATOR OF INTER-AMERICAN ACTIVITIES

President Franklin Delano Roosevelt recognized that the United States required improved relations with Latin America to ensure wartime national security and a strong postwar hemispheric position. The federal government created what became OCIAA in August 1940, with President Roosevelt appointing Nelson A. Rockefeller (whose family had major Latin American financial interests) as its head. The generously funded OCIAA oversaw a program of cultural diplomacy that spanned both North and South America.[33] OCIAA adopted various efforts initiated by the Pan-American movement and combined them into one dedicated government entity. Federal funding for inter-American affairs reached over a billion dollars by 1943, demonstrating the importance of hemispheric security to national defense.[34]

The OCIAA's earliest efforts emphasized hemispheric solidarity so citizens would "realize fully the interdependence of the Nations of the Western Hemisphere." Over the course of the war, OCIAA's purpose and structure would shift repeatedly as the organization responded to new needs and responsibilities.[35] Different divisions developed strategies for domestic and international audiences. The office's multiple international divisions originated programming that included education, health care, economics, and politics designed for audiences outside the United States.[36] The smaller Department of Inter-American Activities in the United States taught U.S. citizens about the language, culture, politics, history, and economy of other American countries.[37] While this program remained small compared to OCIAA's efforts in Latin America, OCIAA's outreach to Americans, especially those in the Southwest, had important implications for Spanish-language education in the United States.

In a 1942 report recounting OCIAA's focus, Nelson Rockefeller described the "four major fields of effort for the people of the United States" as being "popular education" for the American masses, teaching of Spanish and Portuguese, buying products of the Americas, and friendly interaction with visitors and Latin American organizations.[38] As Cranston suggested, OCIAA's early targets neglected Spanish-speaking citizens and immigrants already living in the United States.[39] A preliminary unit conducting this outreach disappeared early in the program's existence, as OCIAA believed other divisions could address the Spanish-speaking community's needs.[40] By responding to the project proposals from educators across the Southwest, the OCIAA moved toward programs that addressed inter-American culture and language alongside the goal of easing local tensions between Anglos and ethnic Mexicans.[41]

The funding and programs of the Department of Inter-American Activities in the United States dwarfed previous federal support for educational programs geared to Latin American culture, history, and the Spanish language.[42] The department worked with both governmental and private agencies as well as all forms of media to accomplish its mission. Importantly, OCIAA's efforts across the United States focused on local community needs. The OCIAA made the Southwest a particular target of its programs because of the poor relations found in the region between the English-speaking majority and the native Spanish-speaking minority.[43]

The Education and Teacher Aid Division spurred Spanish-language use in the United States more than any other federal efforts and benefited from long-running programs funded by private foundations like the General Education Board.[44] It trained teachers in inter-American issues, created and distributed pamphlets and teaching materials, and assisted in the teaching of Spanish and Portuguese. The division's efforts encompassed both far-reaching and local needs.[45] Division head Harold E. Davis wrote in the summer of 1943 that the division hoped to create workshops that would teach Spanish (and Portuguese) language and culture and English as a foreign language and determine important Latin American subjects for each grade level. While Davis saw these workshops as crucial, he identified "in some ways the most significant, and certainly the most distinctive group of workshops" as those dealing with the problems of educating Spanish-speaking communities.[46]

Educator activists in the Southwest quickly mobilized to alert Davis to the educational disparities that magnified the social and economic differences between Anglos and Spanish speakers. Mexican American students often attended segregated schools where districts allocated less funding, employed poorly trained teachers, and stocked inadequate supplies. Leaders throughout the Southwest sent an "almost universal complaint" to OCIAA explaining these differences in a proactive attempt to draw the federal agency's attention and funding.[47] These letters began to arrive as soon as they learned about the federal agency. Even before the OCIAA had officially opened shop in August 1941, educators from Las Vegas's New Mexico Highlands University (NMHU) contacted Rockefeller at the Council of Defense to explain why their particular educational program deserved funding.[48]

The OCIAA listened to these requests, and Davis and his staff began funding programs proposed by local universities. The OCIAA's Spanish-language educational programs represented one of the first cases of a federal agency responding to and respecting the benefits of bilingualism in the Southwest. When the OCIAA opened Spanish-language programs to all students, the desired outcomes extended beyond the classroom. While these programs appeared across the nation, those in New Mexico and Southern California stood out for the disproportionate amount of OCIAA funding and support they received.[49] As NMHU's early proposal in 1941 suggests, New Mexican educators proved particularly adept at securing program funding and led the way in creating curriculum, conferences, and support centers. New Mexico, largely through its own efforts, became a curricular and program development model.[50] A closer look at OCIAA's partnership with New Mexico reveals how the state's educators appealed to the agency to make the state the model for educational programing conducted in Spanish throughout the Southwest.

New Mexico

As longtime advocates for bilingual education, educators in New Mexico were eager to partner with the OCIAA. The OCIAA welcomed their enthusiasm, funding a series of educational conferences, lectures, and programs that featured the work of New Mexicans. The programs funded by OCIAA in New Mexico were wide-reaching and had multiple objectives that ranged from Spanish-language instruction to using intercultural education as a way to foster understanding and more positive relations between Anglos and ethnic Mexicans. These programs mostly targeted youth in a formal educational setting but also included informal educational techniques aimed at adults. They almost universally worked to combat discrimination against Spanish speakers either by teaching Anglos Spanish or by giving ethnic Mexicans the tools to "fit" into U.S. society. The explicit focus on combating discrimination in OCIAA's programs in New Mexico (and also in Texas and to some extent in Los Angeles) differed from the vast majority of OCIAA-sponsored programs, which focused on Spanish and its connection to improving Good Neighbor relations with Latin America.

The University of New Mexico (UNM) was very successful at securing grants, thanks in large part to the efforts of Professor Joaquin Ortega. As director of the newly formed School of Inter-American Affairs, Ortega believed that universal access to quality primary and secondary education and unity between Anglos and *nuevomexicanos* through greater understanding would offer the best protection against discrimination for Spanish speakers.[51] A native Spaniard from Ronda trained in commerce, Ortega came to New Mexico in 1941 after a couple of decades teaching Spanish at the University of Wisconsin. He spent his next ten years at UNM, first as director of the School of Inter-American Affairs and later as editor of the *New Mexico Quarterly*.[52] Ortega held up New Mexico as the model for Spanish-language instruction in the Southwest. He so successfully applied for workshop funding and appealed to OCIAA with such tenacity that OCIAA officials at times criticized what they perceived as his lavish funding requests. They believed he "set [his] sights higher than necessary for the really distinctive job which the University of New Mexico can do."[53]

UNM organized conferences that placed the state at the center of a larger national discussion about the best methods of educating native Spanish speakers. A symposium sponsored by the Bureau of Agricultural Economics and the U.S. Department of Agriculture demonstrates Ortega's success in gaining the interest of non–New Mexicans on this issue. Hosted in August 1942 by the School of Inter-American Affairs, the symposium addressed the difficulties facing native Spanish speakers in New Mexico's Rio Grande valley, "the closest link the United States has with Latin America." Following the conference, the UNM School of Inter-American Affairs published attendees' testimony in a pamphlet it used to solicit further funding and to draw attention to issues related to Spanish speakers' education. For example, the regional representative of the Bureau of Agricultural Economics isolated language as a key to the "problem of accommodating diverse cultural groups one to the other." He noted the "inadequacy of our public education system due to its failure to recognize the importance of this problem." Hugh G. Calkins of the U.S. Department of Agriculture noted his discovery that "racial discrimination and plain lack of understanding" "intensif[ied] the social and economic plight" of residents in the valley. Allan G. Harper of the Bureau of Indian Affairs wrote that he learned about "continuing discrimination in the distribution of school funds" for *nuevomexicano* children.[54]

The conference testimonials also advertised UNM's and New Mexico's contributions to these discussions. They praised UNM for taking the "extremely significant . . . step toward 'social consciousness,' which is so urgently needed in the Rio Grande Valley." New Mexico received accolades for its "wealth of Spanish-American background," which could be used "for developing future U.S. good will representatives for Latin America."[55] Other participants at the conference included progressive activists (e.g., journalist Carey McWilliams), educators (e.g., University of Texas professor George I. Sánchez and former Santa Fe County superintendent Nina Otero-Warren), and government officials (e.g., Carl F. Tacusch, head of the Division of Program Study and Discussion, Bureau of Agricultural Economics, U.S. Department of Agriculture, and director of the School for Rio Grande).[56] The presence of key figures interested in issues surrounding Spanish speakers and education points to how UNM worked to spread news of the social and economic problems of rural *nuevomexicano* children.

The university, along with NMHU, and OCIAA sponsored a second conference in Santa Fe in August 1943. This conference brought together a broad range of education experts from five southwestern states to begin drafting "an authoritative educational plan for Spanish-speaking minorities."[57] The ensuing reports, drafted with the intention that OCIAA would distribute them to educators across the country, detailed both future educational approaches and the current situation of bilingual students in each university in New Mexico.[58]

By 1945, OCIAA trusted Ortega's judgment nearly completely. The agency encouraged him to use the workshop he planned on language instruction to "prepare special materials for the teaching of Spanish to Spanish-speaking children[;] they will be useful not only in New Mexico but throughout the Southwest."[59] UNM had previously taken on this responsibility in 1944, when a research associate for the School of Inter-American Affairs, Lyle Saunders, prepared a bibliography on educating "Spanish American and Mexican children."[60]

OCIAA contracted UNM with tasks even though it was clear that Ortega would push the OCIAA to use its funds in the ways he deemed most useful for New Mexico's students and institutions, regardless of OCIAA opinions. For example, Ortega wrote to Olcott Deming in March 1943 to answer questions posed by OCIAA about speakers. Deming supported more funding for Ortega.[61] The conference in question would build on previous UNM conferences that dealt with "minority" problems or, more specifically, Spanish speakers in the United States, to look at social and economic problems in Latin America, especially in Mexico. Ortega responded to Deming's characterization of the program as "significant and courageous." He went on to offer an explicit critique of inter-American relations. The "Pollyanna picture of Latin-America is doing more harm than good," he argued. Ortega hoped to bring Ernesto Galarza to speak on the topic "Land and Labor Problems" and was pushing to move beyond just a policy of fostering general goodwill with Latin America.[62] In one letter to Ortega in December 1944, Davis tried to steer Ortega back toward Spanish-language instruction but, in general, demonstrated interest and did not bristle at Ortega's critiques.[63]

For programming designed for Spanish-speaking residents in rural parts of New Mexico, OCIAA often turned to NMHU, whose educators knew the population well.[64] NMHU's feeder population from San Miguel County remained over 80 percent Spanish speaking in 1943. In some ways, NMHU described a community where little had changed since the senators' visit in 1902; the English-speaking population confined most of its activities to East Las Vegas, while the Spanish-speaking citizens resided in West Las Vegas. Each town had its own board and mayor. West Las Vegas conducted both its private and public affairs in Spanish. The superintendents of surrounding San Miguel County schools often possessed only a cursory knowledge of English. San Miguel County schools conducted instruction in English as required by state law, but this did little to change the population's habits, since most children dropped out after a few years and returned to a Spanish-speaking society. The community remained segregated by discrimination as well. Educated bilingual *nuevomexicanos* could not work in the schools of northeastern New Mexico "no matter how brilliant their qualifications." The language enclaves were therefore imposed by broader structural discrimination that existed throughout New Mexico that left strong Spanish-speaking language communities but offered few options in the surrounding Anglo-dominated English-language society.[65] The educators at NMHU realized that addressing the needs of adults in San Miguel County and neighboring

Mora and Guadalupe Counties would require an alternative approach from UNM's curriculum- and policy-oriented efforts.

In 1943, educators at NMHU proposed and received funding for the *Institute of the Air*, an adult education radio program created by Spanish professor Antonio Rebolledo and English department chair Quincy Guy Burris. Instead of instructing listeners on culture and formal language training, the *Institute of the Air* broadcast Spanish-language segments that addressed health concerns, soil conservation, rights and responsibilities, and government aid agencies.[66] During the summer of 1943, OCIAA sponsored an intensive training workshop to prepare native Spanish-speaking teachers to lead discussion groups on the material that would be covered in the radio programs. To combat the challenges of transmitting and consuming radio broadcasts in such an isolated region, the institute opened listening centers where residents could gather to hear the thirty-six broadcasts and discuss what they had heard.[67] By November 1943, within two months of starting the program, twenty listening centers in San Miguel, Mora, and Guadalupe Counties claimed to have reached a thousand people.[68] OCIAA praised the practical nature of the information distributed via the *Institute of the Air* and encouraged adding English instruction.[69] By basing the program in the community, and training community leaders, the program helped break down discrimination by instructing rural residents on mainstream standards of U.S. citizenship and the closely connected topics of sanitation and health.[70] Burris hoped to eventually expand the program's offerings to formal English-language instruction for adults.[71]

UNM and NMHU, as well as the OCIAA, recognized that different educational approaches would be needed to address the varied needs of the region's native Spanish-speaking population. The Spanish-speaking population lived in rural and urban regions of the state and included children as well as adults. Some operated in a largely English-language world they did not understand, while others had very little need for the English language. New Mexico provided a great case study for OCIAA of the differences among the native Spanish-speaking community, and the varying social and economic challenges they faced. As NMHU's programs suggested, many of the Spanish-speaking citizens in the rural regions knew little about the resources the federal government had to offer. They had a different means of getting news and living their lives that rarely included consuming English-language mass media, but that made them no less U.S. citizens. If the government wanted to Americanize these Spanish-speaking residents, it would have to develop custom programs that could speak to them in their own language.

California

Both the OCIAA and its local partners recognized and hoped to address the simmering tensions between recent ethnic Mexicans and their Anglo neighbors. Whether through formal educational programs or other kinds of community outreach, the OCIAA's measures in California attempted to integrate ethnic Mexicans into their version of American life and, just as importantly, ensure their support for the war effort.

OCIAA officials criticized urban Spanish-language newspapers for their perceived dearth of news coverage. In November 1942, Walter Laves claimed that Los Angeles County's Spanish speakers had "wholly inadequate sources for information concerning the war of the United Nations." He singled out the Spanish-language press for the deficiency, but he ultimately blamed "the inadequate attention to the problem by the national government."[72] Given that the Spanish-language press in Los Angeles historically addressed a Mexican immigrant community, its lack of interest in war coverage in the first years of the war makes sense. This was a different situation from that in New Mexico, where the Spanish-language press served a readership of U.S. citizens deeply invested in national politics.

Anglo educators in the county proposed to address these supposed deficiencies through conferences and programs meant to alleviate conditions of educational disparity for ethnic Mexicans while simultaneously cultivating cultural tolerance and understanding of native Spanish speakers among Anglos. By 1941 the ethnic Mexicans made up 16 percent of enrolled students in Los Angeles County public schools. The vast majority of California's ethnic Mexicans lived in the southern portion of the state, with the largest cluster in Los Angeles County.[73] In July 1943 the superintendent of Los Angeles Schools and the County Board of Education sponsored a workshop supported by the OCIAA that addressed the educational needs of "Mexican and Spanish-speaking pupils," including providing basic conversational Spanish instruction to teachers who would be meeting Spanish-speaking parents and students.[74] Organizers encouraged schools to adopt a new curriculum and improve teaching strategies to address student language needs. Harold Davis, in an OCIAA article he sent to Los Angeles–based Cultura Panamericana, called the program "in some ways the most significant, and certainly the most distinctive," of the four workshops OCIAA sponsored for teachers that summer. Seven such workshops were planned for the next summer in New Mexico, Arizona, Colorado, Texas, and Southern California.[75]

OCIAA remained a partner in local efforts to improve teaching of Spanish-speaking students. Superintendent C. C. Trillingham hired Marie Hughes, a curriculum coordinator and educational specialist with previous experience in New Mexico's experimental schools, as a curriculum leader with half of her time devoted to the native Spanish-speaking community.[76] Hughes faced the impossible task of solving on a half-time basis the educational disparities that beset ethnic Mexican students, including English-language deficiency for some and segregation for most. For that reason, she reached out to OCIAA to convey the growing "interest in Southern California pertaining to the problems of the Spanish-speaking people." Hughes expressed her interest in sending her "needs and plans" to the OCIAA for support.[77]

In nearby San Dimas, a summer-long program cosponsored by OCIAA and Claremont College in 1943 focused on intercultural understanding through language learning.[78] Claremont's sponsor, Elias Tipton, hoped the program would provide evidence for the claim that desegregating schools would aid the English-language learning of native Spanish-speaking students and at the same time promote bilingualism for all students.[79] The experimental summer program included a morning program for children and an adult program for Mexican nationals. This program grew out of a broader adult community language program that taught Spanish to Anglos and English to Mexican immigrants. The adult evening classes were described as transferring the language "*barrier*" into a language "*bridge* over which understanding and intercultural appreciation can flow." The successful exchanges among participants led to the creation of an Americans All Club that sponsored the creation of the summer program.[80] The summer program, taught largely by former Americanization teachers, was deemed a success by the San Dimas Community Council. As one example of the change in students' opinion, the report described how Anglo participants called all participants "fellow Americans" by the end of the summer rather than drawing distinctions between themselves and "those Mexicans."[81] This program promoted bilingualism and language exposure as one of the keys to intercultural understanding.

The summer educational programs took place in a decidedly tense atmosphere. The "Zoot Suit Riots" of 1943 erupted in Los Angeles in early June, leaving in their wake a new desire among public officials and activists alike to address the social conditions that produced high rates of juvenile delinquency among Mexican American youth. The city's newfound recognition of the barrio's problems presented an opportunity for Mexican American community activists to voice their concerns.[82]

The OCIAA appeared poorly equipped to handle the increased scrutiny, exposure, and urgency of finding a resolution to the city's race relations. The task fell to the OCIAA's local advisory board, which in Los Angeles County took the form of the Southern California Council of Inter-American Affairs (SCCIAA). The board's Anglo-dominated membership included Los Angeles County supervisor John Anson Ford, Los Angeles mayor Bowron Fletcher, and mining engineer Harvey Mudd, among others. Led by its executive secretary, Raymond McKelvey, the SCCIAA devoted its regional efforts almost exclusively to hemispheric relations. The council preferred not to get involved with desegregation campaigns or any efforts to eliminate discriminatory practices. McKelvey explained—six months after the riots—to Manuel Ruiz that the board required firm examples and specific cases that could win in the courts before they would become involved.[83] Ignacio López, who worked for SCCIAA, offered his resignation after allegedly using SCCIAA letterhead to protest police brutality. Victor Borella, director of the Division of Inter-American Activities in the United States at the time, accepted López's resignation. Borella accused López of going too far and reasserted OCIAA's concern about "the problem with Spanish speaking people."[84] As Harry Braverman of Los Angeles's Decorative Fabric Company wrote to Alan Cranston at the OWI, McKelvey "knows about as much about the local Mexican problem as my infant daughter." SCCIAA largely followed McKelvey's lead, which steered them to focus more on language than larger racial issues and gave Mexican American leaders few opportunities to shape the direction of the organization.[85]

SCCIAA's board was not alone in singling out the language gap as a reason for ethnic or racial tensions. The municipal government and local Spanish-speaking leaders joined the board in identifying it as an important place to make change in the Los Angeles landscape. For example, in June 1943, the board supported raises and bonuses for public employees who worked with Spanish-speaking communities and mastered the language, and also encouraged in-service training programs.[86] In July 1944, the SCCIAA board advocated for placing bilingual English-Spanish signs in the train depots of Los

Angeles and encouraged the hiring of civic and public service leaders who could speak Spanish.[87] The newly formed Coordinating Council on Latin American Youth expanded its support for Spanish-speaking employees to police officers and attorneys, as well as state, local, and national officials.[88] They also hoped for more PTA meetings and programs in Spanish for parents.[89]

For the SCCIAA and Mexican American activists alike, language difficulties emerged as a concrete, solvable problem amid the many challenges facing the Mexican American community. Consider an explanation for juvenile delinquency offered by Manuel Ruiz in December 1942. Ruiz argued in an article published in *Crime Prevention Digest* that ethnic Mexican parents, who could not access adult education courses offered in English on hygiene, citizenship, and civics, could never understand the world their Americanized children inhabited. He also faulted the home environment of many Spanish-speaking families, noting that youths' limited exposure to the English language left them with accents that put them at a social and economic disadvantage and therefore more at risk for juvenile delinquency.[90] By focusing on language, Ruiz downplayed the larger socioeconomic factors that led to juvenile delinquency. Marking language as the culprit offered a "fixable" ethnic difference rather than a racial one, which ran deeper. Ruiz's and like-minded SCCIAA members' focus on language gave less weight to the larger systemic problems—economic and racial—that divided ethnic Mexicans from the Anglo Los Angeles community in favor of educational improvement and opportunity. Thirty years later, Ruiz himself acknowledged his tunnel vision, reflecting that his perspective "entirely omitted making reference to those Mexican Americans who had resided in California for many generations who found themselves in the same dilemma, even though possessed of English language skills."[91]

Whether long-standing citizens or new immigrants, California's ethnic Mexicans found themselves in similar straits. While Ruiz may have overestimated the importance of language at the time, his choice to highlight language as the major distinction between Anglos and Mexican Americans is significant. Los Angeles's newly emergent Mexican American political leadership could make community-specific demands, but they focused on ethnic, rather than racial, differences that would attract more positive attention and resources. They made these appeals while speaking English eloquently and persuasively. English-language ability, middle-class status, and citizenship opened up a space in which Los Angeles's Mexican American political leaders argued for recognition, support, and respectability on behalf of those who lacked the language skills to navigate an English-language leadership structure. SCCIAA made Ruiz a board member in January 1944, and in this position he asserted his goal of fully integrating Mexican Americans into society.[92]

During this time, OCIAA's national leadership singled out Los Angeles for attention, in large part because of the riots in the summer of 1943. By fall, OCIAA had shipped an initial twenty thousand copies of a bilingual pamphlet titled *Spanish Speaking Americans in the War* to the SCCIAA for distribution to community members.[93] The pamphlet included pages on agricultural workers and on New Mexico's long-standing citizens and more generally emphasized the patriotism and loyalty of the native Spanish-speaking population.[94] It sought to improve intercultural relations. The fact that it was bilingual was significant. Anglos who read it would see a bilingual pamphlet sponsored by the federal government. Monoglots or bilingual residents could both read it. Maurice Hazan, SCCIAA's field representative, sent the majority of these pamphlets to junior high schools and high schools.[95] With distribution centered in counties where many Mexican Americans resided, the effort encouraged Anglos to take pride in the war service of their Spanish-speaking neighbors—a lesson that needed reinforcement in the post–"Zoot Suit Riots" period.[96]

Spanish-speaking scholars and political activists in New Mexico and California used the federal government's new interest in hemispheric unity to support preexisting goals for their own communities. These included combating segregation and discriminatory practices and creating programs to counter the negative opinions of teachers, administrators, and the larger Anglo community of Spanish speakers in regions guilty of chronic educational neglect. While university professors and grassroots organizers may have had differences over tactics, they collectively told the federal government that the vast Spanish-speaking community of the United States deserved and expected to be addressed in a language they understood. OCIAA and OWI provided channels for Spanish speakers to relay their concerns; to a certain extent, the agencies' funding decisions indicates a respect for these communities' needs.

Both OWI and OCIAA encouraged the federal government to invest in programs that benefited native Spanish speakers in the Southwest. This exposure to federal programs and agencies in turn changed the Spanish-speaking community's relationship to the federal government. But the war's end in 1945 left the future of these programs unclear. Federal support for Spanish-language programs in the Southwest ultimately proved short-lived, drying up by 1945. While the wartime programs encouraged the use of Spanish as propaganda throughout Latin America, other federal initiatives hardened a view of English as the language of the nation by surveilling Spanish speakers as possible subversives.

Still, the federal government's public support for increasing the use of Spanish within U.S. borders produced concrete results. During the war, Spanish surpassed French in college enrollments for language study. Over 82,600 (largely Anglo) college students studied Spanish in 1942 alone, in part due to federal funding that supported the expansion of Spanish as a modern language.[97] These programs supported the nation's bid to promote better relations with Latin America. One of the more famous students of the Spanish language, Vice President Henry Wallace, took his lessons from "a New Mexican boy, Joseph Apodaca"—a point of great pride in the state.[98] The institutional support and personal embrace of figures like Wallace helped increase the national visibility and acceptance of Spanish during the war period, even as countervailing forces opposed the continuing presence of Spanish as a language of instruction in Puerto Rico and New Mexico.

CHAPTER 10

Competing Nationalisms

Puerto Rico and New Mexico

El uso del castellano era el único medio de conservar la cultura y tradiciones de Puerto Rico.*

—Summary of F. J. Richardson's testimony, *La Prensa*, February 21, 1943

WHEREAS, in the present unsettled condition of the world affairs it is essential, . . . that our citizenship acquire a thorough knowledge of the Spanish language.

—1941 N.M. Laws 517–8

In 1942, the U.S. Senate possessed a single native Spanish speaker, Dennis Chávez of New Mexico. Born a U.S. citizen in 1888 to monolingual Spanish-speaking parents in Los Chaves in New Mexico Territory, Chávez's language skills and cultural background made him an important player in the U.S. government's wartime bid for Latin American alliances. In 1942, for example, he traveled to Mexico City at the behest of Nelson Rockefeller, head of OCIAA, and later met Latin American dignitaries when they visited Washington, DC.[1] Chávez attempted to leverage the federal government's newfound interest in the Spanish language for the good of his constituents. "*Our* role in New Mexico seems to be naturally cut out for *us*. We must *use* the priceless gift of the Spanish language which God has given *us* in the *cause of National and Hemispheric Defense*," Chávez proclaimed.[2] But Chávez was not arguing for New Mexico's return to a culture dominated by Spanish. Instead, he saw

---

*"The use of Spanish was the only way to conserve the culture and traditions of Puerto Rico."

instruction in English as the priority for students in his state and in Puerto Rico. Spanish held a singular place among modern languages in the United States, but it remained "foreign" nonetheless.

The politics of how and what languages should be taught in schools, especially primary schools, offers insight into the relationship between language and citizenship in the United States. This chapter explores the divergent stories of educational language policy in New Mexico and Puerto Rico, two areas that retained monolingual Spanish speakers well after their incorporation into U.S. territory. Despite their geographic distance from one another, Puerto Rico and New Mexico have many historical similarities. Both experienced (and one continues to experience) a prolonged territorial period during which the federal government proffered U.S. citizenship status to residents— New Mexicans with the Treaty of Guadalupe Hidalgo in 1848 and Puerto Rico through the Jones Act of 1917—without giving those citizens full control of their affairs. This status separated New Mexicans and Puerto Ricans from the vast majority of noncitizen Spanish speakers in the United States, most of whom were immigrants from Mexico. The educational systems in both locations was spotty and inadequate, the victim of perpetual funding shortages and U.S. government control.[3] Both retained Spanish in all aspects of life during their first forty years as U.S. territories.

New Mexico's ascent to statehood in 1912 set Spanish speakers in New Mexico and Puerto Rico on different paths. Even though the state's school code was enforced unevenly, the state legislature's decision to endorse English as the language of instruction for primary schools in 1919 meant a rapid decline in the number of monolingual Spanish speakers. By the 1940s—thirty years after statehood—New Mexico's government and schools primarily operated in English. Still, the state's long-held political commitments to Spanish speakers thwarted a linear loss of Spanish in the state. New Mexico became an important model of bilingual education at the most basic level—teaching a second language in the primary grades. As a state, New Mexico had the sovereignty to determine its own school code and agenda, and its legislature had the power to tax its citizens to fund the schools. The state's political and educational leaders lobbied for support for bilingual education even while seeking national recognition of New Mexico's potential contribution to the nation's hemispheric goals.[4]

A different path emerged in the territory of Puerto Rico, where locals' efforts to retain Spanish-language schools in the face of intense resistance from the U.S. government contributed to a stronger sense of national identity on the island.[5] After four decades of U.S. influence, mainland native English speakers made up less than 4 percent of Puerto Rico's population, educational funding was sparse, and few Puerto Ricans supported statehood.[6] Puerto Rico's commissioner of education was appointed by the U.S. president, which made local rule less feasible. The presidentially appointed governors did not always consider the preferences of *puertorriqueños*, but neither did *puertorriqueño* teachers and administrators always implement the government's demands.[7]

Both New Mexico and Puerto Rico revisited the role of Spanish in children's education in the 1940s, a period of heightened national interest in the relationship between language and citizenship. In 1941, legislators in New Mexico considered a bill that mandated Spanish-language instruction in primary school classrooms. The pedagogical debates surrounding the bill reveal how the role of Spanish had changed in New Mexico and expose divisions among the native Spanish-speaking population. In 1943, a group of U.S. senators held a series of hearings in Puerto Rico—similar to the 1902 Beveridge hearings—that focused on the island's social and economic conditions but in actuality had a lot to say about the use of Spanish. To understand why these nearly simultaneous discussions produced such different outcomes, the remainder of this chapter offers detailed case studies of the role of Spanish-language instruction in New Mexico and Puerto Rico in the mid-twentieth century. New Mexicans ultimately positioned themselves as U.S. citizens whose ties to Pan-Americanism would aid the nation, whereas Puerto Ricans claimed Spanish-language instruction as a non-negotiable aspect of island identity.

A BILINGUAL FUTURE IN NEW MEXICO

As the leader of the Senate Subcommittee on Territories and Insular Affairs and the senior senator from New Mexico, Dennis Chávez provides the link between Puerto Rico and New Mexico and their sanctioned language policies. Chávez remembered being "in the third grade before I learned to speak English."[8] Although he found his lack of English hindered him in school, his fluency in Spanish facilitated his entrance into politics. Chávez began his career as a court interpreter; in 1911 he interpreted the elected governor's speeches for Spanish-speaking crowds.[9] Even so, Chávez was an early proponent of English-only educational policies. A largely unknown Chávez entered the political fray in 1919 by opposing Governor Octaviano Larrazolo's support for bilingual education. He proclaimed that "a nuestra juventud no debe enseñarsele sino la lengua americana" (our youth should not be taught any but the American language).[10] While Chávez altered his views after 1919, his early support for English-only instruction became typical of New Mexicans in the 1920s.

Chávez's appointment to the Senate in 1935 came during a period of renewed public interest in Spanish-language instruction. Just five years earlier, Santa Fe's county superintendent of public schools, Nina Otero-Warren, had hoped to secure a grant from the Rockefeller Foundation to "preserve the Spanish-American people and their culture."[11] Otero-Warren tied language to cultural identity to argue that New Mexican children could be educated best through the "beauty and charm" of their native Spanish language. She believed that bilingual education would provide an escape from the "fate of all small Colonial Groups" whose vocational options were limited due to their inability to speak the dominant language well and whose cultural identity was erased by a curriculum that omitted any substantive discussion of their culture, art, or literature. Educators' efforts to reintroduce Spanish to New Mexican classrooms came at precisely the same moment that nativists throughout the country focused on other forms of education that emphasized an "English-first" mentality.[12] In a move that recognized the importance of English-language instruction but also valued Spanish, Otero-Warren and others advocated for their mother tongue as a cultural gift to the nation.

During the 1930s, other New Mexican educators had joined Otero-Warren in a broader movement to return Spanish to New Mexico schools. Lloyd Tireman, an educator with a strong belief in the benefits of bilingual education, set up a "laboratory school" in San José, New Mexico, in 1930 to bring a bilingual curriculum to students in New Mexico. The University of New Mexico offered him the institutional support to create these schools. But while Tireman's experimental schools in San José and, later, Nambé were the best known of these experiments in Spanish-language instruction, they served a minuscule number of *nuevomexicano* students.[13] The need for more language-sensitive curricular policies in the state was vast. In Taos County, 70 miles northeast of Santa Fe, the county schools enrolled some 3,500 students, fewer than 3 percent of whom spoke English. The teachers' association fully embraced the benefits of bilingual instruction. Taos County supervisor Ruth Miller

Martínez justified bilingual education using familiar pedagogical arguments from 1919 but with an added layer of Pan-Americanism. New Mexico was in an "ideal situation" to support successful Spanish teaching due to its history, geographic location, and linguistic opportunities, she said. She deemed Spanish the "language of the Americas" and rejected the state's existing educational policy, which officially dismissed Spanish, in favor of a Spanish-first policy that positioned *English* as a foreign language until students learned the basics of reading and writing.[14]

Martínez and other Taos County educators advocated for statewide educational language policies that embraced Spanish, but their position stopped short of favoring Spanish over English. At the 1938 annual meeting of the Taos County Teachers Association (TCTA), members adopted five resolutions relating to language.[15] These resolutions departed from Otero-Warren's 1929 stance: "The first and most important step in the education of these children is . . . the learning of English."[16] Even so, the TCTA recognized the reality of a Spanish-speaking student population and therefore endorsed better teaching strategies that would leave students with a strong base in both Spanish and English. The TCTA's resolutions called for teachers statewide to prove their bilingual proficiency. Members recognized the lack of sound instructional practices regarding bilingual education; for that reason, they wanted to see additional experimental schools in the county to develop "the bilingual method" and requested that the state universities add teacher education courses in both languages. A final resolution suggested that "all Curriculum Revision Committees in the State of New Mexico" consider the possibility of teaching Spanish by the start of third or fourth grade.[17] By calling for bilingual instruction statewide, the TCTA encouraged a broader shift in the way New Mexicans viewed and taught Spanish.

These discussions took place at a moment when the state's official educational policies increasingly emphasized the importance of an English-only approach. Few state educators had previously supported teaching Spanish-language courses outside of high school. Since few native Spanish-speaking students ever reached high school, most had little opportunity to learn the formal mechanics of their native tongue. Many New Mexicans in positions of power simply saw Spanish as unimportant for the economic and social future of students, and they refused to acknowledge how their policies affected monolingual Spanish speakers. These English-only requirements left native Spanish speakers uncertain not only about the place of Spanish in classrooms but also about their place in U.S. society.[18]

Under pressure from both the state's teachers and the broader Pan-Americanism movement, New Mexico legislators began to reconsider its opposition to Spanish-language instruction in 1941. The previous year, Governor John E. Miles recommended the gradual implementation of Spanish courses in New Mexico's grade schools; the state teachers' convention, meanwhile, endorsed Spanish instruction starting in the seventh grade.[19] The Spanish section of the New Mexico Education Association (NMEA) resolved to support compulsory Spanish classes in elementary schools.[20] At the 1940 annual conference of the American Association of Teachers of Spanish and Portuguese in Albuquerque, Secretary of State Cordell Hull sent a message of "Pan-American cultural unity." Beyond New Mexico, the secretary of the National Defense Council, a nonprofit foundation, emphasized Spanish-language instruction throughout the country as "a part of the national defense" effort. Similarly, L. S. Rowe, director general of the Pan-American Union, tasked U.S. Spanish teachers with improving hemispheric relations. These instructors carried the "burden of creating 'a better appreciation'" of the contributions of Latin America.[21] For very different reasons, Spanish-language instruction was gaining defenders from different sectors of society.

In this optimistic climate, state senators Joseph M. Montoya and Ralph Gallegos in January 1941 proposed Senate Bill 3 (S.B. 3), which would require Spanish instruction for all students in the fifth through eighth grade. Born in the tiny northern town of Peña Blanca in Sandoval County in 1915, Montoya joined the state legislature in his early twenties, quickly becoming the majority floor leader in 1939. He became a state senator the following year.[22] Native Spanish-speaking senators were staging and supporting a Spanish linguistic revival. To pass, S.B. 3 would need the votes of the English-speaking majority. Meanwhile House members introduced their own legislation, House Bill 24 (H.B. 24), which would require all students to take a single Spanish course prior to graduation. The bill's sponsors, Representatives Calla A. Eylar and Albert Gonzales of Doña Ana County, felt that compulsory Spanish in the elementary schools lacked universal popularity and that their bill stood a better chance of being signed into law.[23] The fact that this bill was introduced by legislators from the southern counties suggests some regional differences on the question of bilingual education; additional splits soon emerged.

S.B. 3 immediately gained a supporter in Senator Chávez, who now fully recanted his previous support for English-only education. In a letter to state representative Concha Ortiz y Pino written in early February, Chávez outlined the reasons for his support. He emphasized New Mexico's possibly "immeasurable" importance to strengthening Latin American relations, the growing national interest in learning Spanish, and making Spanish a "second official language in order to be good neighbors." He concluded, "New Mexico should be the last State to oppose the trend."[24] New Mexico, the home of so many prominent native Spanish speakers, should advance, rather than hinder, the nation's pursuit of Spanish-language expertise.

Prominent legislators and administrators organized public roundtable discussions of S.B. 3 in Santa Fe, Albuquerque, and Las Cruces to promote and debate the bill. The individuals invited to the roundtable in Santa Fe, held at the historic La Fonda Hotel, included former governor Miguel Antonio Otero Jr., Superintendent of Public Instruction Grace Corrigan, Governor Miles, Representative Gonzales, and Senators Montoya, Gallegos, and George Armijo. Nina Otero-Warren, too, hoped to attend, as "the teaching of Spanish in the elementary grades of the Public Schools of New Mexico is . . . not only desirable but necessary." She saw language as the "strongest tie" between school and home.[25] Publicity for the high-profile New Mexicans planning to attend S.B. 3 roundtables demonstrates the strong feelings the proposed legislation elicited and the visibility of *nuevomexicanos* in the discussion.

S.B. 3 encountered some opposition from educators, particularly those involved in higher education. Prominent opponents included the presidents of four state universities—NMHU, UNM, Eastern New Mexico College (ENMC), and the New Mexico Military Institute—and representatives of the Spanish-American Normal School at El Rito. Most educators concurred that the bill would have little real impact in the schools without adequate teacher training, financial support, and preliminary studies of Spanish-language instruction. The significant population of native Spanish-speaking students at NMHU and the Normal School did not influence its representatives' fiscal and logistical concerns about the bill. With the exception of Donald McKay, president of ENMC, the university presidents agreed with this assessment. McKay, in contrast, based his objection on his belief that Anglos would oppose compulsory courses in Spanish.[26]

The roundtables and other public meetings contributed to a highly charged debate already occurring among native Spanish speakers. Some parents who had attended schools with language restrictions were upset by the prospect of their children learning Spanish even in the 1930s. As one scholar related about Tireman's experimental schools, "The teaching of the Spanish language and singing Spanish songs seemed to Spanish-speaking parents ... to be attempts to keep the children in an inferior, depressed status."[27] Regional civil rights organizations expressed similar concerns. LULAC, founded in 1929, favored an English-focused assimilationist model that supported student advancement, with a stated preference for students to receive Spanish and Latin American cultural instruction at the higher grade levels.[28] LULAC declared its opposition to the senate bill during its national conference, which in 1941 met in Albuquerque. Benjamin Moya, a high school teacher in Santa Fe and chair of LULAC's educational committee, advocated for standard Spanish-language instruction among adults. He blamed parents for New Mexican children's poor Spanish skills. LULAC relegated Spanish to the more private sphere of the home, with parents as the instructors. At that same meeting, however, LULAC passed a conference resolution that required teachers in New Mexico to have Spanish knowledge and spoke of the importance of sending emissaries to Mexico who could speak Spanish "well" and not "in a strictly New Mexican manner."[29] LULAC supported bilingual teachers in primary grades for transitional reasons rather than for Spanish-language maintenance.

LULAC's opposition to the bill placed the organization at odds with other political and educational leaders within the *nuevomexicano* Spanish-speaking community. State representative Concha Ortiz y Pino rejected the "unintelligent group" when she condemned LULAC's move to "throw cold water on one of the greatest opportunities people of Spanish extraction ever had to serve their country." Ortiz y Pino subsequently resigned her LULAC membership. In championing S.B. 3, she outlined reasons to learn Spanish that transcended the home. She explained the role of the language in commercial transactions, hemispheric relations, and increasing the cultural pride of the state's native Spanish speakers.[30] Leo Amador, president of the Central Branch of the NMEA and supervisor of Rio Arriba County Schools, supported as much Spanish as could be taught in schools and claimed LULAC's position was "in direct conflict with the aims and purposes of the league."[31]

S.B. 3 passed into law on April 16, 1941, with an assist from Chávez. The senator spoke at a joint session of the legislature to push legislators to implement the compulsory Spanish-language bill and make New Mexico a "leader in international good will." Chávez argued that not passing the bill would be a missed opportunity for New Mexico "of doing for the United States what no other state can do."[32]

As signed into law, S.B. 3 required Spanish instruction in the fifth through eighth grades in schools with at least three teachers or ninety regularly attending students. The State Board of Education would be responsible for enforcing the act, but "Governing Boards of Education" could name exceptions each school year. The bill also permitted parents who objected to Spanish-language instruction to remove their children from Spanish courses. All of these provisos meant that the originally proposed "compulsory" law was diluted by political compromise. The law's second section outlined new Spanish-language coursework requirements for fifth- to eighth-grade teachers. In the first three school years following passage of S.B. 3, employed teachers would need six, then eight, then ten semester hours of Spanish.[33] The state also passed a small aid bill, S.B. 129, to support the implementation of S.B. 3. It created a Spanish research fund that provided $5,000 a year for two years to test, identify, and learn to teach effective Spanish-teaching strategies.[34]

New Mexico's leaders celebrated passage of the bill, suggesting that New Mexico's schools could model a Spanish-language program that could be implemented throughout the Southwest. They also promoted the state's role in Latin American relations. A joint memorial from New Mexico's House requesting financial aid from Congress recognized Spanish as the "native language" of almost all of Latin America and pleaded for federal funds to help enforce language training as it "will be of great assistance to our people and to the people of the United States." New Mexico's House defined "our people" as largely speaking Spanish—and having done so for "several hundred years"— which continued as the language of "a large percentage of the school children of this state."[35]

Too often, New Mexico's politicians, including Chávez, focused on the state's exceptionalism to further the cause of Spanish instruction. Chávez reinforced the idea that New Mexico's native Spanish speakers could serve as invaluable national assets to either cultural or intelligence agencies.[36] Ortiz y Pino agreed when addressing the bill's detractors: "New Mexico should be a focal point for the betterment of pan-American [sic] relations."[37] These arguments served Ortiz y Pino and Chávez as they came up against fiduciary and ideological opposition to teaching Spanish widely. Instead of suggesting that all Spanish-speaking U.S. citizens had the right to be bilingual—an approach that would include Spanish-language coursework at every stage of public schooling—the state legislature encouraged only successful students in the higher elementary grades to learn Spanish. Policy makers supported language

FIGURE 11. Children in a schoolroom in Questa, New Mexico, in Taos County, 1943. John Collier. Retrieved from the Library of Congress.

instruction patterns that reinforced U.S. language norms. Only after native Spanish-speaking students learned English—and only after they mastered English—could they learn to read and write in the language of their ancestors and home.

As George I. Sánchez wrote in *Forgotten People*, published in 1940, the year before the language debates, *nuevomexicano* students attended chronically underfunded schools where teaching practices often ignored their needs. (See figure 11.) He likely would have argued that the new law failed to do enough, as he believed a student's "limited proficiency in that language [Spanish] is not used as the base for the new language or for the development of proficiency," which contributed to the state's high dropout rate.[38] New Mexico's bill disregarded the needs of the state's rural Spanish-speaking students. Some of the state's educators nevertheless hoped to use the state's new willingness to endorse Spanish-language education as a stepping-stone to help the rural, poor, and monolingual Spanish speakers in the state's remote areas.

One of these champions for New Mexico's rural Spanish-speaking populations was Antonio Rebolledo, the NMHU professor who cofounded the *Institute of the Air*. With funding from S.B. 129, Rebolledo led the state-sponsored New Mexico Research Project to identify the best strategies for teaching Spanish.[39] He advocated more far-reaching Spanish-language practices than S.B. 3 mandated, particularly when teaching native Spanish-speaking students. Rebolledo encouraged language-based segregation in schools with a majority of native Spanish speakers. He believed a heterogeneous classroom of both monolingual English and Spanish speakers would hinder the types of curriculum changes necessary for successful teaching and would only benefit Anglo or monolingual English-speaking students.[40]

Upon submission of the New Mexico Research Project's findings, the state legislature created the new position of state supervisor of Spanish in 1943. But New Mexico did little to enforce Rebolledo's suggestions, and the few mentions of Spanish-language instruction released by the state superintendent of instruction suggested that the new program was largely for the benefit of non-native Spanish speakers.[41] A curriculum development report submitted by the state superintendent of public instruction, Georgia L. Lusk, presumably distributed to New Mexico's educators, emphasized the critical role of Spanish instruction in bilingual fluency. A "Tentative Program for Teaching Spanish" detailed the four general objectives of Spanish language courses:

1. To develop proficiency in speaking and reading the Spanish language.

2. Teaching children to appreciate other peoples' culture.

3. Realization on the part of the students that they possess the ability to learn another language.

4. A better understanding of Latin Americans through a knowledge of their language.[42]

These objectives described a program largely envisioned as a way to form a deeper cultural understanding of Latin America. Lusk expressed a definite desire for students to become bilingual, but the Tentative Program's objectives downplayed the importance of Spanish to the state itself or to its residents. In fact, the phrase "other peoples' culture" implied that students who came from an English-speaking background would continue to view Spanish-speaking culture as different and inferior. Lusk also privileged English-speaking students' presumed monolingual experience over Spanish speakers. Spanish-speaking students would not realize that they "possess[ed] the ability to learn another language" by being taught their mother tongue.

Over time, it became clear that S.B. 3's measured approach to incorporating Spanish into the primary school curriculum had the unintended consequence of rendering Spanish a foreign language, ironically proving more effective at this task than the state's prior English-only regulations. An NMHU grant proposal to the OCIAA from this period suggested that the implementation of the law had forced schools that had previously conducted classes in Spanish to now treat the language as foreign rather than instructional.[43] NMHU made a plea for funding an English-language instruction program that would work in a community with few English speakers. The proposal identified pockets of San Miguel County as having 95 to 98 percent Spanish speakers. NMHU educators used the discriminatory response to Spanish in the broader community as one reason that an OCIAA-sponsored project was needed. The proposal referred to the small number of Spanish speakers who passed the early primary grades and pointed out that those who did enter ninth grade arrived unprepared as "many of them have been taught in Spanish, however illegally." The very existence of this proposal to work on English-language instruction supports that the state's prior attempts to professionalize and regulate the school system had not fully dislodged Spanish as a language of instruction in New Mexico's schools. However, NMHU's summary of the situation since the bill passed described a real shift in the use of Spanish in the schools. While it was never the intent of New Mexican educators that compulsory Spanish-language instruction after 1941 would benefit Anglos over native Spanish speakers, that was the ultimate effect on New Mexico's midcentury educational policies.[44]

A SPANISH STRONGHOLD IN PUERTO RICO

In New Mexico, some Spanish-speaking residents opposed state politicians' push for Spanish as a "compulsory" school subject. In Puerto Rico, citizens, educators, and many territorial officials opposed U.S. politicians' efforts to require instruction in English. Despite U.S. officials' push for English-language instruction since the territory was acquired from Spain in 1898,

Spanish remained the language heard in Puerto Rican homes and among students. In 1942, José M. Gallardo implemented a new language policy that explicitly favored Spanish as the teaching language in the elementary grades.[45] The ensuing debate about Puerto Rico's right to decide its own language of instruction coincided with the visit of a group of senators to the island who judged the situation for themselves.

Language of instruction debates had a long history in Puerto Rico prior to 1943. For example, English-language teaching materials and teachers who were fluent in English could be found in all municipalities by 1902, but Puerto Rican educators pushed back at what they saw as the "height of absurdity" in 1909 when first grade students faced instruction in English instead of Spanish for reading. By 1913, support of Spanish- or English-language instruction could define a person's political sympathies. Those Puerto Ricans who preferred Spanish in schools were viewed as separatists. Language politics in Puerto Rico stood in as a key marker in the debates over Puerto Rico's sovereignty.[46] Its students suffered under the weight of English-only policies, and educators petitioned numerous times for a change in policy.

In 1925, education specialists from Columbia University's International Institute of Teachers College concluded that teaching English in Puerto Rico's lower grades wasted students' time. Federal officials ignored this study and left English as the language of instruction on the island, but in November 1934 Commissioner of Education José Padín announced in Circular No. 10 that Spanish was *a* language of instruction in all the elementary grades and *the* language of instruction in the first and second grades. Padín's own research had confirmed earlier studies that suggested students' poor performance in both languages resulted from ineffective teaching methods.[47] By choosing Spanish, Padín followed the best policy for the vast majority of Puerto Rican children, whatever the consequences for Americanization. Proponents of statehood greatly opposed Padín's policy, while realists warned that "children are being tortured at the lower grades when they are taught English by force."[48]

Puerto Rico's geographic isolation from the continental United States thwarted any federal or booster attempts to attract English-speaking settlers to the island. Even President Roosevelt acknowledged the impossibility of making the island fully English speaking in 1937: "For it is obvious that they always will and should retain facility in the tongue of their inherited culture, Spanish." His concessions to the place of Spanish on the island stopped short of teaching Spanish in the territory's schools, an opinion he enforced by removing Padín from his position in 1934. "It is an indispensable part of American policy that the coming generation of American citizens in Puerto Rico grow up with complete facility in the English tongue. . . . Only through the acquisition of this language will Puerto Rican Americans secure a better understanding of American ideals and principles," the president instructed Gallardo, his new appointee.[49] Roosevelt held a common view of language and citizenship that equated knowing the English language with understanding the government's ideology and an individual's responsibilities as a citizen—the tenets of Americanization. Puerto Ricans would repeatedly hear U.S. authorities invoke this position on the integral relationship between language and citizenship.

Gallardo's new language policies might have resulted in a simple presidential dismissal, as had occurred with Padín, if the change in policy had not coincided with a Senate hearing. Chávez, chair of the Subcommittee on Territories and Insular Affairs, announced that he would hold hearings in the territory in mid-February. Four senators accompanied him to the island: Homer T. Bone of Washington, Allen J. Ellender of Louisiana, Robert A. Taft of Ohio, and Ralph O. Brewster of Maine. The stated goal of the hearings was to improve life on the island.[50] Instead of supporting a vision of the island as a colonial space, Chávez "would like to see Puerto Rico run her own affairs—as Americans."[51] He faced opposition from both Puerto Ricans who preferred not to live as Americans and fellow senators who saw colonial status as a temporary stop on the way to independence. New York's Spanish-language newspaper *Pueblos Hispanos* summed up the diverging views: Chávez saw Puerto Rico as "un problema americano" (an American problem), whereas those on the island saw Chávez as "un problema para Puerto Rico" (a problem for Puerto Rico) or as their "enemigo" (enemy).[52]

The subcommittee became known as the Chávez Committee, in part due to the chair's proficiency in Spanish.[53] "If this committee had come to Puerto Rico without Senator Chavez . . . I would have left Puerto Rico without understanding any of the most tragic problems," admitted committee member Bone.[54] Although the hearing did not set out to investigate Puerto Ricans' use of language, differences of opinion concerning language and bilingualism repeatedly and contentiously emerged during Senate testimony, especially in discussions with education officials.

The hearings on education were largely conducted by Bone, Ellender, and Chávez—three men whose strong opinions intimidated those who disagreed with their vehemently expressed beliefs. Testimony on language instruction began in earnest on February 17, in San Juan. Commissioner of Education Gallardo testified that full bilingualism was impossible for Puerto Rico. Most students received a mere three to four hours of total daily instruction, especially in rural areas. The average student received only two and a half years of schooling. Almost 70 percent of the student population was rural. The high attrition rate left 260,000 unenrolled students between the ages of six and fourteen. Puerto Rico's many pressing educational needs included lack of material facilities and monetary support.[55] Even Senator Taft observed that Cleveland, Ohio, with a population equal to one-fourth of the island's, spent more on education funding than the entire island of Puerto Rico.[56]

Even in the face of these material difficulties, the testimony on language of instruction overshadowed Puerto Rico's other educational policies. The senators expected to hear one line of thought on language—that Americans must be taught first and foremost in English, regardless of pedagogy or custom. The Chávez Committee freely admitted that Puerto Rican schools operated on an extremely low budget, but its members still pressed Gallardo to explain why achieving bilingualism was unlikely. Gallardo believed that the islanders could never truly learn English because few of them spoke fluent English.[57] Asked to estimate the length of time it would take for Puerto Rico to achieve full bilingualism, one educator answered, "A millennium."[58] Lewis C. Richardson, who taught in the English department at the University of Puerto Rico and represented the Puerto Rico Teachers' Association, agreed with Gallardo's assessment. The senators pressed Richardson with the fervor of district attorneys confronting a witness during cross-examination. They frequently interrupted Richardson before he could express his opinion, such as in the following exchange.

> Senator Ellender: I will ask this again . . . they expect to have independence and if they do they will have that culture?
> Richardson: We still—
> Senator Ellender: You will never become a state as long as you retain Spanish as your chief language.[59]

The environment was hostile and intense in part because Richardson himself was a native English speaker. Even if other Puerto Rican educators presumably could not comprehend the importance of learning English, the senators thought that a native English speaker could have been counted on to recognize the language's benefits and oppose the new Spanish-language instructional policy.

Yet Richardson was unwilling to concede that English should take precedence over Spanish: "If you prefer English to their language you would be taking away from the people the means of effective communication, . . . which is the basis of any culture—[here he was interrupted]."[60] The pedagogical rationale for Spanish-language instruction was practical: the island lacked native English speakers to model the language and did not devote enough instruction time for them to learn it well. This argument did not assuage the senators, who instead offered lengthy statements of their disapproval, leading Richardson to interject, "May I answer?"[61] Chávez meanwhile expressed incredulity at Richardson's responses: "You, a professor at the university, at the head of the English department, representative of the Teachers' Association of Puerto Rico[,] . . . tell us point-blank that you are partly responsible for taking away the study of English from children?"[62] While supportive of Spanish as a complement to English-language instruction in New Mexico, Chávez believed all native Spanish-speaking children needed to learn English.

Even at the same moment that federal agencies like the OWI and OCIAA encouraged hemispheric solidarity through Spanish-language communication, the senators sought to downplay the role of Spanish for Puerto Ricans. Senator Bone did so for largely nationalistic reasons. "It is both interesting and starkly revealing to have you refer to teaching kids in English under the American flag, as 'the crime of America,'" Bone responded to former schoolteacher Guillermo Rey's testimony. He ridiculed Rey's testimony on Puerto Rico's attempt to teach students about disease and culture, arguing that the short instruction period left no time for anything other than English-language instruction.[63] Bone failed to recognize, despite Richardson's explanations, that limited instruction time was precisely the reason that the students had such poor knowledge of English.[64]

Bone's core argument defended English as the proper culture for anyone associated with the United States. He had read *Don Quixote*—the quintessential literary example of Spanish culture—in English, and he thoroughly enjoyed and understood the novel. He invoked his knowledge of the Alhambra in Granada, gleaned through the works of Washington Irving, and doubtfully posited, "Would I know more about them if I read them in Spanish?" His assimilationist view extended to his family's immigration experience: "I have never found the traditions of dear old bonny Scotland helping me to understand better the practice of law in my State."[65] Bone ignored the fact that the vast majority of Puerto Rico's residents had not immigrated to Puerto Rico but instead were born in a place where Spanish was a significant aspect of the culture and the language of society. In Puerto Rico, English was the novel language, and the United States was the imposed culture.

Unlike Bone, Senators Chávez and Ellender had personal experience with languages other than English in their home states. They had lived in settings where it was not unusual to hear non-English languages in political, legal, and social settings. They both knew that Americans could speak more than one language, but they each saw a knowledge of English as essential to obtaining the full rights of U.S. citizenship. Chávez explained, "I want the Puerto Ricans to receive every benefit of American citizenship but to accept responsibility. How can a Puerto Rican receive the benefits if he does not know even the language of the country . . . ?" Chávez believed that knowing English empowered students to petition their government in a language that their elected (or appointed) officials could understand. The lack of English relegated citizens to inferior economic and political positions.[66] For this reason, he saw fluency in English as the prerequisite for any sort of worthwhile U.S. education.

Chávez's personal history shaped his stance on English-language acquisition. At one point he asked Richardson, "Do you think that I could be in the United States Senate if I had not learned English?"[67] Chávez's keen awareness of the benefits he received through his ability to write, think, and speak in English led him to believe that the language supported greater opportunities for Spanish-speaking youths. English was required for all communities in the United States: "I cannot reconcile this proposition of speaking Spanish, Italian, Portuguese, or German, or anything other than English in an American community."[68] Despite his pride in his native tongue and his hope that New Mexico would soon play a larger role in hemispheric relations, Chávez did not see the benefit of retaining Spanish as the primary language. "I insist that any language should be secondary to the English wherever the United States predominates or controls," he asserted. Chávez explained that the committee could provide aid for Puerto Rican children solely through U.S. institutions.[69] For this reason, he especially targeted teachers who neglected what he perceived as the educators' primary job—namely, creating an English-speaking citizenry.

Ellender, an Acadian and a member of the Cajun community in Louisiana, encouraged Puerto Ricans to teach exclusively in English. He explained that, even with English instruction, French remained an optional subject in Louisiana schools and was spoken outside schools in certain communities. Ellender believed that English should be taught by those who had learned English from the "cradle up," with Spanish remaining a subject of instruction. He saw statehood as impossible without knowledge of English and echoed Roosevelt's view that monolingual Spanish-speaking Puerto Ricans could not achieve financial success. Lack of English skills left Puerto Ricans without the ability to easily migrate to the United States, obtain a job on the mainland, or follow their commander as members of the army.[70]

To the credit of Puerto Rican educators, they stood fast in their defense of Spanish-language instruction, a position they held with the best interests of their students in mind. Richardson argued that the senators' preferred type of educational program would result in children with little ability to speak English well, and likely even lower levels of Spanish literacy.[71] Pedro A. Cebollero, another representative of the teachers' association, disapproved of the senators' priorities: "The American way is to give people an education, and, secondary, to give them a language. Here you are trying to give them a language and then education." He further asserted, "Preparation for citizenship is not equivalent to learning English. The person can know English and be far from being a good citizen."[72] José Padín, former commissioner of education, criticized the Senate's focus on English instruction in a follow-up report: "The politicians who insist that English should be the language of instruction throughout the school system of Puerto Rico are running out of bounds."[73] He and two other former commissioners of education recommended to the Senate that Spanish remain the language of instruction for at least the first four grades. Paul G. Miller even did so while bringing up the Spanish-language situation in New Mexico in 1890 as an example of how the shift to English could take time.[74]

These top education officials joined a political movement growing since the mid-1930s that pushed back against the United States and held up Puerto Rican culture as something that should be respected and practiced. Led by Luis Muñoz Marín, the Partido Popular Democrático (Popular Democratic Party) turned to the needs of its rural residents. Echoes of this broader political, social, and economic shift in rhetoric are found throughout the Senate hearings and documents.[75] The populism gleaned from Muñoz Marín's rise to political prominence encouraged educators and the general public alike to stand up for the *puertorriqueño* way of life.[76]

For Puerto Rican educators, teaching English was not, and could not be, the sole goal of public education. The island lacked the resources to recruit native English-speaking teachers for the rural districts, where approximately 75 percent of Puerto Rico's population lived.[77] While the senators saw English-language acquisition as necessary for those who might later migrate to the United States, Cebollero explained, "The fact is that the majority of those children will have to make their living here in Puerto Rico. . . . Education cannot be planned for a minority."[78] Educators sought to place the needs of their students above the desires of politicians, and in so doing, they took a larger political stand.

The Chávez Committee's mission to Puerto Rico inadvertently helped solidify Spanish as a permanent part of the territory's national identity. Educators, students, and politicians used language as a political means of distancing themselves from the United States and to advocate for greater autonomy. They did this by coming out in force against the findings and opinions of the committee. Educators wanted local autonomy that would allow them to choose the most appropriate instructional language for their students rather than have it dictated by the federal government. After the hearing, islanders' discussions about the relative merits of Spanish and English no longer focused on the potential of bilingual pedagogy but rather on Spanish's central role in Puerto Ricans' culture and identity.[79]

Puerto Ricans rallied behind educators and politicians who favored Spanish-language instruction. When Commissioner Gallardo submitted his resignation after Secretary of the Interior Harold L. Ickes criticized his testimony before the Senate, the Puerto Rican legislature and educators reinforced their support for him. In response, Ickes apologized and allowed Gallardo to remain in his post.[80] Perhaps this strong show of national solidarity encouraged Senator Millard E. Tydings to submit a bill to secure independence for Puerto Rico in 1943.[81]

The aftermath of the Chávez Committee's trip to Puerto Rico demonstrated the limits of the language discussion in the United States. Following Chávez's visit, Puerto Ricans viewed him negatively, as Juan Minaya's editorial makes clear: "Fuera de Puerto Rico el falangista Chávez . . . y demás enemigos del pueblo puertorriqueño!" (Out of Puerto Rico the fascist Chávez . . . and all other enemies of the Puerto Rican people!)[82] His image on the island was as tarnished as Senator Albert J. Beveridge's had been in New Mexico in the first years of the century. Chávez's conclusions strikingly matched Beveridge's report. Both men extolled fluency in English as a necessary condition of full citizenship in the United States. But unlike Beveridge, Chávez himself acknowledged the importance of retaining Spanish as a language of heritage and culture. Certainly his work in New Mexico demonstrated an acceptance of bilingualism. These mid-twentieth-century senators adopted a broader vision of U.S. citizenship than did their predecessors, but that citizenship still depended on a knowledge of English.[83] Once they knew English, then Spanish became a useful language to learn to take advantage of the increased diplomatic and business opportunities resulting from Latin America's proximity.

Puerto Ricans continued to advocate for their right to dictate their own language choices throughout an exciting decade that moved them toward more self-rule. In both 1945 and 1946, the territorial legislature attempted to mandate Spanish-language instruction; in both cases, the legislation was vetoed by the presidentially appointed territorial governor as well as President Harry Truman himself. Protests erupted in response. The first Puerto Rican appointed to the position of governor, Jesus T. Piñero, made several unsuccessful attempts to place Mariano Villarona as commissioner of education. Villarona openly declared his preference for Spanish as the teaching language; he withdrew from consideration because of Washington's opposition to his language stance. Finally, in 1949, Muñoz Marín, the first independently elected governor, appointed Villarona commissioner of education. Villarona declared Spanish the teaching language by executive order.[84] In Governor Muñoz Marín, Puerto Rico had a vocal advocate for using the Spanish language over English on the island. In 1953, the governor adamantly endorsed Spanish when he spoke to the Puerto Rico Teachers' Association, asking, "If you reject your language, are you not to a certain point rejecting yourself?" He advocated for the use of "Puerto Rican" words in schools and encouraged a Puerto Rican nationalist rather than colonialist mentality.[85] By claiming Spanish for their own, rather than submitting to the pressure and opinions of the federal government, Puerto Ricans irrevocably chose a path different from that of New Mexico.

As the sole native Spanish-speaking senator, Dennis Chávez played a peculiar role in the history of language policy in the United States. Even as he worked to create a united identity among Spanish speakers that elevated New Mexico's status, he denigrated the ability of monolingual Spanish speakers to claim the full benefits of citizenship in Puerto Rico. Chávez regarded himself as a champion of Latin American identity. He gave speeches throughout the country and received appraisals like those offered by the political activist Eduardo Quevedo, who introduced him at a "Good Neighbor" rally in Los Angeles in 1944 as follows: "We have come to pay honor to a man whose native state is the living example of a most successful experiment of good neighborliness." While in California, Chávez gave a speech in each language. His speech in Spanish focused on creating good U.S. citizens.[86] In Puerto Rico, Chávez attempted to use these same credentials to validate his criticisms of local educators. When attacked in the Puerto Rican newspaper *El Mundo*, Chávez conceded, "It is not necessary to speak English for purposes of breathing the free air of the Americas," but he continued to stress that social and economic advancement required using the language.[87] Chávez saw English as the only way to put Puerto Ricans on an equal playing field with other Americans.

In New Mexico, a politician's fluency in Spanish endeared him to native Spanish speakers. In Puerto Rico, knowledge of Spanish was neither novel nor respected. Both regions retained native Spanish-speaking leaders in politics and education through the rest of the twentieth century. Senatorial visits to the island were few and far between; in the long run, Puerto Rico's territorial status allowed its residents to continue their language practices in their everyday lives. While some senators preferred to permit Puerto Ricans to retain Spanish and eventually become independent, Chávez hoped Puerto Ricans would come to enjoy the full benefits of U.S. citizenship, albeit in English. Puerto Ricans chose a third option that permitted a more dynamic relationship with the language than advocates for Americanization could readily imagine.

Native Spanish speakers used the language as a political gift. New Mexicans insisted their citizens' Spanish-language abilities were indispensable to U.S. international policy and goals, hoping to achieve more power for their state within the broader union. Puerto Ricans claimed Spanish as a means to signal their independence from the U.S. government and better position themselves in opposition to it. In allowing Spanish-speaking citizens to pursue two very distinctive goals, the politics of language provides a space for historians to view other cultural markers besides race that Latinos have used to make claims and advocate for different versions of American identity.

Epilogue

Mexico is closer to the Southwest now than when it was theirs. Mexico never left the Southwest, it just learned English.

—José Antonio Burciaga, *Drink Cultura*

Chicano Spanish is a border tongue which develops naturally. Change, *evolución, enriquecimiento de palabras nuevas por invención o adopción* have created variants of Chicano Spanish, *un nuevo lenguaje....* [I]t is a living language.*

—Gloria Anzaldúa, *Borderlands/La Frontera*

Whenever I speak with *nuevomexicanos* about my research, I hear stories of loss and reclamation, generally conflicted and complicated accounts. Many tell me of parents who refused to teach them Spanish out of fear of reprisals in school. These conversations are in contrast to the presence of Spanish in advertisements, on public signs, on television, and in conversations overheard on the streets. Spanish is ubiquitous in major cities like Los Angeles, New York, Houston, or Chicago (see figure 12), but it is also present in small communities and towns throughout the country.[1] The evidence of hard-won victories for language rights—secured either through political mobilization, overall purchasing strength, or just defiant use—abound and coexist with xenophobic rhetoric advocating a monolingual English-speaking nation.

What allows for the current contradictions? What happened between the end of World War II, when the federal government used Spanish-language

---

*"evolution, enrichment through the invention or adoption of new words . . . [,] a new language."

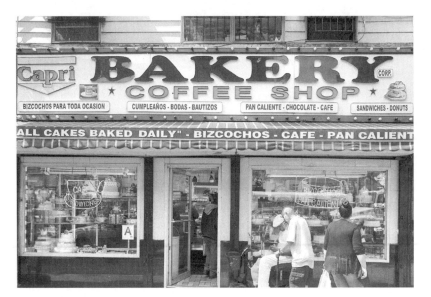

FIGURE 12. Bilingual bakery sign in East Harlem, New York, 2017. Nick Vossbrink, courtesy of Nick Vossbrink.

instruction for the benefit of Pan-Americanism and intercultural exchange, and the present? While this brief epilogue cannot hope to answer that question, it is clear that conflicts over Spanish-language use in the United States have had a lasting impact on contemporary politics. This epilogue, intended to be suggestive rather than conclusive, pinpoints major flashpoints in the post–World War II period. It identifies commonalities with earlier debates over the use of Spanish, but it also acknowledges major gains in civil rights that have altered national politics. These victories have greatly extended the national acceptance of language concessions not only for Spanish speakers but also for American Indians and for immigrant groups.

For middle-class educators and activists in the immediate postwar years, dismantling an unequal educational system that segregated children on the basis of language became an important civil rights goal in California, Arizona, and Texas. The first major court success for Mexican American parents was the now-famous *Mendez v. Westminster* case, won in both the district court and the Ninth Circuit Court of Appeals (1947). In Orange County, administrators had used language heritage as a means of segregating ethnic Mexican children. Although the plaintiffs won their case, the testimony displays embedded prejudices against Spanish speakers. Rather than acknowledging the validity of regional distinctions in pronunciation or accents of students with limited English-language skills, district court judge Paul S. McCormick resorted to generalization. "A person may be of Spanish descent or origin, ancestry, and yet speak English perfectly as far as grammatical expression is concerned and as far as knowledge of the language is concerned, but yet they do have an accent," he opined.[2] Even though Judge McCormick worked to integrate Orange County schools, he held a view of ethnic Mexicans as perpetually foreign and separate from the greater white American population. The courts remained a major site of civil rights activism into the 1950s as numerous court cases filed by Mexican American parents—including, most famously, Texas's *Delgado v. Bastrop* (1948) and Arizona's *Gonzales v. Sheely* (1950)—appeared in the Southwest with mixed results.[3] Access to better educational options increased children's opportunity to learn English well, and for that reason, Mexican American parents and activists sued for access to the best education possible.

Mexican American activists faced another language situation when they turned to the monolingual Spanish-speaking elderly in their midst who had given their working years to labor in the United States but had never naturalized. The Community Service Organization hosted citizenship courses in the mid-1950s explicitly for monolingual Spanish speakers eligible for naturalization. The 1952 Immigration and Naturalization Act included a provision that allowed long-standing citizens over sixty years old to take naturalization exams in their preferred language.[4] Once naturalized, these new voters could qualify for federal aid programs. Today, most federal programs that serve the elderly provide Spanish-language translations or interpreters. Did these translations begin at the local level, as happened in San Miguel County during the Great Depression for New Deal programs? Or did the federal government offer translations in light of other labor and civil rights activism that brought civil rights to the forefront of national consciousness? Or was it a little of both?

Labor movements, building on strong alliances between immigrants that had begun in the early 1900s, continued to use Spanish to reach new Mexican immigrants in the postwar era. For example, Ernesto Galarza employed Spanish to organize and unionize farmworkers throughout the 1940s and 1950s.[5] More generally, the continuation of the U.S.-Mexico Bracero Program, which allowed contracted laborers legal entry into the United States, led to an influx of Spanish-speaking workers who required Spanish-language services.[6] These contracted laborers were joined by increasing numbers of undocumented Mexican laborers. Among Mexican American citizens, civic grassroots activism remained largely based in neighborhoods and unions. Community service organizations of the 1940s and 1950s tended to focus on electoral political engagement during the early Cold War years when political opponents used red-baiting to halt more radical activism.[7]

The citizen- and labor-based politics of the long-standing Spanish-speaking populace shifted dramatically during the post-1965 period. Mexican Americans and the rising Chicano generation addressed language through their efforts to meet a variety of goals. Many middle-class Mexican Americans aspired to assimilation (or at least a more additive cultural acceptance), while Chicanos embraced racial identity and Brown Power. Both groups sought improved political and economic conditions and, ultimately, civil rights, but they approached the issues differently—a split in ethnic Mexicans' approach to activism that has received a lot of attention from historians.[8]

Chicanos militantly advocated for Spanish-language instruction as an act of cultural validation and confirmation. High school students across the Southwest walked out of their schools in 1968. The students' demands included curricular changes that mandated instruction in Chicano culture, which embraced the Spanish language, Mexican history, and the history of ethnic Mexican or Chicano contributions to the United States.[9] Pushing back against earlier middle-class efforts to desegregate schools, Chicano advocates protested for bilingual education programs. These efforts—among other cultural revivals in the arts and entertainment—acknowledged the cultural importance of Spanish and its valuable contribution to the nation. The Crusade for Justice, an important Colorado Chicano organization, called on a key (and familiar) document, the Treaty of Guadalupe Hidalgo, to validate the "protection of our cultural rights" as they demanded bilingual education programs from elementary school through college.[10] Chicanos understood that the Spanish language broadened their connections to a land they claimed ancestrally and renamed Aztlán. While working to educate the masses, they had history on their side. Their treaty citizen predecessors had unapologetically used Spanish as a matter of everyday practice. Chicanos used Spanish as a language of activism and pride, making it once again a political language but with new meaning.

The Civil Rights Movement, federal efforts to find ways to end poverty, and new research that debunked the idea that bilingualism negatively affected intelligence all helped to create the political atmosphere needed for a national act on bilingual education.[11] The Bilingual Education Act, passed in 1968, federally endorsed bilingual education programs for the first time and provided millions of dollars to begin programs through Title VII. Reports written while the bill was under consideration claimed that Spanish speakers accounted for 1.75 million of the 3 million students nationally who could benefit from bilingual education, but the bill itself does not explicitly mention Spanish.[12]

The political discussion surrounding the bill suggested that the terms of debate on language instruction had shifted from either Americanization or Pan-Americanism to the benefit language instruction would provide the student. Proposed by Texas senator Ralph Yarborough, the bill received support from many representatives from the Southwest. In a report prior to passage, the New Mexican–born California representative Edward Roybal cited lower educational achievement rates and a significantly lower median income for "Spanish-speaking persons" as reasons to endorse the bill. Texas's Robert C. Eckhardt expressed his support for the bill's ability to "give dignity to both languages, to extend bilingualism through both languages."[13] Some supporters considered it as important for children to master their "home language" as to obtain an appreciation of others' "cultural heritage."[14] Unlike earlier English-only laws passed in California and Arizona, federal officials here acknowledged the positive attributes of students' "foreign language backgrounds and culture" and encouraged bilingual instruction in part to enhance those "foreign" cultural traits.[15] In spite of support of students retaining their native tongues, the debate centered on vocabulary that cast students' culture apart from the United States.

This historic bill signaled recognition of language rights at the federal level, but it was flawed. Instead of focusing on the cultural or intellectual value of bilingualism, the act emphasized "forward-looking approaches to meet the serious learning difficulties faced" by non-English-speaking students. The educational system, as set up, could not function without knowledge of English, and the act's dominant language labeled limited English-speaking students as having "special education needs"—in other words, a learning deficiency.[16] The bill contained a second major flaw: its inability to reach the students who needed it most. Title VII initially provided funding for approximately one hundred thousand children, leaving millions more at the whim of local funding prioritization.[17] Insufficient federal funding and no mandate for bilingual education allowed many native Spanish-speaking students to enter schools that provided no bilingual language support.

Federal provisions for bilingual education gained strength through the courts. In 1974, in *Lau v. Nichols*, the Supreme Court unanimously ruled that schools had to offer supplemental instruction to English-language learners or otherwise find themselves in violation of the Civil Rights Act of 1964.[18] This ruling effectively secured students' rights to bilingual education if they had limited English skills. Language rights were never just about Spanish, and in this case, ethnic Chinese parents with children in San Francisco public schools brought the case. Their case struck at what the court deemed "the very core of what these public schools teach." The Supreme Court ruled that refusing aid to non-English speakers in an attempt to ensure "the mastery of English by all pupils in the schools" resulted in "classroom experiences wholly incomprehensible and in no way meaningful." The decision quoted a California code that required bilingual curricular approaches that reaffirmed a student's home language if it "does not interfere" with the "regular instruction of all pupils in the English language."[19] While the ruling left open the possibility of studying another language in a public school setting, it nevertheless prioritized English above all other languages and categorized other languages as languages designated to the private rather than public, economic, or political sphere.

Federal language rights during the Civil Rights era extended beyond bilingual education to discussions of political rhetoric—most significantly, the right to participate in elections. The original Voting Rights Act of 1965, largely remembered today as a victory for the Black Civil Rights Movement, included a limited provision that extended voting rights to non-English speakers who attended accredited public or private schools in Washington, DC, or Puerto Rico.[20] As written, the act specifically protected the rights of Puerto Rican students who migrated to the States after attending schools on the island.[21] But since all of the schools in the Southwest had long required English-language instruction, no specific federal concessions were made for Mexican American voters who did not speak English in the Southwest. Those opposing this concession in the bill spoke about "a citizen's ability to read and write our language as a qualification for voting."[22] This opinion establishes citizenship and English, "our language," as mutually constituted. Demands for "literacy" among the electorate was of course part of a longer historical rhetoric that had limited the votes of immigrants and African American voters for decades, but the specific requirement for English-language knowledge demonstrates that literacy itself was not the only criterion for voting expected of "Americans." A citizen's failure to read or write in English meant that an individual who was legally entitled to political participation was marked as culturally unworthy of voting. English, by extension, became the language expected of any immigrant hoping to naturalize.

As Latinos became increasingly identified as a distinct population with specific educational needs and with a powerful political presence over the next two decades, the federal government created agencies and funded studies that aimed at providing them with equal access to the vote. This policy shift is best exemplified in amendments to the Voting Rights Act in 1975 that extended the vote to non-English-speaking language minorities in counties with large numbers of them. The amendment related to language was spelled out in Section 203, which extended the official federal position on language rights to include naturalized citizens, long-standing residents, and American Indians. Section 203 required "registration or voting notices, forms, instructions, [and] assistance . . . including ballots" in other languages if "more than 5 per centum of the citizens of voting age . . . are members of a single language minority." The federal requirement had far-reaching impact. For example, in California, the provision initially extended Spanish-language election material requirements to thirty-seven counties.[23] The lobbying power of language minorities led to the law's successful extension in 1975, but voters' limited use of the concession proved disappointing for many advocates. For example, the *Los Angeles Times* characterized San Francisco's November 1975 election as "a flop," because very few of the "language-handicapped" used the services available. Multilingual notices sent to 271,718 residents asked if they preferred the ballot in another language, yielding only 1,540 affirmative responses. The open survey resulted in many more remarks denouncing the program and advocating for English-only. "This is the United States of America. Vote in English," was one response.[24]

Section 203 remains one of the most important examples of a successful federal language rights provision. Access to the vote, however, remained just one—admittedly underused—language rights issue. Fernando E. C. de Baca worked with President Gerald Ford as the first presidential special assistant on Hispanic affairs. He saw bilingual opportunities as "a formidable obstacle" for Spanish speakers. Most of his concerns involved day-to-day services provided by local municipalities or states, instead of at the federal level.[25] In the 1980s, English-only groups turned their attention to exactly these kinds of programs. U.S. English, an organization focused on legislating English as the official language of the nation, which failed to gain support for a constitutional amendment, found more success in state-level campaigns. By 2010, twenty-nine states had passed legislation making English the official language of the state, including California (1986), Colorado (1988), and Arizona (2006).[26] As of the time of this writing, New Mexico and Texas have not yet joined the list. Latino advocates faced significant losses to language rights at both the local and state levels during this period.

In response to unprecedented levels of migration from Latin American countries, anti-immigration legislation and court decisions curtailed many Spanish-language rights in the 1980s and 1990s. For instance, bilingual strongholds like Florida's Dade County, which includes Miami, banned the use of Spanish in county offices in 1980 after making Spanish the county's official second language in 1973 (Dade County bilingualism was reinstated in 1993).[27] In *Hernández v. New York* (1991), the Supreme Court upheld New York's right to exclude potential jurors because of their bilingualism or multilingualism. The courts feared that knowledge of languages other than English could influence the way jury members interpreted the evidence.[28] In 1998, California passed state legislation dismantling bilingual education (it was reinstated in 2016), which sent the message to non-English-speaking students that their language had no place in schools and likely encouraged negative views of their family environment.[29] Throughout the country, courts heard cases that tested language as a civil right in the workplace, in courts, in schools, on signs, and in public with both successes and setbacks for Spanish speakers.[30]

Judging only from the passage of English-only legislation, the 1980s and 1990s launched a period of relentless attacks on language rights that continued into the first decades of the twenty-first century. Arizona's legislature has often led the call against Mexican American culture and history with state bills such as 2010's H.B. 2281, which worked to dismantle ethnic studies in primary and secondary schools (in 2017, a federal judge found the law racist).[31] Likewise, S.B. 1070 seeded fear of otherwise routine police interactions, as the use of Spanish became a "reasonable" cause for further interrogating individuals to determine their immigration status. "The United States, in the minds of those advancing SB 1070, had only one language: English," explained the National Immigration Law Center.[32]

Supporters of English-only policies often advocated for their cause by denigrating Spanish-language speakers and turning to racist and xenophobic discourse. The recorded statements of Arizona's elected officials help solidify this conclusion. Arizona state senator Russell Pearce denounced "illegal aliens" in Denver for singing the Star Spangled Banner in Spanish, which he summarized as "audacious, arrogant and condescending!" He viewed the display as an "invasion by a foreign country" and did not see that Spanish speakers possibly embraced the country and its national song out of their own sense of patriotism.[33] Similarly, John Huppenthal, Arizona's former superintendent of public instruction, anonymously posted to a website, "We all need to stomp out balkanization. No [S]panish radio stations, no [S]panish billboards, no [S]panish TV stations, no [S]panish newspapers." He recognized the accepted Mexican cultural mainstays but did not extend it to language: "This is America, speak English. . . . I don't mind them selling Mexican food as long as the menus are mostly in English. And, I'm not being humorous or racist."[34] When unmasked, Huppenthal repudiated his comments and broke out in tears at a press conference discussing his diatribes, which included more than just attacks on Spanish.[35] While Huppenthal's tears suggest that such explicitly racist statements are no longer considered acceptable in U.S. political discourse, attacks on language continue to grow.

The politics of the Spanish language offers an opportunity to understand better national discussions about the political rights of Latinos. For example, Kansas's voting guide for the 2016 primary election, which was posted in both English and Spanish on its website and sent out to potential voters in both languages, came under fire for translation discrepancies. The Spanish-language version contained incorrect information regarding registration deadlines—fifteen days before an election instead of twenty-one—and omitted passports from the list of acceptable identification for voters. A *Daily Kos* blogger, Chris Reeves, highlighted the errors on April 7, after hearing from a Spanish speaker in Garden City, a community "about half" of whose population was Latino. The *Kansas City Star* picked up the story from the liberal-leaning blog on April 9. Its major takeaway focused on the fact that the translations could mislead or disenfranchise potential Spanish-speaking voters. Kansas's secretary of state took responsibility for the inaccuracies and claimed they had resulted from administrative error. The state promised to send the text to a professional translating service to eliminate the mismatches in the Spanish- and English-language versions.[36]

The troublesome discrepancies in the translations provided further evidence for critics in Kansas who accused Secretary of State Kris Kobach of attempting to suppress the votes of non-Republicans.[37] The criticism of Kobach gelled with larger national concerns about voter suppression. Yet the Spanish-language press's coverage of Kansas did not revolve around translation errors but instead Kobach's "career-long anti-immigrant crusade." Univision's "Elecciones 2016" section ran stories that included, for example, a letter from Kobach endorsing presidential candidate Donald Trump and his suggestion that Trump's border wall should be paid for by confiscating Mexican remittances.[38]

This anecdote is rich with interpretive possibilities. Its significance is best understood by looking more closely at shifts in Latino voting rights, Latino political strength, and the explosion of the Spanish-language media. First, enforcing Section 203 of the Voting Rights Act has required judicial vigilance. In late 2017 the Department of Justice listed forty-eight "cases raising claims under the language minority provisions of the Voting Rights Act" on its website and provided summaries of many of these. Eighteen of the cases stem from California (eleven), New Mexico (six), and Arizona (one), including the two earliest ones heard between 1978 and 1979. Texas has had ten cases, though all have occurred since 2005. Cases concerning Spanish speakers beyond traditionally accepted enclaves of ethnic Mexican settlement have expanded in the 2000s to encompass Spanish-language rights for Latino voters in New York, Nebraska, Ohio, New Jersey, Illinois, Pennsylvania, Massachusetts, Florida, and Washington.[39] While the Southwest had served as the major legal testing ground for expanding voting rights to non-English-language speakers nationwide, these incidents of successful enforcement from around the country highlight the spread of Spanish-speaking migrants who do not speak English beyond the region.

Spanish-language translations have, at this point, become a political reality in most states, but Latinos rarely mobilize their political strength around translations. They have bigger political fish to fry. Even in Kansas, Kobach did not contest citizens' right to translations. Instead, the state's political establishment accepted the necessity of translations and its responsibility to provide accurate ones. Or their rapid acquiescence was simply a tactical decision to avoid the further scrutiny of either the federal government or Latino activists.

Rather than contracting in the age of U.S. English, federal protections for bilingual voters have actually expanded. As of 2011, county- and even precinct-specific multilingual voting guides were required in 248 of the nation's jurisdictions—accounting for around 65.6 million people, or 30.7 percent of the eligible voting population.[40] New Mexico's Bernalillo County publishes hundreds of individual precinct ballots that offer election material in English and Spanish, along with three indigenous languages—Navajo, Tiwa, and Keres.[41] In California's Santa Clara County, voting guides are available in Spanish, Chinese, Tagalog, and Vietnamese.[42]

While political participation is a crucial factor in the politics of language, millions of Spanish speakers are undocumented and cannot vote—though they do use the language daily to participate in society. The politics of the Spanish language has huge economic ramifications and is audible (and visible) in communities across the country. The spread of Spanish is apparent in the many opportunities to consume Spanish-language media. Spanish-language newspapers flourish in thirty-nine states, and U.S. Spanish speakers can view 321 distinct digital dailies.[43] Spanish-language newspapers cover the latest U.S. and Latin American political stories with great regularity and with a deep knowledge of the U.S. political system, just as they did in the Southwest in the nineteenth century, but they now inform an ever-growing Latino electorate. Univision, which focused on the election and major issues concerning Latinos in Kansas, is a recognized national media force, with which politicians must reckon in each election season. Since their inception in the 1980s, Univision and the other major Spanish-language network, Telemundo, have grown to become ratings powerhouses. Univision's *Noticiero Univisión* averaged 1.86 million viewers in 2014, which surpassed all other major broadcast networks (ABC, CBS, NBC, and Fox).[44] More recently, other media outlets have vied for Spanish-language viewers. Netflix, the major video streaming service, has expanded its Spanish-language offerings and subtitle capabilities to include novelas, movies, stand-up, and television shows.[45] Last but not least, forty-one states host one of the 699 local Spanish-language radio stations in the United States, which include programs on national politics and immigration law.[46] Spanish-speaking migrants to the United States are introduced to the country's legal and political realities through an extensive Spanish-language media that is unavoidable to anyone using a remote control or scanning through radio stations.

Latinos have rising political strength and visibility within the United States. The border, the ramifications of migration and immigration policy, and the place of Latinos in the nation have become unavoidable national issues. Latinos made up 11 percent of national voting power in 2012 and are expected to increase by 40 percent by 2030.[47] In sheer numbers, Latino residents make up 56.6 million, or 17.8 percent, of the population and have various language abilities and needs.[48] While the scope of the Latino electorate has blossomed, *An American Language* has shown that it is not a new political force. Bolstered by the many migrant booms of the post–World War II period, the heterogeneous Latino community bears little resemblance to the population of treaty citizens. And yet the country's long history of multilingualism, particularly the way it has privileged and responded to Spanish, encouraged and facilitated the extension of language rights to other groups. Multilingualism in the United States has a deep history and very real current relevance. Non-English speakers' fight for language rights in the nation's political, social, and legal spheres is a significant marker of migrant power and a strong indicator of their voice and presence in shaping the nation.

––––––––

Federal language rights for Spanish speakers were never automatic or guaranteed. Spanish speakers received language concessions because they retained a political voice and presence on state and territorial legislatures and chose to advocate for treaty citizens' language rights. There are few legacies of these treaty citizens' efforts outside of New Mexico. In 2013, New Mexico's supreme court reaffirmed a constitutional protection from 1910 that allowed monolingual Spanish-speaking jurors into the state's jury boxes. It is the only state that permits limited- or non-English-speaking jurors.[49]

A major point of this book is that the United States has historically viewed Spanish as distinct from other immigrant languages. The federal courts and Congress have at times recognized language rights as a civil right, but English-only court decisions and laws point to the ambivalence many U.S. citizens feel about guaranteeing language rights. As long as there remain significant numbers of citizens and residents who do not speak English, language politics will persist at the local, state, territorial, and federal levels. It may be that the Spanish language's unique history will continue to distinguish itself from other language struggles in the United States, or it may serve as a model for how non-English speakers can secure and fight for language rights through shifting periods of nationalism and what it means to be American.

English-only activists advocate for eradicating Spanish and other "immigrant" languages from political and sometimes even social settings. "Speak English. You're in America." "Speak American." These are common refrains, with variations yielding numerous tweets, blog posts, and even an attack in a Kentucky JC Penney's in 2016 and a student walkout in New Jersey protesting against a teacher in 2017.[50] Xenophobic rhetoric and assimilation pressures across the country have succeeded to some degree, as Spanish monolingualism has declined sharply among U.S.-born Latinos, the majority of whom now speak English well (though they remain more likely than non-Latinos to be bilingual).[51] These efforts have not, however, succeeded at eradicating the use of Spanish among tens of millions of individuals in their homes in the United States.

Advocates for language rights have won significant legal victories in establishing language as a civil right. Instead of denouncing or fearing the use of Spanish in the United States, politicians and English-only advocates could better expend their energies by viewing Spanish-language concessions for what they are—a form of protection for otherwise vulnerable citizens (or potential future citizens) who live in an English-dominated nation. The United States could reconsider an older political vision that encouraged greater acceptance of non-English-language citizens. Previous language policies encouraged higher voter turnouts, higher levels of citizen participation, and a better general sense of national belonging, which ultimately resulted in Spanish speakers investing in the political system and adopting the English language (though not necessarily rejecting Spanish). The long history of language use in the U.S. Southwest exemplifies the possibilities of an electorate formed in Spanish that voted, testified, served as judges, and held public office. Spanish-language political culture has a long precedent in the United States. Spanish is an American language, not just because of its place in the Americas and the future of the nation, but also because of its pivotal role in the United States for over a century.

ACKNOWLEDGMENTS

I am upending traditional acknowledgments by thanking Nick Vossbrink first. Nick believed in me and this project from the outset of the dissertation. He agreed to a long-distance marriage at times, moved across the country, from our native California to New Jersey—leaving his job as an engineer to do so—and became a stay-at-home father so that I could work on this book and follow this career. Our joint decision has worked well for our family, but I am incredibly grateful for his support, sacrifice, and love. The book is between covers because he was my rock who took care of our family and our home, and served as my final reader and typesetting expert. Gracias mi amor.

I would not be where I am today without the constant love and support of my family. My parents, Noé and Vira Lozano, have always encouraged me to excel and succeed at everything I put my mind to and they have provided me with the tools and unconditional love to do so. I am so lucky to call my siblings Celina, Noé, and Pablo best friends. We have learned and grown together and our long talks and check-ins provide the best sort of trust in one another. My family has always pushed me forward with words of pride and encouragement. They are my greatest cheerleaders. Marriage has expanded my circle of support and I thank Audrey Wong, David and Emma Vossbrink, and Gabriel Serrano for championing my work; and my nieces and nephews, Elena, Gabriela, and Pablo for giving me California summers to eagerly anticipate. My sons Walter and Tomás helped me sit back and learn from their growth and discovery. We had "reading marathons" together as I worked and they served as a welcome distraction that reminded me what was truly most important in life, namely bringing up compassionate, strong, and informed members of the next generation.

This book began as a dissertation under the guidance of two extraordinary mentors who have become wonderful friends. George Sánchez and Bill Deverell complemented one another and offered a richly nuanced mentoring experience that provided everything I needed as a graduate student and in the years since. Thank you for leaving the door open after I graduated. I've accumulated other mentors, including Al

Camarillo and Lorena Oropeza, who have offered sage advice and close readings of my work. Muy agradecido. I will pay it forward to future students and younger colleagues who come up the ranks. Thank you also to Mary Dudziak and Félix Gutiérrez for providing guidance as this project moved from dissertation to book.

I am very grateful that I worked through the major revisions of this book at Princeton. I have enjoyed and benefited from countless discussions with my colleagues, some of whom read multiple iterations of the manuscript. In the history department, Jeremy Adelman, Margot Canaday, Vera Candiani, Janet Chen, Angela Creager, Shel Garon, Dirk Hartog, Tera Hunter, Alison Isenberg, Bill Jordan, Kevin Kruse, Regina Kunzel, Michael Laffan, Erika Milam, Yair Mintzker, Phil Nord, Gyan Prakash, Teresa Shawcross, and Emily Thompson; in other departments on campus: Marta Tienda, Ali Valenzuela, Brian Herrera, Anne Cheng, Paul Frymer, Alan Patten, Desmond Jagmohan, Sandy Bermann, and Wendy Belcher. Believe it or not, I met with each and every one of these colleagues to discuss this book. They offered me resources, comments, publication advice, and writing advice and overall believed in the potential of the project. I would especially like to thank Keith Wailoo, Marni Sandweiss, and Michael Gordin, who read numerous versions of drafts and offered key insights on the West and language politics. Keith, my Princeton mentor, gracefully provided his wisdom at each stage of the revisions and improved my thinking each time. I have benefited immeasurably from the generosity of my senior colleagues, and this book reflects their investment in me. I also thank my writing group comrades for providing a safe place to share new ideas and support one another as friends: Alec Dun, Joe Fronczak, Caley Horan, Rob Karl, Matt Karp, Jon Levy, Beth Lew-Williams, Ronny Regev, Rebecca Rix, and Wendy Warren.

I thank the National Academy of Education and the Spencer Foundation for granting me a postdoctoral fellowship, which provided me with the financial means to travel to archives and work without distraction. I'm appreciative of the Andrew W. Mellon Foundation for funding research at the Huntington Library. Special thanks to the Center for Comparative Studies in Race and Ethnicity at Stanford University for hosting me for the 2012–13 school year while I began these revisions. Ramón Saldívar, José David Saldívar, Chris Queen, Ana Minian, and Kathryn Gin Lum, among others, offered a wonderfully supportive and engaging scholarly community.

Early versions of specific chapters of this book benefited from close readings at a dissertation workshop held at Yale in 2009, an American Studies Works in Progress Workshop held at Princeton in April 2014, a presentation at the Language and Authority Workshop held by PIIRS in February 2015, the Bancroft Seminar on Latino and Borderlands History that met at UC Berkeley in November 2015, and a History Colloquium and manuscript review held at the University of New Mexico in November 2016. I thank John Mack Faragher, Richard White, Louis Warren, Steve Aron, Jay Gitlin, David Montejano, Raúl Coronado, Brian DeLay, Mark Brilliant, Lisbeth Haas, Fay Yarbrough, Geraldo Cadava, and Monica Martínez Muñoz, among others, for reading my early work and for their generous comments, suggestions, and enthusiasm for the project. I wish to highlight the time and effort of Felipe Gonzales,

A. Gabriel Meléndez, Samuel Truett, Cathleen Cahill, Anna María Nogar, and Andrew Sandoval-Strausz, each of whom read the entire manuscript and offered keen insights on New Mexico that have strengthened the book. Andrew in particular provided the right mix of tough questions and writing advice that has now made its way into my best practices and is evident in my revisions. Mil gracias.

Several research assistants aided me as I researched. José Argueta Funes read an early draft of the manuscript and offered wonderful suggestions. I am appreciative of graduate students Adrian Masters, Lucinda Grinnell, and Robert Gross, who collected photos and evidence from the archives. My undergraduate RAs, Candelaria Duran, Lafayette Matthews, and Marlyn Bruno, scoured newspapers and session laws thanks to a grant from Princeton University's Anonymous, Undergraduate Research Assistants in Humanities and Social Sciences Fund. Lafayette and Marlyn diligently worked with me over three years, and their enthusiasm proved rejuvenating as I worked through revisions. I also thank students in my undergraduate and graduate courses who embraced, accepted, and encouraged the use of "treaty citizens" first.

Writing a book would be very lonely without friends. I am fortunate to have friends who have supported me since I began this career path. Thanks to my Huntington "crew," Veronica Castillo-Muñoz, Jerry González, Margie Brown-Coronel, José Alamillo, Natalia Molina, Alicia Perez, and Miriam Pawel, who brought joy to an intensive writing period in the archives. I am happy to call so many fellow historians friends, including Lori Flores, Ruben Flores, Adam Goodman, Andrew Highsmith, Emily Hobson, Jason LaBau, Gerardo Licon, Gustavo Licon, Katherine Marino, Julia Ornelas-Higdon, Mark Padoongpatt, Abigail Rosas, Ana Rosas, Andie Reid, Vicki Ruiz, Barbara Soliz, and Serena Sprungl. Shout-outs in solidarity to my fellow scholars interested in language politics: Claire Gilbert, Zevi Gutfreund, John Nieto-Phillips, Carlos Blanton, John Bezis-Selfa, Brendan Shanahan, Ying Ying Tan, Priti Mishra, Helder De Schutter, Mary Pratt, and Farina Mir. Thanks for the dynamic conversations about the politics of language. Last but not least, I want to thank my longtime writing accountability partner, Sarah Keyes, whose book I eagerly await.

Archivists hold a very special place in my heart for their dedication to preservation and to scholars. While I am grateful to each archivist I worked with, I wish to especially thank Teresa Salazar, Roberto Trujillo, Sibel Melik, Samuel Sisneros, and Nancy Brown-Martinez for answering and researching my questions and requests.

I am also appreciative of Jolene Torr, Dore Brown, Peter Perez, and Sheila Berg, who worked with me at the University of California Press, and especially my editor and advocate, Niels Hooper, who saw the promise of this project from the outset. Thanks for fielding questions about time line and work process from this ardent planner. My production team Katherine Harper and Sandy Sadow made me confident that my book was ready to print and accessible. Special thanks to Audra Wolfe, who made a daunting revision process enjoyable. I am grateful for the funding I received to support these professionals. Thanks to the Frank D. Graham Research Fund administered by Princeton's University Committee on Research in the Humanities and Social Sciences and to PIIRS for its support of the interdisciplinary research group, Migration: People and Cultures Across Borders, which gave me additional research funding.

Thanks to each of the editors of the American Crossroads series—which I have admired for over a decade and am honored to join. George Lipsitz offered sage advice, read closely, and prodded me to make this book better. Reconocimiento a Steve Pitti, who went above and beyond with his thorough and helpful comments and suggestions as my formerly anonymous reader.

This book would not have been possible without a strong support network. My parents told me that reading my introduction brought them to tears. They reminded me of just how important this history is to so many who have lived for decades in the United States almost entirely in the Spanish language, including my grandparents, Amelia and Arturo Colmenero and Antonia and Salvador Lozano. My goal as I wrote this book was to write in such a way that my extended family—mis abuelos, tíos, tías, primas y primos, and friends—would enjoy the book. I thank you all for your encouragement, places to stay when I was working in the archives (I'm looking at you, Anthony and Sabrina Chen Lozano, Brynne Lazarus, Heidi and Aaron Perea, Celina and Gabe, and Noé), love, and support. Gracías a todos por su apoyo, amor, y consejos. Your pride in me and my work serves as a buoy when I have a crisis of confidence. Thank you for believing in me.

ABBREVIATIONS

AHN	Readex: America's Historical Newspapers
BFP	Bergere Family Papers
CP	Thomas B. Catron Papers
DCP	Dennis Chávez Papers
DoE	Department of Education, New Mexico Papers
GFC	Guerra Family Collection
EGP	Ernesto Galarza Papers
HBP	Holm O. Bursum Papers
HRL	Helen and Robert W. Long collection of Moreno documents
LOC-CA	Library of Congress–Chronicling America
MC	Monterey Collection
MD	Marion Dargan Papers
MRP	Manuel Ruiz Papers
NACP	National Archives at College Park, Maryland
NARA	National Archives and Records Administration
NARS	National Archives and Records Administration—Pacific Region (Riverside)
NewsARC	NewspaperARCHIVE
NMJE	*New Mexico Journal of Education*
NSB	*New Statehood Bill*
OLP	Governor Octaviano Larrazolo Papers

RC   William Gillet Ritch Collection
SRP   Secundino Romero Papers
TANM   Territorial Archives of New Mexico
VFP   Vallejo Family Papers

NOTES

INTRODUCTION

1. United Nations Office of the High Commissioner for Human Rights, "Language Rights to Linguistic Minorities: A Practical Guide for Implementation," draft.

2. UNESCO, Universal Declaration of Linguistic Rights, art. 3.1, http://culturalrights.net/descargas/drets_culturals389.pdf.

3. The others are the United Kingdom, Pakistan, Costa Rica, Ethiopia, Somalia, Eritrea, and Bosnia-Herzegovina. Henry Hitchings, *The Language Wars: A History of Proper English* (New York: Farrar, Straus and Giroux, 2011), 252.

4. Jill Lepore, *A Is for American: Letters and Other Characters in the Newly United States* (New York: Alfred A. Knopf, 2002), 28.

5. Heinz Kloss, *The American Bilingual Tradition: Language in Education* (McHenry, IL: Delta Systems, 1998); Dennis Baron, *The English-Only Question: An Official Language for Americans* (New Haven, CT: Yale University Press, 1990); Paul Ramsey, *Bilingual Public Schooling in the United States: A History of America's "Polyglot Boardinghouse"* (New York: Palgrave MacMillan, 2010), 40–173.

6. There is no universally agreed upon term for the Latino or Hispanic population. Using "Hispanic" to refer to Spanish speakers suggests that Spain itself is a language of Spanish speakers and omits indigenous migrants from Latin America. Some indigenous-language speakers learn Spanish while in the United States to help them survive in their adopted nation. For these reasons, I use "Latino" to refer to individuals who entered the United States from Latin America, with the understanding that the vast majority came with some familiarity with the Spanish language. Pew Research Center: Hispanic Trends, www.pewhispanic.org/2015/09/28/modern-immigration-wave-brings-59-million-to-u-s-driving-population-growth-and-change-through-2065/ph_2015–09–28_immigration-through-2065-a2–05/.

7. The number of Spanish speakers is expected to grow to between thirty-nine and forty-three million by 2020. Jennifer M. Ortman, "Language Projections: 2010 to 2020" (Paper presented at the Annual Meeting of the American Sociological Association, Las Vegas, NV, 20–23 August 2011), 9, 17.

8. Pilar Meléndez, "United States Has More Spanish Speakers than Spain Does, Report Says," CNN, www.cnn.com/2015/07/01/us/spanish-speakers-united-states-spain/.

9. Reynaldo Macías, "Minority Languages in the United States, with a Focus on Spanish in California," in *The Other Languages of Europe: Demographic, Sociolinguistic, and Educational Perspectives*, ed. Guus Extra and Durk Gorter (Buffalo, NY: Multilingual Matters, 2001), 333–34.

10. Early Spanish Empire settlers in Florida largely came from Minorca and spoke Spanish and a Minorcan dialect originally from Catalán. Philip D. Rasico, *The Minorcans of Florida: Their History, Language, and Culture* (New Smyrna Beach, FL: Luthers, 1990), 96–98.

11. José E. Fernández, *The Biography of Casimiro Barela*, trans. A. Gabriel Meléndez (Albuquerque: University of New Mexico Press, 2003; orig. pub. 1911), viii, 72.

12. This estimate does not include Texas or those eligible for citizenship but born in Mexico. U.S. Census Bureau, *The Seventh Census of the United States: 1850* (Washington, DC: Robert Armstrong, Public Printer, 1853), 996, 972.

13. "American" is a highly problematic term, because its common-use definition in the United States excludes all Americans residing outside the borders of the United States in North and South America. Due to its ubiquitous use within the United States as the defining identity of the country, however, I use the term to signify a sense of belonging to the nation but not as an adjective, e.g., American government.

14. Reies López Tijerina was perhaps the most famous figure to do so. Lorena Oropeza, "The Heart of Chicano History: Reies López Tijerina as a Memory Entrepreneur," *The Sixties: A Journal of History, Politics and Culture* 1, no. 1 (2008): 51–56.

15. For their racialization, see Tomás Almaguer, *Racial Fault Lines: The Historical Origins of White Supremacy in California* (Berkeley: University of California Press, 1994); Laura E. Gómez, *Manifest Destinies: The Making of the Mexican American Race* (New York: New York University Press, 2007), 6.

16. The literature on the Fourteenth Amendment is voluminous. A sampling: William Nelson, *The Fourteenth Amendment: From Political Principle to Judicial Doctrine* (Cambridge, MA: Harvard University Press, 1988); Garrett Epps, *Democracy Reborn: The Fourteenth Amendment and the Fight for Equal Rights in Post–Civil War America* (New York: Holt Books, 2006). A broader look at citizenship that pays scant attention to language or treaty citizens is Rogers M. Smith, *Civic Ideals: Conflicting Visions of Citizenship in U.S. History* (New Haven, CT: Yale University Press, 1997).

17. A social reality encountered by other white ethnics at the time. See, e.g., Matthew Frye Jacobson, *Whiteness of a Different Color: European Immigrants and the Alchemy of Race* (Cambridge, MA: Harvard University Press).

18. Earl S. Pomeroy, *The Territories and the United States, 1861–1890* (Philadelphia: University of Pennsylvania Press, 1947), 28–30.

19. Stephanie D. Moussalli, *The Fiscal Case against Statehood: Accounting for Statehood in New Mexico and Arizona* (Lanham, MD: Lexington Books, 2012), 37.

20. For more on the United States as empire, see Steven Hahn, *A Nation without Borders: The United States and Its World in An Age of Civil Wars* (New York: Viking, 2016), 7–8; Paul Frymer, *Building an American Empire: The Era of Territorial and Political Expansion* (Princeton, NJ: Princeton University Press, 2017).

21. In 1870, Canada had 2 million English speakers to 1 million French speakers—a ratio never reached nationally in the United States. William F. Mackey, "History and Origins of Language Policies in Canada," in *Canadian Language Policies in Comparative Perspective*, ed. Michael A. Morris (Montreal: McGill-Queen's University Press, 2010), 28–29; Claude-Armand Sheppard, *The Law of Languages in Canada* (Ottawa: Crown, Studies of the Royal Commission on Bilingualism and Biculturalism, 1971), 62–68.

22. For more on German use: Charles Hart Handschin, *The Teaching of Modern Languages in the United States* (Washington, DC: Government Printing Office, 1913); Ramsey, *Bilingual Public Schooling*.

23. In 2013, 40.1 million individuals in the United States were migrants or immigrants. U.S. Census Bureau, Foreign Born Data Table 2.1, www.census.gov/data /tables/2013/demo/foreign-born/cps-2013.html; Kavita R. Khory, ed., *Global Migration: Challenges in the Twenty-First Century* (New York: Palgrave Macmillan, 2012); Bernadette Hanlon and Thomas J. Vicino, *Global Migration: The Basics* (Abingdon, U.K.: Routledge, 2014); Thomas Nail, *Theory of the Border* (Oxford: Oxford University Press, 2016).

24. Jefferson Martenet Correspondence Finding Aid, The Huntington Library, San Marino, CA.

25. Jefferson Martenet to Pump[?], 26 November 1853, Jefferson Martenet Correspondence, mssMartenet, Correspondence–1853, The Huntington Library, San Marino, CA.

26. Tom Prezelski, "Lives of the California Lancers: The First Battalion of Native California Cavalry, 1863–1866," www.californiamilitaryhistory.org/1stNatCavCV .html.

27. Porfirio J. Jimeno to Pablo de la Guerra, 3 August 1865, Guerra Family Papers, box 12, FAC 667, The Huntington Library, San Marino, CA (hereafter GFC).

28. ANLE, "Bienvenido a la página del español de los Estados Unidos," www.anle .us/303/El-espanol-de-los-Estados-Unidos.html.

29. Almost a dozen Spanish-speaking historians read parts of the book, and all suggested slightly different translations.

30. Jesús Alarid, "El idioma español," in *Los pobladores nuevo mexicanos y su poesía, 1889–1950*, ed. Anselmo F. Arellano (Albuquerque, NM: Pajarito Publications, 1976), 38.

31. A vast literature exists on this topic. A sampling: Gilbert González, *Chicano Education in the Era of Segregation* (Denton: University of North Texas Press, 1990); Guadalupe San Miguel Jr. and Richard Valencia, "From the Treaty of Guadalupe

Hidalgo to Hopwood: The Educational Plight and Struggles of Mexican Americans in the Southwest," *Harvard Educational Review* 68 (1998): 353–405.

32. Andrew Sandoval-Strausz, "Latino Landscapes: Postwar Cities and the Transnational Origins of a New Urban America," *Journal of American History* 101 (2014): 804–31; Dominic Vitiello and Thomas Sugrue, eds., *Immigration and Metropolitan Revitalization in the United States* (Philadelphia: University of Pennsylvania Press, 2017).

33. Olusola O. Adesope et al., "A Systematic Review and Meta-Analysis of the Cognitive Correlates of Bilingualism," *Review of Educational Research* 80 (2010): 207–45; Ellen Bialystok, "Reshaping the Mind: The Benefits of Bilingualism," *Canadian Journal of Experimental Psychology* 65 (2011): 229–35.

34. Calif. AB-82 (2017), http://leginfo.legislature.ca.gov/faces/billNavClient .xhtml?bill_id=201720180AB82; Jazmine Ulloa, "What's in a Name? This Bill Would Allow Accent Marks on California Birth Certificates," *Los Angeles Times*, January 13, 2017.

35. Claude Goldenberg and Kristin Wagner, "Bilingual Education: Reviving an American Tradition," www.aft.org/ae/fall2015/goldenberg_wagner.

36. This trend differs from other nations that turned in the mid-twentieth century to preserving indigenous and other European settler languages, a practice exemplified by both neighbors of the United States, Mexico and Canada. Claire Mar-Molinero, *The Politics of Language in the Spanish-Speaking World: From Colonization to Globalization* (New York: Routledge, 2000), 134–37; Mackey, "History and Origins of Language Policies in Canada," 54.

37. Sam Howe Verhovek, "Mother Scolded by Judge for Speaking in Spanish," *New York Times*, August 30, 1995, www.nytimes.com/1995/08/30/us/mother-scolded-by-judge-for-speaking-in-spanish.html?mcubz=0.

38. Mahita Gajanan, "Oklahoma Republican Suggests Turning Kids over to ICE If They Don't Speak English," *Time*, May 12, 2017, http://time.com/4778082/oklahoma-republican-ice-students-mike-ritze/.

39. Gwinnett County, Board of Registrations and Elections, Minutes, January 19, 2016, 2, www.gwinnettcounty.com/static/upload/bac/6/20160119/m_j1min.pdf.

1. UNITED BY LAND

1. Maurilio E. Vigil, *Los Patrones: Profiles of Hispanic Political Leaders in New Mexico History* (Washington, DC: University Press of America, 1980), 42.

2. Contested Election—New Mexico, H.R. Mis. Doc., 34–114, at 1 (1856) (José M. Gallegos).

3. For more on the 1855 Gallegos-Otero election, see Phillip Gonzales, *Política: Nuevomexicanos and American Political Incorporation, 1821–1910* (Lincoln: University of Nebraska Press, 2016), 300–316.

4. For racialization, see Almaguer, *Racial Fault Lines*, 45–72.

5. Omar Valerio-Jiménez, *River of Hope: Forging Identity and Nation in the Rio Grande Borderlands* (Chapel Hill, NC: Duke University Press, 2013), 1, 41–46.

6. Anne Hyde, *Empires, Nations, and Families: A History of the North American West, 1800–1860* (New York: HarperCollins, 2012), 200–219; Raúl Ramos, *Beyond the Alamo: Forging Mexican Ethnicity in San Antonio, 1821–1861* (Chapel Hill: University of North Carolina Press, 2010), 85–97, 193–98.

7. One, José Antonio Navarro, served two terms as a Texas senator. Ramos, *Beyond the Alamo*, 170.

8. 1837 Repub. Tex. Laws 99–100.

9. Spanish translations were approved in 1841, only to be suspended a week later. 1841 Repub. Tex. Laws 35, 38.

10. 1846 Tex. Laws 85.

11. Texas's unsettled boundary initiated the U.S.-Mexican War. Richard Griswold de Castillo, *The Treaty of Guadalupe Hidalgo: A Legacy of Conflict* (Norman: University of Oklahoma Press, 1990), 11–13.

12. Louise Pubols, "Becoming Californio: Jokes, Broadsides, and a Slap in the Face," in *Alta California: Peoples in Motion, Identities in Formation, 1769–1850*, ed. Steven W. Hackel (Berkeley and San Marino: Published for Huntington-USC Institute on California and the West by the University of California Press, 2010), 131–56.

13. Steven W. Hackel, *Children of Coyote, Missionaries of Saint Francis: Indian-Spanish Relations in Colonial California, 1769–1850* (Chapel Hill: University of North Carolina Press, 2005), 388–407.

14. Andrés Reséndez, *Changing National Identities at the Frontier: Texas and New Mexico, 1800–1850* (Cambridge: Cambridge University Press, 2004), 33–34; Maria Montoya, *Translating Property: The Maxwell Land Grant and the Conflict over Land in the American West, 1840–1900* (Berkeley: University of California Press, 2002), 29–38; David Correia, *Properties of Violence: Law and Land Grant Struggle in Northern New Mexico* (Athens: University of Georgia Press), 19.

15. Speech, Stephen W. Kearney, August 18/19, 1846, RI 240, William G. Ritch Collection, The Huntington Library, San Marino, CA (hereafter RC).

16. Gonzales, *Política*, 126.

17. Lisbeth Haas, "War in California, 1846–1848," in *Contested Eden: California before the Gold Rush*, ed. Ramón A. Gutiérrez and Richard J. Orsi (Berkeley: University of California Press, 1998), 341–46.

18. Treaty of Guadalupe Hidalgo, Art. IX.

19. There is a difference between those Congress thought owned land and those who actually controlled the land. See, e.g., Pekka Hämäläinen, *The Comanche Empire* (New Haven, CT: Yale University Press, 2009); Brian DeLay, *War of a Thousand Deserts: Indian Raids and the US-Mexican War* (New Haven, CT: Yale University Press, 2008).

20. For the limitation of political rights to white men, see Louisiana State Constitution of 1812, art. III; Julien Vernet, *Strangers on Their Native Soil: Opposition to United States' Governance in Louisiana's Orleans Territory, 1803–1809* (Jackson: University of Mississippi Press, 2013), 28, 34; Perry H. Howard, *Political Tendencies in Louisiana, 1812–1952* (Baton Rouge: Louisiana State University Press, 1957), 25–28.

21. U.S. Immigration Legislation Online, www.library.uwb.edu/guides/USimmigration/1790_naturalization_act.html.

22. Griswold de Castillo, *Treaty of Guadalupe Hidalgo*, 51.

23. DeLay, *War of a Thousand Deserts*, xiv; David Weber, *The Mexican Frontier: The American Southwest under Mexico* (Albuquerque: University of New Mexico Press, 1982), 16.

24. James S. Calhoun, Notice to Pueblos, 20 May 1850, RI 388, RC.

25. Anthony Mora, *Border Dilemmas: Racial and National Uncertainties in New Mexico, 1848–1912* (Durham, NC: Duke University Press, 2011), 60–64.

26. Hackel, *Children of Coyote*, 59–60; Ramón Gutiérrez, *When Jesus Came the Corn Mothers Went Away: Marriage, Sexuality, and Power in New Mexico, 1500–1846* (Stanford, CA: Stanford University Press, 1991), 193–94.

27. 1850 U.S. Census, 996, 966, 505.

28. Oregon, Minnesota, and Utah each had fewer than 15,000 inhabitants. Ibid., 993.

29. Ibid., 994–95; Reséndez, *Changing National Identities*, 32–36.

30. Reséndez, *Changing National Identities*, 34–37; 1850 U.S. Census, 994.

31. 1850 U.S. Census, 1869.

32. In 1850, 84 percent of New Mexico's adult population could not read or write. *Californios* lived in a more literate state. Michael Haines, ed., Social Explorer Dataset, Census 1850, Digitally transcribed by Inter-University Consortium for Political and Social Research.

33. Two exceptions: Platon Vallejo, *Memoirs of the Vallejos: New Light on the History, before and after the "Gringos" Came* (1914 serial; orig. 1943, repr. Fairfield, CA: J. D. Stevenson in cooperation with Napa County Historical Society, 1994), 25; Alfonso Griego, *Voices of the Territory of New Mexico* (Albuquerque, NM: Alfonso Griego, 1984), 25.

34. Rachel St. John, *A Line in the Sand: A History of the Western U.S.-Mexico Border* (Princeton, NJ: Princeton University Press, 2011), 67.

35. DeLay, *War of a Thousand Deserts*, 235–43, 297–310; Karl Jacoby, *Shadows at Dawn: A Borderlands Massacre and the Violence of History* (New York: Penguin Books, 2008), 100–105.

36. Francisco Ramírez, "Mas sobre la Emigracion a Sonora," *El Clamor Público* (Los Angeles), May 17, 1856.

37. José Francisco Leyva to Donaciano Vigil, 31 August 1848, RI 344, RC; José Francisco Leyva to Donaciano Vigil, 4 September 1848, RI 346, RC.

38. Martín González de la Vara, "The Return to Mexico: The Relocation of New Mexican Families to Chihuahua and the Confirmation of a Frontier Region, 1848–1854," in *The Contested Homeland: A Chicano History of New Mexico*, ed. Erlinda Gonzales-Berry and David R. Maciel (Albuquerque: University of New Mexico Press, 2000), 46–51; Mora, *Border Dilemmas*, 70–71.

39. The recolonization efforts in California largely moved treaty citizens into Baja California and Sonora. The harsh conditions (particularly in Sonora) led many to

return or to request U.S. annexation. Paul Bryan Gray, *A Clamor for Equality: Emergence and Exile of Californio Activist Francisco P. Ramírez* (Lubbock: Texas Tech University Press, 2012), 69–82; José Angel Hernández, *Mexican American Colonization during the Nineteenth Century: A History of the U.S.-Mexico Borderlands* (Cambridge: Cambridge University Press, 2012), 150.

40. Pedro Bautista Pino, *Noticias históricas y estadisticas de la antigua provincia de la Nueva México* (México: Imprenta de Lara, 1849), 93–95, quoted in González de la Vara, "The Return of Mexico," 45.

41. Mora, *Border Dilemmas*, 72; Hernández, *Mexican American Colonization*, 105–6.

42. Chihuahua was the largest state in Mexico in terms of area, with the majority of its settlers residing farther south of the border. Hernández, *Mexican American Colonization*, 104–9.

43. González de la Vara, "Return to Mexico," 48.

44. Hernández, *Mexican American Colonization*, 125–29. For more on one of the largest resettlement colonies, La Mesilla, see Mora, *Border Dilemmas*, 70–102.

45. González de la Vara, "The Return of Mexico," 46.

46. Mora, *Border Dilemmas*, 72–74.

47. Art. VIII promises Mexican citizens that they "shall be free to continue where they now reside, or to remove at any time to the Mexican Republic." It is correct that the treaty did not discuss or sanction recruiting individuals. Treaty of Guadalupe Hidalgo, art. VIII; Hernández, *Mexican American Colonization*, 113–14.

48. Ernesto Chávez, *The U.S. War with Mexico: A Brief History with Documents* (Boston: Bedford/St. Martin's, 2008), 24; John C. Calhoun, "Speech on the War with Mexico," January 4, 1848, in Chávez, *U.S. War with Mexico*, 119–20.

49. DeLay, *War of a Thousand Deserts*, 235–43, 297–310; Jacoby, *Shadows at Dawn*, 100–105.

50. The early legislature spent much of its resources combating Indian raids.

51. *An Act to Establish the Offices of Surveyor-General of New Mexico . . .* , 33rd Cong., 1st sess., ch. 103 §8 (1854).

52. Gonzales, *Política*, 797–99.

53. See various muster rolls, Box 12, RG.

54. 1852 N.M. Laws 81–82.

55. Henry Hilgert to William F. M. Arny, 25 October 1865, Reel 25, Territorial Archives of New Mexico (hereafter TANM); Henry Hilgert to William F. N. Arny, 2 January 1866, reel 25, TANM.

56. See reel 25, TANM for individual claims.

57. Montoya, *Translating Property*, 11–12; Correia, *Properties of Violence*, 28–29.

58. 1872 N.M. Laws 70.

59. 1880 N.M. Laws 108–9; 1882 N.M. Laws 194–95; 1887 N.M. Laws 243–44.

60. An Act to establish a court of private land claims, 51st Cong., sess. II, ch. 539, §1–2, 10.

61. For more complete stories of Tierra Amarilla and the Maxwell Land Grant that detail landownership, struggles, and occupation, see Correia, *Properties of Violence;* Montoya, *Translating Property.*

62. 1850 U.S. Census, xxxvi, 976.

63. California, . . . Governor's message; and report of the Secretary of State on the census of 1852, of the State of California (San Francisco: G. K. Fitch & Co. and V. E. Geiger & Co., State Printers, 1853), 6.

64. For Anglo views of Mexican land grants, see Tamara Venit Shelton, *A Squatter's Republic: Land and the Politics of Monopoly in California, 1850–1900* (Berkeley and San Marino: Published for Huntington-USC Institute on California and the West by the University of California Press, 2013), 14–18, 66, 89–94.

65. Missing from these census accounts is the Native American population. Settlers waged brutal campaigns against the indigenous populations that remained in much of the Southwest. In California, miners helped to "clear" these lands in a "genocide" of the Native population. See Benjamin Madley, *An American Genocide: The United States and the California Indian Catastrophe, 1846–1873* (New Haven, CT: Yale University Press, 2015); Jacoby, *Shadows at Dawn,* 95–101; Hämäläinen, *The Comanche Empire,* 293–361.

66. Treaty of Guadalupe Hidalgo; Griswold del Castillo, *Treaty of Guadalupe Hidalgo,* 44.

67. Peter H. Burnett, "Governor's Message," *Calif. Sen. Journal,* 1st sess. (1850), 36.

68. *Cong. Globe,* 31st Cong., 2nd sess. 2046 (1850) CG–1850–0927; William W. Morrow, *Spanish and Mexican Private Land Grants* (San Francisco and Los Angeles: Bancroft-Whitney Company, 1923), 12–14. For more on Gwin, see Kevin A. Waite, "The Slave South in the Far West: California, the Pacific, and Proslavery Visions of Empire" (PhD diss., University of Pennsylvania, 2016).

69. Eugene Casserly to Pablo de la Guerra, 28 July 1851, FAC 164, GFC.

70. See especially Miroslava Chávez-García, *Negotiating Conquest: Gender and Power in California, 1770s to 1880s* (Tucson: University of Arizona Press, 2004), 123–50; Hackel, *Children of Coyote,* 369–419; Rose Marie Beebe and Robert M. Senkewicz, *Testimonios: Early California through the Eyes of Women, 1815–1848* (Berkeley, CA: Heyday Books, 2006), 165–67, 184; Lisbeth Haas, *Conquests and Historical Identities in California, 1769–1936* (Berkeley: University of California Press, 1995), 3–4. Some women continued to control land after the Mexican period, even when married to Anglos. Widows who controlled land included Ysabel del Valle, Arcadia Bandini de Stearns, Josefa Fitch, María Ignacia de Bale, and Isidora Bandini Couts. See Fitch Family Papers, C-B 357, Bancroft Library, University of California, Berkeley; Bale Family Papers, BANC MSS C-B 746, Bancroft Library, University of California, Berkeley; Jesus M. Estudillo, *Sketches of California in the 1860s: The Journals of Jesus M. Estudillo* (Fredericksburg, TX: Awani Press, 1988), 122.

71. M. M. Sexton to Josefa Fitch, 19 June 1851, volume 1, folder 7, Fitch Family Papers.

72. Chávez-García, *Negotiating Conquest*, 124–50; Margie Brown-Coronel, "Beyond the Rancho: Four Generations of del Valle Women in Southern California, 1830–1940" (PhD diss., University of California, Irvine, 2011), 55–58.

73. M. G. Vallejo to María, 21 February 1878, box 1, folder 9, Vallejo Family Papers, BANC MSS C-B 441, Bancroft Library, University of California, Berkeley (hereafter VFP).

74. Henry W. Halleck to Pablo de la Guerra, 2 April 1852, FAC 602, GFC.

75. Leonard Pitt, *The Decline of the Californios: A Social History of the Spanish-Speaking Californians, 1846–1890*, rev. ed. (1966; repr. Berkeley: University of California Press, 1999), 97–98.

76. Chávez-García, *Negotiating Conquest*, 125.

77. Henry W. Halleck to Pablo de la Guerra, 23[?] April 1853, FAC 487, GFC.

78. Anglos brought 46.8 percent of the cases before the land commission, though they represented only 17.7 percent of the grantees during the Mexican period. Venit Shelton, *A Squatter's Republic*, 41.

79. Pablo de la Guerra, speech, 1860s[?], FAC 438, GFC.

80. California. Courts. District Court, 12th Judicial District, William M. Stafford v. James Lick, 28 September 1857, HM 43002, The Huntington Library, San Marino, California.

81. Letter from Juan Luco to Pío Pico, 11 July 1888, box 1, folder 43, Pío Pico Papers, MSS 68/115c, Bancroft Library, University of California, Berkeley (hereafter Pico Papers).

82. George H. Smith to Pío Pico, 17 September 1891, box 1, folder 45 [translated], Pico Papers; Alfred Stokes, Document list, May 1894, box 1, folder 60, Pico Papers.

83. Speech, de la Guerra, 1860s[?].

84. Ibid., 7.

85. Ibid., 8; emphasis in original.

86. Juan Montenegro to María Ysabel Bale, 18 November 1868, box 1, folder 3, Bale Family Papers.

87. Landowners, "Subscripcion," Los Angeles County, 22 March 1855, box 13, vol. 11, Abel Stearns Collection I, The Huntington Library, San Marino, California.

88. Venit Shelton, *A Squatter's Republic*, 12.

89. Henry Nash Smith, *Virgin Land: The American West as Symbol and Myth*, rev. ed. (1950; repr. Cambridge, MA: Harvard University Press, 1970).

90. María Ruiz de Burton, *The Squatter and the Don*, rev. ed. (1885; repr. New York: Modern Library, 2004), 391.

91. For more on squatters' political power, see Venit Shelton, *A Squatter's Republic*.

92. Andrés Garriza to M.G. Vallejo, 27 December 1874, box 4, folder 20, VFP.

93. Pitt, *Decline of the Californios*, 83–119; Chávez-García, *Negotiating Conquest*, 125.

94. Chávez-García, *Negotiating Conquest*, 149–50; Albert Camarillo, *Chicanos in a Changing Society: From Mexican Pueblos to American Barrios in Santa Barbara and Southern California, 1848–1930* (Cambridge, MA: Harvard University Press, 1978), 118; Robert M. Fogelson, *The Fragmented Metropolis: Los Angeles, 1850–1930* (Berkeley: University of California Press, 1993), 63–84.

2. TRANSLATION, A MEASURE OF POWER

1. Translations, at their best, were legally precise; at worst, literal, "on account of the many law terms." California, *Report of the Debates in the Convention of California on the Formation of the State Constitution, in September and October, 1849* (Washington, DC: J. T. Towers, 1850), xxxvii. Future studies of Spanish-language translations made throughout the Southwest will offer a greater understanding of how treaty citizens understood the new U.S. political system. For a better understanding of the promise of this sort of translation study, see Lawrence Venuti, *Translation Changes Everything: Theory and Practice* (New York: Routledge, 2013); David Bellos, *Is That a Fish in Your Ear? Translation and the Meaning of Everything* (New York: Farrar, Straus and Giroux, 2011).

2. Charles Montgomery, *The Spanish Redemption: Heritage, Power, and Loss on New Mexico's Upper Rio Grande* (Berkeley: University of California Press, 2002), xii; William Deverell, *Railroad Crossing: Californians and the Railroad, 1850–1910* (Berkeley: University of California Press, 1994), 62.

3. The research on state government translation is incomplete. This conclusion stems from Kloss, *American Bilingual Tradition,* 100–105.

4. Ibid., 133–57, 178–83.

5. Ibid., 137–41.

6. E.g., Michael Perman, *Struggle for Mastery: Disfranchisement in the South, 1888–1908* (Chapel Hill: University of North Carolina Press, 2001); Beth Lew-Williams, *The Chinese Must Go: Violence, Exclusion, and the Making of the Alien in America* (Cambridge, MA: Harvard University Press, 2018).

7. The town had 1,092 inhabitants. 1850 U.S. Census, 970.

8. Teofilo C. Echeverria to Camito Borondas, 13 January 1850, MR 120, Monterey Collection, 1785–1877, MSSMR 1–407, The Huntington Library, San Marino, CA (hereafter MC); Rafael Sánchez, List of Liquor Duty, 31 December 1849, MR 351, MC; Various Bills and Disbursements, August–December 1849, MR 7, MC.

9. José Santos Abarca to Prefect and Town Council, 9 February 1850, MR 354, MC; Rafael Sánchez to Monterey Common Council, 15 April 1850, MR 352, MC.

10. Monterey Common Council, Minutes of Sessions, 1850?, MR 262, MC; W. H. Chevers to Mayor and Common Council of Monterey, 14 June 1851, MR 83, MC; W. H. Chevers et al. to Common Council and Mayor of Monterey, 5 July 1851, MR 84, MC; Monterey Common Council, City Ordinances, 1850, MR 261, MC; Monterey Common Council to Residents of Monterey, 9 December 1851, MR 266, MC.

11. José Abrego to Common Council of Monterey, 15 April 1853, MR 34, MC.

12. For translation requests, see California, *Report of the Debates,* 25, 31, 218–19, 331. They considered taxed California Indians as voters because of Pablo de la Guerra's efforts (305–7). The decision to be counted as white contrasted with the treatment of Blacks. Almaguer, *Racial Fault Lines,* 35–38.

13. Considered at $16 per diem and ending at $28, the interpreter's salary was equal only to the secretary's. California, *Report of the Debates*, 95, 107, 25.

14. Ibid., 163–64, 398.

15. Ibid., 478–79.

16. Ibid., 475.

17. Ibid., 7, 478–79, 407, 14.

18. Although J. M. Covarrubias was French born, the proceedings claimed he was born in California. He spoke in Spanish during the convention. John Sutter, a native German speaker, confessed his poor English speaking ability. Ibid., 478–79, 187.

19. Ibid., 18.

20. Susanna Bryant Dakin, *The Lives of William Hartnell* (Stanford, CA: Stanford University Press, 1949), 134, 242–45.

21. California, *Report of the Debates*, 19.

22. Ibid., 478–79.

23. E.g., California, *Report of the Debates*, 305, 273–74, 17, 22; Madley, *An American Genocide*, 149–56, 163–64.

24. California, *Report of the Debates*, 21–23.

25. Nine other delegates also settled in Mexican California.

26. Votes included those by Henry Tefft, Hugo Reid, Abel Stearns, and Henry Hill. California, *Report of the Debates*, 23.

27. Pitt, *Decline of the Californios*, 43.

28. The convention recorder used Carillo/Carrillo, and Pablo de la Guerra was sometimes listed as Noriego. California, *Report of the Debates*, 14, 26, 63.

29. Ibid., 303.

30. One motion was related to Spanish-language translations. Ibid., 451, 456–57, 290–91, 153.

31. Ibid., 11–12, 23.

32. Ibid., 157, 274. Dimmick became a respected Los Angeles district attorney and judge.

33. Ibid., 23.

34. Ibid., 31. Requests failed at times because translators had proactively created translations.

35. Ibid., 37, 38; California, *Relacion de los Debates de la convencion de California* (Nueva York: Imprenta de S. W. Benedict, 1851), 62. The slash (/) here and elsewhere indicates that both the Spanish and the English exist in documents. In official bilingual documents, Spanish and English might appear on opposing pages or in separate versions.

36. California, *Report of the Debates*, 390, 398. Vallejo, Jones, and Carrillo made up the committee dealing with the Spanish-language constitution.

37. Ibid., 94–95.

38. Ibid., 399. Botts suggested a physical division by speaking of "one of the gentleman on the other side (a member of the native California delegation)" (400).

39. Ibid.

40. Ibid., 404–14.

41. Ibid., 273; California, *Relacion de los debates*, 268.

42. California, *Report of the Debates*, 273–74.

43. Cal. Const. of 1849, art. XI, §21 (superseded 1879).

44. Antonio de la Guerra to Pablo de la Guerra, 9 March 1850, box 8, FAC 351, GFC.

45. Cal. Leg. Journal, 1st sess. (1850), 551, 776.

46. Ibid., 150, 551. Lourie's name was spelled inconsistently: Lowry/Lowrie/Lourie.

47. Ibid., 1172.

48. Ibid., 346; 1850 Cal. Stat. 466.

49. Cal. Leg. Journal, 1st sess. (1850), 1034–35, 1172.

50. 1850 Cal. Stat. 466.

51. 1850 Cal. Stat. 466, 64.

52. 1850 Cal. Stat. 466, 83.

53. 1851 Cal. Stat. 529.

54. 1853 Cal. Stat. 144.

55. Minority Report, Joint Committee of the Senate and Assembly on the Translation of the Laws into the Spanish Language in Appendix to Journal of Senate and Assembly, 21st sess., vol. 5 (Sacramento, CA: State Printing Office, 1876).

56. Ibid.; Cal. Sen. Journal, 22nd sess. (1878), 200.

57. 1870 Cal. Stat. 909.

58. Cal. Pol. Code, §§415, 528 (1876).

59. 1870 Cal. Stat. 737.

60. Cal. Leg. Journal, 2nd sess. (1851), 1449–52; Cal. Leg. Journal, 7th sess. (1856), 152.

61. Andrés Pico, "Discurso de Don Andrés Pico," *El Clamor Público*, April 10, 1858.

62. For example, during the eighth session, Edward Harrison inquired about missing translations. Cal. Leg. Journal, 8th sess. (1857), 563.

63. Minority Report, Joint Committee of the Senate and Assembly on the Translation of the Laws into the Spanish Language.

64. E.g., George D. Fisher, County Clerk, and J. Carrillo, Juez del 2° Distrito (2nd District judge), Certification County Court of Santa Barbara, 21 April 1854, box 6, folder 292, GFC.

65. G. A. Pendleton, San Diego County Clerk, legal document, 3 July 1866, mssHLG 918, Helen and Robert W. Long collection of Moreno documents, The Huntington Library, San Marino, CA (hereafter HRL).

66. "The City of Language," *San Francisco Chronicle*, September 16, 1878.

67. W. W. H. Davis, *El Gringo: New Mexico and Her People* (Lincoln: University of Nebraska Press, 1982; orig. pub. 1857), 171.

68. Ibid., 253.

69. New Mexico, *Laws for the Government of the Territory of New Mexico*, 22 September 1846, Records and Seals, §4, http://avalon.law.yale.edu/19th_century/kearney .asp; *New Statehood Bill: Hearings Before the Subcommittee of the Committee on*

Territories on H.B. 12543, to Enable the People of Oklahoma, Arizona, and New Mexico to Form Constitutions and State Governments and be Admitted into the Union on an Equal Footing with the Original States, 57th Cong. 36 (1902) (statement of Charles M. Conklin, justice of the peace), 40 (hereafter *NSB*); Pablo Mitchell, *Coyote Nation: Sexuality, Race, and Conquest in New Mexico, 1880–1920* (Chicago: University of Chicago Press, 2005), 73.

70. E.g., 1860 N.M. Laws 30; 1882 N.M. Laws 40.

71. E.g., Legislative Assembly, Joint Resolution [from Translator's Office], 20 July 1851, RI 441, box 8, RC.

72. E.g., Resolution of the New Mexico Legislative Assembly, 13 December 1851, RI 472, box 9, RC; Facundo Pino to James S. Calhoun, 10 December 1851, RI 471, box 9, RC; Enrique Connelly to Diego Archuleta, 4 February 1864, RI 1308, box 21, RC; New Mexico Act, 23 December 1863, RI 1545, box 21, RC.

73. A sampling: James S. Calhoun, "Proclamation," 18 March 1851, No. 2, Rare book 49545, The Huntington Library, San Marino, CA (hereafter 49545); Lewis Wallace, "Proclamation by the Governor, 13 December 1878, No. 12, 49545.

74. Henry Connelly, "Proclamation by the Governor," 9 September 1861, nos. 3, 4; William A. Pile, "Governor's Proclamation," 8 September 1869, No. 6, 49545.

75. A sampling: Charles Leib, "Juramento de Oficio y Lealtad," 16 October 1863, RI 1203, box 21, RC; Ambrosio Pino, "Juramento de Lealtad," 21 October 1863, RI 1215, box 21, RC.

76. E.g., Esmeregildo Sanches, "Territorial Oath of Office and Allegiance," 24 September 1864, RI 1573, box 22, RC.

77. H.Misc. 4, 32nd Cong, 1st sess., §§1, 4–5, pp. 5–6.

78. Elisha Whittlesey to William S. Allen, 11 September 1851, RI 451, box 8, RC.

79. Elisha Whittlesey to William S. Allen, 29 April 1851, RI 425, box 8, RC; Pomeroy, *Territories and the United States*, 28–32.

80. New Mexico, *Report of the Secretary of the Territory, 1903–1904, and Legislative Manual* (Santa Fe: New Mexican Printing Company, 1905), 126.

81. W. W. H. Davis to Elisha Whittlesey, 21 February 1855, TANM, reel 27, frames 101–2.

82. Elisha Whittlesey to W. W. H. Davis, 20 October 1855, RI 765, box 13, RC.

83. W. W. H. Davis to Elisha Whittlesey, 25 August 1854, TANM, reel 27, frames 81–84.

84. W. W. H. Davis to Elisha Whittlesey, 15 January 1855, TANM, reel 27, frames 97–98.

85. Elisha Whittlesey to W. W. H. Davis, 21 March 1855, RI 710, box 13, RC.

86. Elisha Whittlesey to W. W. H. Davis, 21 March 1855, RI 710, box 13, RC.

87. W. W. H. Davis to Elisha Whittlesey, 27 March 1857, TANM, reel 27, frames 154–55.

88. The 1868 N.M. Laws are an exception.

89. 1863 N.M. Laws 113–14.

90. 1867 N.M. Laws 179–80.

91. 1870 N.M. Laws 193–94; 1869 N.M. Laws Joint Resolution 1; 1893 N.M. Laws 32.

92. 1872 N.M. Laws, Appendix 15.

93. By contrast, in Lower Canada the bilingual legislature voted on both French and English texts. 1874 N.M. Laws 17; Sheppard, *The Law of Languages in Canada*, 59–61.

94. See, e.g., 1861 N.M. Laws 118.

95. See, e.g., 1887 N.M. Laws 18; 1889 N.M. Laws 9; 1891 N.M. Laws 245; 1893 N.M. Laws 151.

96. Correia, *Properties of Violence*, 54–67, 74–75; Deutsch, *No Separate Refuge*, 24–25.

97. See, e.g., 1891 N.M. Laws 98, 165; 1893 N.M. Laws 51.

98. See, e.g., 1891 N.M. Laws 22.

99. Richard L. Nostrand, *The Hispano Homeland* (Norman: University of Oklahoma Press, 1992), 82–88.

100. C. Dominguez to H. P. Bennet, 30 May 1862, box 128, vol. 6, Records of the Accounting Officers of the Department of the Treasury, Record Group 217, National Archives and Records Administration (hereafter RG 217, NARA).

101. Elisha Whittlesey to H. P. Bennet, 16 June 1862, box 129, vol. 7, RG 217, NARA.

102. 1862 Colo. Sess. Laws 151.

103. Elisha Whittlesey to Samuel Hitt Elbert, 23 December 1862, box 129, vol. 7, RG 217, NARA.

104. 1863 N.M. Laws 104–5.

105. 1863 N.M. Laws 104–5; 1864 Colo. Sess. Laws 256.

106. Colo. Council Journal, 3rd sess. (1864), 15.

107. 1864 Colo. Sess. Laws 219–20.

108. Colo. Council Journal, 9th sess. (1872), 271.

109. Colo. Council Journal, 8th sess. (1870), 6.

110. Colo. Council Journal, 8th sess. (1870), 6.

111. Colo. Council Journal, 8th sess. (1870), 263.

112. Fernández, *Biography of Casimiro Barela*, 39.

113. Colo. Const. art. XVIII, §8 (1876).

114. The legislature at times downgraded or failed to print English-language reports, suggesting cost influenced votes; e.g., Colo. House Journal, 2nd sess. (1879), 54–56, 118.

115. Colo. Sen. Journal, 5th sess. (1885), 237, 351, 653, 1242, 1275; Colo. Sen. Journal, 6th sess. (1887), 201, 213, 321.

116. Colo. Sen. Journal, 6th sess. (1887), 13, 325.

117. Colo. Sen. Journal, 8th sess. (1892).

118. Gadsden Purchase art. V, www.avalon.law.yale.edu/19th_century/mx1853.asp.

119. Eric Meeks, *Border Citizens: The Making of Indians, Mexicans, and Anglos in Arizona* (Austin: University of Texas Press, 2007), 11, 18.

120. Ibid., 70–73. Thomas Sheridan, *Los Tusconenses: The Mexican Community in Tucson, 1854–1941* (Tucson: University of Arizona Press, 1986), 33–40.

121. No Spanish-surnamed individuals served in either chamber in 1866, 1867, and 1879.

122. Ariz. Sess. Laws 67 (1864).

123. Ariz. Sess. Laws 94 (1865).

124. Ariz. Assembly Journal, 3rd sess. (1867), 32.

125. Ariz. Assembly Journal, 3rd sess. (1867), 221.

126. Spanish-surnamed students remained the majority into the early 1900s. Ariz. Sess. Laws 41 (1875); Laura Muñoz, "Desert Dreams: Mexican American Education in Arizona, 1870–1930" (PhD diss., Arizona State University, 2006), 78–79.

127. Muñoz, "Desert Dreams," 8–53.

128. Ariz. Sess. Laws 119 (1877); Ariz. Sess. Laws 68 (1879).

129. San Francisco's Cosmopolitan Schools remained an exception to the law. 1870 Cal. Stat. 820; 1929 Cal. Stat. 134.

130. California, *Debates and Proceedings of the Constitutional Convention of the State of California, Convened at the City of Sacramento, Saturday, September 28, 1878*, vol. 1 (Sacramento: State Office, J. D. Young, sup't. 1880), 50.

131. See Carl Brent Swisher, *Motivation and Political Technique in the California Constitutional Convention, 1878–79* (New York: Da Capo Press, 1969).

132. California, *Debates and Proceedings*, 220, 89, 110.

133. Alexander Keyssar, *The Right to Vote: The Contested History of Democracy in the United States* (New York: Basic Books, 2000), 142.

134. Cal. Const. art. IV, § 24.

135. California, *Debates and Proceedings of the Constitutional Convention of the State of California*, vol. 2 (Sacramento: State Office, J. D. Young, sup't, 1880), 801–2.

136. Ibid., 802–3, 829; California, *Debates and Proceedings of the Constitutional Convention of the State of California*, vol. 3 (Sacramento: State Office, J. D. Young, sup't, 1880), 1269.

137. California, *Debates and Proceedings*, 3:1282.

138. "Kanaka" is a term used by native Hawaiians to refer to themselves. Francisco Ramírez, [Untitled], *El Clamor Público*, March 7, 1857.

3. CHOOSING LANGUAGE

1. Mariano Guadalupe Vallejo to Jovita Vallejo, 17 January 1864, Part III, box 1, folder 4, VFP.

2. The original letter has not been found. Madie Brown Emparan, *The Vallejos of California* (San Francisco: Gleeson Library Associates, University of San Francisco, 1968), 330.

3. "it is important to test in one, and then in another language, because . . ." M. G. Vallejo to W. W. Chipman, 7 December 1872, box 1, folder 6, VFP. This version is an incomplete draft, which Vallejo wrote in both Spanish and English.

4. *La invasión norteamericana* is the Mexican name for the U.S.-Mexican War.

5. Emparan, *Vallejos of California*, 430–31.

6. Vallejo, *Memoirs of the Vallejos*, 22.

7. Mariano Guadalupe Vallejo to Francisca Carrillo Vallejo, 4 February 1850, Part III, box 1, folder 3, VFP.

8. Emparan, *Vallejos of California*, 259.

9. Ibid., 262; Alan Rosenus, *General Vallejo and the Advent of the Americans* (Berkeley, CA: Heyday Books, 1999), 231.

10. Emparan, *Vallejos of California*, 255, 260–66; Benicia C. Frisbie to Francisca Vallejo, 21 November 1864, box 4, folder 9, VFP.

11. Mariano Guadalupe Vallejo to Francisca Benicia Vallejo, 28 January 1850, Part III, box 1, folder 3, VFP.

12. Andrónico Vallejo to Mariano Guadalupe Vallejo, 27 February 1851, Part III, box 6, folder 3, VFP.

13. Napoleon Vallejo to Francisca Benicia Vallejo, 26 February 1868, Part III, box 6, folder 11, VFP.

14. Henry Vallejo to Platón Vallejo, 4 April 1861, Part III, reel 1, VFP; Uladislao Vallejo to M. G. Vallejo, 21 June 1860, Part III, box 6, folder 15, VFP.

15. Mariano Guadalupe Vallejo to Francisca [Benicia] Vallejo, 18 March 1878, Part III, box 1, folder 9, VFP.

16. Platón Vallejo to Francisca Benicia Vallejo, 20 July 1862, Part III, box 6, folder 13, VFP.

17. Emparan, *Vallejos of California*, 225.

18. Mariano Guadalupe Vallejo to Romualdo Velázquez, 23 September 1880, Part III, box 1, folder 9, VFP.

19. Emparan, *Vallejos of California*, 324–25.

20. María Vallejo to M. G. Vallejo, 15 January, 18??, postcard, box 3, folder 34, VFP.

21. María Vallejo to Francisca Vallejo, 6 February 1873, box 3, folder 34, VFP.

22. María Vallejo to Mariano Guadalupe Vallejo, 29 May 1889?, box 3, folder 34, VFP.

23. Bernardo Frisbie to Mariano Guadalupe Vallejo, 14 May 1889, Part III, box 4, folder 10, VFP.

24. Adela and Fannie Frisbie et al. to Mariano Guadalupe Vallejo, 1 July 1887, Part III, box 4, folder 8, VFP.

25. Beebe and Senkewicz, *Testimonios*, 17.

26. Vallejo Leese's words come to us in English since Cerruti recorded them only in English. Ibid., 20.

27. Frank Jordan, *California Blue Book or State Roster, 1911* (Sacramento: Superintendent of State Printing, 1913), 190.

28. Pablo de la Guerra to Archibald Cary Peachy, 14 December 1851, FAC413, GFC.

29. Ibid.

30. Ibid.

31. Vigil, *Los Patrones*, 56.

32. Montgomery, *Spanish Redemption*, 39.

33. Vigil, *Los Patrones*, 53, 74, 77, 80.

34. "Jose Francisco Chavez," *El Nuevo Mexicano* (Santa Fe), October 18, 1890. Readex: America's Historical Newspapers (hereafter AHN).

35. These quotes provide selected corrections. Nicolás Armijo to Juan Armijo, 7 April 1880, box 1, folder 3, Armijo-Borradaile Family, MSS 359BC, Center for Southwest Research, University Libraries, University of New Mexico.

36. Matthew Gardner Kelly, "Schoolmaster's Empire: Race, Conquest, and the Centralization of Common Schooling in California, 1849–1879," *History of Education Quarterly* 56, no. 3 (2016): 446, 448, 454–55.

37. John Marvin to John Bigler, 10 April 1851, John G. Marvin Scrapbook 1, The Huntington Library, San Marino, CA.

38. 1870 Cal. Stat. 838–39.

39. John G. Marvin to John Bigler, 10 April 1851, 5, Marvin Scrapbook I.

40. James D. Hutton to John G. Marvin, 7 January 1852, in John Marvin to John Bigler, Marvin Scrapbook 1.

41. Ibid.

42. For more on intermarriage, see Raquel Casas, *Married to a Daughter of the Land: Spanish-Mexican Women and Interethnic Marriage in California, 1820–1880* (Reno: University of Nevada Press, 2007), 169–70.

43. Robert Nelson Christian, "A Study of the Historical Development of the Santa Barbara School District" (Master's thesis, University of Southern California, 1963), 40–44.

44. H. W. Splitter, "Education in Los Angeles, 1850–1900," *Historical Society of Southern California Quarterly* 33 (1951): 101.

45. H. D. Barrows, "Pioneer Schools of Los Angeles," *Annual Publications of the Historical Society of Southern California* 8 (1911): 61–66.

46. The major educational points of contention of the era centered on coeducation, whether to teach abolition, and the creation of sectarian versus nonsectarian schools. 1852 Cal. Stat. 125; Splitter, "Education in Los Angeles, 1850–1900," 109–10.

47. An 1880 Spanish-language letter to California assemblyman Reginaldo del Valle suggested a network of Spanish-speaking parents. Frederic Francois Vicomte Mondran to Reginaldo del Valle, 5 January 1880, HM43860, Reginaldo del Valle Papers, The Huntington Library, San Marino, CA.

48. *1880 Report of the Superintendent of Common Schools*, San Francisco School District, 34–35, box 51, M43, folder 4, San Francisco Unified School District Records (SFH 3), San Francisco History Center, San Francisco Public Library.

49. John Swett, *History of the Public School System of California* (San Francisco: A. L. Bancroft and Company, 1876), 73–74.

50. 1870 Cal. Stat. 838–39, 235.

51. The entire state embraced Cosmopolitan Schools in 1909 when state law recommended one in each "first class" city. The legislature expected French, Spanish, Italian, and German instruction at the schools. 1909 Cal. Stat. 412; *1880 Report of Superintendent of Common Schools*, 34–35.

52. Ygnacio del Valle to Joseph Lancaster Brent, 8 March 1866, box 2, folder 220, Papers of Joseph Lancaster Brent, The Huntington Library, San Marino, CA.

53. F. John Nobili, letter to the editor, "Education," *Daily Evening Picayune* (San Francisco), February 18, 1852, Marvin Scrapbook 1.

54. Moussalli, *Fiscal Case against Statehood*, 36–37.

55. Victoria-María MacDonald, *Latino Education in the United States: A Narrated History from 1513–2000* (New York: Palgrave, 2004), 69.

56. Lynne Marie Getz, *Schools of Their Own: The Education of Hispanos in New Mexico, 1850–1940* (Albuquerque: University of New Mexico Press, 1997), 13–17.

57. A. Gabriel Meléndez, *So All Is Not Lost: The Poetics of Print in Nuevomexicano Communities, 1834–1958* (Albuquerque: University of New Mexico Press, 1997), 6–7, 45–46.

58. 1891 N.M. Laws 45–59; Getz, *Schools of Their Own*, 16–17.

59. Amado Chaves to James F. Cannon, 29 April 1905, roll 66, TANM.

60. 1891 NM Laws 47–48, 51.

61. "Transitional" and "maintenance" are standard terms used in current modern discussions of bilingual education. They differ from English as a Second Language, which privileges English.

62. The difficulty continued into the early decades of the twentieth century. E. D. Leon to Amado Chaves, 23 December 1895, roll 65, TANM; Hiram Hadley to Arthur Bloche, 14 April 1905, roll 66, TANM; Lois Edith Huebert, "History of Presbyterian Church in New Mexico" (Master's thesis, University of New Mexico, 1964), Main Findings.

63. 1891 N.M. Laws 48.

64. Amado Chaves, Annual Report Territory of New Mexico Superintendent of Public Instruction from January 1, 1893, to December 31, 1893, 8–9, roll 72, TANM.

65. Plácido Sandoval, Report of the Superintendent of Public Instruction, Year Endings December 31, 1897, 14, 9, roll 72, TANM.

66. Amado Chaves, Annual Report Territory of New Mexico Superintendent of Public Instruction from January 1, 1896, to December 31, 1896, 8–9, roll 72, TANM.

67. 1907 N.M. Laws 200.

68. J. E. Clark chose to adopt no textbooks in Spanish in 1907, because "this Territory belongs to an English speaking people." J. E. Clark to Abraham Kempenich, 12 July 1907, roll 67, TANM.

69. Edwin A. Sherman to Mariano Guadalupe Vallejo, 15 July 1886, box 5, folder 55, VFP.

70. In another speech, Vallejo stated his preference for Spanish but, "warming with the subject," gave it in "pure unadulterated Anglo-Saxon." Aug. Rodgers to Mariano Guadalupe Vallejo, 19 May 1886, box 6, folder 1, VFP; R. A. Thompson to Mariano Guadalupe Vallejo, 28 September 1878, box 4, folder 198, Mariano Guadalupe Vallejo Papers, The Huntington Library, San Marino, CA; Emparan, *Vallejos of California*, 270.

71. Sherman to Vallejo, 15 July 1886; P. J. Thomas to Mariano Guadalupe Vallejo, 25 June 1877, box 4, folder 196, Mariano Guadalupe Vallejo Papers.

72. Addison A. Pollard to Susy, 24 February 1870, box 17, folder 2, California State Library Collection, California State Library, Sacramento.

73. California, *Report of the Debates*, 171.

74. "California and the Dictionary," Newspaper clipping, box 1, folder 1, Gertrude Atherton Papers, MMC-3164, Library of Congress.

75. "The Language Made Him Mad," newspaper clipping, undated, box 50, folder 3, L. Bradford Prince Papers, MSS 1959–174, Courtesy of the New Mexico State Records Center and Archives.

76. Leonardo Ver Mehr to María Ygnacia Bale de Soberanos, 26 June 1876, box 1, folder 1, Bale Family Papers.

77. Leonardo Ver Mehr to M. Y. Bale de Soberanos, 30 December 1861, box 1, folder 1, Bale Family Papers.

78. Ad, "Avisos a Las Familias," *Voz del Nuevo Mundo* (San Francisco), April 29, 1882, AHN.

79. Corrections are presented in brackets for clarity. Guillermo [William] Leighton to Augustín Olvera, 3 April 1858, HLG217, HRL.

80. Ysabel del Valle to Joseph Lancaster Brent, 7 April 1880, box 3, BT227, Brent Papers.

81. Mary Refugio Carpenter Diaries, 1860–1865, box 1, folder 6, Pleasants Family Papers, Special Collections and Archives, The UC Irvine Libraries, Irvine, CA; Tahireh Hicks, "'Refugio en el campo': The Persistence of Californio Identity in Rural Southern California, 1850–1900" (Senior thesis, Princeton University, 2017).

82. On this trip, both men also expressed their aspirations to be U.S. senators—a feat they both accomplished. "How He Learned Spanish: Interesting Sidelight on Mr. Catron's Character," *New Mexican* (Santa Fe), May 16, 1921, box 5, folder 11, Marion Dargan Papers, MSS 120BC, Center for Southwest Research, University Libraries, University of New Mexico (hereafter MD).

83. Governor Mitchell's reason for the promotion remains debatable, but the incident's use in sources emphasizes the territorial interest in language acquisition. Vioalle Clark Hefferman, "Thomas Benton Catron" (Master's thesis, University of New Mexico, 1940), 10.

84. Victor Westphall, *Thomas Benton Catron and His Era* (Tucson: University of Arizona Press, 1973), 26.

85. James B. Morrow, " Senator Catron Dubbed Prophet," *Washington DC Herald*, September 6, 1914, Chronicling America: Historic American Newspapers, sponsored by the Library of Congress and the National Endowment for the Humanities, (hereafter LOC-CA); Westphall, *Thomas Benton Catron*, 22.

86. Morrow, "Senator Catron Dubbed Prophet."

87. David H. Stratton, "New Mexican Machiavellian? The Story of Albert B. Fall," *Montana: The Magazine of Western History* 7, no. 4 (October 1957): 4; Westphall, *Thomas Benton Catron*, 22.

88. Montgomery, *Spanish Redemption*, 223.

89. Margaret S. Hereford Wilson to Esther Sale Hereford, August 1848, WN1825, Benjamin Davis Wilson Papers, The Huntington Library, San Marino, CA.

4. A LANGUAGE OF CITIZENSHIP

1. Pico et al., "Al honorable senado y casa de los Estados Unidos de America," 1859.

2. An estimated 2,000 of over 50,000 *nuevomexicanos* retained Mexican citizenship. Griswold del Castillo, *Treaty of Guadalupe Hidalgo*, 65–66.

3. For more, see Griswold del Castillo, *Treaty of Guadalupe Hidalgo*, 51; William J. Novak, "The Legal Transformation of Citizenship in Nineteenth-Century America," in *The Democratic Experiment: New Directions in American Political History*, ed. Meg Jacobs, William J. Novak, and Julian M. Zelizer (Princeton, NJ: Princeton University Press, 2003); Laura F. Edwards, *The People and Their Peace: Legal Culture and the Transformation of Inequality in the Post-Revolutionary South* (Chapel Hill: University of North Carolina Press, 2009); J. Morgan Kousser, *The Shaping of Southern Politics: Suffrage Restriction and the Establishment of the One-Party South, 1880–1910* (New Haven, CT: Yale University Press, 1974).

4. Marta Tienda, "Demography and the Social Contract," *Demography* 39, no. 4 (November 2002): 602.

5. Ron Hayduk, *Democracy for All: Restoring Immigrant Voting Rights in the United States* (New York: Routledge, 2006), 19–20.

6. Two classics in the field barely consider language: Smith, *Civic Ideals*; Keyssar, *Right to Vote*, 145.

7. Ariz. Sess. Laws 64 (1877).

8. Quote from Senator Casimiro Barela speech. Fernández, *Biography of Casimiro Barela*, 81. The original version of Article IX had stronger protective language: "as soon as possible" instead of "at the proper time." It promised individual rights beyond property by maintaining "the civil rights not vested in them according to Mexican Law." References to civil rights or Mexican law are absent from the final treaty. Griswold del Castillo, *Treaty of Guadalupe Hidalgo*, 179–80, 189–90.

9. Francisco Ramírez, Editorial, *El Clamor Público*, July 25, 1857.

10. For a brief history of these political practices in Texas, see David Montejano, *Anglos and Mexicans in the Making of Texas, 1836–1986* (Austin: University of Texas Press, 1987), 39–40; Valerio-Jiménez, *River of Hope*, 237–39.

11. Francisco Ramírez, Editorial, *El Clamor Público*, December 18, 1857.

12. Paul Bryan Gray, *A Clamor for Equality: Emergence and Exile of Californio Activist Francisco P. Ramírez* (Lubbock: Texas Tech University Press, 2012), 59.

13. Howard W. Allen and Kay Warren Allen, "Vote Fraud and Data Validity," in *Analyzing Electoral History: A Guide to the Study of American Voter Behavior*, ed. Jerome Clubb, William Flanigan, and Nancy Zingale (Beverly Hills, CA: Sage, 1981), 153–54.

14. Mark Lawrence Kornbluh, *Why America Stopped Voting: The Decline of Participatory Democracy and the Emergence of Modern American Politics* (New York: New York University Press, 2000), 11, 27–33.

15. Richard Franklin Bensel, *The American Ballot Box in the Mid-Nineteenth Century* (New York: Cambridge University Press, 2004), 295; Kornbluh, *Why America Stopped Voting,* 163, 42, 48–49, 80.

16. Voters responded to these tactics by voting at levels unthinkable today. The national average was 79 percent between 1880 and 1896. Kornbluh, *Why America Stopped Voting,* 27–33, 12–15.

17. Ibid., 36–43, 123.

18. Harris Newmark, *Sixty Years in Southern California* (Los Angeles: Zeitlin & Ver Brugge, 1970; orig. pub. 1916), 41–43.

19. Ibid., 43.

20. Pitt, *Decline of the Californios,* 202–4.

21. Tom Sitton, *The Courthouse Crowd: Los Angeles County and Its Government, 1850–1950* (Los Angeles: Historical Society of Southern California), 60, 85.

22. U.S. Census Office, Report on Population of the United States at the Eleventh Census, Part II, lxii.

23. Literacy requirements began in the Northeast in the 1850s as a method of disenfranchising illiterate and poor immigrants. In southern states, literacy tests served as one tactic of many to disenfranchise African American voters during the rise of Jim Crow laws. Mississippi enacted a literacy test in 1890, prior to California. But California's 1894 requirement that voters had to read the Constitution in English and be able to write their names preceded literacy test requirements elsewhere in the South. Catherine Prendergast, *Literacy and Racial Justice: The Politics of Learning after Brown v. Board* (Carbondale: Southern Illinois University Press, 2003), 5–6; Kousser, *The Shaping of Southern Politics,* 238–65.

24. 1880 Cal. Stat. 173–74.

25. An 1891 provision allowed voters to determine voting restrictions on language. 1891 Cal. Stat. 115; Cal. Const. art. II, §1 (adopted 1894, superseded 1970).

26. Cal. Civ. Proc. Code, §1184 (1876).

27. After 1862, only the first five counties listed permitted court proceedings in Spanish. By 1876 only the first four received the exemption. Cal. Title XVII, 5575, §646 (1865); Cal. Civ. Proc. Code, §185 (1876).

28. 1870 Cal. Stat. 820–21.

29. 1880 Cal. Stat. 182.

30. 1880 Cal. Code of Civil Procedure, 43, 45.

31. 1899 Cal. Stat. 86, 326, 336.

32. The California legislature struck the act allowing Spanish translations of laws in 1897 in what was likely a procedural cleanup of California's Political Code (it passed 52 to 1). After the 1879 constitution, California only considered posting notices in Chinese regarding exclusion laws and allowing the employment of Japanese

(withdrawn) interpreters for criminal proceedings. In 1899 the legislature gave superior court judges the authority to hire interpreters in any required language. 1897 Cal. Stat. 99; 1891 Cal. Stat. 189; 1895 Cal. Stat. 37; Calif. Leg. Journal, 32nd sess. (1897), 420; 1899 Cal. Stat. 250, 276.

33. Camarillo, *Chicanos in a Changing Society*; Pitt, *Decline of the Californios*.

34. Fernández, *Biography of Casimiro Barela*, 4, 93–94; Meléndez, Introduction to Fernández, *Biography of Casimiro Barela*, xxxiii–xxxiv.

35. 1891 Colo. Sess. Laws 160. Fernández also credits Barela with pushing through symbols on ballots to aid illiterates in 1899. Fernández, *Biography of Casimiro Barela*, 127–28.

36. Benjamin Read, in José Emilio Fernández, *Cuarenta años de legislador: Biografía del senador Casimiro Barela*, Chicano Heritage (New York: Arno Press, 1976); Fernández, *Biography of Casimiro Barela*, li.

37. Phillip Gonzales, "La Junta de Indignación: Hispano Repertoire of Collective Protest in New Mexico, 1884–1933," *Western Historical Quarterly* 31 (Summer 2000): 162–64.

38. Fernández, *Biography of Casimiro Barela*, 49–50.

39. Fernández, *Cuarenta años de legislador*; Fernández, *Biography of Casimiro Barela*, 51.

40. My estimate of at least 10 percent is a conservative one to account for rapid growth. 1880 U.S. census, 52; 1890 U.S. census, 78.

41. [Untitled], *Colorado Springs Gazette*, March 7, 1884, AHN.

42. Fernández, *Biography of Casimiro Barela*, 52, 54; Meléndez, in Fernández, *Biography of Casimiro Barela*, xxxvi; 1885 Colo. Sess. Law 263.

43. Fernández, *Biography of Casimiro Barela*, 53–54.

44. A later case filed to secure ethnic Mexican rights to sit on a jury went all the way to the Supreme Court but did not consider language. See *Hernández v. Texas* (1954).

45. Fernández, *Biography of Casimiro Barela*, 53.

46. 1890 U.S. Census Report, v. 2, lxii.

47. 1870 U.S. Census, xvii.

48. Ariz. Sess. Laws, 1864–1900.

49. Ariz. Sess. Laws, JR 67–68 (1864).

50. The 2nd session of the Assembly had a translator. Ariz. Ass. Journal, 2nd sess. (1866), 60, 64; Ariz. Ass. Journal, 3rd sess. (1867), 56, 68, 215.

51. Ariz. Sess. Laws 36 (1875); Ariz. Sess. Laws 456 (1887); Ariz. Sess. Laws 161–62 (1881).

52. Ariz. Sess. Laws 59 (1889).

53. Ariz. Sess. Laws 93 (1891).

54. 1890 U.S. Census Report, v. 2, lxii.

55. W. G. Ritch to Lew Wallace, 7 December 1878, reel 25, TANM; Gonzales, *Política*, 6–7.

56. 1889 N.M. Laws 18.

57. 1882 N.M. Laws 40; 1889 N.M. Laws 276.

58. Laura Gómez, "Race, Colonialism, and Criminal Law: Mexicans and the American Criminal Justice System in Territorial New Mexico," *Law & Society Review* 34 (2000): 1130, 1139, 1192.

59. For party dynamics in the territory, see Gonzales, *Política.*

60. Davis, *El Gringo,* 252.

61. Election Roll for Valencia County, 4 September 1865, RI 2269, RC.

62. Ibid. More examples from Valencia County exist in the RC.

63. 1890 U.S. Census Report, v. 2, lxii.

64. For a detailed history of each early election, see Gonzales, *Política.*

65. The secretary of the territory, solicitor general, treasurer, and superintendent of the penitentiary did not have Spanish surnames. B. M. Thomas to S. H. Macy, 9 September 1892, reel 27, TANM.

66. Amado Chaves, Territory of New Mexico Superintendent of Public Instruction, Amado Chaves, from January 1, 1894, to December 31, 1894, report for territorial governor, 7, reel 72, TANM.

67. For more, see Gonzales, *Política.*

68. For more on the role of territorial delegates, see Pomeroy, *The Territories and the United States,* 80–88; Gonzales, *Política.*

69. In 1890, *nuevomexicanos* criticized Joseph for not fully supporting them or Spanish. Marion Dargan, "New Mexico's Fight for Statehood, Part III: The Opposition within the Territory (1888–1890)," *New Mexico Historical Review* 15, no. 2 (April 1940): 136; Doris Meyer, *Speaking for Themselves: Neomexicano Cultural Identity and the Spanish-Language Press, 1880–1920* (Albuquerque: University of New Mexico Press, 1996), 23–25.

70. Jesus Lucero and Demostenes Martínez to Hon. Antonio Trujillo, 20 August 1892, box 401, folder 3, Thomas B. Catron Papers, MSS 29BC, Center for Southwest Research (hereafter CP).

71. Newspaper clipping, August 22, 1892, box 401, folder 3, CP.

72. "¡Joseph renominado! En medio del mas grande entusiasmo," *El Estandarte de Springer* (Springer, NM), September 15, 1892, AHN.

73. "The Battle Begun . . . ," *Springer Banner,* September 8, 1892, AHN.

74. "The Democratic Convention," *Las Vegas Daily Optic,* September 7, 1892, NewsARC.

75. L. A. Riley to T. B. Catron, 29 September 1892, box 401, folder 3, CP.

76. J. C. Berry to [?] Wright, 3 October 1892, box 401, folder 3, CP.

77. Samuel C. Week [Wick?] to R. E. Twitchell, 19 October 1892, box 401, folder 3, CP.

78. Hughes to Thomas Hughes, 17 October 1892, box 401, folder 3, CP.

79. T. B. Catron to John Daily, 30 March 1892, box 6, folder 6, MD.

80. Porter A. Stratton, *The Territorial Press of New Mexico, 1834–1912* (Albuquerque: University of New Mexico Press, 1969), 24–26.

81. Political cartoon and "La intrépida campaña . . . ," *La Voz del Pueblo,* October 29, 1892, LOC-CA.

82. For more on editors and the literary quality of Spanish-language newspapers: Meyer, *Speaking for Themselves*; Meléndez, *So All Is Not Lost*.

83. "El informe aquel," *El Estandarte de Springer*, September 15, 1892, AHN.

84. 1891 N.M. Laws 58; "El Pueblo es burlado y Desfranquiciado de Votar," *La Opinion Pública* (Albuquerque, NM), September 10, 1892, AHN; David Holtby, *Forty-Seventh Star: New Mexico's Struggle for Statehood* (Norman: University of Oklahoma Press, 2012), 14–15.

85. Holtby, *Forty-Seventh Star*, 88.

86. Novak, "Legal Transformation of Citizenship in Nineteenth-Century America," 92.

87. An unsecure archive led to the improper loss of many papers from the Territorial Archives of New Mexico. Executive Branch papers recovered by William T. Ritch demonstrate that the governor received few letters. See William Ritch papers, box 12, for monthly letter logs.

88. The governor kept official records in English, which could explain the inconsistency. Facundo Pino to James S. Calhoun, 10 December 1851, RI 471, box 9, RC; Enrique Connelly to Diego Archuleta, 4 February 1864, RI 1308, box 21, RC.

89. Petition, Doña Ana County Inhabitants to William Carr Lane, 22 March 1853, RI 578, box 10, RC.

90. Cecilia Lucero López to Henry Connelly, ca. May 1866, RI 1477, box 24, RC.

91. For example, Maximo Baca to B. M. Thomas, 15 July 1889, reel 25, TANM.

92. F. E. Montoya to B. M. Thomas, August 1890, reel 25, TANM.

93. Jesus María Chávez to Lewis Wallace, 2 May 1880, RI 1895, box 27, RC.

94. "el pueblo Reunido En masa" to Secretary of the Territory, 11 February 1890, reel 25, TANM.

95. Lucas E. Gallegos to M. A. Otero, 17 March 1901, reel 130, frame 362, TANM.

96. Martín Alfaro to Miguel A. Otero, 13 March 1901, reel 130, frame 345, TANM; R. Ortiz to M. A. Otero, 26 April 1901, reel 130, frame 584, TANM; Celso Baca to M. A. Otero, 8 July 1901, reel 131, frame 39, TANM.

97. Kornbluh, *Why America Stopped Voting*, 53–54.

98. B. D. Rodey to Fourth Assistant Post Master General and Miguel A. Otero, 11 July 1901, reel 131, frames 54–55, TANM.

99. For more on statehood attempts: Robert Larson, *New Mexico's Quest for Statehood: 1846–1912* (Albuquerque: University of New Mexico, 1968); Gonzales, *Política*.

100. An 1876 minority report from the House also highlighted representatives' discomfort with the poor educational system in the territory and small number of English speakers. H.R. Rep. No. 44–503, Pt. 1 at 7 (1876); Pt. II at 7.

101. Baron, *English-Only Question*, 96.

102. Dargan, "New Mexico's Fight for Statehood, Part III," 151–53.

103. Ibid., 136.

104. H.R. Rep. No. 52–736, at 43 (1892).

105. H.R. Rep. No. 52–736, at 43–44 (1892).

106. "Statehood," *Las Vegas Optic*, March 16, 1888, box 3, folder 1, MD.

107. Ibid.

108. William M. Stewart, "The Stumbling Block," *Las Vegas Optic*, February 23, 1889, box 4, folder 1, MD.

109. Meyer, *Speaking for Themselves*, 124–26.

110. California, *Report of the Debates*, 22.

5. THE UNITED STATES SEES LANGUAGE

1. "To Investigate Territories' Claims to Statehood," *Boston Post* (MA), November 10, 1902, NewsARC.

2. [Untitled], *Daily Ardmoreite* (Ardmore, OK), November 11, 1902, NewsARC.

3. *NSB* (statement of Albert Beveridge, chairman of subcommittee), 10.

4. *NSB* (statement of Beveridge), 33.

5. *NSB* (Enrique Salasar, West Las Vegas postmaster), 11; (William J. Mills, Chief Justice, Supreme Court of New Mexico), 1.

6. *NSB* (Bernard Rodey, New Mexico territorial representative), 332.

7. Sandoval, *Report of the Superintendent . . . 1897*, 14.

8. These sentiments were further solidified and entrenched in the next generation. For more on middle-class understandings of citizenship, see Valerio-Jimenez, *River of Hope*, 153–58, 238–39; Mitchell, *Coyote Nation*, 127–36.

9. For more on previous statehood attempts, see Larson, *New Mexico's Quest*; Gonzales, *Política*.

10. Howard Lamar, *The Far Southwest, 1846–1912: A Territorial History* (New Haven, CT: Yale University Press, 1966), 337–44.

11. Baron, *English-Only Question*, 99.

12. "Territory Statehood Junket," *Muskogee Phoenix* (AZ), November 13, 1902, NewsARC.

13. 56 Cong. Rec. S. at 704–11 (9 January 1900). See also Albert Beveridge, "The March of the Flag," speech, Indianapolis, IN, September 16, 1898.

14. "The Omnibus Bill," *Galveston Daily News* (TX), November 26, 1902, News-ARC; [Untitled], *Titusville Herald* (PA), December 12, 1902, NewsARC.

15. Senator Dillingham later chaired the Immigration Commission and became a proponent of restrictive immigrant quotas. Baron, *English-Only Question*, 99.

16. "Oppose Statehood Bill," *New York Times*, November 8, 1902, NewsARC.

17. "Presidential Talk," *Mansfield News* (OH), January 7, 1903, NewsARC.

18. "To Investigate Territories' Claims to Statehood," *Boston Post*; "No Junketing Tour," *Arizona Republican* (Phoenix), November 12, 1902, NewsARC.

19. "The Senators Finished Work," *Santa Fe New Mexican*, November 14, 1902, NewsARC.

20. The late addition suggests how little the senators knew about language use in New Mexico. "Oppose Statehood Bill," *New York Times*; S. Rep. No. 57–2206, part 1, at 8 (1902).

21. "Senators Finished Work," *Santa Fe New Mexican*.

22. *NSB*, 309–16. The transcript includes 120 pages on New Mexico, with 84 interviews conducted. Arizona's section is only 54 pages with 31 interviews. Oklahoma has 39 pages and 26 interviews. The vast exhibits, appendixes, and committee meeting transcripts largely consist of New Mexico documents.

23. Other sources are more localized or describe language use over a longer period.

24. Baron, *English-Only Question*, 99.

25. [Illegible], *Arizona Republican*, November 18, 1902, NewsARC.

26. L. Bradford Prince, *New Mexico's Struggle for Statehood: Sixty Years of Effort to Obtain Self-Government* (Santa Fe: New Mexican Printing Co., 1910), 98.

27. See the interviews of Albuquerque's N. E. Hickey and Phoenix's Benjamin A. Fowler and Joseph H. Kibbey. *NSB*, 93–96, 132–44.

28. "Arizona Hotel Owner Will Renovate Historic New Mexico Property," *Arizona Republic* (Phoenix, AZ), April 22, 2014, www.azcentral.com/story/money/real-estate/2014/04/21/northern-arizona-hotelier-buys-historic-hotel-las-vegas-nm/7978975/; *NSB* (Mills, chief justice), 1, 10.

29. Representative Rodey proactively brought five New Mexican boosters to the June 28 hearings. They downplayed Spanish use but encouraged a favorable view of *nuevomexicanos*. *NSB* (statement of Bernard S. Rodey, New Mexico congressional representative), 332, 347.

30. *NSB* (statement of H. S. Wooster, justice of the peace), 18.

31. Aurelio Espinosa, *The Spanish Language in New Mexico and Southern Colorado* (Santa Fe: New Mexican Printing Company, 1911).

32. *NSB* (statement of Rodey), 329–30, 342.

33. *NSB* (statements of Pablo Ulibarri, Damo Deo Sena, José Lino Rivera, Eugenio Rodolph, Pablo Jaramillo, Rafael Gallegos, census enumerators), 13–14, 15–17, 19–20, 22.

34. *NSB* (statement of Maggie J. Bucher, superintendent of schools of East Las Vegas), 24.

35. *NSB* (statements of Francesca Zana, teacher; Enrique Armijo, superintendent of West Las Vegas Schools; Wooster), 9–11, 18.

36. *NSB* (statement of Baca y García), 25.

37. *NSB*, 8–11, 24, 30, 33, 55–56, 89–91, 101, 108.

38. "Senators Finished Work," *Santa Fe New Mexican*.

39. *NSB* (statements of Beveridge), 27, 24; (statement of William P. Dillingham, senator), 24. For the increasing adoption of "Spanish" as an identifier, see John Nieto-Phillips, *The Language of Blood: The Making of Spanish-American Identity in New Mexico, 1880s–1930s* (Albuquerque: University of New Mexico Press, 2004).

40. They code-switched who was "foreign." *NSB* (statement of Beveridge), 6, 50.

41. *NSB* (statement of Mills, chief justice), 2. Albuquerque's Benjamin Baker confirmed, "When I use the term 'American,' I mean all other nationalities except Mexicans," *NSB* (statement of Benjamin S. Baker, associate justice of the territorial supreme court), 46.

42. *NSB* (statement of Nepomuceno Segura, court interpreter), 6. I follow their convention in descriptions of their testimony observations; otherwise I use *nuevomexicano* or Anglo.

43. For the double colonization process, see Gómez, *Manifest Destinies*, 47–79.

44. *NSB* (statement of Enrique Armijo), 10.

45. For two examples, see *NSB* (statement of Beveridge), 28, 44. For a more nuanced examination of the meanings that "Mexican" served for native Spanish speakers, see Mora, *Border Dilemmas*, 9–15.

46. *NSB* (statement of José María García, former justice of the peace), 41.

47. "Senators Finished Work," *Santa Fe New Mexican*.

48. *NSB* (statement of José D. Sena, assistant interpreter), 33.

49. *NSB* (statement of Paul A. F. Walters, postmaster), 44.

50. *NSB* (statement of James D. Hughes, businessman), 38.

51. *NSB* (statement of Walters), 43.

52. *NSB* (statement of Charles M. Conklin, justice of the peace), 40.

53. "Senators Finished Work," *Santa Fe New Mexican*.

54. Ibid.

55. *NSB* (statement of Camilo Padilla, census enumerator), 42.

56. *NSB* (statements of Facundo Ortiz and Barbara Perea y [Y]risarri, census enumerators), 30–31.

57. *NSB* (statement of Clementa P. Ortiz, census enumerator), 35.

58. Unfortunately, the senators did not ask whether Conklin spoke Spanish. *NSB* (statement of Joseph P. Conklin), 37.

59. Ultimately, Beveridge determined the census was largely accurate, validating Sánchez's work. Beveridge's opposition to statehood benefited from a low census count. S. Rep. No. 57–2206, part 1, at 5 (1902).

60. *NSB* (statement of Pedro Sánchez, census supervisor), 44–45.

61. In addition to the 13 Spanish-language interpreters, one German, one Italian, and 17 "Indian" interpreters served on the census staff. The senators did not ask about these other language groups. *NSB*.

62. "Senators Finished Work," *Santa Fe New Mexican*.

63. For more on politics and legal proceedings, see *NSB*, 28–29, 31–33, 39–43.

64. Griego, *Voices of the Territory*, 65, 83.

65. Holtby, *Forty-Seventh Star*, 88.

66. Taken from Mayor C. F. Myers's statement and the 1900 census. *NSB* (statement of C. F. Myers, mayor of Albuquerque), 59; 1900 U.S. Census, 271.

67. *NSB* (statement of Thomas Hughes, newspaperman), 65.

68. For a sampling, see *NSB* (statement of William George Tight, University of New Mexico president), 82; (statement of Rodey), 84.

69. *NSB* (statements of Senator Henry Burnham and O. N. Marron), 90.

70. *NSB* (statement of Rodey), 85.

71. *NSB* (statement of Dillingham), 81.

72. *NSB* (statement of Beveridge), 8, 10.

73. *NSB* (statement of A. A. Sedillo, former court interpreter), 81.

74. *NSB* (statement of Rodey), 84.

75. The precinct numbers recorded only 850. *NSB* (statement of Seferino Crollott, census enumerator), 51; *1900 U.S. Census Report*, 271.

76. *NSB* (statement of Crollott), 52.

77. *NSB* (statements of Modesto C. Ortiz and Eslavio Vigil, census takers), 53–55.

78. *NSB* (statements of Beveridge and Vigil), 54.

79. The district identified as precinct no. 2, reports only 613 residents. *NSB* (statement of G. W. Metzgar, census enumerator), 50–51; *1900 U.S. Census Report*, 271.

80. Montoya also wavers and uses "Spanish-Americans" before switching back to "what we call Mexicans." *NSB* (statement of Montoya), 49.

81. *NSB* (statement of Anastasio C. Torres, county superintendent of schools), 79.

82. *NSB* (statement of H. G. Baca, probate clerk), 80.

83. *NSB* (statement of Tight), 82.

84. "Committee Was Pleased," *Alamogordo News* (NM), November 29, 1902, NewsARC.

85. *NSB* (statement of Beveridge), 101, 108.

86. *NSB* (statement of Allen J. Papen, postmaster), 103.

87. *NSB* (statement of Martin Lohman, storeowner), 108.

88. *NSB* (statement of Isidor Armijo, probate clerk), 101.

89. *NSB* (statement of Armijo), 104.

90. *NSB* (statement of "Martinez" Amador, farmer), 105. Martín Amador was listed as a farmer but also owned a downtown hotel, was active in politics, and had held several patronage government positions.

91. Marion Dargan, "New Mexico's Fight for Statehood, 1895–1912, V: The Silencing of Opposition at Home," *New Mexico Historical Review* 16 (October 1941): 397–400.

92. Ibid., 396.

93. *NSB* (statement of Daniel H. McMillan), 112.

94. *NSB* (statement of McMillan), 111.

95. *NSB* (statement of James O. Cameron, attorney), 120.

96. *NSB* (statement of L. O. Fullen, postmaster), 115; (statement of R. W. Tansill, land speculator), 119; (statement of Cameron), 120.

97. "De mal agüero," *El Independiente* (Las Vegas, NM), November 27, 1902, LOC-CA.

98. "Taft y estado," *El Eco del Valle* (Las Cruces, NM), June 16, 1910, AHN; "La Admisión de Nuevo Mexico," *El Tiempo* (Las Cruces, NM), December 6, 1902, AHN.

99. Phillip B. Gonzales, *Forced Sacrifice as Ethnic Protest: The Hispano Cause in New Mexico and the Racial Attitude Confrontations of 1933* (New York: Peter Lang, 2001), 132.

100. "Una cuestión de importancia nacional," *El Independiente*, January 1, 1903, LOC-CA.

101. [Untitled], *Decatur Semi-Weekly Herald* (ID), December 5, 1902.

102. "Statehood Committee Through," *Salt Lake Tribune* (UT), November 27, 1902, NewsARC; "Statehood Bill," *Evening News* (Jeffersonville, IN), December 8, 1902, NewsARC.

103. "Black Eye," *Indianapolis Sun* (IN), November 25, 1902, NewsARC.

104. "The Statehood Fight," *New York Times*, December 5, 1902, NewsARC.

105. 1900 U.S. Census, ccxv–ccxvi.

106. Other western territories and states recognized this distinction. Colo. Sen. Journal (1889), 522; Richard Melzer, "New Mexico in Caricature: Images of the Territory on the Eve of Statehood," *New Mexico Historical Review* 62 (1987): 335–60.

107. *NSB* (statement of Lohman), 107.

108. *NSB* (appendix, letter from J. Francisco Chaves, Superintendent of Public Instruction), 304. For a Spanish-language version of the same sentiments, see "Noticias," *Bandera Americana* (Albuquerque, NM), March 7, 1902.

109. *NSB* (appendix, Chaves), 304.

110. "Noticias," *Bandera Americana*, May 2, 1902.

111. *NSB* (statement of John L. Gay, Railway Mail Service), 366.

112. *NSB* (statement of Rodey), 88.

113. The author preemptively saw the senators' opposition as an attack on the far West's increasing powers. "The Statehood Report," *Santa Fe New Mexican*, December 9, 1902, NewsARC.

114. The partisan factors are extensively covered; see Holtby, *Forty-Seventh Star*; Larson, *New Mexico's Quest*; Lamar, *Far Southwest*.

115. [Untitled], *Muskogee Daily News*, December 20, 1902, NewsARC.

116. "New States," *New York Times*, December 18, 1902.

117. "Opposed to Quay," *Dubuque Telegraph-Herald* (IA), December 8, 1902. Reports of the president's change of heart appeared almost immediately after the subcommittee returned to Washington. "Statehood Bill's Prospect," *New York Times*, November 30, 1902, NewsARC.

118. "Sectional Statesman," *Arizona Republican*, December 15, 1902, NewsARC.

119. S. Rep. No. 57–2206, part 1, at 9 (1902).

120. S. Rep. No. 57–2206, part 1, at 8 (1902).

121. Larson, *New Mexico's Quest*, 222–23; "La lucha por el estado," *El Independiente*, December 11, 1902, LOC-CA.

122. S. Rep. No. 57–2206, part 3, at 7–8, 2 (1902).

123. S. Rep. No. 57–2206, part 3, at 4–5, 2 (1902).

124. S. Rep. No. 57–2206, part 2, at 2–3 (1902).

125. "New States and Theories," *Washington Post*, December 18, 1902, Proquest.

126. "Not Fit for Statehood," *Philadelphia Telegraph*, original publisher, December 22, 1902, reprint in NM, box 1, folder 14, MD.

127. "New Mexico vs. Pennsylvania," *Alamogordo News* (NM), November 29, 1902, NewsARC.

128. "Ignorance Is Not Bliss," *Santa Fe New Mexican*, December 11, 1902, box 1, folder 14, MD.

129. Senator Elkins, speaking on Statehood Bill, on 9 February 1903, 57th Cong., 2nd sess., Cong. Rec., app. 166; "Discurso del Senador Elkins . . . ," *La Voz del Pueblo* (Las Vegas, NM), March 14, 1903, LOC-CA.

130. "Refutación categórica," *El Labrador* (Las Cruces, NM), March 20, 1903, stanza 2, AHN.

131. Ibid., stanza 7.

132. Ibid., stanza 11.

133. Ibid., stanza 9.

134. Ibid., stanza 12.

135. Larson, *New Mexico's Quest*, 205–25.

136. Ibid., 225; Lamar, *Far Southwest*, 428.

6. A LANGUAGE OF IDENTITY

1. Aurora Lucero, "Shall the Spanish Language Be Taught in the Schools of New Mexico," *New Mexico Normal University Bulletin* 23 (January 1911).

2. Ibid.

3. Ibid.

4. Mae Ngai, *Impossible Subjects: Illegal Aliens and the Making of Modern America* (Princeton, NJ: Princeton University Press, 2004), 52.

5. On Jim Crow policies: Leon F. Litwack, *Trouble in Mind: Black Southerners in the Age of Jim Crow* (New York: Vintage, 1999); Jane Dailey and Glenda Elizabeth Gilmore, *Jumpin' Jim Crow: Southern Politics from Civil War to Civil Rights* (Princeton, NJ: Princeton University Press, 2000). For ethnic Mexican lynchings: Benjamin Johnson, *Revolution in Texas: How a Forgotten Rebellion and Its Bloody Suppression Turned Mexicans into Americans* (New Haven, CT: Yale University Press, 2003); William D. Carrigan and Clive Webb, *Forgotten Dead: Mob Violence against Mexicans in the United States, 1848–1928* (Oxford: Oxford University Press, 2013), 64–96; Monica Muñoz Martínez, "'Inherited Loss': Tejanas and Tejanos Contesting State Violence and Revising Public Memory, 1910–Present" (PhD diss., Yale University, 2012), 33–79.

6. An Act to Establish a Bureau of Immigration and Naturalization . . . , ch. 3592, H.R. 15442, 59th Cong., sess. 1, §8 at 599 (1906).

7. 59 Cong. Rec., S9088 (daily ed. June 25, 1906).

8. Camarillo, *Chicanos in a Changing Society*, 67–70; George Sánchez, *Becoming Mexican American: Ethnicity, Culture, and Identity in Chicano Los Angeles, 1900–1945* (New York: Oxford University Press, 1993), 69–70.

9. 1900 U.S. Census, 2. California's population was 1.485 million. The best estimates for the Latino population in 1900 hover around 50,000. These are rough estimates since Mexico was not listed for parentage in the census tables and there was no racial or ethnic indicator for Spanish speakers in 1900. Armando Navarro, *Mexicano Political Experience in Occupied Aztlán: Struggles and Change* (Walnut Creek, CA: Altamira Press, 2005), 136.

10. Phoebe Kropp, *California Vieja: Culture and Memory in a Modern American Place* (Berkeley: University of California Press, 2008); William Deverell, *Whitewashed Adobe: The Rise of Los Angeles and the Remaking of Its Mexican Past* (Berkeley: University of California Press, 2004), 49–90, 207–49.

11. Sánchez, *Becoming Mexican American*, 20–29; Douglas Monroy, *Rebirth: Mexican Los Angeles from the Great Migration to the Great Depression* (Berkeley: University of California Press, 1999), 75–95.

12. By 1930, the census recorded the first- and second-generation figures for Mexican Americans at 1.2 percent of the population. This census formulation could have omitted most treaty citizen families. Cybelle Fox, *Three Worlds of Relief: Race, Immigration, and the American Welfare State from the Progressive Era to the New Deal* (Princeton, NJ: Princeton University Press, 2012), 20, 39.

13. An exception was Colorado, where workers had to use more English because fewer farmers knew Spanish than in California. E-9 Kersey Colony, G. W. S. Company, interviewed by Paul Taylor (?), 1927, field notes, box 11, folder 16, Paul Schuster Taylor Papers, 1860–1997, MSS 84/38c, Bancroft Library, University of California, Berkeley (hereafter Taylor Papers).

14. Ngai, *Impossible Subjects*, 50; Natalia Molina, *How Race Is Made in America: Immigration, Citizenship, and the Historical Power of Racial Scripts* (Berkeley: University of California Press, 2014), 74–75; David Gutiérrez, *Walls and Mirrors: Mexican Americans, Mexican Immigrants, and the Politics of Ethnicity* (Berkeley: University of California Press, 1995), 43–44.

15. By 1930, 167,000 ethnic Mexicans lived in Los Angeles County; 84 percent of the city's ethnic Mexican population was born in Mexico. Devra Weber, *Dark Sweat, White Gold: California Farm Workers, Cotton, and the New Deal* (Berkeley: University of California Press, 1994), 53–57.

16. Also to southern Colorado, Arizona, and New Mexico. Deutsch, *No Separate Refuge*, 109; Meeks, *Border Citizens*, 78.

17. Manuel Gamio, *The Mexican Immigrant: His Life-Story* (Chicago: University of Chicago Press, 1931), 65; E-9 Kersey Colony, G. W. S. Company notes, Taylor Papers.

18. Steve Pitti, *The Devil in Silicon Valley: Northern California, Race, and Mexican Americans* (Princeton, NJ: Princeton University Press, 2003), 80–86; Gutiérrez, *Walls and Mirrors*, 46–65; Mark Reisler, "Always the Laborer, Never the Citizen: Anglo Perceptions of the Mexican Immigrants during the 1920s," *Pacific Historical Review* 2 (May 1976): 231–54.

19. Zaragosa Vargas, *Labor Rights Are Civil Rights: Mexican American Workers in Twentieth-Century America* (Princeton, NJ: Princeton University Press, 2005), 38.

20. José Solís (alias Pablo Flores), interview by Robert J. Jones, transcript, June 25, 1928, box 11, folder 70, Taylor Papers.

21. Pitti, *Devil in Silicon Valley*, 97.

22. Camarillo, *Chicanos in a Changing Society*, 147–51.

23. Gamio, *Mexican Immigrant*, 168–70.

24. Pitti, *Devil in Silicon Valley*, 97.

25. Ngai, *Impossible Subjects*, 21–55.

26. For more on the creation of the border: Kelly Lytle Hernández, *Migra! A History of the Border Patrol* (Berkeley: University of California Press, 2010).

27. Gutiérrez, *Walls and Mirrors*, 52–56; Reisler, "Always the Laborer," 231–54.

28. Gutiérrez, *Walls and Mirrors*, 48–49.

29. Reisler, "Always the Laborer," 236.

30. Weber, *Dark Sweat, White Gold*, 49–51; Vargas, *Labor Rights Are Civil Rights*, 5.

31. Almaguer, *Racial Fault Lines*, 187–204; Frank Barajas, "Resistance, Radicalism, and Repression on the Oxnard Plain: The Social Context of the *Betabelero* Strike of 1933," *Western Historical Quarterly* (Spring 2004): 32–34.

32. Praxedis G. Guerrero, "Algo Mas," *Regeneración* (Los Angeles), September 3, 1910.

33. For proposed constitutional provisions related to workers speaking English: Katherine Benton-Cohen, *Borderline Americans: Racial Division and Labor War in the Arizona Borderlands* (Cambridge, MA: Harvard University Press, 2009), 201–3, 202–11.

34. Ibid., 205.

35. More on the strike, see Benton-Cohen, *Borderline Americans*, 206–11.

36. Benton-Cohen, *Borderline Americans*, 211–16, 225, 228.

37. Ibid., 227.

38. Ibid., 83–85, 236, 223–24.

39. Quoted in Pitti, *Devil in Silicon Valley*, 88.

40. Vargas, *Labor Rights Are Civil Rights*, 66, 89–90.

41. Vicki Ruiz, *Cannery Women, Cannery Lives: Mexican Women, Unionization, and the California Food Processing Industry, 1930–1950* (Albuquerque: University of New Mexico Press, 1987), 49.

42. International Garment Workers' Union, *El Organizador*, 1933, Code Inquiries and Complaints, 1933–1935, Needle Trade Union, Records of the National Labor Relations Board District 15 (Los Angeles), Record Group 25, Pacific Region of the National Archives and Records Administration, Riverside, CA (hereafter Needle Trade Union, RG 25, NARS).

43. Needle Trades Workers Industrial Union, "To All Dressmakers!," flyer, 1933, Needle Trade Union, RG 25, NARS; Needle Trades Workers Industrial Union, *La Costurera de Los Angeles*, newsletter, Needle Trade Union, RG 25, NARS; Sánchez, *Becoming Mexican American*, 227.

44. Dolores Nuno to Lou Kornhandler, Inc., undated, Needle Trade Union, RG 25, NARS.

45. Ruiz, *Cannery Women, Cannery Lives*.

46. See Vargas, *Labor Rights are Civil Rights*, 16–61.

47. Fernando Saúl Alanís Enciso, *Voces de la repatriación: La sociedad mexicana y la repatriación de mexicanos de Estados Unidos 1930–1933* (San Luis Potosí, Mexico: Colegio de San Luis, 2015), 66–67.

48. Francisco Balderrama and Raymond Rodriguez, *Decade of Betrayal: Mexican Repatriation in the 1930s* (Albuquerque: University of New Mexico Press, 2006), 71–72.

49. Alanís Enciso, *Voces de la repatriación*, 67; Sánchez, *Becoming Mexican American*, 213.

50. Sánchez, *Becoming Mexican American*, 211.

51. Alanís Enciso, *Voces de la repatriación*, 80; Balderrama and Rodriguez, *Decade of Betrayal*, 150.

52. Alanís Enciso, *Voces de la repatriación*, 88, 82.

53. Deutsch, *No Separate Refuge*, 136–37; Rubén Donato, *Mexicans and Hispanos in Colorado Schools and Communities, 1920–1960* (Albany: State University of New York Press, 2007), 5–11.

54. T. Aragon, interview with Paul Taylor (?), 1927, summary, box 11, folder 10, Taylor Papers.

55. Fred Holmes, interview with Paul Taylor (?), 1927, report, box 11, folder 25, Taylor Papers.

56. Gutiérrez, interview with Paul Taylor (?), 1927, box 11, folder 25, Taylor Papers.

57. "La Legislatura de Colorado: Proyectos buenos y perniciosos introducidos," *El Anunciador* (Trinidad, CO), January 29, 1921, AHN.

58. 1925 Colo. Sess. Laws 340.

59. Gamio, *Mexican Immigrant*, 266.

60. Ibid., 262–63.

61. Ibid., 268.

62. Ibid., 271, 275.

63. J. M. Guajardo, interview with Paul Taylor (?), 1927, box 10, folder 5, Taylor Papers.

64. For the rise of the Republican Party: Gonzales, *Política*.

65. For more on the politics to keep *nuevomexicano* votes, see Montgomery, *Spanish Redemption*, 79–86.

66. "Inventory of the Secundino Romero Papers," Rocky Mountain Online Archive, http://rmoa.unm.edu/docviewer.php?docId=nmu1mss287bc.xml.

67. The six counties and their percentages are Rio Arriba (95), Taos (93), Sandoval (93), San Miguel (85), Mora (82), and Santa Fe (78). Valencia County (90) was the only central New Mexico county above 75 percent. Three other counties also had a "Spanish-speaking vote" of more than 70 percent. Montgomery, *Spanish Redemption*, 67; 1910 U.S. census, vol. 3, 165.

68. 1910 U.S. Census, vol. 3, 166.

69. Gonzales, *Política*, 802–3.

70. Antonio Archuleta y Flores to Secundino Romero, 17 March 1908, box 3, folder 34, Secundino Romero Papers, MSS287BC, Center for Southwest Research, University of New Mexico (hereafter SRP).

71. Apolonio Coronado to Wm. H. Andrews, 23 October 1904, box 2, folder 4, Holm O. Bursum Papers, 92BC, Center for Southwest Research, University of New Mexico (hereafter HBP).

72. Balentín Sena to Señor elector del ēco Republicano, 5 February 1902, box 1, folder 2, SRP.

73. Gonzales, *Política*, 789–90; Correia, *Properties of Violence*, 152.

74. E.g., Grand Jury Interpreter: N. Segura to Secundino Romero, 25 April 1899, box 1, folder 5, SRP; Justice of the peace: José T. Domínguez to Secundino Romero, 27 August 1910, box 3, folder 38, SRP; Petition supporting deputy nominee: Petition, Félix Salmerón, et. al to Secundino Romero, box 3, folder 39, SRP.

75. For a sample Romero letter to precinct officials sharing the preferred party slate, see Secundino Romero to Tito Meléndez Mora, 6 November 1908, box 3, folder 36, SRP.

76. Anglos often avoided jury duty, but Spanish speakers attempted to secure these positions. *NSB* (Statement of William J. Mills, 4th district judge), 2.

77. For example, Benigno Trujillo to Secundino Romero, 1 April 1908, box 3, folder 35, SRP; Emilio M. Martínez to Secundino Romero, 10 April 1911, box 3, folder 40, SRP. Grand Jury requests: Pedro A. Tafoya to Secundino Romero, 15 November 1908, box 3, folder 36, SRP.

78. Deutsch, *No Separate Refuge*, 29–34, 40, 128; Suzanne Forrest, *The Preservation of the Village: New Mexico's Hispanics and the New Deal* (Albuquerque: University of New Mexico Press, 1998), 21, 28–30.

79. District court interpreter: Cristoval Sánchez to Secundino Romero, 30 January 1902, box 1, folder 12, SRP; Cecilio Valverde to Secundino Romero, 27 September 1908, box 3, folder 36, SRP.

80. E.g., legislative representative, Faustin Trujillo to Secundino Romero, 22 October 1908, box 3, folder 36, SRP; legislative translator, Juan D. Kavanaugh to Secundino Romero, 9 November 1908, box 3, folder 36, SRP.

81. Telesfor Martínez to Secundino Romero, 8 January 1909, box 3, folder 37, SRP.

82. E.g., Pablo A. Sena and Antonio Archuleta y Flores, 8 August 1910, box 3, folder 38, SRP.

83. Juan Ortiz to Secundino Romero, 23 August 1910, box 3, folder 38, SRP. Another sought funds to travel: Félix Vernal to Wm. H. Andrews, 30 October 1904, box 2, folder 6, HBP.

84. Abenicio Rodríguez to Secundino Romero, 3 August 1908, box 3, folder 36, SRP.

85. A Recommendation for a musician, Pelagio Arquello to Secundino Romero, 9 October 1908, box 3, folder 36, SRP. Supporting a local dance, Antonio Portillo to Secundino Romero, 16 November 1908, box 3, folder 36, SRP.

86. José S. Chávez to H. O. Bursum, 23 October 1904, box 2, folder 4, HBP.

87. Cecilio Valverde to Secundino Romero, 28 March 1902, box 1, folder 12, SRP.

88. For examples, see Holm Bursum Papers, boxes 2, 8, and 9.

89. Mariano Larragoite to H. O. Bursum, 14 October 1906, box 4, folder 7, HBP.

90. W. W. H. Llewellyn to H. O. Bursum, 8 October 1904, box 2, folder 2, HBP.

91. Depending on the location, speeches could be monolingual in either language. They were not always bilingual.

92. Ed Kavelle to Holm Bursum, 5 October 1904, box 2, folder 1, HBP.

93. E. H. Biernbaum to H. O. Bursum, 25 October 1904, box 2, folder 3, HBP.

94. Pablo Martínez to H. O. Bursum, 25 October 1904, box 2, folder 4, HBP.

95. Max Frost, "Plan of 1906 Republican Challenge," 1906, box 2, folder 7, HBP. For Guadalupe County's distribution list: H. O. Bursum to Max Frost, 12 October 1906, box 4, folder 7, HBP.

96. The general strategy for encouraging the monolingual Spanish vote can be read at Unsigned letter to W. H. Andrews, 15 October 1906, box 4, folder 7, HBP.

97. The $3,000 estimate included five thousand copies of the *New Mexican Review*.

98. Llewellyn to Bursum, 8 October 1904, HBP.

99. "Plan of 1906 Republican Challenge."

100. Larrazolo remained a Democratic Party member until 1911. [Holm Bursum?] to W. H. Andrews, 15 October 1906, box 4, folder 7, HBP.

101. S. Rep. No. 61–454 (1910), 25.

102. Larson, *New Mexico's Quest*, 274.

103. N.M. Const., art. VII, §3.

104. New Mexico, *Proceedings of the Constitutional Convention … New Mexico* (Albuquerque: Press of the Morning Journal, 1910), 22–23, 73, 76, 96, 189, 201. Delegate Malaquías Márquez resolved that a committee of three oversee the Spanish version of the proceedings. Two of the three selected members had Spanish surnames. Ibid., 237.

105. S. Rep. No. 61–454, Joseph H. Kibbey, Governor of Arizona (1910), 10.

106. Ariz. Sess. Laws 20 (1909).

107. S. Rep. No. 61–454 (1910), 15.

108. "En Arizona," *El Independiente*, October 20, 1910, LOC-CA.

109. N.M. Const. art. XX, §12.

110. N.M. Const. art. XII, §8.

111. N.M. Const. art. VII, §3, and art. XII, §10, are specifically mentioned for this strict amendment criteria (art. XIX, §1).

112. N.M. Const. art. II, §5.

113. Ariz. Const. (1912); "En Arizona," *La Independiente*.

114. Ariz. Sess. Laws, Spec. Sess. 258 (1912); Meeks, *Border Citizens*, 42. The primaries showed little sign of not occurring in the Spanish-language newspaper *El Hijo de Frontizero*. Candidates paid for ads in the newspaper, perhaps to appeal to the bilingual voting public who preferred Spanish. C. I. Velasco, Ads, *El Hijo de Frontizero* (Tucson, AZ), October 29, 1912, University of Arizona Libraries Digital Collection.

115. 1912 N.M. Laws 274.

116. Lamar, *Far Southwest*, 433.

117. Larson, *New Mexico's Quest*, 273, 283–86.

118. Rebecca J. Mead, *How the Vote Was Won: Woman Suffrage in the Western United States, 1868–1914* (New York: New York University Press, 2004), 2.

119. N.M. Const. art. XII, §10.

120. 1912 N.M. Laws 272.

121. The translator or interpreter requirements and responsibilities were not specified.

122. A school poll tax implemented in 1917 threatened to limit Spanish-speaking voters, though it had no real disenfranchising powers. The legislature repealed all poll taxes in 1925. 1917 N.M. Laws 300; 1925 N.M. Laws 17.

123. 1919 N.M. Laws 148–49.

124. "Gentleman from State of Mississippi Gets in Bad," *Santa Fe New Mexican*, September 27, 1918.

125. Ibid.

126. Fernando V. Padilla and Carlos B. Ramírez, "Patterns of Chicano Representation in California, Colorado, and Nuevo Mexico," *Aztlán* 5, no. 1 (Winter 1974): 211–12.

127. The state laws only required a newspaper "of general circulation" for most notices, which included the branding of cattle, roundup of abandoned horses, irrigation, and land cases. 1921 N.M. Laws 71, 165, 257, 262; 1931 N.M. Laws 263. By 1928 only thirteen Spanish-language newspapers remained in the state. Meléndez, *So All Is Not Lost*, 208.

128. 1927 N.M. Sess. Laws, 64–68, 76, 83, 89–91, 98–99, 113, 132.

129. 1927 N.M. Sess. Laws, 122, 132; Maurilio Vigil, "The Political Development of New Mexico Hispanas," in *The Contested Homeland: A Chicano History of New Mexico*, ed. Erlinda Gonzales-Berry and David R. Maciel (Albuquerque: University of New Mexico Press, 2000), 207.

130. 1938 N.M. Laws 299.

131. 1938 N.M. Laws 5, 12, 290, 292, 299, 312–19.

132. Each of these citations represents the last time that the New Mexico Session Laws included specific language provisions. 1931 N.M. Laws 263; 1933 N.M. Laws 138, 431; 1935 N.M. Laws 345.

133. Padilla and Ramírez, "Patterns of Chicano Representation," 218–19.

134. 1940 N.M. Laws 48–49.

135. Fox, *Three Worlds of Relief*, 58–59.

136. Ibid.

137. Forrest, *Preservation of the Village*, 17; Deutsch, *No Separate Refuge*, 164–66.

138. Forrest, *Preservation of the Village*, 79–101.

139. Ibid., 104, 170; Deutsch, *No Separate Refuge*, 144–45.

140. Maria Montoya, "The Roots of Economic and Ethnic Divisions in Northern New Mexico," *Western Historical Quarterly* 26, no. 1 (April 1995): 21–29.

141. Ibid., 25.

142. *Aids to Teachers of Literacy Naturalization and Elementary Subjects for Adults*, W.P.A. Technical Series, Educational Circular No. 5, January 13, 1938 (Washington, DC: Works Progress Administration, Division of Education Projects), 38–40, Serial 8182, folder 50, Bergere Family Papers, MSS 1975–024, Courtesy of the New Mexico State Records Center and Archives (hereafter BFP).

143. Political parties drew many literate villagers' interest as they offered a path for modest upward mobility and aid.

144. Montoya, "Roots of Economic and Ethnic Divisions in Northern New Mexico," 13–17.

145. 1923 N.M. Law 356; 1925 N.M. Laws.

146. Jennifer Leeman, "Categorizing Latinos in the History of the US Census: The Official Racialization of Spanish," in *A Political History of Spanish: The Making of a Language,* ed. José del Valle (Cambridge: Cambridge University Press, 2013), 315.

147. There is a longer history of Spanish letters to U.S. senators Octaviano Larrazolo (1928–29), Thomas B. Catron (1912–19), Holm Bursum (1921–25), Bronson Cutting (1927–28), and Dennis Chávez (1936–62). Each of their archives includes letters from villagers in Spanish.

148. For examples of the use of petitions by *nuevomexicanos,* see Forrest, *Preservation of the Village,* 104, 118–19.

149. Fox, *Three Worlds of Relief,* 262–67.

150. Ibid., 189–206; Forrest, *Preservation of the Village,* 86, 96–99.

151. Forrest, *Preservation of the Village,* 122–23; Meléndez, *So All Is Not Lost,* 202–3.

152. Meléndez, *So All Is Not Lost,* 202–3.

153. For a more comprehensive history of ethnic Mexican labor activism: Vargas, *Labor Rights Are Civil Rights.*

154. David M. Kennedy, *Freedom from Fear: The American People in Depression and War, 1929–1945,* Oxford History of the United States (New York: Oxford University Press, 2001), 151; Weber, *Dark Sweat, White Gold,* photo insert.

155. Vicki Ruiz, "Una Mujer sin Fronteras: Luisa Moreno and Latina Labor Activism," *Pacific Historical Review* 73, no. 1 (2004): 2, 4, 6, 13.

156. "First National Congress of the Mexican and Spanish American People of the United States," 28–30 April 1939, box 13, folder 4, Ernesto Galarza Papers, Department of Special Collections, Stanford University (hereafter EGP).

157. Gutiérrez, *Walls and Mirrors,* 114.

158. "Preparation for the Second Congress," Special Bulletin, 9 and 10 December 1939, box 13, folder 9, EGP.

159. Vargas, *Labor Rights Are Civil Rights,* 181–84.

160. "First National Congress . . . ," EGP.

161. George I. Sánchez, *Forgotten People: A Study of New Mexicans,* rev. ed. (1940; repr. Albuquerque: University of New Mexico Press, 1967), 38–39, 79.

162. Rafaela G. Castro, *Chicano Folklore: A Guide to the Folktales, Traditions, Rituals and Religious Practices of Mexican-Americans* (New York: Oxford University Press, 2001), 35.

163. "Aims and Purposes of the League of United Latin American Citizens," enclosed in E. B. Duarte to Tom Connally, 18 June 1940, box 6, folder 8, Dennis Chávez Papers, MSS 394BC, Center for Southwest Research, University Libraries, University of New Mexico (hereafter DCP); Meeks, *Border Citizens,* 116.

7. THE LIMITS OF AMERICANIZATION

1. Benjamin M. Read, "Porvenir y hegemonia mundial de los idiomas inglés y castellano," *El Eco del Valle* (Las Cruces, NM), September 2, 1911, AHN.

2. Jeffrey Mirel, *Patriotic Pluralism: Americanization Education and European Immigrants* (Cambridge, MA: Harvard University Press, 2010), 2–4; Cliff Stratton, *Education for Empire: American Schools, Race, and the Paths of Good Citizenship* (Berkeley: University of California Press, 2016), 8–11.

3. Ramsey, *Bilingual Public Schooling*, 39–48; Wayne J. Urban and Jennings L. Wagoner Jr., *American Education: A History*, 5th ed. (New York: Routledge, 2014), 95.

4. 1899 Ariz. Sess. Laws 14; M. S. Katz, *A History of Compulsory Education Laws*, Fastback Series, No. 75 (Bloomington, IN: Phi Delta Kappa, 1976), 17–18.

5. New Mexico brought the average in the "Western Division" down. For comparison, California had an average of 158, Arizona 130, and Colorado 145 days. H.R. Misc. Doc. No. 340, Part 18, at 1028; "Report on the Population of the United States at the Eleventh Census: 1890, Part II," 52nd Cong., 1st sess. (1897).

6. Alvan N. White, *Report of the Superintendent of Public Instruction: For the Biennial Period Ending November 30th 1914*, Alvan N. White to Governor William McDonald, 6–9, 15–16.

7. Mark Wild, *Street Meeting: Multiethnic Neighborhoods in Early Twentieth-Century Los Angeles* (Berkeley: University of California Press, 2005), 106–12.

8. There is a vast literature on this topic; for a sampling, see James Anderson, *The Education of Blacks in the South, 1860–1935* (Chapel Hill: University of North Carolina Press, 1988), 148–278; Benjamin Justice, "Education at the End of a Gun: The Origins of American Imperial Education in the Philippines," in *American Post-Conflict Educational Reform: From the Spanish-American War to Iraq*, ed. Noah W. Sobe (New York: Palgrave Macmillan, 2009), 22–27; Smith, *Civic Ideals*, 466–67; Stratton, *Education for Empire*.

9. Stratton, *Education for Empire*, 1–9; Anderson, *The Education of Blacks in the South*, 110–47; A. J. Angulo, *Empire and Education: A History of Greed and Goodwill from the War of 1898 to the War on Terror* (New York: Palgrave Macmillan, 2012), xvi, 28.

10. Urban and Waggoner, *American Education*, 184; Smith, *Civic Ideals*, 463.

11. Stratton, *Education for Empire*, 8.

12. Angulo, *Empire and Education*, 1–50; Sobe, *American Post-Conflict Educational Reform*, 19–74.

13. White, *Report of the Superintendent . . . 1914*, 11; David Wallace Adams, *Education for Extinction: American Indians and the Boarding School Experience, 1875–1925* (Lawrence: University of Kansas Press, 1995), 21–24.

14. Angulo, *Empire and Education*, 22–23, 39.

15. John B. Mondragón and Ernest S. Stapleton, *Public Education in New Mexico* (Albuquerque: University of New Mexico Press, 2005), 87; Alvan N. White, "Relation of Good Roads to the Schools," *NMJE* 9, no. 3 (November 15, 1914): 33.

16. Julian Go, *American Empire and the Politics of Meaning: Elite Political Cultures in the Philippines and Puerto Rico during U.S. Colonialism* (Durham, NC: Duke University Press, 2008), 19–22.

17. Angulo, *Empire and Education*, 5–6, 15–16, 22–5, 36–41.

18. Ibid., 41.

19. Juan José Osuna, *History of Education in Puerto Rico*, 2nd ed. (Río Piedras: Editorial de la Universidad de Puerto Rico, 1949), 341–64.

20. Solsiree del Moral, *Negotiating Empire: The Cultural Politics of Schools in Puerto Rico, 1898–1952* (Madison: University of Wisconsin Press, 2013), 87–88; Nancy Morris, *Puerto Rico: Culture, Politics, and Identity* (Westport, CT: Praeger, 1995), 29–34.

21. Urban and Waggoner, *American Education*, 199.

22. Ibid., 178–87.

23. Carlos Kevin Blanton, "The Rise of English-Only Pedagogy: Immigrant Children, Progressive Education, and Language Policy in the United States, 1900–1930," in *When Science Encounters the Child: Education, Parenting, and Child Welfare in 20th-Century America*, ed. Barbara Beatty, Emily D. Cahan, and Julia Grant (New York: Teacher's College, Columbia University, 2006), 60–69; Ramsey, *Bilingual Public Schooling*, 150–51.

24. "Address of [S]enator O. A. Larrazolo in the Senate of the United States, 1929, in support of S. 5374, to establish a Military and Industrial School for boys and girls in New Mexico," III–V, box 1, folder 11, Octaviano Larrazolo Papers, MSS 614BC, Center for Southwest Research, University Libraries, University of New Mexico.

25. "Address of [S]enator O. A. Larrazolo in the Senate of the United States, 1929," IV–V, Octaviano Larrazolo Papers.

26. John Jay used the term *Americanize* as early as 1797. It has been a constant throughout United States history but became a movement in the early twentieth century. Robert A. Carlson, *The Quest for Conformity: Americanization through Education* (New York: Wiley, 1975), 6–8.

27. This nationalism, tied to the schools, existed in countries throughout Europe at the same time. See, e.g., Tara Zahra, *Kidnapped Souls: National Indifference and the Battle for Children in the Bohemian Lands, 1900–1948* (Ithaca, NY: Cornell University Press, 2011).

28. Carlson, *Quest for Conformity*, 8. This end point for the height of Americanization coincided with the immigration quota laws of the 1920s—though efforts continued through World War II. See Mirel, *Patriotic Pluralism*.

29. Ariz. Leg. Journal (1918), 20.

30. Donato, *Mexicans and Hispanos*, 50–54.

31. State-funded efforts in California, New York, Illinois, and Massachusetts were broad and particularly well supported. 1913 Cal. Stat. 608–12; 1918 Ariz. Sess. Laws 28–29; Christina Ziegler-McPherson, *Americanization in the States: Immigrant Social Welfare Policy, Citizenship, and National Identity in the United States, 1908–1929* (Gainseville: University Press of Florida, 2009).

32. Ariz. Leg. Journal (1918), 20.

33. Sánchez, *Becoming Mexican American*, 95–107; Zevi Gutfreund, "Language, Education, Race and the Remaking of American Citizenship in Los Angeles, 1900–1968" (PhD diss., University of California, Los Angeles, 2013), 10–11.

34. George J. Sánchez, "'Go after the Women': Americanization and the Mexican Immigrant Woman, 1915–1929," in *Unequal Sister: A Multi-Cultural Reader in U.S. Women's History*, ed. Vicki Ruiz and Ellen Carol DuBois (New York: Routledge, 1990), 288–95.

35. 1914 Colo. Sess. Laws 22.

36. 1913 Colo. Sess. Laws 167–68, 181.

37. Ramsey, *Bilingual Public Schooling*, 146–53.

38. Jonathan Zimmerman, "Ethnics against Ethnicity: European Immigrants and Foreign-Language Instruction, 1890–1940," *Journal of American History* 88, no. 4 (March 2002): 1392–93; Michael Gordin, *Scientific Babel: How Science Was Done before and after Global English* (Chicago: University of Chicago Press, 2015), 6–7.

39. "Americanization or America First," *NMJE* 15, no. 1 (September 1918): 23.

40. Noriko Asato, *Teaching Mikadoism: The Attack on Japanese Language Schools in Hawaii, California, and Washington* (Honolulu: University of Hawaii Press, 2006).

41. Ariz. Sess. Laws 49 (1883); 1870 Cal. Stat. 838–39.

42. Zimmerman, "Ethnics against Ethnicity," 1387.

43. Ramsey, *Bilingual Public Schooling*, 156.

44. 1919 N.M. Laws 299–300.

45. Neb. Const. art. 1, §27 (amended 1919); William G. Ross, *Forging New Freedoms: Nativism, Education, and the Constitution, 1919–1927* (Lincoln: University of Nebraska Press, 1994), 3–5, 115.

46. For a more complete analysis of *Meyer v. Nebraska* and other Supreme Court language of instruction decisions, see Ross, *Forging New Freedoms*, 115–33.

47. Kloss, *American Bilingual Tradition*, 206–7.

48. González, *Chicano Education*, 12. I use this statistic with hesitation. The figure was based on a survey that only counted districts that responded. New Mexico's constitution prohibited segregation of Spanish-speaking students. Some Southwest localities did not have enough children to create separate schools, though they may have separated students by class.

49. David Torres-Rouff, "Becoming Mexican: Segregated Schools and Social Scientists in Southern California, 1913–1946," *Southern California Quarterly* 94, no. 1 (March 2012): 99, 101.

50. 1917 Cal. Stat. 667.

51. By the 1920s, ethnic Mexican students made up 90 percent of the student population in ten Los Angeles schools. Weber, *Dark Sweat, White Gold*, 55.

52. Torres-Rouff, "Becoming Mexican," 100–103; Wild, *Street Meeting*, 106–12.

53. MacDonald, *Latino Education in the United States*, 136.

54. Maria Fleming, *A Place at the Table: Struggles for Equality in America* (Oxford: Oxford University Press, 2001), 96.

55. Educational studies proving the detriment of segregation emerged in the 1940s. George I. Sánchez to Marie M. Hughes, 13 November 1947, box 19, folder 17, George Sánchez Papers, MSS 1983–30, Benson Library, University of Texas, Austin.

56. Torres-Rouff, "Becoming Mexican," 97.

57. Sánchez, *Becoming Mexican American*, 115–20.

58. Torres-Rouff, "Becoming Mexican," 103, 119–22.

59. Rubén Donato, Gonzalo Guzmán, and Jarrod Hanson, "Francisco Maestas et al. v. George H. Shone et al.: Mexican American Resistance to School Segregation in the Hispano Homeland, 1912–1914," *Journal of Latinos and Education* 16, no. 1 (2017): 3–17.

60. Quoted in Donato, Guzmán, and Hanson, "Francisco Maestas et al. v. George H. Shone et al.," 17.

61. Robert J. Alvárez Jr., "The Lemon Grove Incident: The Nation's First Successful Desegregation Court Case," *Journal of San Diego History* 32, no. 2 (Spring 1986); 131.

62. Colo. Const. art. IX, sec. 8.

63. Donato, *Mexicans and Hispanos*, 70–82, 90–98.

64. New Mexican–born George I. Sánchez attended integrated schools in the poor mining town of Jerome, Arizona. Generalizations are difficult to make with such local disparities. Carlos Kevin Blanton, *George I. Sánchez: The Long Fight for Mexican American Integration* (New Haven, CT: Yale University Press, 2014), 17; Jeanne M. Powers, "Forgotten History: Mexican American School Segregation in Arizona from 1900–1951," *Equity & Excellence in Education* 41 (2008): 469–71.

65. Muñoz, "Desert Dreams," 78, 94, 41–46, 23–24.

66. Determined after searching Arizona's session laws in the period 1900–1920.

67. Ramsey, *Bilingual Public Schooling*, 182; Carlos Kevin Blanton, *The Strange Career of Bilingual Education in Texas, 1836–1981* (College Station: Texas A&M University Press, 2004), 73.

68. 1907 N.M. Laws 200; New Mexico, Comp. of the Public School Laws of New Mexico, §§4824, 4827, 4829 (White 1916).

69. White, "Relation of Good Roads to the Schools," 33.

70. White, *Biennial Report . . . 1914*, 6.

71. N.M. Const. art. 12, §8.

72. 1909 N.M. Laws 254.

73. White, *Biennial Report . . . 1914*, 17.

74. Alvan N. White, State Superintendent, "Report of the Department of Education," 18 December 1912, box 7698, folder 8, Department of Education Papers, MSS 1970 004, courtesy of the New Mexico State Records Center and Archives (hereafter DoE).

75. Frank H. Roberts, "Dos errores fundamentales en el sistema educacional de Nuevo Mexico," newspaper clipping, November 21, 1914, box 14019, folder 46, Prince Papers.

76. "El Problema de la Enseñanza del Idioma Español . . . ," *La Estrella* (Las Cruces, NM), December 5, 1914, reprint from *La Revista de Taos* (NM), AHN.

77. Agrippina Carreras, "Súplica a los Hispanos-Americanos," *La Estrella* (Hatch, NM), November 4, 1916, AHN.

78. Ella C. W. G. Ward, "El idioma inglés en las escuelas rurales y lo que dice acerca de Ella C. W. G. Ward el procurador de este distrito," *El Combate* (Wagon Mound, NM), November 29, 1913, AHN.

79. 1915 N.M. Laws 133.

80. 1915 N.M. Laws 134.

81. Filadelío Baca's articles are published in the December 1915–April 1916 issues. Editorial, *NMJE* 12, no. 8 (April 1, 1916): 1.

82. For a description of different methods employed to teach language, see Blanton, "The Rise of English-Only Pedagogy," 56–76; Ramsey, *Bilingual Public Schooling*, 133–34.

83. D. B. Morrill, "Lesson Outlines for Teaching English to Spanish-American Child," *NMJE* 13, no. 10 (June 1917): 16.

84. D. B. Morrill, "Teaching the Spanish-American Child," *NMJE* 13, no. 8 (April 1917): 10.

85. Ibid.

86. White, *Biennial Report . . . 1914*, 5.

87. 1917 N.M. Laws 50–51.

88. Phillip Gonzales and Ann Massmann, "Loyalty Questioned: Nuevomexicanos in the Great War," *Pacific Historical Review* 75, no. 4 (November 2006): 649.

89. For Spanish word acceptance in cartoon and poem form, see George Moody, *Mexican Words We Have Met in the West* (Albuquerque, NM: George Moody, 1935).

90. Carreras, "Súplica a los Hispano-Americanos."

91. Ibid.

92. 1920 U.S. Census, vol. 2, 664, 667.

93. "English Must Come First," *NMJE* 14, no. 9 (May 1918): 27.

94. "Address by Governor Larrazolo," General Education News, *NMJE* 15, no. 5 (January 1919): 9.

95. O. A. Larrazolo, "Governor of New Mexico to the Fourth State Legislature," Santa Fe, New Mexico, January 15, 1919, box 6, folder 12, Governor Octaviano A. Larrazolo Papers, 1918–1920, MSS1959–097, Courtesy of New Mexico State Records and Archives, Santa Fe, New Mexico (hereafter OLP)

96. Elza White to Hon. O. A. Larrazolo, 17 January 1919, box 14120, folder 5, OLP.

97. A Teacher to O. A. Larrazolo, March 1919, box 14120 fol 11, OLP.

98. For example: Gilbert Cosulich to Octaviano A. Larrazolo, 15 January 1919, box 14120, folder 11, OLP; Juan P. Montaño to Hon. Governador A. Laraolo [sic], 20 February 1919, box 14120, folder 10, OLP.

99. W. N. Beacon to Hon. O. A. Larrazolo, 27 March 1919, box 14120, folder 19, OLP.

100. Frank Brady to Chief Executive of the State of New Mexico [Octaviano Larrazolo], April 1919, box 14120, folder 19, OLP.

101. "El Mensaje del Gobernador O. A. Larrazolo," *El Independiente* (Mountainair, NM), January 25, 1919, AHN.

102. 1919 N.M. Laws 300. An exception was made if the requirement would leave a school without a teacher.

103. "Resolution by the State Board of Education," April 26, 1919, box 14127. folder 150, OLP.

104. Minutes of the State Board of Education for the State of New Mexico, April 25–26, 1919, serial 14127, folder 125, OLP.

105. "Resolutions of the N.M.E.A.–1919," *NMJE* 16, no. 4 (December 1919): 30.

106. "A Local Survey of Educational Conditions in San Miguel County," *NMJE* 16, no. 11 (July 1920): 5–7.

107. Getz, *Schools of Their Own*, 38.

108. Isabel Lancaster Eckles, *Thirty-Third and Thirty-Fourth Annual Reports of the State Superintendent of Public Instruction to the Governor of New Mexico, 1923–1924* (Santa Fe: State Superintendent of Instruction, 1924), 18.

109. Georgia L. Lusk, *Código escolar de Nuevo Mexico aumento del código original* (Santa Fe: Superintendent of Public Instruction, 1931), 44.

110. Ruth Miller Martínez, "Forecast of Language Instruction . . . ," *New Mexico School Review* 17, no. 1 (September 1938): 16–17; E. L. Drake, "Class III A Bernalillo County-Education," Albuquerque Office WPA, April 13, 1936, box 1, WPA5–5–52#26, WPA New Mexico Collection, MSS AC228, Fray Angélico Chávez History Library, Santa Fe, NM.

111. For curricular examples, see serial 8181, BFP.

112. Adelina Otero(-Warren), "My People," 23 September 1929, serial 8182, folder 45, BFP.

113. "Spanish American Normal," *New Mexico School Review* 3, no. 1 (September 1923): 16.

8. STRATEGIC PAN-AMERICANISM

1. California, *Debates and Proceedings*, 1:1399.

2. Other terms existed, too, like "Good Neighbor." During World War II, for instance, the federal government chose "Inter-American" rather than "Pan-American" for its federal agency, the Office of Inter-American Affairs.

3. "Se celebra hoy el día Pan-Americano por primera vez," *El Tucsonense* (Tucson, AZ), April 14, 1931; Philip Leonard Green, *Pan American Progress* (New York: Hastings House, 1942), 182.

4. This strategy emerged in both California and New Mexico at earlier points but was mostly aimed at economic opportunity. California, *Debates and Proceedings*, 2:802; *NSB*, at 358 (statement of W. W. Llewellyn, district attorney); Chaves, *Annual Report . . . Superintendent . . . 1896*, 8–9.

5. Walter Johnson, *River of Dark Dreams: Slavery and Empire in the Cotton Kingdom* (Cambridge, MA: Belknap Press, 2013), 307–13; Gordon S. Brown, *Latin American Rebels and the United States, 1806–1822* (Jefferson, NC: McFarland, 2015).

6. James L. Morrison, *"The Best School": West Point, 1833–1866* (Kent, OH: Kent State University Press, 1998), 116; Patricia B. Genung, "Teaching Foreign Languages at West Point," in *West Point: Two Centuries and Beyond*, ed. Lance A. Betros (Abilene, TX: McWhiney Foundation Press, 2004), 510–12.

7. Juan Pablo Scarfi, "In the Name of the Americas: The Pan American Redefinition of the Monroe Doctrine and the Emerging Language of American International Law in the Western Hemisphere, 1898–1933," *Diplomatic History* 40 (2016): 5–7. doi: 10.1093/dh/dhu071.

8. Walter LaFeber, *The American Age: United States Foreign Policy at Home and Abroad Since 1750* (New York: Norton, 1989), 221.

9. The interest in Pan-Americanism grew exponentially. By 1943, an estimated 123 groups and organizations in the United States interested in inter-American affairs had a total membership of 9 million people. Over 1,000 "civic clubs, youth clubs, women's clubs, labor organizations, agricultural associations, fraternal, patriotic, and other groups in the United States" focused on inter-Americanism. Victor Borella to Nelson A. Rockefeller, memorandum, 6 September 1943, CIAA Central Files, box 57, folder 1, Records of the Office of Inter-American Affairs, Record Group 229; National Archives College Park (hereafter cited as RG 229, NACP).

10. "Spanish Courses Offered to the Public," *NMJE* 12, no. 8 (April 1, 1916): 14.

11. "The Spanish Language: . . . Great Importance in a Commercial Sense to Americans," *San Francisco Examiner*, December 26, 1878, Proquest; D. R. Morrill, "Spanish," *NMJE* 14, no. 6 (February 1918): 4.

12. "Spanish the Most Popular Language," *New Mexico School Review* 1, no. 2 (September 1921): 18.

13. Board of Education, City of New York, Office of the Superintendent of Schools, 19 October 1931, report, box 98, folder 1, John Barrett Papers, LOC 1, Library of Congress, Washington, DC.

14. *Polytechnic Student*, Polytechnic High School Yearbook, 1911, box 73, folder: Los Angeles Polytechnic High School, 56, Ephemera collection, Los Angeles City, Seaver Center for Western History Research, Natural History Museum, Los Angeles.

15. Mexican immigration to California began in earnest during the revolution and continued in the 1920s. By 1930, Los Angeles would become home to the largest number of Mexican-born residents in the country (190,000). Gutiérrez, *Walls and Mirrors*, 57; Torres-Rouff, "Becoming Mexican."

16. Editorial, "El Castellano en los E.U.," *Southwestern Catholic*, no. 3 (October 1921), box 11, folder 71, Benjamin Read Collection, MSS 1959–179, Courtesy of the New Mexico State Records Center and Archives.

17. Green, *Pan American Progress*, 148–50.

18. The *Southwestern Catholic* published passages of the original *El Norte Americano* article, "El Castellano en los E.U.," October 1921.

19. Charles Lomnitz, *The Return of Comrade Flores Magón* (Brooklyn, NY: Zone Books, 2014), 122, 153–70.

20. E. D. McQueen Gray, "The Spanish Language in New Mexico: A National Resource," *Bulletin University of New Mexico, Sociological Series* 1, no. 2 (February 1912): 1–2.

21. Ibid., 3.

22. The article was originally printed in *La Crónica* (San Francisco, CA). "El Idioma Español en los Estados Unidos," *La Estrella* (Las Cruces, NM), September 4, 1915, AHN.

23. Gray, "Spanish Language in New Mexico," 4, 6.

24. "Training in Spanish," *NMJE* 12, no. 2 (October 1915): 30.

25. D. R. Morrill, "Spanish," *NMJE* 14, no. 6 (February 1918): 4.

26. "Nuestra Herencia," *La Estrella* (Las Cruces, NM), March 15, 1919, AHN. Originally published in *El Progreso* (Santa Fe, NM).

27. Carreras, "Súplica a los Hispano-Americanos."

28. Hiram Hadley, "What Next?," *NMJE* 14, no. 7 (March 1918): 4.

29. "El Problema de la Enseñanza . . . ," December 5, 1914.

30. Editorial, "El Castellano en los E.U.," October 1921.

31. "Hon. Anastacio Medina," *El Combate* (Wagon Mound, NM), September 5, 1914, AHN.

32. For more, along with harsh interpretations of Spanish-language bans, see Torres-Rouff, "Becoming Mexican," 91–127; González, *Chicano Education in the Era of Segregation*, 1–144; Muñoz, "Desert Dreams"; Blanton, *Strange Career of Bilingual Education*, 59–110; Guadalupe San Miguel Jr., *"Let All of Them Take Heed": Mexican Americans and the Campaign for Educational Equality in Texas, 1910–1981* (Austin: University of Texas Press, 1987), 1–90.

33. Roberts, "Dos errores fundamentales," box 14019, folder 46, Prince Papers.

34. Stratton, *Education for Empire*, 186–87; Morris, *Puerto Rico*, 31–38.

35. Edith Algren Gutiérrez, *The Movement against Teaching English in Schools of Puerto Rico* (Lanham, MD: University Press of America, 1987); MacDonald, *Latino Education in the United States*, 93–100, 113–16; Angulo, *Empire and Education*, 33–49; Osuna, *History of Education in Puerto Rico*, 341–418.

36. Meléndez, *So All Is Not Lost*, 63–99.

37. It stopped publication in 1952. Nicolás Kanellos, *Hispanic Periodicals in the United States Origins to 1960: A Brief History and Comprehensive Bibliography* (Houston, TX: Arte Público Press, 2000), 35–36, 20–23, 199.

38. Lomnitz, *Return of Comrade Flores Magón*, 432–35, 452–54.

39. "El Congreso del Periodismo es el primero en la Historia del Continente Americana," *El Heraldo de México* (Los Angeles), March 30, 1926.

40. "Se Constituyo la Asociación de la Prensa Mexicana de California," *El Heraldo de México*, February 3, 1927, AHN; Armando Vargas de la Maza, "La Unión de Periodistas," *El Heraldo de México*, February 6, 1927, AHN.

41. De la Maza, "La Unión de Periodistas"; "Fueron Aprobados los Estatutos de la A. Mexicana de la Prensa de California," *El Heraldo de México*, February 17, 1927, AHN.

42. For more on *México de afuera* in Los Angeles, see Monroy, *Rebirth*.

43. De la Maza, "La Unión de Periodistas."

44. Kanellos, *Hispanic Periodicals in the United States*, 35.

45. For more, see Weber, *Dark Sweat, White Gold*; Mario García, *Memories of Chicano History: The Life and Narrative of Bert Corona* (Berkeley: University of

California Press, 1994), 87–134; Sánchez, *Becoming Mexican American*, 188–208; Vargas, *Labor Rights Are Civil Rights*, 16–157.

46. Alanís Enciso, *Voces de la Repatriación*, 66–67; Balderrama and Rodríguez, *Decade of Betrayal*, 129, 310; Sánchez, *Becoming Mexican American*, 220–23.

47. Edward J. Escobar, *Race, Police, and the Making of a Political Identity: Mexican Americans and the Los Angeles Police Department, 1900–1945* (Berkeley: University of California Press, 1999), 195–96.

48. The American-born population jumped from 45 to 65 percent of the ethnic Mexican population in 1940. Sánchez, *Becoming Mexican American*, 228; Elizabeth Escobedo, *From Coveralls to Zoot Suits: The Lives of Mexican American Women on the World War II Homefront* (Chapel Hill: University of North Carolina Press, 2013), 5.

49. Escobedo, *From Coveralls to Zoot Suits*, 17–44.

50. Stephen Keating of the Los Angeles Coordinating Council claimed only about 3 percent of Mexican American youth could be categorized as pachucos; but "gangs" and "juvenile crime" remained key features of the press. "Delinquency War Mapped," *Los Angeles Times*, April 20, 1943, Proquest. For more on the Zoot Suit Riots, see Escobedo, *From Coveralls to Zoot Suits*, 42–43; Escobar, *Race, Police, and the Making of a Political Identity*, 233–53; Luis Alvarez, *The Power of the Zoot: Youth Culture and Resistance during World War II* (Berkeley: University of California Press, 2008), 155–99.

51. Anthony Macías, *Mexican American Mojo: Popular Music, Dance, and Urban Culture in Los Angeles, 1935–1968* (Durham, NC: Duke University Press, 2008), 87–89.

52. Octavio Paz, *Labyrinth of Solitude: Life and Thought in Mexico* (New York: Grove Press, 1961), 14.

53. V. M. Egas to Robert Neeb Jr., 25 June 1941, box 2, folder 4, Manuel Ruiz Papers, MSS M0295, Department of Special Collections, Stanford University (hereafter MRP).

54. In 1977, Ruiz remembered the goals concerned both juvenile delinquency and the infiltration of South American communist agents. Ruiz comment, 25 January 1977, box 1, folder 1, MRP; Egas to Neeb, 25 June 1941, MRP.

55. Ila Dixon Buntz to Mrs. Franklin D. Roosevelt, 28 March 1941, Washington, DC, box 2, folder 3, MRP.

56. Trustee Manuel Ruiz Jr. sent letters inquiring about financial support to the World Peace Foundation, the Guggenheim, the Carnegie Foundation, and the General Education Board, among others, which can be found in box 2, folder 4 of the MRP. Cultura Panamericana, Inc. to Raymond T. Rich, 20 June 1940, box 2, folder 6, MRP.

57. Ruiz comment, 25 January 1977; Dr. Carreon, Manuel Ruiz, Dr. Victor Egas to Clarence H. Matson, 3 June 1940, box 2, folder 2, MRP.

58. Charles Thomson to Victor Egas, 29 March 1940, box 2, folder 2, MRP.

59. Cultura Panamericana to Rich, 20 June 1940; Cultura Panamericana, Inc. to L.S. Row, 25 April 1941, box 2, folder 3, MRP; Manuel Ruiz Jr. to Freeman Hall, 2 April 1940, box 2, folder 2, MRP.

60. Victor Egas to Robert Neeb, 18 June 1941, box 2, folder 4, MRP.

61. Manuel Ruiz, Corporate Article of Incorporation, 1940, box 2, folder 1, MRP.

62. Abraham Hoffman, *Unwanted Mexican Americans in the Great Depression: Repatriation Pressures, 1929–1939* (Tucson: University of Arizona Press, 1974), 68–70.

63. Carreon, Ruiz, and Egas to Matson, 3 June 1940.

64. Leonard E. Read to Club Cultura Pan-Americano [*sic*], 17 June 1940, box 2, folder 2, MRP.

65. Buntz to Roosevelt, 28 March 1941.

66. Buntz to Roosevelt, 28 March 1941.

67. Carreon, Ruiz, Egas to Matson, 3 June 1940; Buntz to Roosevelt, 28 March 1941.

68. Cultura Panamericana, Inc. to Los Angeles Board of Education, 30 July 1941, box 2, folder 2, MRP.; Cultura Panamericana, Inc. to Los Angeles Board of Education, 21 September 1940, box 2, folder 2, MRP; Cultura Panamericana, Event Program, 22 August 1940, box 2, folder 10, MRP.

69. "Latin-Americans Plan Entertainment," *Los Angeles Times*, April 8, 1941, Proquest.

70. Ruiz to Hall, 2 April 1940.

71. Egas to Neeb, 18 June 1941.

72. These details come from a last-ditch effort to get Pan-American Union support. Cultura Panamericana to Rowe, 25 April 1941.

73. Egas to Neeb, 25 June 1941.

74. Cultura Panamericana, Inc., petition, undated [1940?], box 2, folder 6, MRP.

75. Asato, *Teaching Mikadoism*, 44–49.

76. Schedule for All Spanish Classes at Black-Foxe Military Institute, 1942–43, undated, box 2, folder 9, MRP.

77. Cultura Panamericana, Inc., handout, undated [1942?], box 2, folder 9, MRP.

78. Miles Sanford to V. M. Egas, 2 October 1942, box 2, folder 9, MRP.

79. Cultura Panamericana, Circular, 8 September 1942, box 2, folder 9, MRP.

80. Ruiz comment, 25 January 1977.

81. Cultura Panamericana to Rich, 20 June 1940.

82. Cultura Panamericana to Rich, 20 June 1940.

83. García, *Memories of Chicano History*, 70–73.

84. Other organizations uniting to organize the day included the Los Angeles Chamber of Commerce, El Salón Español, el Círculo Mexicano, and the Pan American League. Manuel Ruiz Jr. to Harold Sugarman, 20 March 1942, box 2, folder 4, MRP; "Pan-American Day Programs Completed Here," *Los Angeles Times*, April 13, 1943, Proquest.

85. "Unity Hailed in Pan-American Day Festivities," *Los Angeles Times*, April 15, 1942, Proquest.

86. For movement from the historical plaza to East Los Angeles, see Sánchez, *Becoming Mexican American*, 80–89.

87. "Gay Gets Indorsements [*sic*] from Prominent Persons," *Los Angeles Times*, April 30, 1943, Proquest.

88. Ibid.

9. THE FEDERAL GOVERNMENT REDISCOVERS SPANISH

1. Manuel Abeyta to Dennis Chávez, 18 February 1944, box 9, folder 1, DCP.

2. Blanton, *Strange Career of Bilingual Education*, 96; González, *Chicano Education in the Era of Segregation*, 157–61.

3. Ezequiel Padilla to Coke R. Stevenson, 20 July 1943, in "The Good Neighbor Policy and Mexicans in Texas: Letters by Coke R. Stevenson and Ezequiel Padilla, Department of State Foreign Affairs and Bureau of International News Service," National and International Problems Series, Mexico City, 1943, 18–19, box 5, folder 7, EGP.

4. A standard "American" English perfected in the schools results in socially expected language use and encourages xenophobic reactions to objectionable accents. For more, see Rosina Lippi-Green, *Language, Ideology and Discrimination in the United States* (New York: Routledge, 1997), 104–32, 218–39.

5. Padilla to Stevenson, 20 July 1943, 17–22, EGP.

6. 1943 Tex. Laws 1119.

7. J. T. Williamson to Ernesto Galarza, 12 April 1944, box 5, folder 7, M224, EGP; E. B. Perry to Ernesto Galarza, 18 April 1944, box 5, folder 7, EGP; L. W. Horning to Ernesto Galarza, 21 April 1944, box 5, folder 7, EGP; Ernesto Galarza to E. B. Perry, 25 April 1944, box 5, folder 7, EGP.

8. Lori Flores, *Grounds for Dreaming: Mexican Americans, Mexican Immigrants, and the California Farmworker Movement* (New Haven, CT: Yale University Press, 2016), 42.

9. John Herling, "English Language Guide for Mexican Workers," 1–2, report, undated [1944?], Central Files o. IAA, Educational Programs-Teaching Aids, A-IA–4381, RG 229, NACP.

10. Ernesto Galarza to Dorothy Knowles, 19 July 1945, box 5, folder 8, EGP.

11. Herling, "English Language Guide for Mexican Workers," 2, RG 229, NACP.

12. "Department of U.S. Activities and Special Labor Relations Division to Project Committee," memorandum, 22 June 1944, Central Files o., IAA, Educational Programs-Teaching Aids, A-IA–4381, RG 229, NACP.

13. Report [Inter-American Centers in the U.S.], undated, Central Files o., Inter-American Centers in the U.S., Inter-American Centers in the U.S. Printed Matter, RG 229, NACP.

14. Office of Strategic Services to Volunteer Helpers, memorandum, 13 July 1942, serial 8560, folder 490, Dorothy Woodward Collection, MSS 1959–231, Courtesy of the New Mexico State Records Center and Archives, Santa Fe (hereafter Woodward Collection).

15. Richard V. Lindabury to Dorothy Woodward, 14 June 1943, serial 8560, folder 490, Woodward Collection; Robert L. Reynolds to Joaquin Ortega, 28 October 1942, serial 8560, folder 490, Woodward Collection.

16. OCIAA distributed the pamphlet *Spanish Speaking Americans in the War* widely but especially to students.

17. The sole exception was *El Continental* (El Paso, TX), which had some articles of a suspicious nature. [Dorothy Woodward] to Richard V. Lindabury, 3 July 1944, file copy, serial 8560, folder 490, Woodward Collection.

18. Report [Inter-American Centers in the U.S.], RG 229, NACP.

19. "Notes on Meeting Held in Mr. Cranston's Office," minutes, 4 March 1943, NC-148 E-222, Records of the Office of War Information, Record Group 208; National Archives College Park (hereafter RG 208, NACP).

20. Eleanor Herring to Alan Cranston, Chief, Foreign Language Division, memorandum, 24 February 1943, NC-148 E-221, Joseph Saldana, RG 208, NACP.

21. Ignacio López to Alan Lomax, memorandum, 30 January 1943, 5, NC-148 E-222, RG 208, NACP.

22. Alan Cranston to Raymond Rich, memorandum, 6 February 1942, NC-148 E-222, RG 208, NACP.

23. Herring to Cranston, 24 February 1943, RG 208, NACP.

24. OCIAA wrote the copy for Spanish-language news releases. Joseph E. Weckler to Victor Borella, 21 January 1943, memorandum, Records Relating to Minorities (E-155), Spanish Speaking Minorities Projects–General Correspondence, RG 229, NACP.

25. Alan Cranston to Mr. Hetinger, "Foreign Language Division and Transportation Campaign," memorandum, 21 October 1942, NC-148, E-222, RG 208, NACP; Herring to Cranston, 24 February 1943, RG 208, NACP.

26. For more on Ignacio López, see Matt Garcia, *A World of Its Own: Race, Labor, and Citrus in the Making of Greater Los Angeles, 1900–1970* (Chapel Hill: University of North Carolina Press, 2001), 230–40.

27. Ignacio L. López to Lee Falk, memorandum, 18 November 1942, NC-148 E-222, RG 208, NACP; Ignacio López to LULAC, 29 January 1943, NC-148 E-222, Latin America, RG 208, NACP.

28. In 1930, 52 percent lived in rural regions. Fox, *Three Worlds of Relief*, 40.

29. López to Falk, 18 November 1942, RG 208, NACP.

30. Original in all caps. Manuel Ruiz to Alan Cranston, telegram, 20 January 1943, NC-148 E-221, S-Foreign Lang., RG 208, NACP.

31. For more on the agencies roles and relationship, see Darlene J. Sadlier, *Americans All: Good Neighbor Cultural Diplomacy in World War II* (Austin: University of Texas Press, 2012), 184–94.

32. Cranston left in 1944 after enlisting in the army as a private. Alan Cranston to Harry Braverman, 26 November 1943, E-221 NC-148, Foreign Lang. B, RG 208, NACP; Alan Cranston to Walter H. C. Laves, memorandum, 17 September 1942, Records Relating to Minorities (E-155), OWI-Miscellaneous, RG 208, NACP.

33. William Rex Crawford, "Cultural Relations in 1941," in *Inter-American Affairs 1941: An Annual Survey No. 1*, ed. Arthur P. Whitaker (New York: Columbia University Press, 1942), 123.

34. Arthur P. Whitaker, "Pan-American Détente," in *Inter-American Affairs 1943: An Annual Survey No. 3* (New York: Columbia University Press, 1944), 41, 219. It is not clear how much of that money was directly funneled into OCIAA, but the number

of programs, projects, and personnel affiliated with the organization suggests a rich source of funding.

35. "Functions of the Department of Inter-American Activities in the United States," report, OCIAA Central Files o, Inter-American Centers in the U.S., Printed Matter, Inter-American Centers in the U.S., RG 229, NACP.

36. For more on the OCIAA's cultural programming, see Sadlier, *Americans All.*

37. OCIAA compiled lists of Pan-American organizations and turned to them for aid. Womens' organizations had worked since the 1920s to form liaisons with like-minded Latin American womens' organizations. Mary N. Winslow, "Report of the Division for Civic Projects Office of the Coordinator of Inter-American Affairs January 1941–March 15, 1942," report, OCIAA Central Files o, Inter-American Activities in the U.S., Civic Programs Misc., RG 229, NACP; Megan Threlkeld, *Pan American Women: U.S. Internationalists and Revolutionary Mexico* (Philadelphia: University of Pennsylvania Press, 2014).

38. Winslow, "Report of the Division for Civic Projects . . . ," RG 229, NACP.

39. Cranston to Laves, memorandum, 17 September 1942, RG 208, NACP.

40. Cranston's letter most likely refers to the demise of the Resident Latin American Unit, which never got off the ground. Davis J. Saposs, "Program for Cooperation with Spanish-speaking Minorities in the United States: Progress Report of Latin American Unit," report, 1 July 1942, NC-148 Entry E-222, RG 208, NACP.

41. One example of the community pushing OCIAA away from language and toward tolerance: Elis M. Tipton to Walter H. C. Laves, 23 October 1942, Central Files o. IAA, Educational Programs-Teachers, Teacher Workshops Claremont & San Dimas Sch. B-SE-1647, RG 229, NACP.

42. OCIAA documents use both "department" and "division." For clarity, "department" is used throughout. For more on federal interest in Mexican Americans, see Richard Steele, "The Federal Government Discovers Mexican Americans," in *World War II and Mexican American Civil Rights,* ed. Richard Griswold del Castillo (Austin: University of Texas Press, 2008), 19–33.

43. For the scope of these programs, see "Functions of the Department of Inter-American Activities in the United States," RG 229, NACP.

44. For more on the General Education Board's programs, see Ruben Flores, *Backroads Pragmatists: Mexico's Melting Pot and Civil Rights in the United States* (Philadelphia: University of Pennsylvania Press, 2014), 112–55.

45. "Functions of the Department of Inter-American Activities in the United States," RG 229, NACP.

46. Harold E. Davis, "Inter-American Workshops for Teachers," Summer 1943, box 2, folder 5, MRP.

47. David J. Saposs to Walter H. C. Laves, memorandum, 28 November 1942, Spanish Speaking Minorities in Speaker's Service, RG 229, NACP.

48. Edward Eyring to Nelson Rockefeller, 28 July 1941; Central Files o. IAA, Educational Programs–Teachers, B-SE-1647 OEMcra-89 OEMcra-108 (Teacher Workshops NMHU & UNM), RG 229, NACP.

49. Texas also stood out in terms of OCIAA funding and support. Its more pronounced discrimination against native Spanish speakers led OCIAA to often discuss it separately rather than as a plausible model for the Southwest. Blanton, *George Sánchez*, 99–101.

50. Connie Brockette to Georgia Lusk, 12 January 1944, Central Files o. IAA, Educational Programs–Language Teaching, Language Teaching-Misc, RG 229, NACP.

51. Joaquin Ortega, *New Mexico's Opportunity: A Message to My Fellow New Mexicans* (Albuquerque: University of New Mexico Press, 1942), 14.

52. F. V. Scholes, "Joaquin Ortega," *News Bulletin of the Rocky Mountain Modern Language Association* 9, no. 1 (October 1955): 3.

53. See Harold E. Davis to Joaquin Ortega, 12 November 1943, Central Files o. Spanish and Portuguese Speaking Minorities in US Speaker's Service, A-IA-1718, RG 229, NACP.

54. School of Inter-American Affairs, "The School of the Rio Grande Valley," symposium report, undated, 1–4, Central Files o. IAA, Educational Programs-Lectures, B-SE-1042 LA-32 (New Mexico University Lectures), RG229, NACP.

55. Ibid., 3.

56. Ibid., 1–4.

57. Division of Inter-American Activities in the U.S., "Conference on the Spanish-speaking minority program in the Southwest," 12–14 July 1943, Washington, DC, Spanish Speaking Minorities in Speaker's Service, RG 229, NACP.

58. Coordinator of Inter-American Affairs, UNM & New Mexico Highlands University, "Recent Educational and Community Experiments and Projects in New Mexico Affecting the Spanish Speaking Population," conference minutes, 19–26 August 1943, v & vi, box 1, folder 1, John Philip Wernette Presidential Papers, UA 018, Center for Southwest Research, University Libraries, University of New Mexico (hereafter Wernette Papers).

59. In 1944 Ortega proposed uniting different New Mexico universities in the program. Harold Davis to Joaquin Ortega, 7 December 1944, New Mexico University Lectures, RG 229, NACP; Connie Garza Brockette to Joaquin Ortega, 27 April 1945, New Mexico University Lectures, RG 229, NACP.

60. For OCIAA interest in a UNM-prepared bibliography, see Churchill Murray to Harold E. Davis, memorandum, 14 January 1944, Educational Programs, RG 229, NACP; Lyle Saunders, "The Education of Spanish-American and Mexican Children: A Selected Bibliography," undated, School of Inter-American Affairs, box 1, folder 1, Wernette Papers.

61. Olcott H. Deming to Joaquin Ortega, 24 February 1943, Central Files o. IAA, Educational Programs-Lectures, Inter-American Lectures New Mexico University B-SE-1042 LA-32, RG 229, NACP (hereafter Inter-American Lectures).

62. Joaquin Ortega to Olcott H. Deming, 2 March 1943, Inter-American Lectures.

63. Harold E. Davis to Joaquin Ortega, 7 December 1944, Inter-American Lectures.

64. The New Mexico State Department of Education also supported bilingual education but appears less in OCIAA papers. Social studies courses used Spanish as a way to encourage bilingualism and support understanding of "Latin Americans." Coordinator of Inter-American Affairs, UNM & New Mexico Highlands University, "Recent Educational and Community Experiments and Projects in New Mexico Affecting the Spanish Speaking Population," 19–26 August 1943, box 1, folder 1, Wernette Papers.

65. Quincy Guy Burris to Kenneth Holland, 23 February 1943, Teacher Workshops NMHU & UNM, RG 229, NACP.

66. OCIAA, UNM & NMHU, "Recent Educational and Community Experiments . . . ," box 1, folder 1, Wernette Papers.

67. New Mexico Highlands University, "Report of the Summer Workshop Institute of the Air for Three Counties," Central Files 0. IAA, Educational Programs–Teachers, B-SE-1647, RG 229, NACP.

68. Harold Davis to Antonio Rebolledo, 6 November 1943, Central Files 0. IAA, Educational Programs–Language Teaching, B-SE-4243, RG 229, NACP.

69. Harold E. Davis to Quincy Guy Burris, 13 March 1943, Teacher Workshops NMHU & UNM, RG 229, NACP.

70. The report where NMHU discussed a typical visitor is riddled with racist presumptions and terms that would offend most individuals today. For example: "clannishness," "crude," "garbled Spanish tradition, speaks a bastard Spanish, breeds copiously." NMHU, "Report of the Summer Workshop Institute . . . ," RG 229, NACP.

71. Quincy Guy Burris to Harold E. Davis, 29 February 1944, Central Files 0. IAA, Educational Programs–Teachers, B-SE-1647, RG 229, NACP.

72. Laves also recognized that the living and health conditions of Mexican Americans would "militate against the development of any strong attachment by this minority to the larger American community." Walter H. C. Laves to William G. McLean, 7 November 1942, Spanish and Portuguese Speaking Minorities in US Speaker's Service, Spanish & Portuguese Speaking Minorities, RG 229, NACP.

73. Sánchez, *Becoming Mexican American*, 259.

74. Board of Education of the City of Los Angeles, "LA City and County Schools workshop on Mexican and Spanish-speaking Pupils," 10 July 1943, box 2, folder 18, MRP.

75. Harold E. Davis, "Inter-American Workshops for Teachers," Summer 1943, box 2, folder 5, MRP.

76. Marie Hughes to Kenneth Holland, 20 September 1943, Central Files 0. IAA, Educational Programs–Teachers, B-SE-1647, RG 229, NACP; Getz, *Schools of Their Own*, 83.

77. Hughes to Holland, 20 September 1943, RG 229, NACP.

78. Elias Tipton to Walter H.C. Laves, 23 October 1942; Central Files 0. IAA, Educational Programs–Teachers, B-SE-1647 OEMcra-93 (Claremont & San Dimas Teacher Workshops), RG 229, NACP (hereafter Claremont Teacher Workshops).

79. Elias Tipton to Peter L. Spencer, 27 April 1943, Claremont Teacher Workshops.

80. San Dimas Schools?, "San Dimas Intercultural School and Recreational Program, June 21–September 10, 1943[?], Claremont Teacher Workshops.

81. San Dimas Schools Community Council, "The San Dimas Intercultural School and Recreational Program," report, 1943, Claremont Teacher Workshops.

82. Escobedo, *From Coveralls to Zoot Suits*, 1–43; Alvarez, *The Power of the Zoot*, 155–99; Escobar, *Race, Police, and the Making of a Political Identity*, 257–84.

83. Raymond G. McKelvey to Manuel Ruiz, 27 November 1943, box 5, folder 7, MRP.

84. Victor Borella to Ignacio López, 12 May 1943, box 1, folder 2, MRP.

85. Harry Braverman to Alan Cranston, 7 May 1943, E-221 NC-148, Foreign Lang. B, RG 208, NACP.

86. "Recommendations from Southern California Council of Inter-American Affairs," 22 June 1943, box 76, folio i, John Anson Ford Papers, 1832–1971, mssFordPapers, The Huntington Library, San Marino, CA (hereafter Ford Papers).

87. Raymond G. McKelvey, "Minutes of the Board of Directors Meeting Southern California Council of Inter-American Affairs," 17 July 1944, box 76, folder i, Ford Papers.

88. "Resolution of Coordinating Council for Latin American Youth," box 3, folder 15, MRP.

89. Manuel Ruiz, "Minutes for Regular Meeting of Coordinating Council of Latin-American Youth," 3 May 1943, box 3, folder 8, MRP.

90. Manuel Ruiz, "Latin-American Juvenile Delinquency in Los Angeles Bomb or Bubble!," December 1942, box 1, folder 6, MRP.

91. "Comment by Ruiz on Crime Prevention Article RE: Juvenile Delinquency," [1977?], box 1, folder 1, MRP.

92. Raymond G. McKelvey, "Minutes of the Board of Directors Meeting Southern California Council of Inter-American Affairs," 19 January 1944, box 76, folder i, Ford Papers.

93. The total distribution of the pamphlet in California and Arizona was originally expected to be 325,000. Camille Ross to Churchill Murray, 10 August 1943, Central Files 0. Inter-American Activities in the U.S., Distribution of Materials, Misc., RG 229, NACP; Maurice Hazan to Camille Ross, 20 October 1943, Central Files 0. Inter-American Activities in the U.S., Distribution of Materials, Misc., RG 229, NACP.

94. Charles Olson, *Spanish Speaking Americans in the War: The Southwest* (Washington, DC: Office of the Coordinator of Inter-American Affairs, 1943). OCIAA had high hopes for the pamphlet but initially distributed only 75,000 of the 600,000 pamphlets produced. Letters between Cranston and McKelvey called them the "bloody pamphlets," especially when McKelvey heard he was to receive 325,000. Raymond McKelvey to Alan Cranston, 27 July 1943, NC-148 E-221, B-l-a, RG 208, NACP; Alan Cranston to Raymond McKelvey, 14 October 1943, NC-148 E-221, B-l-a, RG 208, NACP.

95. Maurice Hazan to Calvin Lauderbach, 29 October 1943, Central Files 0. Inter-American Activities in the U.S., Distribution of Materials, Misc. Oct. 1943, RG 229, NACP.

96. Ross to Murray, 10 August 1943, RG 229, NACP.

97. William Rex Crawford, "Cultural Relations," in *Inter-American Affairs 1942: An Annual Survey: No.2*, ed. Arthur P. Whitaker (New York: Columbia University Press, 1943), 111.

98. Dennis Chávez, "New Mexico's Role in Hemispheric Defense," typed speech, 3 February 1942, 6, box 71, folder 40, DCP.

10. COMPETING NATIONALISMS

1. "Dennis Chávez comenta sobre el buen vecino," *La Prensa*, January 8, 1943.

2. Chávez, "New Mexico's Role in Hemispheric Defense," DCP (emphasis in original).

3. John Nieto-Phillips, "Citizenship and Empire: Race, Language, and Self-Government in New Mexico and Puerto Rico, 1898–1917," *Centro de Estudios Puertorriqueños Journal* 11, no. 1 (Fall 1999): 51–57; Sánchez, *Forgotten People*, 21–22; Osuna, *A History of Education in Puerto Rico*.

4. Texas activists began using these arguments during World War II. Blanton, *Strange Career of Bilingual Education*, 96.

5. Sharon Clampitt-Dunlap, "Nationalism and Native-Language Maintenance in Puerto Rico," *International Journal of the Sociology of Language*, no. 142 (2000): 25–34; Algren de Gutiérrez, *Movement against Teaching English in Schools of Puerto Rico*.

6. Economic and Social Conditions in Puerto Rico: Hearings Before a Subcommittee of the Committee on Territories and Insular Affairs Pursuant to S. Res. 26 . . . , 78th Cong. 232 (1943) (statement of Robert A. Taft) (hereafter S. Res. 26); Elise Marie DuBord, "La Mancha del Plátano: The Effect of Language Policy on Puerto Rican National Identity in the 1940s" (Master's thesis, University of Arizona, 2004), 30.

7. Stratton, *Education for Empire*, 186–87, 192.

8. Dennis Chávez to teacher, 4 April 1952, box 74, folder 19, DCP.

9. Maurilio Vigil and Roy Lujan, *Parallels in the Careers of Two Hispanic U.S. Senators* (El Paso: Chicano Studies, University of Texas at El Paso, 1985), 5.

10. "Van entrando poco a poco en razón," *La Estrella* (Las Cruces, NM), March 15, 1919, AHN.

11. Nina Otero-Warren to Hermon M. Bumpus, 30 January 1930, serial 8181, folder 41, BFP.

12. Blanton, "The Rise of English-Only Pedagogy," 56–76.

13. Flores, *Backroads Pragmatists*, 108–15.

14. Ruth Miller Martínez, "Forecast of Language Instruction—Both English and Spanish—in the Taos County Rural Schools," *New Mexico School Review* 18 (September 1938): 16–17, serial 8182, folder 47, BFP.

15. Ruth Miller Martínez, "The Bi-Lingual Method and the Improvement of Instruction," 4–5, serial 8181, folder 43, BFP.

16. A. Otero-Warren, "Curriculum for Elementary Schools of Santa Fe County," 1929, serial 8181, folder 42, BFP.

17. Martínez, "Bi-Lingual Method," 4–5, BFP.

18. San Miguel and Valencia, "From the Treaty of Guadalupe Hidalgo to Hopwood," 354–412; Blanton, *Strange Career of Bilingual Education*, 74–91.

19. "Teachers' Group Urges Compulsory Classes in Spanish Language," *Albuquerque Journal*, October 26, 1940; Antonio Rebolledo, "Teaching Spanish in Elementary Grades," *New Mexico School Review* 19 (March 1940): 2.

20. "Teachers' Group . . . ," *Albuquerque Journal*.

21. "Teachers of Spanish Get Hull Message," *Christian Science Monitor*, December 30, 1940.

22. Vigil and Lujan, *Parallels*, 9; "Bills Affecting Schools Introduced in Fifteenth Legislature: Senate Bills, House Bills," *New Mexico School Review* 20 (March 1941): 21.

23. "Bills Affecting Schools," *New Mexico School Review*; "[Hidden?] Representative Defends Bill [to?] Compel Spanish in High School," *Albuquerque Journal*, March 16, 1941.

24. Chávez also criticized the Spanish spoken in homes across New Mexico. Chávez to Concha Ortiz y Pino, 6 February 1941, Ortiz y Pino Family Papers, 1696–1984, MSS 336BC, Center for Southwest Research, University Libraries, University of New Mexico (hereafter Ortiz y Pino Family Papers).

25. "Meets Planned on Spanish Bill," newspaper clipping, [February 1941?], Scrapbook, 1930–40, Ortiz y Pino Family Papers; Otero-Warren to Ortiz y Pino, 20 February 1941, serial 8181, folder 43, BFP.

26. "Spanish Proposal Meets Opposition: Educators Object to Compulsory Classes," *Albuquerque Journal*, February 28, 1941.

27. David J. Bachelor, *Educational Reform in New Mexico: Tireman, San José, and Nambé* (Albuquerque: University of New Mexico Press, 1991), 98.

28. UNM encouraged diplomatic courses. Cynthia E. Orozco, "Regionalism, Politics, and Gender in Southwest History: The League of United Latin American Citizens' Expansion into New Mexico from Texas, 1929–1945," *Western Historical Quarterly* 29 (Winter 1998): 471.

29. "Lulacs Reject Spanish Proposal: Compulsory Classes Held 'Not Feasible,'" *Albuquerque Journal*, February 2, 1941.

30. "Miss Ortiz Hits Back at LULAC Group," newspaper clipping, n.d., box 1, folder 15, Ortiz y Pino Family Papers; "No Resignation Needed, says Lulacs," newspaper clipping, n.d., Scrapbook 1930–40, Ortiz y Pino Family Papers.

31. "No Resignation Needed, Says Lulacs," February 5, 1941, newspaper clipping, Scrapbook 1930–1940, Ortiz y Pino Family Papers.

32. Chávez, quoted in "Chavez Irked by Men in 'Power': Hits Failure to Enact Spanish Teaching Law," *Albuquerque Journal*, April 9, 1941.

33. 1941 N.M. Laws 250–51.

34. 1941 N.M. Laws 238.

35. 1941 N.M. Laws 517.

36. Chávez, "New Mexico's Role," February 3, 1942, box 71, folder 40, DCP.

37. "For Spanish Teaching," February 11, 1941, newspaper clipping, scrapbook, Ortiz y Pino Family Papers.

38. Sánchez, *Forgotten People*, 79, 21–22.

39. Because of its name and time of creation, the New Mexico Research Project has been linked with the Spanish research fund.

40. Antonio Rebolledo, "Shall Language Groups Be Segregated for Teaching Spanish," *New Mexico School Review* 22 (December 1942): 3.

41. 1943 N.M. Laws 123.

42. Georgia L. Lusk, Curriculum Development in the Elementary Schools of New Mexico (Santa Fe, 1944), serial 7736, folder 8, DoE.

43. New Mexico Highlands University Committee, "Project for the Teaching of English to Spanish Speaking People of New Mexico," 3, Educational Programs—Teachers, Teacher Workshops New Mexico Highlands & New Mexico University, Inter-American Activities in the U.S., B-SE-1647, RG 229, NACP.

44. For a more full history on how Spanish-language instruction aided Anglo students to the detriment of *nuevomexicanos*: Lynne Marie Getz, "Lost Momentum: World War II and the Education of Hispanos in New Mexico," in *Mexican Americans and World War II*, ed. Maggie Rivas-Rodriguez (Austin: University of Texas Press, 2005), 93–113.

45. S. Res. 26, 554–6 (exhibit 113).

46. Morris, *Puerto Rico*, 25–35.

47. S. Res. 26, 560–1 (exhibit 114); Osuna, *History of Education in Puerto Rico*, 365–66.

48. S. Res. 26, 291 (statement of Guillermo Rey).

49. S. Res. 26, 230 (statement by Franklin Roosevelt read by Robert A. Taft).

50. S. Res. 26, 199 (statement of subcommittee).

51. "U.S. Senate Investigators In Puerto Rico," *Christian Science Monitor*, February 10, 1943.

52. Don Goyo, "Ajilimojili," *Pueblos Hispanos* (New York), August 21, 1943, AHN; Juan José Bernales, "El Senador Chávez es un enemigo de Puerto Rico," *Pueblos Hispanos*, December 11, 1943, AHN.

53. S. Res. 26, 20 (statement of E. C. Masson).

54. S. Res. 26, 283 (statement of Homer T. Bone).

55. S. Res. 26, 228–29, 232–37 (statement of José M. Gallardo); Exhibit 92, 484–86.

56. S. Res. 26, 232 (statement of Taft).

57. S. Res. 26, 230–32 (statement of Gallardo).

58. S. Res. 26, 285 (statement of Pedro A. Cebollero).

59. S. Res. 26, 281 (statements of Allen J. Ellender and Lewis C. Richardson).

60. S. Res. 26, 275 (statement of Richardson).

61. S. Res. 26, 275–80, 277 (statement of Richardson).

62. S. Res. 26, 279 (statement of Dennis Chávez).

63. S. Res. 26, 291, 283–85 (statement of Bone).

64. S. Res. 26, 283 (statement of Richardson).

65. S. Res. 26, 280, 282, 289 (statement of Bone).

66. S. Res. 26, 235–36, 277 (statement of Chávez).

67. S. Res. 26, 280 (statement of Chávez)

68. S. Res. 26, pt. II, 619 (statement of Chávez).

69. S. Res. 26, 277 (statement of Chávez).

70. Thomas Becnel, *Senator Allen Ellender of Louisiana: A Biography* (Baton Rouge: Louisiana State University Press, 1996), 5, 24; S. Res. 26, 281, 276, 278, 230, 277 (statement of Ellender).

71. S. Res. 26, 280–83 (statement of Richardson).

72. S. Res. 26, 290, 288 (statement of Cebollero).

73. S. Res. 26, 560 (exhibit 114).

74. S. Res. 26, 547, 557 (exhibits 112, 113).

75. Morris, *Puerto Rico*, 40–41.

76. Stratton, *Education for Empire*, 206–9.

77. S. Res. 26, 295 (statement of Francisco Vizcarrondo).

78. S. Res. 26, 289 (statement of Cebollero).

79. DuBord, "Mancha del Plátano," 58–78.

80. "Intensa la protesta contra Ickes," *Pueblos Hispanos*, April 24, 1943, AHN; Algren de Gutiérrez, *Against Teaching English*, 108.

81. Roscoe Drummond, "New Rights for Puerto Rico Outlined in Senate's Study," *Christian Science Monitor*, September 27, 1943.

82. Juan Minaya, "Fuera de Puerto Rico el Comité Chavez," *Pueblos Hispanos*, February 27, 1943, AHN.

83. S. Rep. No. 57–2206, pt. 1, at 8–9 (1902); Florence Kerr to H. N. Baker and Ethel Perryman, 5 October 1940, Puerto Rico and Virgin Islands, 651.314, Spanish Teaching, 1942–43, Administrative and Operational Correspondence Relating to Puerto Rico and the Virgin Islands, 1935–1944, Records of the Work Progress Administration, 1922–44, Record Group 69, National Archives College Park.

84. DuBord, "Mancha del Plátano," 66–8, 73.

85. A. W. Maldonado, *Luis Muñoz Marín: Puerto Rico's Democratic Revolution* (San Juan: Universidad de Puerto Rico, 2006), 344.

86. Eduardo Quevedo, Chávez rally speech, October 19, 1944, box 2, folder 3, Eduardo Quevedo Papers, MSS M0295, Department of Special Collections, Stanford University Libraries.

87. "Says Puerto Rico Clings to Spanish: Chavez Reports Much Opposition . . . ," *New York Times*, March 14, 1943.

EPILOGUE

1. The Los Angeles metropolitan area has over 5.7 million Latino inhabitants; New York's has over 4.2 million; Houston's over 2.0 million; and Chicago's 1.9 million. "Hispanic Population in Select U.S. Metropolitan Areas, 2010," www.pewhispanic.org/hispanic-population-in-select-U-S-metropolitan-areas/.

2. Reporter's Transcript of Proceedings at 34, Mendez v. Westminster, 64 F. Supp. 544 (S.D. Cal. 1946)(No. 4292–M-Civil) (McCormick), Records of District Court of

the United States, Record Group 21, National Archives and Records Administration—Pacific Region (Riverside).

3. San Miguel and Valencia, "From the Treaty of Guadalupe to Hopwood," 376–77; J. M. Powers and Lirio Patton, "Between *Mendez* and *Brown: Gonzales v. Sheely* (1951) and the Legal Campaign against Segregation," *Law & Social Inquiry* 3 (Winter 2008): 127–71.

4. Pitti, *Devil in Silicon Valley*, 162.

5. Ibid., 136–45.

6. The literature on braceros is extensive. A select few are Flores, *Grounds for Dreaming*; Julie Weise, *Corazón de Dixie: Mexicanos in the U.S. South since 1910* (Chapel Hill: University of North Carolina Press, 2015); Ana Elizabeth Rosas, *Abrazando el Espíritu: Bracero Families Confront the U.S.-Mexico Border* (Berkeley: University of California Press, 2014); Mireya Loza, *Defiant Braceros: How Migrant Workers Fought for Racial, Sexual, and Political Freedom* (Chapel Hill: University of North Carolina Press, 2016).

7. Kenneth Burt, *The Search for a Civic Voice: California Latino Politics* (Claremont, CA: Regina Books, 2007); Pitti, *Devil in Silicon Valley*, 148–72; Mario García, *Mexican Americans: Leadership, Ideology, and Identity, 1930–1960* (New Haven, CT: Yale University Press, 1989).

8. A select few: Lorena Oropeza, *Raza sí! Guerra no! Chicano Protest and Patriotism during the Viet Nam War Era* (Berkeley: University of California Press, 2005); García, *Mexican Americans*, 199–230; Rubén Donato, *The Other Struggle for Equal Schools: Mexican Americans during the Civil Rights Era* (Albany: State University of New York Press, 1997).

9. Ian F. Haney López, *Racism on Trial: The Chicano Fight for Justice* (Cambridge, MA: Belknap Press, 2003), 19–22; Mario T. García and Sal Castro, *Blowout! Sal Castro and the Chicano Struggle for Educational Justice* (Chapel Hill: University of North Carolina Press, 2011).

10. Christine Marín, *A Spokesman of the Mexican American Movement: Rodolfo "Corky" Gonzales and the Fight for Chicano Liberation, 1969–1972* (San Francisco: R. and E. Research Associates, 1977), 9.

11. Guadalupe San Miguel Jr., *Contested Policy: The Rise and Fall of Federal Bilingual Education in the United States, 1960–2001* (Denton: University of North Texas Press, 2004), 5–10.

12. H.R. 915, 90th Cong. (1967) at 3–4; H.R. 7810, 90th Cong. (1967).

13. H.R. 915, 6–7.

14. H.R. 915, 39–40.

15. H.R. 915, 24.

16. H.R. 7819, sec. 702, 90th Cong. (1967).

17. By 1972, five million students qualified for bilingual education. Natalia Mehlman Petrzela, *Classroom Wars: Language, Sex, and the Making of Modern Political Culture* (New York: Oxford University Press, 2015), 36.

18. MacDonald, *Latino Education in the United States*, 253–57.

19. Ibid., 255–56.

20. S. 1564, sec. 4 (e) 1–2, 89th Cong. (1965).

21. Sandra del Valle, *Language Rights and the Law in the United States: Finding Our Voices* (Clevedon, U.K.: Multilingual Matters, 2003), 88.

22. H.R. 6219, "An Act to Amend the Voting Rights Act of 1965," sec. 203, 94th Congress, 1st sess. (1975).

23. "State Seeks Solution on Multilingual Pamphlets," December 20, 1975, *Los Angeles Times*, Proquest.

24. Philip Hager, "S.F. Multilingual Voting Effort Admittedly a Flop: Critics Put Blame on the City," *Los Angeles Times*, November 7, 1975, Proquest.

25. "Latinos' Big Obstacle Is Language, Says Ford Aide Honored Here," November 27, 1975, *Chicago Tribune*, Proquest.

26. Jacques Maurais, "The Language Issue in the United States, Canada, and Quebec: Some Comparative Aspects," in *Canadian Language Politics in Comparative Perspective*, ed. Michael A. Morris (Montreal: McGill-Queen's University Press, 2010), 167.

27. María Cristina García, *Havana USA: Cuban Exiles and Cuban Americans in South Florida, 1959–1994* (Berkeley: University of California Press, 1996), 114.

28. Cristina M. Rodríguez, "Accommodating Linguistic Difference: Toward a Comprehensive Theory of Language Rights in the United States," *Harvard Civil Rights-Civil Liberties Law Review* 36 (2001): 133.

29. Daniel Martinez Hosang, *Racial Propositions: Ballot Initiatives and the Making of Postwar California* (Berkeley: University of California Press, 2010), 201–42.

30. Del Valle, *Language Rights and the Law in the United States*.

31. H.B. 2281 Ariz. Laws (2010); Julie Depenbrock, "Federal Judge Finds Racism Behind Arizona Law Banning Ethnic Studies," August 22, 2017, www.npr.org/sections /ed/2017/08/22/545402866/federal-judge-finds-racism-behind-arizona-law-banning-ethnic-studies.

32. National Immigration Law Center, "Along Racial Lines: The Genesis of Arizona's SB 1070 Is a Cautionary Tale of Race-Based Immigration Policy," 5, www.nilc .org/issues/immigration-enforcement/along-racial-lines-arizonas-sb1070/.

33. Ibid.

34. Mary Beth Faller, "Overview of Huppenthal's Anonymous Comments," *Arizona Republic*, June 30, 2014, www.azcentral.com/story/news/arizona/politics/2014/06/30 /huppenthal-anonymous-comments-overview/11781139/.

35. Mary Beth Faller and Cathryn Creno, "Huppenthal Breaks Down in Tears over Blog Posts," *Arizona Republic*, June 26, 2014, www.azcentral.com/story/news/arizona /politics/2014/06/25/arizona-huppenthal-blog-posts-tears-press/11373231/.

36. Chris Reeves, "Kansas' New Play on Voter Disenfranchisement: Voter Guidelines Are Different in Spanish," *Daily Kos Blog*, April 7, 2016, http://m.dailykos.com /stories/2016/4/7/1512132/-Kansas-New-Play-On-Voter-Disenfranchisement-Voter-Guidelines-Are-Different-In-Spanish; Dion Lefler, "Errors in Kansas Spanish Voting Guide Include Wrong Registration Deadline," *Kansas City Star* (MO), April 9, 2016, www.kansascity.com/news/politics-government/article70943892.html.

37. Ibid.

38. "Univision Recaps Trump Ally Kris Kobach's Career-Long Anti-Immigrant Crusade," April 14, 2016, http://mediamatters.org/blog/2016/04/14/univision-recaps-trump-ally-kris-kobachs-career-long-anti-immigrant-crusade/209918; "Kris Kobach, el hombre que asesoró el plan del muro frontizero de Donald Trump," April 12, 2016, http://www.univision.com/noticias/elecciones-2016/kris-kobach-el-hombre-que-asesoro-el-plan-del-muro-fronterizo-de-donald-trump.

39. U.S. Department of Justice, "Cases Raising Claims under the Language Minority Provisions of the Voting Rights Act," www.justice.gov/crt/voting-section-litigation.

40. U.S. Census Bureau, "Census Bureau Releases 2011 Determinations of Political Jurisdictions Subject to Minority Language Assistance Provisions of Section 203 of the Voting Rights Act," www.census.gov/newsroom/releases/archives/2010_census/cb11-cn189.html.

41. Bernalillo County Clerk, "Native American & Spanish Language Assistance," www.bernco.gov/clerk/native-american-spanish-language-assistance.aspx.

42. California, Santa Clara County, November 8, 2016, General Election: *Official Voter Information Guide*, back cover.

43. Daniel A. Martínez, *Mapa hispano de los Estados Unidos, 2016* (Cambridge, MA: Instituto Cervantes at the Faculty of Arts and Sciences at Harvard University, 2016), 82.

44. Ibid., 88.

45. Netflix en español, http://netflixenespanol.com/; Kelly Carrion, "Netflix Increases Its Spanish Language Content," June 17, 2015.

46. Clara González Tosat, *La radio en español en los Estados Unidos* (Cambridge, MA: Instituto Cervantes at the Faculty of Arts and Sciences at Harvard University, 2016), 15; Dolores Inés Casillas, *Sounds of Belonging: U.S. Spanish-Language Radio and Public Advocacy* (New York: New York University Press, 2014).

47. Idelisse Malavé and Esti Giordani, *Latino Stats: American Hispanics by the Numbers* (New York: New Press, 2015), 25.

48. Martínez, *Mapa hispano de los Estados Unidos, 2016*, 5.

49. New Mexico Courts, "For Jurors," https://languageaccess.nmcourts.gov/for-jurors.aspx; New Mexico v. Samora, 2013-NMSC-038 (N.M. 2013).

50. Lindsey Bever, "'Tell Them to Go Back Where They Belong': J.C. Penney Customer's Racist Tirade Caught on Video," *Washington Post*, December 22, 2016, www.washingtonpost.com/news/post-nation/wp/2016/12/22/tell-them-to-go-back-where-they-belong-j-c-penney-customers-racist-tirade-caught-on-video/; Valerie Strauss, "N.J. Students Walk Out of High School to Protest Teachers' 'Speak American' Comments," *Washington Post*, October 17, 2017, www.washingtonpost.com/news/answer-sheet/wp/2017/10/17/n-j-students-walk-out-of-high-school-to-protest-teachers-speak-american-comments/.

51. Cindy Carcamo, "Spanish Declines and English Is on the Rise among U.S. Latinos," April 20, 2016, *Los Angeles Times*, www.latimes.com/nation/immigration/la-me-latino-immigration-english-language-20160419-story.html.

SELECT BIBLIOGRAPHY

MANUSCRIPT COLLECTIONS AND DOCUMENTS

Armijo-Borradaile Family. Papers. MSS 359BC. Center for Southwest Research, University Libraries, University of New Mexico, Albuquerque.

Atherton, Gertrude. Papers. MMC-3164. Library of Congress, Washington, DC.

Bale Family. Papers. BANC MSS C-B 746. Bancroft Library, University of California, Berkeley.

Barrett, John. Papers. LOC 1. Library of Congress, Washington, DC.

Bergere Family. Papers. MSS 1975–024. New Mexico State Records Center and Archives, Santa Fe.

Brent, Joseph Lancaster. Papers. MSS BT 1–300. The Huntington Library, San Marino, CA.

Bursum, Holm O. Papers. 1867–1953. MSS 92 BC. Center for Southwest Research, University Libraries, University of New Mexico, Albuquerque.

California State Library Collection. California State Library, Sacramento.

Catron, Thomas B. Papers. MSS 29BC. Center for Southwest Research, University of New Mexico, Albuquerque.

Chávez, Dennis. Papers. 1921–63. MSS 394BC. Center for Southwest Research, University of New Mexico, Albuquerque.

Dargan, Marion. Papers. MSS 120BC. Center for Southwest Research, University Libraries, University of New Mexico, Albuquerque.

Department of Education. Papers. MSS 1970–004. New Mexico State Records Center and Archives, Santa Fe.

District Court of the United States Records. Record Group 21. National Archives and Records Administration—Pacific Region, Riverside, CA.

Fitch Family. Papers. BANC MSS C-B 357. Bancroft Library, University of California, Berkeley.

Ford, John Anson. Papers. 1832–1971. mssFord Papers. The Huntington Library, San Marino, CA.

Galarza, Ernesto. Papers. 1936–84. MSS M0224. Department of Special Collections, Stanford University.

Guerra Family. Collection. 1752–1955 (bulk 1806–86). mssFAC1–1194. The Huntington Library, San Marino, CA.

Larrazolo, Governor Octaviano. Papers. 1918–20. MSS 1959–097. New Mexico State Records and Archives, Santa Fe.

Larrazolo, Octaviano. Papers. MSS 614BC. Center for Southwest Research, University Libraries, University of New Mexico, Albuquerque.

Long, Helen, and Robert W. Long collection of Moreno documents, 1818–1974. mss HLG 1–1132. The Huntington Library, San Marino, CA.

Los Angeles City. Ephemera collection. Seaver Center for Western Research, Natural History Museum, Los Angeles.

Martenet, Jefferson. Correspondence, 1837–92. mssMartenetcorrespondence. The Huntington Library, San Marino, CA.

Marvin, John G. Scrapbook I. HM51846. The Huntington Library, San Marino, CA.

Monterey Collection. 1785–1877. mss MR1–407. The Huntington Library, San Marino, CA.

National Labor Relations Board District 15 (Los Angeles) Records. Record Group 25. National Archives and Records Administration—Pacific Region, Riverside, CA.

Office of Inter-American Affairs Records. Record Group 229. National Archives, College Park, MD.

Office of War Information Records. Record Group 208. National Archives, College Park, MD.

Ortiz y Pino Family. Papers. 1696–1984. MSS 336 BC. Center for Southwest Research, University Libraries, University of New Mexico, Albuquerque.

Pico, Pío. Papers: Additions. 1836–94. BANC MSS 68/115c. Bancroft Library, University of California, Berkeley.

Pleasants Family. Papers. 1856–1973. MS.R.044. University of California, Irvine.

Prince, Bradford. Papers. MSS 1959–174. New Mexico State Records Center and Archives, Santa Fe.

Quevedo, Eduardo. Papers. MSS 0395. Department of Special Collections, Stanford University Libraries.

Ritch, William Gillet. Collection. RI 1–2270. The Huntington Library, San Marino, CA.

Romero, Secundino. Papers. MSS 287BC. Center for Southwest Research, University of New Mexico, Albuquerque.

Ruiz, Manuel. Papers. MSS M0295. Department of Special Collections, Stanford University Libraries.

Sánchez, George. Papers. 1919–86. MSS 1983–30. Benson Library, University of Texas, Austin.

San Francisco Unified School District. Records. SFH 3. San Francisco History Center, San Francisco Public Library.

Stearns, Abel. Papers. mssStearnspapers. The Huntington Library, San Marino, CA.

Taylor, Paul Schuster. Papers. 1860–1997. MSS 84/38c. Bancroft Library, University of California, Berkeley.

Territorial Archives of New Mexico. New Mexico State Records and Archives, Santa Fe.

U.S. Department of Treasury. Records of the Accounting Officers of the Department of the Treasury. Record Group 217. National Archives and Records Administration, Washington, DC.

del Valle, Reginaldo F. Papers. 1854–1938. The Huntington Library, San Marino, CA.

Vallejo Family. Papers. ca. 1824–1938. C-B 441. Bancroft Library, University of California, Berkeley.

Vallejo, Mariano Guadalupe. Papers. 1833–88. MSS VA 1–257. The Huntington Library, San Marino, CA.

Wernette, John Philip. Presidential Papers. UA 018. Center for Southwest Research, University Libraries, University of New Mexico, Albuquerque.

Wilson, Benjamin Davis. Papers. 1836–1941. mss WN 1–2419. The Huntington Library, San Marino, CA.

Woodward, Dorothy. Collection. MSS 1959–231. New Mexico State Records Center and Archives, Santa Fe.

Works Projects Administration. Records. Record Group 69. National Archives and Records Administration, Washington, DC.

WPA. New Mexico Collection. MSS AC228. Fray Angélico Chávez History Library, Santa Fe, NM.

NEWSPAPERS

Alamogordo News
Albuquerque Journal
El Anunciador
Arizona Republic
Arizona Republican
Bandera Americana
Boston Post
Chicago Tribune
Christian Science Monitor
El Clamor Público
Colorado Springs Gazette
El Combate
El Continental
La Crónica
Las Cruces Sun-News

Daily Ardmoreite
Daily Evening Picayune
Decatur Semi-Weekly Herald
Dubuque Telegraph-Herald
El Eco del Valle
El Estandarte de Springer
La Estrella
Evening News
Galveston Daily News
El Heraldo de México
El Hijo de Frontizero
El Independiente
Indianapolis Sun
Kansas City Star
El Labrador
Las Vegas Daily Optic
Los Angeles Times
Mansfield News
Muskogee Daily News
Muskogee Phoenix
New Mexican
New York Times
El Nuevo Mexicano
La Opinión Pública
Philadelphia Telegraph
La Prensa
El Progreso
Pueblos Hispanos
Regeneración
La Revista de Taos
Salt Lake Tribune
San Francisco Chronicle
San Francisco Examiner
Santa Fe New Mexican
Southwestern Catholic
Springer Banner
El Tiempo
Titusville Herald
El Tucsonense
Voz del Nuevo Mundo
La Voz del Pueblo
Washington DC Herald
Washington Post

HISTORICAL JOURNALS

New Mexico Journal of Education
New Mexico School Review

GOVERNMENT DOCUMENTS

Arizona. *Journal of the Legislative Assembly of the State of Arizona.* Phoenix: State Government Publication, 1912–45.

———. *Journal of the Legislative Assembly of the Territory of Arizona.* Phoenix: Territorial Government Publication, 1864–1911.

———. *State of Arizona Session Laws.* Phoenix: State Government Publication, 1912–45.

———. *Territory of Arizona Session Laws.* Phoenix: Territorial Government Publication, 1864–1911.

Browne, J. Ross, and California. *Report of the Debates in the Convention of California on the Formation of the State Constitution, in September and October, 1849.* Washington, DC: J. T. Towers, 1850.

California. *Journal of the Legislature of California.* Sacramento: State Government Publication, 1850–1945.

———. *Report of the Superintendent of Public Instruction of the State of California.* Sacramento: State Government Publication, 1880.

———. *State of California Session Laws.* Sacramento: State Government Publication, 1850–1945.

California. Constitutional Convention. *Debates and Proceedings of the Constitutional Convention of the State of California. Convened at the City of Sacramento, Saturday, September 28, 1878, v. 1–3.* Sacramento: State office, J. D. Young, sup't, 1974.

Colorado. *Journal of the Legislative Assembly of the State of Colorado.* Denver: State Government Publication, 1876–1945.

———. *Journal of the Legislative Assembly of the Territory of Colorado.* Denver: Territorial Government Publication, 1861–74.

———. *State of Colorado Session Laws.* Denver: State Government Publication, 1876–1945.

———. *Territory of Colorado Session Laws.* Denver: Territorial Government Publication, 1861–75.

Constitutional Convention, 1849 (Calif.), and J. Ross Browne. *Relacion de los Debates de la Convencion de California sobre la Formacion de la Constitucion de Estado, en Septiembre y Octubre de 1849.* Nueva York: S. W. Benedict, 1851.

Eckles, Isabel Lancaster. *Thirty-Third and Thirty-Fourth Annual Reports of the State Superintendent of Public Instruction to the Governor of New Mexico, 1923–1924.* Santa Fe: State Superintendent of Instruction, 1924.

Handschin, Charles Hart. *The Teaching of Modern Languages in the United States.* Washington, DC: Government Printing Office, 1913.

Jordan, Frank. *California Blue Book or State Roster, 1911.* Sacramento: Superintendent of State Printing, 1913.

Lusk, Georgia L. "Código Escolar de Nuevo Mexico Aumento del Código Original." Santa Fe, NM: Superintendent of Public Instruction, 1931.

New Mexico. Department of Education. *Compilation of the Public School Laws of New Mexico, 1915.* Denver, CO: W. H. Courtright Pub. Co., 1916.

———. *Journal of the Legislature of the State of New Mexico.* Santa Fe: State Government Publication, 1912–45.

———. *Journal of the Legislature of the Territory of New Mexico.* Santa Fe: Territorial Government Publication, 1850–1911.

———. Office of the Secretary of State. *Report of the Secretary of the Territory, 1903–1904, and Legislative Manual, 1905.* Santa Fe: New Mexican Printing Company, 1905.

———. *Proceedings of the Constitutional Convention of the Proposed State of New Mexico Held at Santa Fe, New Mexico, October 3rd, 1910, to November 21st, 1910.* Albuquerque: Press of the Morning Journal, 1910.

———. *State of New Mexico Session Laws.* Albuquerque: State Government Publication, 1912–45.

———. Superintendent of Instruction. *Annual Report Territory of New Mexico Superintendent of Public Instruction.* Santa Fe: Territorial Government Publication, 1891–1900.

———. *Territory of New Mexico Session Laws.* Santa Fe: Territorial Government Publication, 1850–1911.

Texas. *Republic of Texas Session Laws.* Houston: Government Document, 1836–1845.

———. *State of Texas Session Laws.* Houston: State Government Publication, 1846.

United States Congress. Senate and Committee on Territories and Insular Affairs. *Economic and Social Conditions in Puerto Rico: Hearings Before a Subcommittee of the Committee on Territories and Insular Affairs, United States Senate, Seventy-Eighth Congress, First Session, Pursuant to S. Res. 26 . . . Parts I–IV.* Washington, DC: Government Printing Office, 1943.

———. Inter-American Affairs Office and Charles Olson. *Spanish Speaking Americans in the War.* Washington, DC: National Government Publication, 1943.

———. Senate. Committee on Territories. *Hearings before the Subcommittee of the Committee on Territories on House Bill 12543, to Enable the People of Oklahoma, Arizona, and New Mexico to Form Constitutions and State Governments and Be Admitted into the Union on an Equal Footing with the Original States,* 57th Cong. 36 (1902).

United States Census. *Census Reports Volume 1: Twelfth Census of the United States, Taken in the Year 1900.* Washington, DC: United States Census Office, 1901.

———. *Fourteenth Census of the United States: 1920, v. 2 Population.* Washington, DC: Government Printing Office, 1922.

———. *Report on Population of the United States at the Eleventh Census, Part II.* Washington, DC: Government Printing Office, 1897.

———. *The Seventh Census of the United States: 1850.* Washington, DC: Robert Armstrong, Public Printer, 1853.

———. *The Statistics of the Population of the United States, Embracing the Tables of Race, Nationality, Sex . . .* Washington, DC: Government Printing Office, 1872.

———. *Thirteenth Census of the United States: 1910, v. 3 Population.* Washington, DC: Government Printing Office, 1913.

White, Alvan. *Report of the Superintendent of Public Instruction: For the Biennial Period Ending November 30th 1914.* Santa Fe: State Government Publication, 1914.

MISCELLANEOUS DOCUMENTS

California Citizens. *Al Honorable Senado y Casa de Representantes, de los Estados Unidos de America* (Signed Petition). San Francisco: Greenwood, California Imprints, 1859, 28094, The Huntington Library, San Marino, CA.

Martínez, Luis S. "En las Islas filipinas." Music by Felipe H. Martínez. War Anderson Co., Albuquerque, 1942.

Stevenson, Coke R., and Ezequiel Padilla. *The Good Neighbor Policy and Mexicans in Texas.* Mexico City: Cooperativa Talleres Gráficos de la Nación, 1943.

UNESCO. Universal Declaration of Human Rights. www.linguistic-declaration.org /versions/angles.pdf.

United Nations Office of the High Commissioner for Human Rights. "Language Rights to Linguistic Minorities: A Practical Guide for Implementation." Draft.

ARTICLES AND CHAPTERS IN BOOKS

Adesope, Olusola, Tracy Lavin, Terri Thompson, and Charles Ungerleider. "A Systematic Review and Meta-Analysis of the Cognitive Correlates of Bilingualism." *Review of Educational Research* 80, no. 2 (2010): 207–45.

Alvarez, Robert J. "The Lemon Grove Incident: The Nation's First Successful Desegregation Court Case." *Journal of San Diego History* 32, no. 2 (Spring 1986), www .sandiegohistory.org/journal/1986/april/lemongrove/.

Barajas, Frank P. "Resistance, Radicalism, and Repression on the Oxnard Plain: The Social Context of the Betabelero Strike of 1933." *Western Historical Quarterly* 35, no. 1 (April 1, 2004): 28–51. doi:10.2307/25442925.

Barrows, Henry D. "Pioneer Schools of Los Angeles." *Annual Publications of the Historical Society of Southern California* 8, no. 24 (1911).

Bialystok, Ellen. "Reshaping the Mind: The Benefits of Bilingualism." *Canadian Journal of Experimental Psychology* 65, no. 4 (2011): 229–35.

Blanton, Carlos Kevin. "The Rise of English-Only Pedagogy: Immigrant Children, Progressive Education, and Language Policy in the United States, 1900–1930." In *When Science Encounters the Child: Education, Parenting, and Child Welfare in 20th–Century America,* edited by Barbara Beatty, Emily D. Cahan, and Julia Grant, 56–76. New York: Teachers College, Columbia University, 2006.

Clampitt-Dunlap, Sharon. "Nationalism and Native-Language Maintenance in Puerto Rico." *International Journal of the Sociology of Language* 142, no. 3 (2000): 25–34.

Dargan, Marion. "New Mexico's Fight for Statehood, 1895–1912, Part I–VI." *New Mexico Historical Review* 16, no. 4 (October 1, 1941): 379.

Donato, Rubén, Gonzalo Guzmán, and Jarrod Hanson. "Francisco Maestas et al. v. George H. Shone et al.: Mexican American Resistance to School Segregation in the Hispano Homeland, 1912–1914." *Journal of Latinos and Education* 16, no. 1 (January 2, 2017): 3–17. doi:10.1080/15348431.2016.1179190.

Genung, Patricia B. "Teaching Foreign Languages at West Point." In *West Point: Two Centuries and Beyond*, edited by Lance A. Betros, 507–32. Abilene, TX: McWhiney Foundation Press, 2004.

Getz, Lynne Marie. "Lost Momentum: World War II and the Education of Hispanos in New Mexico." In *Mexican Americans and World War II*, edited by Maggie Rivas-Rodríguez, 93–113. Austin: University of Texas Press, 2005.

Gómez, Laura. "Race, Colonialism, and Criminal Law: Mexicans and the American Criminal Justice System in Territorial New Mexico." *Law and Society Association* 34, no. 4 (2000): 1129–1202.

Gonzales, Phillip B. "'La Junta de Indignación': Hispano Repertoire of Collective Protest in New Mexico, 1884–1933." *Western Historical Quarterly* 31, no. 2 (September 30, 2000): 161–86.

Gonzales, Phillip, and Ann Massmann. "Loyalty Questioned: Nuevomexicanos in the Great War." *Pacific Historical Review* 75, no. 4 (November 30, 2006): 629–66.

Gray, E. D. McQueen. "The Spanish Language in New Mexico: A National Resource." *Bulletin University of New Mexico* 1, no. 2 (February 1, 1912): 1–12.

Haas, Lisbeth. "War in California, 1846–1848." In *Contested Eden: California before the Gold Rush*, edited by Ramón A. Gutiérrez and Richard J. Orsi, 331–55. California History Sesquicentennial Series 1. Berkeley: University of California Press, 1998.

Kelly, Matthew Gardner. "Schoolmaster's Empire: Race, Conquest, and the Centralization of Common Schooling in California, 1848–1879." *History of Education Quarterly* 56, no. 3 (2016): 445–72.

Leeman, Jennifer. "Categorizing Latinos in the History of the U.S. Census: The Official Racialization of Spanish." In *A Political History of Spanish: The Making of a Language*, edited by José del Valle, 305–26. Cambridge: Cambridge University Press, 2013.

Lucero, Aurora. "Shall the Spanish Language Be Taught in the Schools of New Mexico." *New Mexico Normal University Bulletin* 23 (January 1911).

Macías, Reynaldo. "Minority Languages in the United States, with a Focus on Spanish in California." In *The Other Languages of Europe: Demographic, Sociolinguistic, and Educational Perspectives*, edited by Guus Extra and Durk Gorter, 333–54. Buffalo, NY: Multilingual Matters, 2001.

Melzer, Richard. "New Mexico in Caricature: Images of the Territory on the Eve of Statehood." *New Mexico Historical Review* 62, no. 4 (October 1, 1987): 335–60.

Montoya, Maria E. "The Roots of Economic and Ethnic Divisions in Northern New Mexico: The Case of the Civilian Conservation Corps." *Western Historical Quarterly* 26, no. 1 (April 1, 1995): 15–34. doi:10.2307/971280.

Nieto-Phillips, John. "Citizenship and Empire: Race, Language, and Self-Government in New Mexico and Puerto Rico, 1898–1917." *Centro de Estudios Puertorriqueños Journal* 11, no. 1 (Fall 1999): 51–74.

Oropeza, Lorena. "The Heart of Chicano History: Reies López Tijerina as a Memory Entrepreneur." *The Sixties* 1, no. 1 (June 1, 2008): 49–67.

Orozco, Cynthia E. "Regionalism, Politics, and Gender in Southwest History: The League of United Latin American Citizens' Expansion into New Mexico from Texas, 1929–1945." *Western Historical Quarterly* 29, no. 4 (December 1, 1998): 459–83. doi:10.2307/970404.

Padilla, Fernando V., and Carlos B. Ramírez. "Patterns of Chicano Representation in California, Colorado and Nuevo México." *Aztlán: A Journal of Chicano Studies* 5, no. 1–2 (November 1, 1974): 189–234.

Powers, Jeanne M. "Forgotten History: Mexican American School Segregation in Arizona from 1900–1951." *Equity & Excellence in Education* 41, no. 4 (October 21, 2008): 467–81. doi:10.1080/10665680802400253.

Powers, Jeanne M., and Lirio Patton. "Between Mendez and Brown: Gonzales v. Sheely (1951) and the Legal Campaign against Segregation." *LSI Law & Social Inquiry* 33, no. 1 (2008): 127–71.

Pubols, Louise. "Becoming Californio: Jokes, Broadsides, and a Slap in the Face." In *Alta California: Peoples in Motion, Identities in Formation, 1769–1850*, 131–56. Western Histories 1. Berkeley: Huntington–USC Institute on California and the West by University of California Press and The Huntington Library, San Marino, CA, 2010.

Reisler, Mark. "Always the Laborer, Never the Citizen: Anglo Perceptions of the Mexican Immigrant during the 1920s." *Pacific Historical Review* 45, no. 2 (1976): 231–54. doi:10.2307/3638496.

Rodríguez, Cristina M. "Accommodating Linguistic Difference: Toward a Comprehensive Theory of Language Rights in the United States." *Harvard Civil Rights–Civil Liberties Law Review* 36, no. 1 (2001): 133–223.

Ruiz, Vicki. "Una Mujer sin Fronteras: Luisa Moreno and Latina Labor Activism." *Pacific Historical Review* 73, no. 1 (2004): 1–20.

Sánchez, George J. "'Go after the Women': Americanization and the Mexican Immigrant Woman, 1915–1929." In *Unequal Sister: A Multi-Cultural Reader in U.S. Women's History*, edited by Vicki Ruiz and Ellen Carol DuBois, 284–97. New York: Routledge, 1990.

Sandoval-Strausz, Andrew K. "Latino Landscapes: Postwar Cities and the Transnational Origins of a New Urban America." *Journal of American History* 101, no. 3 (December 1, 2014): 804–31.

San Miguel, Guadalupe Jr., and Richard R. Valencia. "From the Treaty of Guadalupe Hidalgo to Hopwood: The Educational Plight and Struggle of Mexican

Americans in the Southwest." *Harvard Educational Review* 68, no. 3 (January 1, 1998): 353–412.

Scarfi, Juan Pablo. "In the Name of the Americas: The Pan-American Redefinition of the Monroe Doctrine and the Emerging Language of American International Law in the Western Hemisphere, 1898–1933." *Diplomatic History* 40, no. 2 (April 1, 2016): 189–218. doi:10.1093/dh/dhu071.

Scholes, F. V. "Joaquín Ortega." *News Bulletin of the Rocky Mountain Modern Language Association* 9, no. 1 (1955): 3.

Splitter, Henry Winfred. "Education in Los Angeles: 1850–1900." *Historical Society of Southern California Quarterly* 33, no. 2 (1951): 101–18.

Steele, Richard. "The Federal Government Discovers Mexican Americans." In *World War II and Mexican American Civil Rights*, 19–33. Austin: University of Texas Press, 2008.

Stratton, David H. "New Mexican Machiavellian? The Story of Albert B. Fall." *Montana: The Magazine of Western History* 7, no. 4 (October 1, 1957): 2–14.

Tienda, Marta. "Demography and the Social Contract." *Demography* 39, no. 4 (November 1, 2002): 587–616. doi:10.1353/dem.2002.0041.

Torres-Rouff, David. "Becoming Mexican: Segregated Schools and Social Scientists in Southern California, 1913–1946." *Southern California Quarterly* 94, no. 1 (March 19, 2012): 91– 127.

White, Alvan N. "Relation of Good Roads to the Schools." *New Mexico Journal of Education* 9, no. 3 (November 15, 1914): 33.

Zimmerman, Jonathan. "Ethnics against Ethnicity: European Immigrants and Foreign-Language Instruction, 1890–1940." *Journal of American History* 88, no. 4 (March 1, 2002): 1383–1404. doi:10.2307/2700602.

DISSERTATIONS, THESES, AND UNPUBLISHED PAPERS

Brown-Coronel, Margie. "Beyond the Rancho: Four Generations of del Valle Women in Southern California, 1830–1940." PhD diss., University of California, Irvine, 2011.

Christian, Robert Nelson. "A Study of the Historical Development of the Santa Barbara School District." Master's thesis, University of Southern California, 1963.

DuBord, Elise Marie. "La Mancha del Plátano: The Effect of Language Policy on Puerto Rican National Identity in the 1940s." Master's thesis, University of Arizona, 2004.

Gutfreund, Zevi. "Language, Education, Race and the Remaking of American Citizenship in Los Angeles, 1900–1968." PhD diss., University of California, Los Angeles, 2013.

Hefferan, Vioalle Clark. "Thomas Benton Catron." Master's thesis, University of New Mexico, 1940.

Hicks, Tahireh. "'Refugio en el Campo': The Persistence of Californio Identity in Rural Southern California, 1850–1900." Senior thesis, Princeton University, 2017.

Huebert, Lois Edith. "A History of Presbyterian Church Schools in New Mexico." Master's thesis, University of New Mexico, 1964.

Martínez, Monica Muñoz. "'Inherited Loss' : Tejanas and Tejanos Contesting State Violence and Revising Public Memory, 1910–Present." PhD diss., Yale University, 2012.

Muñoz, Laura K. "Desert Dreams: Mexican American Education in Arizona, 1870–1930." PhD diss., Arizona State University, 2006.

Ortman, Jennifer. "Language Projections: 2010 to 2020." Paper presented at the annual meeting of the American Sociological Association, Las Vegas, NV, 2011.

BOOKS

Adams, David Wallace. *Education for Extinction: American Indians and the Boarding School Experience, 1875–1928.* Lawrence: University Press of Kansas, 1997.

Alanís Enciso, Fernando Saúl. *Voces de la repatriación: La sociedad mexicana y la repatriación de mexicanos de los Estados Unidos 1930–1933.* San Luis Potosí, Mexico: Colegio de San Luis, 2015.

Almaguer, Tomás. *Racial Fault Lines: The Historical Origins of White Supremacy in California.* Berkeley: University of California Press, 1994.

Alvarez, Luis. *The Power of the Zoot: Youth Culture and Resistance during World War II.* Berkeley: University of California Press, 2008.

Anderson, James D. *The Education of Blacks in the South, 1860–1935.* Chapel Hill: University of North Carolina Press, 1988.

Angulo, A. J. *Empire and Education: A History of Greed and Goodwill from the War of 1898 to the War on Terror.* New York: Palgrave Macmillan, 2012.

Anzaldúa, Gloria. *Borderlands: The New Mestiza/La Frontera.* San Francisco: Aunt Lute Books, 1987.

Arellano, Anselmo, ed. *Los pobladores nuevo mexicanos y su poesía, 1889–1950.* Albuquerque, NM: Pajarito Publications, 1976.

Asato, Noriko. *Teaching Mikadoism: The Attack on Japanese Language Schools in Hawaii, California, and Washington, 1919–1927.* Honolulu: University of Hawaii Press, 2006.

Bachelor, David. *Educational Reform in New Mexico: Tireman, San José, and Nambé.* Albuquerque: University of New Mexico Press, 1991.

Balderrama, Francisco, and Raymond Rodriguez. *Decade of Betrayal: Mexican Repatriation in the 1930s.* Albuquerque: University of New Mexico Press, 1995.

Baron, Dennis E. *The English-Only Question: An Official Language for Americans?* New Haven, CT: Yale University Press, 1990.

Becnel, Thomas. *Senator Allen Ellender of Louisiana: A Biography.* Baton Rouge: Louisiana State University Press, 1995.

Beebe, Rose Marie, and Robert M. Senkewicz. *Testimonios: Early California through the Eyes of Women, 1815–1848.* Berkeley, CA: Heyday Books, 2006.

Bellos, David. *Is That a Fish in Your Ear? Translation and the Meaning of Everything.* London: Particular Books, 2011.

Bensel, Richard Franklin. *The American Ballot Box in the Mid-Nineteenth Century.* New York: Cambridge University Press, 2004.

Benton-Cohen, Katherine. *Borderline Americans: Racial Division and Labor War in the Arizona Borderlands*. Cambridge, MA: Harvard University Press, 2009.

Blanton, Carlos Kevin. *George I. Sánchez: The Long Fight for Mexican American Integration*. New Haven, CT: Yale University Press, 2014.

———. *The Strange Career of Bilingual Education in Texas, 1836–1981*. College Station: Texas A&M University Press, 2004.

Burciaga, José Antonio. *Drink Cultura: Chicanismo*. Santa Barbara, CA: Capra Press, 1993.

Burt, Kenneth C. *The Search for a Civic Voice: California Latino Politics*. Claremont, CA: Regina Books, 2007.

Camarillo, Albert. *Chicanos in a Changing Society: From Mexican Pueblos to American Barrios in Santa Barbara and Southern California, 1848–1930*. Cambridge, MA: Harvard University Press, 1978.

Carlson, Robert A. *The Quest for Conformity: Americanization through Education*. New York: Wiley, 1975.

Carrigan, William D., and Clive Webb. *Forgotten Dead: Mob Violence against Mexicans in the United States, 1848–1928*. Oxford: Oxford University Press, 2013.

Casas, María Raquél. *Married to a Daughter of the Land: Spanish-Mexican Women and Interethnic Marriage in California, 1820–1880*. Reno: University of Nevada Press, 2007.

Casillas, Dolores Inés. *Sounds of Belonging: U.S. Spanish-Language Radio and Public Advocacy*. Critical Cultural Communication. New York: New York University Press, 2014.

Castro, Rafaela. *Chicano Folklore: A Guide to the Folktales, Traditions, Rituals and Religious Practices of Mexican Americans*. New York: Oxford University Press, 2001.

Chávez, Ernesto. *The U.S. War with Mexico: A Brief History with Documents*. Boston: Bedford/St. Martin's Press, 2008.

Chávez-García, Miroslava. *Negotiating Conquest: Gender and Power in California, 1770s to 1880s*. Tucson: University of Arizona Press, 2004.

Clubb, Jerome, William Flanigan, and Nancy Zingale, eds. *Analyzing Electoral History: A Guide to the Study of American Voter Behavior*. Beverly Hills, CA: Sage.

Correia, David. *Properties of Violence: Law and Land Grant Struggle in Northern New Mexico*. Geographies of Justice and Social Transformation 17. Athens: University of Georgia Press, 2013.

Dailey, Jane Elizabeth, Glenda Elizabeth Gilmore, and Bryant Simon, eds. *Jumpin' Jim Crow: Southern Politics from Civil War to Civil Rights*. Princeton, NJ: Princeton University Press, 2000.

Dakin, Susanna Bryant. *The Lives of William Hartnell*. Stanford, CA: Stanford University Press, 1949.

Davis, W. W. H. *El Gringo: New Mexico and Her People*. Repr. Lincoln: University of Nebraska Press, [1857] 1982.

DeLay, Brian. *War of a Thousand Deserts: Indian Raids and the U.S.-Mexican War*. New Haven, CT: Yale University Press, 2008.

Deutsch, Sarah. *No Separate Refuge: Culture, Class, and Gender on an Anglo-Hispanic Frontier in the American Southwest, 1880–1940.* New York: Oxford University Press, 1987.

Deverell, William. *Railroad Crossing: Californians and the Railroad, 1850–1910.* Berkeley: University of California Press, 1994.

———. *Whitewashed Adobe: The Rise of Los Angeles and the Remaking of Its Mexican Past.* Berkeley: University of California Press, 2004.

Donato, Rubén. *Mexicans and Hispanos in Colorado Schools and Communities, 1920–1960.* Albany: State University of New York Press, 2007.

———. *The Other Struggle for Equal Schools: Mexican Americans during the Civil Rights Era.* Albany: State University of New York Press, 1997.

Edwards, Laura F. *The People and Their Peace: Legal Culture and the Transformation of Inequality in the Post-Revolutionary South.* Chapel Hill: University of North Carolina Press, 2009.

Emparan, Madie Brown. *The Vallejos of California.* San Francisco: Gleeson Library Associates, University of San Francisco, 1968.

Epps, Garrett. *Democracy Reborn: The Fourteenth Amendment and the Fight for Equal Rights in Post–Civil War America.* New York: H. Holt, 2006.

Escobar, Edward J. *Race, Police, and the Making of a Political Identity: Mexican Americans and the Los Angeles Police Department, 1900–1945.* Berkeley: University of California Press, 1999.

Escobedo, Elizabeth Rachel. *From Coveralls to Zoot Suits: The Lives of Mexican American Women on the World War II Home Front.* Chapel Hill: University of North Carolina Press, 2013.

Espinosa, Aurelio Macedonio. *The Spanish Language in New Mexico and Southern Colorado.* Santa Fe: New Mexican Printing Co., 1911.

Estudillo, Jesús María, and Margaret Schlichtmann. *Sketches of California in the 1860s: The Journals of Jesús M. Estudillo.* Fredericksburg, TX: Awani Press, 1988.

Fernández, José Emilio. *The Biography of Casimiro Barela.* Translated by A. Gabriel Meléndez. Albuquerque: University of New Mexico Press, 2003.

———. *Cuarenta años de legislador: Biografía del senador Casimiro Barela.* The Chicano Heritage. New York: Arno Press, 1976.

Fleming, Maria, and Southern Poverty Law Center. *A Place at the Table: Struggles for Equality in America.* Oxford: Oxford University Press in association with the Southern Poverty Law Center, 2001.

Flores, Lori A. *Grounds for Dreaming: Mexican Americans, Mexican Immigrants, and the California Farmworker Movement.* New Haven, CT: Yale University Press, 2016.

Flores, Ruben. *Backroads Pragmatists: Mexico's Melting Pot and Civil Rights in the United States.* Politics and Culture in Modern America. Philadelphia: University of Pennsylvania Press, 2014.

Fogelson, Robert M. *The Fragmented Metropolis: Los Angeles, 1850–1930.* Cambridge, MA: Harvard University Press, 1967.

Forrest, Suzanne. *The Preservation of the Village: New Mexico's Hispanics and the New Deal.* Albuquerque: University of New Mexico Press, 1998.

Fox, Cybelle. *Three Worlds of Relief: Race, Immigration, and the American Welfare State from the Progressive Era to the New Deal.* Princeton Studies in American Politics. Princeton, NJ: Princeton University Press, 2012.

Frymer, Paul. *Building an American Empire: The Era of Territorial and Political Expansion.* Princeton, NJ: Princeton University Press, 2017.

Gamio, Manuel. *The Mexican Immigrant, His Life-Story; Autobiographic Documents Collected by Manuel Gamio.* Chicago: University of Chicago Press, 1931.

García, María Cristina. *Havana USA: Cuban Exiles and Cuban Americans in South Florida, 1959–1994.* Berkeley: University of California, 1996.

García, Mario T. *Memories of Chicano History: The Life and Narrative of Bert Corona.* Berkeley: University of California Press, 1994.

———. *Mexican Americans: Leadership, Ideology & Identity, 1930–1960.* Yale Western Americana Series 36. New Haven, CT: Yale University Press, 1989.

Garcia, Matt. *A World of Its Own: Race, Labor, and Citrus in the Making of Greater Los Angeles, 1900–1970.* Chapel Hill: University of North Carolina Press, 2001.

Getz, Lynne Marie. *Schools of Their Own: The Education of Hispanos in New Mexico, 1850–1940.* Albuquerque: University of New Mexico Press, 1997.

Gómez, Laura E. *Manifest Destinies: The Making of the Mexican American Race.* New York: New York University Press, 2007.

Gonzales, Phillip. *Forced Sacrifice as Ethnic Protest: The Hispano Cause in New Mexico and the Racial Attitude Confrontation of 1933.* Politics, Media & Popular Culture 5. New York: Peter Lang, 2001.

———. *Política: Nuevomexicanos and American Political Incorporation, 1821–1910.* Lincoln: University of Nebraska Press, 2016.

Gonzales-Berry, Erlinda, and David R. Maciel, eds. *The Contested Homeland: A Chicano History of New Mexico.* Albuquerque: University of New Mexico Press, 2000.

González, Gilbert G. *Chicano Education in the Era of Segregation.* Philadelphia: Balch Institute Press, 1990.

Gordin, Michael D. *Scientific Babel: How Science Was Done before and after Global English.* Chicago: University of Chicago Press, 2015.

Gray, Paul Bryan. *A Clamor for Equality: Emergence and Exile of Californio Activist Francisco P. Ramírez.* Lubbock: Texas Tech University Press, 2012.

Green, Philip Leonard. *Pan American Progress.* New York: Hastings House, 1942.

Griego, Alfonso. *Voices of the Territory of New Mexico.* Albuquerque, NM: A. Griego, 1985.

Griswold del Castillo, Richard. *The Treaty of Guadalupe Hidalgo: A Legacy of Conquest.* Norman: University of Oklahoma Press, 1990.

Gutiérrez, David G. *Walls and Mirrors: Mexican Americans, Mexican Immigrants, and the Politics of Identity.* Berkeley: University of California Press, 1995.

Gutiérrez, Edith. *The Movement against Teaching English in Schools of Puerto Rico.* Lanham, MD: University Press of America, 1987.

Gutiérrez, Ramón A. *When Jesus Came, the Corn Mothers Went Away: Marriage, Sexuality, and Power in New Mexico, 1500–1846.* Stanford, CA: Stanford University Press, 1991.

Haas, Lisbeth. *Conquests and Historical Identities in California, 1769–1936.* Berkeley: University of California Press, 1995.

Hackel, Steven W. *Children of Coyote, Missionaries of Saint Francis: Indian-Spanish Relations in Colonial California, 1769–1850.* Chapel Hill: University of North Carolina Press, 2005.

Hahn, Steven. *A Nation without Borders: The United States and Its World in an Age of Civil Wars, 1830–1910.* New York: Viking Books, 2016.

Hämäläinen, Pekka. *The Comanche Empire.* Lamar Series in Western History. New Haven, CT: Yale University Press, 2008.

Haney López, Ian. *Racism on Trial: The Chicano Fight for Justice.* Cambridge, MA: Belknap Press, 2003.

Hanlon, Bernadette, and Thomas J. Vicino. *Global Migration: The Basics.* London: Routledge, 2014.

Hayduk, Ronald. *Democracy for All: Restoring Immigrant Voting Rights in the United States.* New York : Routledge, 2006.

Hernández, José Angel. *Mexican American Colonization during the Nineteenth Century: A History of the U.S.-Mexico Borderlands.* New York: Cambridge University Press, 2012.

Hernández, Kelly Lytle. *Migra! A History of the U.S. Border Patrol.* Berkeley: University of California, 2010.

Hitchings, Henry. *The Language Wars: A History of Proper English.* London: John Murray, 2011.

Hoffman, Abraham. *Unwanted Mexican Americans in the Great Depression: Repatriation Pressures, 1929–1939.* Tucson: University of Arizona Press, 1974.

Holtby, David V. *Forty-Seventh Star: New Mexico's Struggle for Statehood.* Norman: University of Oklahoma Press, 2012.

HoSang, Daniel Martinez. *Racial Propositions: Ballot Initiatives and the Making of Postwar California.* Berkeley: University of California Press, 2010.

Howard, Perry H. *Political Tendencies in Louisiana, 1812 1952.* Baton Rouge: Louisiana State University Press, 1957.

Hyde, Anne Farrar. *Empires, Nations, and Families: A History of the North American West, 1800–1860.* History of the American West. Lincoln: University of Nebraska Press, 2011.

Jacobs, Meg, William J. Novak, and Julian E. Zelizer, eds. *The Democratic Experiment: New Directions in American Political History.* Princeton, NJ: Princeton University Press, 2003.

Jacobson, Matthew Frye. *Whiteness of a Different Color: European Immigrants and the Alchemy of Race.* Cambridge, MA: Harvard University Press, 1998.

Jacoby, Karl. *Shadows at Dawn: A Borderlands Massacre and the Violence of History.* New York: Penguin Press, 2008.

Johnson, Benjamin H. *Revolution in Texas: How a Forgotten Rebellion and Its Bloody Suppression Turned Mexicans into Americans*. New Haven, CT: Yale University Press, 2003.

Johnson, Walter. *River of Dark Dreams: Slavery and Empire in the Cotton Kingdom*. Cambridge, MA: Belknap Press, 2013.

Kanellos, Nicolás. *Hispanic Periodicals in the United States, Origins to 1960: A Brief History and Comprehensive Bibliography*. Recovering the U.S. Hispanic Literary Heritage Project Publication. Houston, TX: Arte Público Press, 2000.

Katz, Michael S. *A History of Compulsory Education Laws*. Fastback Series, No. 75. Bicentennial Series. Bloomington, IN: Phi Delta Kappa, 1976.

Keyssar, Alexander. *The Right to Vote: The Contested History of Democracy in the United States*. New York: Basic Books, 2000.

Khory, Kavita R. *Global Migration: Challenges in the Twenty-First Century*. New York: Palgrave Macmillan, 2012.

Kloss, Heinz. *The American Bilingual Tradition*. Language in Education: Theory and Practice No. 88. McHenry, IL: Delta Systems, 1998.

Kornbluh, Mark Lawrence. *Why America Stopped Voting: The Decline of Participatory Democracy and the Emergence of Modern American Politics*. New York: New York University Press, 2000.

Kousser, J. Morgan. *The Shaping of Southern Politics: Suffrage Restriction and the Establishment of the One-Party South, 1880–1910*. Yale Historical Publications. Miscellany 102. New Haven, CT: Yale University Press, 1974.

Kropp, Phoebe S. *California Vieja: Culture and Memory in a Modern American Place*. Berkeley: University of California Press, 2006.

LaFeber, Walter. *The American Age: United States Foreign Policy at Home and Abroad since 1750*. New York: Norton, 1989.

Lamar, Howard. *The Far Southwest, 1846–1912: A Territorial History*. New Haven, CT: Yale University Press, 1966.

Larson, Robert W. *New Mexico's Quest for Statehood, 1846–1912*. Albuquerque: University of New Mexico Press, 1968.

Lepore, Jill. *A Is for American: Letters and Other Characters in the Newly United States*. New York: Alfred A. Knopf, 2002.

Lippi-Green, Rosina. *English with an Accent: Language, Ideology, and Discrimination in the United States*. New York: Routledge, 1997.

Litwack, Leon F. *Trouble in Mind: Black Southerners in the Age of Jim Crow*. New York: Alfred A. Knopf, 1998.

Lomnitz, Claudio. *The Return of Comrade Ricardo Flores Magón*. Brooklyn, NY: Zone Books, 2014.

Loza, Mireya. *Defiant Braceros: How Migrant Workers Fought for Racial, Sexual, and Political Freedom*. David J. Weber Series in the New Borderlands History. Chapel Hill: University of North Carolina Press, 2016.

MacDonald, Victoria María. *Latino Education in the United States: A Narrated History from 1513–2000*. New York: Palgrave Macmillan, 2004.

Macías, Anthony F. *Mexican American Mojo: Popular Music, Dance, and Urban Culture in Los Angeles, 1935–1968*. Durham, NC: Duke University Press, 2008.

Madley, Benjamin. *An American Genocide: The United States and the California Indian Catastrophe, 1846–1873*. Lamar Series in Western History. New Haven, CT: Yale University Press, 2016.

Malavé, Idelisse. *Latino Stats: American Hispanics by the Numbers*. New York: New Press, 2015.

Maldonado, A. W. *Luis Muñoz Marín: Puerto Rico's Democratic Revolution*. San Juan: Editorial Universidad de Puerto Rico, 2006.

Marín, Christine. *A Spokesman of the Mexican American Movement: Rodolfo "Corky" Gonzales and the Fight for Chicano Liberation, 1966–1972*. San Francisco: R and E Research Associates, 1977.

Mar-Molinero, Clare. *The Politics of Language in the Spanish-Speaking World*. The Politics of Language. New York: Routledge, 2000.

Martínez, Daniel A. *Mapa hispano de los Estados Unidos, 2016*. Cambridge, MA: Instituto Cervantes at the Faculty of Arts and Sciences at Harvard University, 2016.

Mead, Rebecca J. *How the Vote Was Won: Woman Suffrage in the Western United States, 1868–1914*. New York: New York University Press, 2004.

Meeks, Eric V. *Border Citizens: The Making of Indians, Mexicans, and Anglos in Arizona*. Austin: University of Texas Press, 2007.

Meléndez, Anthony Gabriel. *So All Is Not Lost: The Poetics of Print in Nuevomexicano Communities, 1834–1958*. Albuquerque: University of New Mexico Press, 1997.

Meyer, Doris. *Speaking for Themselves: Neomexicano Cultural Identity and the Spanish-Language Press, 1880–1920*. Albuquerque: University of New Mexico Press, 1996.

Mirel, Jeffrey. *Patriotic Pluralism: Americanization Education and European Immigrants*. Cambridge, MA: Harvard University Press, 2010.

Mitchell, Pablo. *Coyote Nation: Sexuality, Race, and Conquest in Modernizing New Mexico, 1880–1920*. Chicago: University of Chicago Press, 2005.

Molina, Natalia. *How Race Is Made in America: Immigration, Citizenship, and the Historical Power of Racial Scripts*. Berkeley: University of California Press, 2014.

Mondragón, John B. *Public Education in New Mexico*. Albuquerque: University of New Mexico Press, 2005.

Monroy, Douglas. *Rebirth: Mexican Los Angeles from the Great Migration to the Great Depression*. Berkeley: University of California Press, 1999.

Montejano, David. *Anglos and Mexicans in the Making of Texas, 1836–1986*. Austin: University of Texas Press, 1987.

Montgomery, Charles. *The Spanish Redemption: Heritage, Power, and Loss on New Mexico's Upper Rio Grande*. Berkeley: University of California Press, 2002.

Montoya, Maria E. *Translating Property: The Maxwell Land Grant and the Conflict over Land in the American West, 1840–1900*. Berkeley: University of California Press, 2002.

Moody, George W. *Mexican Words We Have Met in the West*. Albuquerque, NM: George Moody, 1935.

Mora, Anthony. *Border Dilemmas: Racial and National Uncertainties in New Mexico, 1848–1912*. Durham, NC: Duke University Press, 2011.

Moral, Solsiree del. *Negotiating Empire: The Cultural Politics of Schools in Puerto Rico, 1898–1952*. Madison: University of Wisconsin Press, 2013.

Morris, Michael A., ed. *Canadian Language Policies in Comparative Perspective*. Montreal: McGill-Queen's University Press, 2010.

Morris, Nancy. *Puerto Rico: Culture, Politics, and Identity*. Westport, CT: Praeger, 1995.

Morrison, James L. *"The Best School in the World": West Point, the Pre–Civil War Years, 1833–1866*. Kent, OH: Kent State University Press, 1986.

Morrow, William W. *Spanish and Mexican Land Grants*. San Francisco: Bancroft-Whitney Company, 1923.

Moussalli, Stephanie. *The Fiscal Case against Statehood : Accounting for Statehood in New Mexico and Arizona*. Lanham, MD: Lexington Books, 2012.

Nail, Thomas. *Theory of the Border*. New York: Oxford University Press, 2016.

Navarro, Armando. *Mexicano Political Experience in Occupied Aztlán: Struggles and Change*. Walnut Creek, CA: Altamira Press, 2005.

Nelson, William E. *The Fourteenth Amendment: From Political Principle to Judicial Doctrine*. Cambridge, MA: Harvard University Press, 1988.

Newmark, Harris. *Sixty Years in Southern California, 1853–1913; Containing the Reminiscences of Harris Newmark*. Introduction and Notes by W. W. Robinson. 4th ed. Los Angeles: Zeitlin & Ver Brugge, 1970.

Ngai, Mae. *Impossible Subjects: Illegal Aliens and the Making of Modern America*. Princeton, NJ: Princeton University Press, 2004.

Nieto-Phillips, John M. *The Language of Blood: The Making of Spanish-American Identity in New Mexico, 1850–1940*. Albuquerque: University of New Mexico Press, 2004.

Nostrand, Richard L. *The Hispano Homeland*. Norman: University of Oklahoma Press, 1992.

Oropeza, Lorena. *Raza Sí! Guerra No! Chicano Protest and Patriotism during the Viet Nam War Era*. Berkeley: University of California Press, 2005.

Ortega, Joaquín. *New Mexico's Opportunity: A Message to My Fellow New Mexicans*. Albuquerque: University of New Mexico Press, 1942.

Osuna, Juan José. *A History of Education in Puerto Rico*. Río Piedras: Editorial de la Universidad de Puerto Rico, 1949.

Paz, Octavio. *Labyrinth of Solitude: Life and Thought in Mexico*. New York: Grove Press, 1961.

Petrzela, Natalia Mehlman. *Classroom Wars: Language, Sex, and the Making of Modern Political Culture*. New York: Oxford University Press, 2015.

Pino, Pedro Bautista. *Noticias historicas y estadisticas de la antigua provincia del Nuevo-México . . .* Mexico City: Imprenta de Lara, 1849.

Pitt, Leonard. *The Decline of the Californios: A Social History of the Spanish-Speaking Californians, 1846–1890*. Berkeley: University of California Press, 1966.

Pitti, Stephen J. *The Devil in Silicon Valley: Northern California, Race, and Mexican Americans*. Princeton, NJ: Princeton University Press, 2003.

Pomeroy, Earl S. *The Territories and the United States, 1861–1890.* Philadelphia: University of Pennsylvania Press, 1947.

Prendergast, Catherine. *Literacy and Racial Justice: The Politics of Learning after Brown v. Board of Education.* Carbondale: Southern Illinois University Press, 2003.

Prince, L. Bradford. *New Mexico's Struggle for Statehood: Sixty Years of Effort to Obtain Self Government.* Santa Fe: New Mexican Printing Co., 1910.

Ramos, Raúl A. *Beyond the Alamo: Forging Mexican Ethnicity in San Antonio, 1821–1861.* Chapel Hill: Published in association with the William P. Clements Center for Southwest Studies, Southern Methodist University, by the University of North Carolina Press, 2008.

Ramsey, Paul J. *Bilingual Public Schooling in the United States: A History of America's "Polyglot Boardinghouse."* New York: Palgrave Macmillan, 2010.

Rasico, Philip D. *The Minorcans of Florida: Their History, Language, and Culture.* New Smyrna Beach, FL: Luthers, 1990.

Reséndez, Andrés. *Changing National Identities at the Frontier: Texas and New Mexico, 1800–1850.* Cambridge: Cambridge University Press, 2004.

Rosas, Ana Elizabeth. *Abrazando el Espíritu: Bracero Families Confront the U.S.-Mexico Border.* Berkeley: University of California Press, 2014.

Rosenus, Alan. *General Vallejo and the Advent of the Americans.* Berkeley, CA: Heyday Books, 1999.

Ross, William G. *Forging New Freedoms: Nativism, Education, and the Constitution, 1917–1927.* Lincoln: University of Nebraska Press, 1994.

Ruiz, Vicki. *Cannery Women, Cannery Lives: Mexican Women, Unionization, and the California Food Processing Industry, 1930–1950.* Albuquerque: University of New Mexico Press, 1987.

Ruiz de Burton, María Amparo. *The Squatter and the Don.* New York: Modern Library, 2004.

Sadlier, Darlene J. *Americans All: Good Neighbor Cultural Diplomacy in World War II.* Austin: University of Texas Press, 2012.

St. John, Rachel. *Line in the Sand: A History of the Western U.S.-Mexico Border.* America in the World. Princeton, NJ: Princeton University Press, 2011.

San Miguel, Guadalupe, Jr. *Contested Policy: The Rise and Fall of Federal Bilingual Education in the United States, 1960–2001.* Denton: University of North Texas Press, 2004.

———. *"Let All of Them Take Heed": Mexican Americans and the Campaign for Educational Equality in Texas, 1910–1981.* Vol. 11. Austin: University of Texas Press, 1987.

Sánchez, George I. *Forgotten People: A Study of New Mexicans.* Repr. Albuquerque: University of New Mexico Press, [1940] 1996.

Sánchez, George J. *Becoming Mexican American: Ethnicity, Culture, and Identity in Chicano Los Angeles, 1900–1945.* New York: Oxford University Press, 1993.

Sheppard, Claude Armand. *The Law of Languages in Canada.* Ottawa: Crown, 1971.

Sheridan, Thomas E. *Los Tucsonenses: The Mexican Community in Tucson, 1854–1941.* Tucson: University of Arizona Press, 1986.

Sitton, Tom. *The Courthouse Crowd: Los Angeles County and Its Government, 1850–1950*. Los Angeles: Historical Society of Southern California, 2013.

Smith, Henry Nash. *Virgin Land: The American West as Symbol and Myth*. Cambridge, MA: Harvard University Press, 1950.

Smith, Rogers. *Civic Ideals: Conflicting Visions of Citizenship in U.S. History*. New Haven, CT: Yale University Press, 1997.

Sobe, Noah W., ed. *American Post-Conflict Educational Reform: From the Spanish-American War to Iraq*. New York: Palgrave Macmillan, 2009.

Stratton, Cliff. *Education for Empire: American Schools, Race, and the Paths of Good Citizenship*. Berkeley: University of California Press, 2016.

Stratton, Porter A. *The Territorial Press of New Mexico, 1834–1912*. Albuquerque: University of New Mexico Press, 1969.

Swett, John. *History of the Public School System of California*. San Francisco: A. L. Bancroft and Company, 1876.

Swisher, Carl Brent. *Motivation and Political Technique in the California Constitutional Convention, 1878–79*. New York: Da Capo Press, 1969.

Threlkeld, Megan. *Pan American Women: U.S. Internationalists and Revolutionary Mexico*. Politics and Culture in Modern America. Philadelphia: University of Pennsylvania Press, 2014.

Urban, Wayne J., and Jennings L. Wagoner. *American Education: A History*. 5th ed. New York: Routledge, 2014.

Valerio-Jiménez, Omar S. *River of Hope: Forging Identity and Nation in the Rio Grande Borderlands*. Durham, NC: Duke University Press, 2013.

Valle, Sandra del. *Language Rights and the Law in the United States: Finding Our Voices*. Clevedon, U.K.: Multilingual Matters, 2003.

Vallejo, Platon Mariano Guadalupe. *Memoirs of the Vallejos: New Light on the History, before and after the "Gringos" Came, Based on Original Documents and Recollections*. Fairfield, CA: James D. Stevenson in cooperation with the Napa County Historical Society, 1994.

Vargas, Zaragosa. *Labor Rights Are Civil Rights: Mexican American Workers in Twentieth-Century America*. Politics and Society in Twentieth-Century America. Princeton, NJ: Princeton University Press, 2005.

Venit Shelton, Tamara. *A Squatter's Republic: Land and the Politics of Monopoly in California, 1850–1900*. Western Histories. Berkeley: Huntington–USC Institute on California and the West by University of California and the Huntington Library, San Marino, CA, 2013.

Venuti, Lawrence. *Translation Changes Everything: Theory and Practice*. New York: Routledge, 2013.

Vernet, Julien. *Strangers on Their Native Soil: Opposition to United States' Governance in Louisiana's Orleans Territory, 1803–1809*. Jackson: University Press of Mississippi, 2013.

Vigil, Maurilio E. *Parallels in the Careers of Two Hispanic U.S. Senators*. El Paso: University of Texas at El Paso, 1985.

———. *Los Patrones: Profiles of Hispanic Political Leaders in New Mexico History.* Washington, DC: University Press of America, 1980.

Vitiello, Domenic, and Thomas J. Sugrue, eds. *Immigration and Metropolitan Revitalization in the United States. City in the Twenty-First Century.* Philadelphia: University of Pennsylvania Press, 2017.

Weber, David J. *The Mexican Frontier, 1821–1846: The American Southwest under Mexico.* Albuquerque: University of New Mexico Press, 1982.

Weber, Devra. *Dark Sweat, White Gold: California Farm Workers, Cotton, and the New Deal.* Berkeley: University of California Press, 1994.

Weise, Julie M. *Corazón de Dixie: Mexicanos in the U.S. South since 1910.* David J. Weber Series in the New Borderlands History. Chapel Hill: University of North Carolina Press, 2015.

Westphall, Victor. *Thomas Benton Catron and His Era.* Tucson: University of Arizona Press, 1973.

Whitaker, Arthur P., ed. *Inter-American Affairs 1942–44: An Annual Survey No. 1–3.* New York: Columbia University Press, 1942–44.

Wild, Mark. *Street Meeting: Multiethnic Neighborhoods in Early Twentieth-Century Los Angeles.* Berkeley: University of California Press, 2005.

Zahra, Tara. *Kidnapped Souls: National Indifference and the Battle for Children in the Bohemian Lands, 1900–1948.* Ithaca, NY: Cornell University Press, 2008.

Ziegler-McPherson, Christina A. *Americanization in the States: Immigrant Social Welfare Policy, Citizenship, and National Identity in the United States, 1908–1929.* Working in the Americas. Gainesville: University Press of Florida, 2009.

INDEX

AMERICAN CROSSROADS

Edited by Earl Lewis, George Lipsitz, George Sánchez, Dana Takagi, Laura Briggs, and Nikhil Pal Singh